AUTHENTICITY AND VICTIMHOOD AFTER THE SECOND WORLD WAR

GERMAN AND EUROPEAN STUDIES

General Editor: Jennifer L. Jenkins

Authenticity and Victimhood after the Second World War

Narratives from Europe and East Asia

EDITED BY RANDALL HANSEN,
ACHIM SAUPE, ANDREAS WIRSCHING,
AND DAQING YANG

UNIVERSITY OF TORONTO PRESS
Toronto Buffalo London

Toronto Buffalo London
utorontopress.com

ISBN 978-1-4875-2821-8 (cloth) ISBN 978-1-4875-2823-2 (EPUB)
ISBN 978-1-4875-2822-5 (PDF)

Library and Archives Canada Cataloguing in Publication

Title: Authenticity and victimhood after the Second World War : narratives from Europe and East Asia / edited by Randall Hansen, Achim Saupe, Andreas Wirsching, and Daqing Yang.
Names: Hansen, Randall, editor. | Saupe, Achim, editor. | Wirsching, Andreas, editor. | Yang, Daqing, 1964– editor.
Series: German and European studies.
Description: Series statement: German and European studies | Includes bibliographical references and index.
Identifiers: Canadiana (print) 20210207752 | Canadiana (ebook) 20210207906 | ISBN 9781487528218 (cloth) | ISBN 9781487528232 (EPUB) | ISBN 9781487528225 (PDF)
Subjects: LCSH: World War, 1939–1945 – Europe – Historiography. | LCSH: World War, 1939–1945 – East Asia – Historiography. | LCSH: World War, 1939–1945 – Atrocities – Historiography. | LCSH: War victims – Europe. | LCSH: War victims – East Asia. | LCSH: Collective memory – Europe. | LCSH: Collective memory – East Asia.
Classification: LCC D744.7.E8 A98 2021 | DDC 940.53/1 – dc23

The German and European Studies series is funded by the DAAD with funds from the German Federal Foreign Office

Deutscher Akademischer Austauschdienst
German Academic Exchange Service

University of Toronto Press acknowledges the financial assistance to its publishing program of the Canada Council for the Arts and the Ontario Arts Council, an agency of the Government of Ontario.

Canada Council for the Arts Conseil des Arts du Canada

Funded by the Government of Canada Financé par le gouvernement du Canada

For Dr. Jürgen Zarusky, 1958–2019

Scholar. Colleague. Friend.

Contents

Acknowledgments

This volume began with a conversation over *Kaffee und Kuchen* at the Institute for Contemporary History (IfZ) in Munich in 2012. There, Randall Hansen met Magnus Brechtken and Andreas Wirsching to discuss possibilities for collaboration between the IfZ and the Centre for European, Russian, and Eurasian Studies (CERES) at the University of Toronto's Munk School of Global Affairs and Public Policy. There was enthusiasm on all sides, and we were delighted when Achim Saupe of the Leibniz Centre for Contemporary History in Potsdam and Daqing Yang from George Washington University gave the project essential early support and agreed to serve as editors. Two conferences – one at the Munk School in October 2013 and one at Berlin's Topography of Terror in December 2014 – followed. This volume is the result of this years-long transatlantic collaboration.

Along the way, we have acquired many debts. Our first word of thanks goes to our funders: the IfZ, CERES, the German Academic Exchange Service (DAAD), and the Leibniz Association. For event organization, and moving this project along, we are grateful to Joseph Hawker in Toronto as well as Agnes Bresselau von Bressensdorf, Elke Seefried, and Nadine Recktenwald of the IfZ. Joseph Hawker served as our primary point of contact with the University of Toronto Press and offered invaluable assistance after the manuscript was submitted for publication. His editorial talents and scrupulous eye ensured proper documentation of a vast array of sources in multiple languages and have improved this work immeasurably. We are also grateful for the support of Jennifer Jenkins, general editor of the German and European Studies Series, in which this volume appears, and Stephen Shapiro, history and Slavic studies editor at the University of Toronto Press.

AUTHENTICITY AND VICTIMHOOD AFTER THE SECOND WORLD WAR

Introduction: War, Genocide, and Forced Migration

RANDALL HANSEN, ACHIM SAUPE, ANDREAS WIRSCHING, AND DAQING YANG

"This filthy twentieth century. I hate its guts," declared a British historian of Elizabethan England, A.L. Rowse, in 1978.[1] There was certainly much to hate: war, genocide, forced migration, forced labour, human-made famine, mass rape, forced sterilizations, and dispossession – none of which was new but all of which occurred on an unprecedented scale. Were one adjective to be assigned to these extreme experiences, it would be "total." Some fifty million persons worldwide lost their lives in the Second World War alone, over half of whom were civilians, including millions of Jews as well as Sini, Roma, and LGBTQ people murdered in Nazi camps. An estimated thirteen million people lost their lives in the Asia Pacific War, not including those who died of war-related famine and disease in China, French Indochina, the Dutch Indies, and the Philippines.[2] An estimated thirty million Europeans were rendered refugees, a figure that does not include approximately twenty million more who were subjected to deportation. And, with the view to East Asia, more than ninety million Chinese became internally displaced persons during the Sino-Japanese War.[3]

All these horrors, and many others, have entered the public consciousness to varying degrees and at different times, but still others have not entered it at all. Until the 1960s, the Holocaust was marginal to public memory and the commemoration of the Second World War; it is now central. The wartime experiences of Roma and Sinti remain marginal, as do the lives of the 200,000 mentally handicapped people murdered by Nazi Germany and some 500,000 individuals forcibly sterilized not only under the Third Reich but also in Scandinavia, the United States, and Canada.[4] Since the early 1970s, the Nanjing Massacre has been a highly contentious issue in Sino-Japanese relations and, more recently, has become part of Chinese collective memory. In contrast, forced migration does not play a significant role in narratives of internal Chinese politics of the 1930s and 1940s and similarly lacks a prominent place in Chinese memory of the Sino-Japanese War. And while it is still difficult for some Japanese to acknowledge their country's wartime violence in China and Korea (as part of commemoration culture), many Japanese have emphasized their own victimhood: as victims of the atomic bombings, aerial firebombing, or violence enacted by their own regime. As this book will show, similar processes of victimization and self-victimization have played out in Germany and many other countries in Europe and East Asia. They have become a signature of memory cultures in the twentieth and twenty-first centuries, in particular for those related to the Second World War.

For the process through which events become remembered, recorded, and commemorated, historical "authentication" is of great significance: by drawing on new evidence, by giving marginalized witnesses a voice, or by creating new narratives about the past, those events are ascribed a sense of validity and legitimacy.[5] These authentication processes are necessary for the recognition of historical events as part of public consciousness or collective memory. In the absence of some form of authentication, past events remain the tree that fell in the forest. Self-identification and authentication are important strategies for gaining recognition as a victim or as a part of a group of victims in the culture of commemoration. In a European perspective, self-identification as a victim – seeing ourselves as sacrifices, casualties, and victims – has functioned as a central part of a "European collective identity," as German historians Ulrike Jureit and Christian Schneider have remarked.[6] This book aims to investigate how the construction of victim groups and their authentication took place in the shadow of the Second World War. By doing so, we hope to shed more light on the role that victim groups have played in postwar culture and politics. This book also seeks to understand to what extent the invocation of victim status as a primary element of a postwar identity can be generalized to encompass examples from East Asian countries. Finally, the chapters collectively address the relative lack of comparative studies in the abundant literature on victimhood processes after the Second World War. While the comparison of postwar commemorative cultures has recently become an important topic in European historiography,[7] there is still a lack of intercontinental perspectives.[8] The book combines, therefore, comparative aspects with European and Asian case studies. The two approaches are not mutually exclusive but, rather, complement each other.

In an essay published shortly after the end of the Cold War, historian Charles Maier laments what he termed "the surfeit of memory" and asks whether there might be something inauthentic and unhealthy about the canonization of memory. He was referring to a particular kind of memory: memory of grievance. If such memory can bring about a sense of sweet melancholy at the individual level, Maier argues, it became, at the collective level, part of a trend of "competition for enshrining grievances at the end of the 20th century," when Western society has retreated from future-oriented "transformative politics."[9] Maier was writing against the background of a new wave of museums and memorials devoted to such grievances, in particular the United States Holocaust Memorial Museum and the Holocaust Memorial in the centre of Berlin.

A few years later, journalist and writer Ian Buruma tackled the issue head-on in an essay entitled "The Joy and Peril of Victimhood."[10] Buruma's intervention was prompted by, among other things, the publication of Chinese-American author Iris Chang's bestseller, *The Rape of Nanking: The Forgotten Holocaust of Asia*. Chang's book demonstrates that elements of the Chinese diaspora, with no connection to the mid-twentieth-century catastrophe in Europe, seem to aspire to a victim status.[11]

Both Maier and Buruma note the sense of satisfaction and even joy resulting from the respect associated with victimhood. Echoing Maier, Buruma points out that identity has increasingly come to rest on what he calls the "pseudo-religion of victimhood." Like Maier, he also underscores the implication of such memory in our understanding of the past: "When truth is subjective, only feelings are authentic, and only the subject can know whether his or her feelings are true or false."[12] If Maier and Buruma were addressing a growing trend in Europe and North America, especially among hyphenated Americans, it is natural to wonder whether this phenomenon applies in other parts of the world.

Some twenty years after Buruma's essay was published, the study of memory and victimhood has become something of a boom phenomenon, embracing virtually every discipline, from law to psychology and literature.[13] Such a phenomenon certainly reflects what Maier called "the epistemological transition" after the postmodern revolution, but it was also a response to democratic transitions in Latin America and elsewhere as well as to the post–Cold War transformations of Eastern Europe and the concomitant end, at least in portions of Europe, to the suppression of memory of human rights abuses.

East Asia is no exception to such a phenomenon, but it has its own dynamics. Since the mid-1980s, East Asian countries seem to be entangled in what some have called a "memory war."[14] The visit of Japanese prime minister Nakasone Yasuhiro[15] in 1985 to the controversial Yasukuni Shinto shrine – which commemorates Japanese war dead, including convicted war criminals – was the first widely publicized official visit by a Japanese prime minister, and it sparked protests in China, South Korea, and elsewhere. A debate had been going on in Japan since the early 1970s over the exact extent of Japanese military atrocities in the Chinese city of Nanjing during the Second Sino-Japanese War, but they now spilled over into the diplomatic arena between the two countries. In the early 1990s, Korean survivors of the wartime Japanese military's "comfort women" system spoke out and demanded an official apology from Japan. They were soon joined by victims of such sexual exploitation in many other countries in Asia and elsewhere. The demand for redress also came from other victims of wartime Japan, including survivors of forced labour, aerial bombing, as well as chemical and biological weapons attacks.

At the heart of this "memory war" lie the competing narratives of victimhood related to the Second World War as well as perceived or real attempts to exaggerate or deny such status. While such a "war" plays out very publicly in the international arena, internal factors within the concerned countries shape the discourse. There is ample evidence of China's drive to use the "century of humiliation" to strengthen patriotism and loyalty within its one-party state. Looking outward, Asian victims of atrocities and exploitation demanding recognition often find supporters within Japan, but those demands are still sometimes dismissed as being exaggerated, based on distorted facts, and motivated by financial or other ulterior motives. On another level, such demands are also seen as threats to Japan's own sense of victimhood in that war, particularly with respect to the atomic bombing. Finally, the quest for victim status can intensify internal conflicts – for example, within South Korea. As anthropologist Chunghee Sarah Soh has shown, demands by former Korean comfort women and their supporters for public recognition at home encountered opposition from Korean veteran groups who considered the former's experience of sexual violence a stain on the national honour.[16]

Claiming authenticity in memory conflicts can have multiple goals. In some cases, a claim to authenticity is simply a claim to historical recognition: a place in the history books, in school curricula, or in public monuments. In other cases, these claims are strategies designed to further political, social, and/or economic objectives. The process is characterized by a high degree of feedback: individuals and groups pursue authenticity, but that goal is in part determined by authority itself, since the state, which generally controls education policy and public commemoration, determines the contours of acceptable authenticity claims. In this respect, "authority" and "authorization" are both intimately linked with the concept of authenticity, in that they largely determine which historical subjects societies will perceive as part of "their" cultural heritage. Given the centrality of authentication and the benefits it brings – recognition, sympathy, a place in the history books, and sometimes more material advantages such as reparations – it is inevitable and understandable that victims strive to achieve it. But so do others. In some cases, the victim designation is not especially clear-cut. It is self-evident in the case of Holocaust survivors, forced labourers, and survivors of massacres that their status as victims is authenticated merely by ascribing this label to them. The situation proves more problematic when those with more complicated claims seek a similar status: should we sympathize with groups who, for example, were expelled from their homes when they had earlier advocated the expulsion of others?

Such processes involve contestation of the past (that is, what actually happened) and of collective commemoration (that is, how that past is to be officially and publicly recalled, spoken of, taught, and memorialized as history). The conflict between history as an academic discipline and history as memory and commemoration can, in part, be traced back to the discourse about perpetrators and victims. When individuals identify themselves as victims or are recognized as such by others, and when prevailing narratives about the past are challenged, collective memory becomes reconfigured and expanded, which in turn shapes academic historiography. Until relatively recently, for instance, historians excluded queer history from histories of Nazi Germany (and, to some degree, still do). As the *Simon Wiesenthal Center Annual* put it in 1990:

> In the immediate postwar period, many of those who wrote about concentration camps ... treated homosexuals as common criminals, justly punished for violating the penal code of the Third Reich. Postwar historians of the Holocaust, especially those asserting the exclusivist view that the Holocaust was a historical experience unique to the Jewish people, have taken a similar position. Thus Lucy S. Dawidowicz, a leading exclusivist, has dismissed as not worthy of mention the "prostitutes, homosexuals, perverts, and common criminals" incarcerated by the Nazis.[17]

Following lobbying by activists, lesbian, gay, bisexual, and transgender people have since gained a place in collective memory of the Holocaust, in public memorialization (the Memorial to the Homosexuals Persecuted under the National Socialist Regime in Berlin), and in historical scholarship.[18]

Victimization, as Tami Jacoby has argued, is an act of harm perpetrated against a person or group, and victimhood is a form of collective identity based on that harm.[19] In all instances of human suffering, there were perpetrators (those who precipitated expulsions, massacres, mass rapes, and mass sterilization) and victims (those who were expelled, massacred, raped, and sterilized). The categories of perpetrator and victim are, to be sure, contested (perpetrators deny being such, others deny the legitimacy of victims' status), blurred (victims may become perpetrators), and problematic (some victims – those of the bombing of Hiroshima, for example – claim unmerited moral equivalence with other victims, such as those of the Holocaust). In the second half of the twentieth century, when claiming victim status became a strategy for recognition and exculpation, we can observe many examples of "self-victimization," not only by perpetrators but also in discourses about guilt, responsibility, and reconciliation. But the categories are at least recognizable to historians and their readers. The same is not obvious regarding the terms "authentic" and "authenticity." This is partly because authenticity is a highly emotive and contingent concept: what is regarded as authentic in one context or period might be considered inauthentic in others. Until now, authenticity has been studied primarily by those in the fields of philosophy, literature, art history, aesthetics, tourism studies, anthropology, and film, media, and theatre studies.[20] In addition, those involved in the preservation of historic monuments and in the study of material culture have devoted attention to questions of how to define authenticity – for example, as a characteristic of historic buildings.[21] By contrast, historians have hardly touched the concept. Only a handful of intellectual historians and scholars of commemorative culture and memory research have examined how perceptions of the authentic have changed over time.[22]

As a starting point, there are two basic forms of authenticity. The first is subject-oriented, "existential," or "expressive" authenticity – that is, authentic in the sense of being true to oneself or demonstrating trustworthiness and credibility. The second form is object-oriented authenticity, in the sense of confirming material genuineness of an original entity, or verifying whether – or the extent to which – entities are what they are purported to be. When these concepts of authenticity are applied to ideas of victimhood and victimization, it is important whether one's status as a victim is genuine in one's own mind and whether others recognize it as such. Here, there is a tension between lived history – what people actually experienced and witnessed – and its academic study. The questions for historians are traditionally rather binary and causal: Did it happen or did it not? Why did it happen and to what effect? Historians can also look at the representation of the voice and the "truth of the telling"[23] – that is, what oral testimonies and other (ego) documents reveal about how memories are related by individual narrators or groups. The idea and attribution of authenticity is key here: What makes testimony true or trustworthy in the eyes of the recipients? What makes something authentic and therefore credible and convincing? Do victim testimonies claim or even possess more "moral authenticity" than those of perpetrators?

From a methodological perspective, any attribution of authenticity to a particular experience – a claim, for instance, that some suffering was more or less real, more or less authentic – is a construct.[24] Nonetheless, claims to historical and expressive authenticity are a crucial point for receiving recognition in media societies. To cite one example, the decimation of likely tens of millions of Indigenous people in North America happened, and sources confirm this. Nonetheless, this fact was for many years not fully recognized or commemorated in the United States or Canada (and arguably is still not today). An important shift was that, in the 1970s, members of several tribes (or First Nations in Canada) – representing the "authentic voice" of the people and the victims – increasingly made claims for recognition by the state, the public, and scholars that genocidal violence had in fact occurred. The ascription or denial of historical authenticity is thus a contingent and highly political process that extends beyond mere verification through the assessment of sources.

This book explores social processes of authentication through an examination of victims' histories and of the construction of victimhood narratives in multiple social, political, ethnic, ideological, and religious memory conflicts in Europe and East Asia in the twentieth and twenty-first centuries. It is the result of a comparative examination of global trends in commemorative culture at the conference "Authenticity and Victimhood in Twentieth-Century History and Commemorative Culture," which took place in Berlin in December 2014 and is part of an ongoing collaboration between the Centre for European, Russian & Eurasian Studies, the Munk School at the University of Toronto and the Leibniz Institute of Contemporary History Munich-Berlin, in cooperation with the Leibniz Research Alliance Historical Authenticity. At this conference, international researchers aimed to analyse claims of authenticity and processes of authentication and the role they play in memory politics and public commemorative culture.

The chapters investigate how notions of historical authenticity and authentication influence self-identification and public recognition of a given social group as victims, the tensions arising from individual and group experiences of victimhood, and the resulting, sometimes divergent, interpretation of historical events. They look at the relationship of authentication and victimization found in the politics of memory and commemorative culture, including public ceremonies, museums and memorial sites, and documentaries and other films, and in the development of educational curricula and school textbooks. The case studies pertain to the experience and recognition of victimhood in Europe and East Asia in several contexts, which also build the framework for the second, third, and fourth sections of the book: genocide and massacres, war victims, and forced migration and deportations.

The contributors ask if there are specific moments in the aftermath of war crimes in which certain groups of victims achieve societal relevance and interpretational authority, and what form rivalries between different victims take. They also focus on the roles of victim organizations and the narratives they promote as well as state-led narratives in public commemoration. How is victimhood constructed, and what are its characteristics? Is it closely linked with what some have called a "global memory culture"?[25] What implications does this trend have for victims themselves as well as for our understanding of the past in general? And finally, the contributors ask whether East Asia, like Europe, is witnessing a shift from heroic to post-heroic memories.[26]

Structure of the Book

This book contains four sections. The first examines theoretical and methodological issues. Andreas Wirsching's opening chapter asks whether, and to what degree, a "monumental" conception of history (to draw on Friedrich Nietzsche) might have shifted from a "heroic" to a "post-heroic" age.[27] Is there a global trend towards a post-heroic understanding of history, and, if so, what roles do the narratives of victimhood play in that? What consequences do competing interests of different groups of victims have for the conceptualization of national history, collective memory, and identity? Is it possible to pinpoint events and identify periods that were of pivotal importance for post-heroic and victim narratives? And are there any contemporary societies in which a post-heroic understanding of history remains unusual or even is viewed as inappropriate?

Michael Schwartz's chapter examines the shifting hierarchies and framings of victimhood in postwar Germany. In the early postwar years, Germans placed themselves at the top of the victim pyramid by developing an internal German hierarchy of authenticity: first, the war wounded, their dependants, and the dependants of the dead; then bombing victims; and, finally, refugees. The first decades after 1945 showed a preference for "active," "heroic" victims (e.g., the 20 July military resisters), little interest in passive victims (Roma and Sinti), and no interest at all in passive, "socially deviant" German victims (gay and bisexual men, whose oppression continued until the late 1960s and beyond).

Despite German victims' efforts to retain their place at the top of this hierarchy, the conceptualization started to shift in the 1960s. Those victimized by Germany became the focus of understandings of victimhood and authenticity, and Germans themselves were understood as the perpetrators. This process was a slow and graduated one, focusing first on Jewish victims and only recently – and belatedly – on Roma and Sinti, people with mental and physical disabilities, and LGBT people.

The second section surveys war victims of genocide and massacres. Ingo Loose examines Jewish survivors of the Holocaust and the formation of Jewish identity in its aftermath. Loose distinguishes three periods. In the first, from 1945 to 1948, Jewish identity was greatly fragmented, as there was little coherence among the identities of the shattered Jewish communities of Europe. The second period spanned from 1948 until the Eichmann trial in 1961, when global Jewish identity coalesced around the state of Israel. Finally, since 1961, Jewish identity has increasingly anchored itself to memory of the Holocaust.

In the next contribution, Jürgen Zarusky analyses the history of "ghetto pensions," in which the most horrific aspects of twentieth-century German history – the concentration camps – intersect with one of the most positive: Germany's *Rechtsstaat* (state based on procedural justice and the rule of law). In 1997, a Jewish Holocaust survivor who had lived in the Łódź ghetto before being deported to the camps brought a suit before the German federal court, arguing that she deserved a pension because she had worked voluntarily in the ghetto. She won, and the result was a great anomaly: the court determined that she was entitled to a pension because Łódź had been located in the portion of Poland annexed by Germany; those who had worked in the Warsaw ghetto, however, would not be so entitled, as Warsaw belonged to the territory under the General Government. Such an anomaly could not stand, and the German government responded by generalizing the entitlement. In the 2002 law on "ghetto pensions," the German Bundestag made it possible for anyone who had worked voluntarily in any German-controlled ghetto to receive a pension.

Centring on the most publicized wartime atrocity during the Japanese invasion of China in the 1930s, the Nanjing Massacre, Daqing Yang traces the factors that led to the first-ever national commemoration of this incident. Although state-led construction of victimhood in China in recent decades has received much outside critical attention, Yang shows that subnational and quasi-state actors often played significant roles. Moreover, he shows that, even though victimhood has become a strong motif in China's collective memory of modern history, including events associated with the Second World War, it has by no means displaced the heroic narrative, which has undergone its own transformation.

The final chapter in this section, by Nakano Satoshi, shows a different dynamic at work in postwar Japanese-Filipino relations. Both sides suffered greatly from the devastation of the Second World War, and the two countries managed to move toward reconciliation by acknowledging mutual victimhood from war. As Nakano points out, however, it is doubtful that reconciliation through amnesia can work for other parts of Asia.

The third section of the book deals with war crimes and, in particular, the controversies surrounding the aerial bombing of Japan as well as the politics of remembrance in the Soviet Union and Russia. In the first chapter in this section, James Orr provides a comparative genealogy that examines Japanese victim narratives resulting from, on the one hand, atomic bombing and, on the other, conventional aerial bombing. He traces the rise of Japanese narratives of nuclear victimhood after 1954 and then examines the attention given much later to victims of firebombing, despite the latter being an experience shared by more people. He attributes these developments to multiple actors – the state, victims, and activists – as well as shifts in domestic and international contexts. Orr confirms that, in Japan, too, an "older trope of heroism is still strong" and that war victims are regarded as having contributed to the peace and prosperity of the postwar era.

Tatiana Voronina examines a group of victims whose place in the collective memory blurs the heroic and victimized histories of victimhood: those who lived through the Siege of Leningrad in 1941–4. Some siege survivors sought meaning, even a sort of redemption, in suffering because they understood their experience as a sacred and, thus, meaningful sacrifice for ideals, their future, and their homeland. Other survivors, by contrast, avoided invoking the discourse of victimhood because they saw it as being in tension with their status as heroes: the role of victim would have implied passivity, thus equating them with victims of the Holodomor or political repression rather than with the heroic veterans of the Great Patriotic War. Many siege survivors clearly rejected passive victimhood. Their motivation was partly principled and ideological, partly pragmatic: few in Russia were eager to grant special social benefits on the basis of starvation and harsh living conditions, since those conditions had affected the majority of elderly people in the Soviet Union. The siege survivors distinguished themselves by asserting that they had actively sacrificed themselves in order to defeat the enemy and determine the ultimate outcome of the war. On this basis, they were entitled to more generous assistance from the state. These themes of heroism and sacrifice thus merged into a coherent narrative without contradiction.

The third section ends with a chapter by Barbara Christophe that observes the ways in which narrative films, documentaries, and other educational media portrayed, and, in such portrayals, authenticated and constructed, victims and victimhood. Christophe explores the ways in which Lithuanian textbooks and teachers have addressed wartime partisans, whom the Soviet Union defined as murderers, fascists, and war criminals. Global recognition of the Holocaust has encouraged both increased attention in Lithuania to that genocide as well as the casting of non-Jewish Lithuanians as victims. Under the spell of cosmopolitan discourses on victimhood, textbooks vie for the public's attention by telling stories of hitherto ignored victims. All these stories emphasize some facts and omit others. Conservative textbooks, for example, portray the partisans as victims and the communists as perpetrators. In order to preserve the dichotomy, they mention neither cruel acts of violence committed by the former nor the suffering endured by the latter. Textbooks closer to the post-communist version of the past dissolve those dichotomies. In their accounts, partisans turn into collaborators, Lithuanian communists fall victim to the Soviets, and ordinary people suffer from the violence exercised by all. As a result, boundaries are blurred, and who did what to whom almost gets lost. Both accounts serve political aims, but neither has emerged as a dominant narrative.

The fourth section of the book focuses on forced migration and deportations. Mathias Beer's contribution discusses one of the numerically largest and most politically charged forced migrations in Europe: the expulsion of 12.5 million ethnic Germans from former German territories and East European states. Beer traces the evolution of expellees' claims, including the language in which those claims were made. The process began with demands for legal recognition and reparations, and ended, in 2014, with a claim to a place within historiography on official commemoration of forced migrants. This process, Beer argues, was not linear but rather tortuous, hitting many bumps along the way.

Tobias Hof then explores the under-researched topic of forced population movements in and by Italy, with a focus on northeastern

Italy, South Tyrol, and the Balkans. Examining the period from the end of the First World War to the aftermath of the Second, Hof argues that the "cultural politics" of "forced removal" effected through the power of images and discourses, had a decisive role in forging the Italian us-versus-them mentality that made removals meaningful and acceptable. Both perpetrators and victims relied on such cultural politics, as propaganda campaigns in South Tyrol demonstrated. In both Italy and the Balkans, language was a feature of the *Kulturnation* and played a vital role in determining if someone belonged to the "Italian race" or not. In the Balkans, racial antagonism was further aggravated by other considerations such as ideology, class, and religion.

Moritz Florin examines the experience of the Chechen, an ethnic group situated between Asia and Europe, who were subject to persecution and forced migration under Stalin during the Second World War. Although most were returned to their homeland after Stalin's death, Chechen demands for commemoration were not addressed until the late 1990s. After a brief renaissance in recognition for their ethnic victimhood, however, the Chechen had to accept that they would not receive a special place within current Russian commemorative culture. Florin thus sees commemoration of Chechen victimhood intrinsically tied to the fate of the Chechen nation inside Russia.

Finally, the contribution by Lori Watt examines efforts by China, Japan, and Korea to secure international recognition of their respective victims by nominating collections of documentary heritage to the UNESCO Memory of the World Register in 2014. This was perhaps the closest thing to an East Asian rivalry for victimhood in the international arena – known as the "memory wars in East Asia," which have been slowly emerging since the 1980s – and such rivalry has often disrupted diplomatic relations among close neighbours.

The different contributions and case studies of this volume show that there is a clear European *and* Asian trend toward a victim-centred collective memory. Accordingly, we can speak of comparative developments, parallels, and even convergences in European and East Asian history. On the other hand, strong differences remain not only between Europe and East Asia but also within European and East Asian countries and cultures. For example, although non-heroism and victimhood seem to be the dominant mode of commemoration in Germany and South Korea, things are more complex in Russia, Japan, and China. This book contributes to the knowledge of convergences, ambivalences, and irreducible peculiarities in the political culture of continents, regions, and nation states.

NOTES

1 Robert Andrews, ed., *New Penguin Dictionary of Modern Quotations* (London: Penguin Books, 2001), 585.
2 J.M. Winter, "Demography of the War," in *Oxford Companion to World War II*, ed. I.C:B. Dear and M.R.D. Foot (Oxford: Oxford University Press, 2001), 224–7.
3 Rana Mitter, *China's War with Japan, 1937–1945: The Struggle for Survival* (London: Allen Lane, 2013), 387.
4 The numbers of mentally handicapped persons murdered by Nazi Germany in East Central Europe remain in particular uncertain. See Ingo Loose, "Aktion T4 Die 'Euthanasie'-Verbrechen im Nationalsozialismus 1933 bis 1945," https://www.gedenkort-t4.eu/de/wissen/aktion-t4; Alison Bashford and Philippa Levine, eds., *The Oxford Handbook of the History of Eugenics* (Oxford: Oxford University Press, 2010); Thorsten Noack, "William L. Shirer and International Awareness of the Nazi 'Euthanasia' Program," *Holocaust and Genocide Studies* 30 (2016): 433–57; Alexander Friedman and Rainer Hudemann, eds., *Diskriminiert – Vvernichtet – Vvergessen: Behinderte in der Sowjetunion, unter nationalsozialistischer Besatzung und im Ostblock 1917–1991* (Stuttgart: Franz Steiner Verlag, 2016).
5 Martin Sabrow and Achim Saupe, "Historische Authentizität: Zur Kartierung eines Forschungsfeldes," in *Historische Authentizität*, ed. Martin Sabrow and Achim Saupe (Göttingen: Wallstein, 2016), 7–28.
6 Ulrike Jureit and Christian Schneider, *Gefühlte Opfer: Illusionen der Vergangenheitsbewältigung*, 2nd ed. (Stuttgart: Klett-Cotta, 2011).
7 See Jörg Echternkamp and Stefan Martens, eds., *Experience and Memory: The Second World War in Europe* (New York: Berghahn, 2010); Manuel Bragança and Peter D. Tame, eds., *The Long Aftermath: Cultural Legacies of Europe at War, 1936–2016* (New York: Berghahn, 2016); K. Erik Franzen and Martin Schulze Wessel, eds., *Opfernarrative: Konkurrenzen und Deutungskämpfe in Deutschland und im östlichen Europa nach dem Zweiten Weltkrieg* (Munich: Oldenbourg, 2012): Stefan Troebst, *Erinnerungskultur – Kulturgeschichte – Geschichtsregion: Ostmitteleuropa in Europa* (Stuttgart: Franz Steiner Verlag, 2013).
8 Important studies include Daniel Chirot, Gi-Wook Shin, and Daniel Sneider, eds., *Confronting Memories of World War II: European and Asian Legacies* (Seattle: University of Washington Press, 2014); Wilfried Wilms and William Rasch, eds., *Bombs Away: Representing the Air War over Europe and Japan* (Amsterdam: Rodopi, 2006); Sebastian Conrad, "Entangled Memories: Versions of the Past in Germany and Japan, 1945–2001," *Journal of Contemporary History* 38, no. 1 (2003): 85–99. Christoph Cornelißen, Lutz Klinkhammer, and Wolfgang Schwentker, eds., *Erinnerungskulturen:*

Deutschland, Italien und Japan seit 1945 (Frankfurt: Fischer-Taschenbuch-Verlag, 2003).

9 Charles Maier, "Surfeit of Memory? Reflections on History, Melancholy, and Denial," *History and Memory* 5, no. 2 (1993): 136–52.

10 Ian Buruma, "The Joys and Perils of Victimhood," *New York Review of Books*, 8 April 1999.

11 Iris Chang, *The Rape of Nanking: The Forgotten Holocaust of Asia* (New York: Basic Books, 1997).

12 Buruma, "Joys and Perils," 7.

13 See, for example, Nigel C. Hunt, *Memory, War and Trauma* (Cambridge: Cambridge University Press, 2010); Ian Buruma, *Theater of Cruelty: Art, Film, and the Shadows of War* (New York: New York Review of Books, 2014); Peter Gray and Kendrick Oliver, eds., *The Memory of Catastrophe* (Manchester: Manchester University Press, 2004).

14 See, for example, Sheila Miyoshi Jager, ed., *Ruptured Histories: War, Memory, and the Post–Cold War in Asia* (Cambridge, MA: Harvard University Press, 2007); Franziska Seraphim, *War Memory and Social Politics in Japan, 1945–2005* (Cambridge: Harvard University Asia Center, 2006).

15 Unless otherwise noted, names of individuals in this volume follow the order typically used in their country of origin. Author names in works cited are replicated as given in the source.

16 C. Sarah Soh, *The Comfort Women: Sexual Violence and Postcolonial Memory in Korea and Japan* (Chicago: University of Chicago Press, 2008).

17 Quoted in Warren Johansson and William A. Percy, *Outing: Shattering the Conspiracy of Silence* (New York: Haworth Press, 1994), 226.

18 Dagmar Herzog, ed., *Sexuality and German Fascism* (New York: Berghahn, 2005); Geoffrey Giles, "Männerbund mit Homo-Panik: Die Angst der Nazis vor der Rolle der Erotik," *Nationalsozialistischer Terror gegen Homosexuelle: Verdrängt und ungesühnt*, ed. Burkhard Jellonnek and Rüdiger Lautmann (Paderborn: Schöningh, 2002), 105–18; Geoffrey Giles, "Legislating Homophobia in the Third Reich: The Radicalization of Prosecution against Homosexuality by the Legal Profession," *German History* 23, no. 3 (2005): 339–54; Clayton J. Whisnant, *Queer Identities and Politics in Germany: A History, 1880–1945* (New York: Harrington Park Press, 2016).

19 Tami Amanda Jacoby, "A Theory of Victimhood: Politics, Conflict and the Construction of Victim-based Identity," *Millennium: Journal of International Studies* 43, no. 2 (2015): 511–30.

20 See, for example, Charles Taylor, *The Ethics of Authenticity* (Cambridge, MA: Harvard University Press, 1995); Marshall Berman, *The Politics of Authenticity: Radical Individualism and the Emergence of Modern Society*, new ed. (London: Verso, 2009); Wolfgang Funk, Florian Gross, and Irmtraud Huber, eds., *The Aesthetics of Authenticity: Medial Constructions of the Real* (Bielefeld:

Transcript, 2012); Susanne Knaller and Harro Müller, eds., *Authentizität: Diskussion eines ästhetischen Begriffs* (Munich: Fink, 2006); Regina Bendix, *In Search of Authenticity: The Formation of Folklore Studies* (Madison: University of Wisconsin Press, 1997); Ning Wang, "Rethinking Authenticity in Tourism Experience," *Annals of Tourism Research* 26, no. 2 (1999): 349–70; Gunn Enli, *Mediated Authenticity: How the Media Constructs Reality* (New York: Peter Lang, 2015); Erika Fischer-Lichte and Isabel Pflug, eds., *Inszenierung von Authentizität (Theatralität)*, vol. 1, 2nd ed. (Tübingen: Francke, 2007).

21 David Lowenthal, "Changing Criteria of Authenticity," in *Nara Conference on Authenticity: Proceedings of the Conference in Nara, Japan, 1–6 November 1994*, ed. Knut Einar Larsen (Trondheim: Tapir, 1995), 121–35; Tino Mager, *Schillernde Unschärfe: Der Begriff der Authentizität im architektonischen Erbe* (Berlin: de Gruyter, 2016); Christoph Bernhardt, Martin Sabrow, and Achim Saupe, eds., *Gebaute Geschichte: Historische Authentizität im Stadtraum* (Göttingen: Wallstein, 2017).

22 Charles Lindholm, *Culture and Authenticity* (Oxford: Blackwell Publishing, 2008); Charles Lindholm, "The Rise of Expressive Authenticity," *Anthropological Quarterly* 86, no. 2 (2013): 361–95; Sabrow and Saupe, *Historische Authentizität*; Achim Saupe, "Authenticity," Docupedia-Zeitgeschichte, https://docupedia.de/zg/Saupe_authentizitaet_v3_en_2016. See also Barbara Christophe, Christoph Kohl, and Heike Liebau, eds., *Geschichte als Ressource: Politische Dimensionen historischer Authentizität* (Berlin: Klaus Schwarz Verlag, 2017).

23 Lynn Abrams, *Oral History Theory*, 2nd ed. (Abingdon, UK: Routledge, 2016), 46.

24 "Um es gleich vorweg zu nehmen: Authentische Erinnerung gibt es nicht. Die Rede beschwört vielmehr einen zählebigen Mythos," in *Erlebnis – Gedächtnis – Sinn. Authentische und konstruierte Erinnerung*, ed. Hanno Loewy and Bernhard Moltmann (Frankfurt: Campus, 1996), 7; Helmut Lethen, "Versionen des Authentischen: sechs Gemeinplätze," in *Literatur und Kulturwissenschaften: Positionen, Theorien, Modelle*, ed. Hartmut Böhme and Klaus R. Scherpe (Reinbek: Rowohlt, 1996), 205–31. See also Michael Rössner and Heidemarie Uhl, eds., *Renaissance der Authentizität? Über die neue Sehnsucht nach dem Ursprünglichen* (Bielefeld: Transcript, 2012).

25 Aleida Assmann and Sebastian Conrad, eds., *Memory in a Global Age: Discourses, Practices and Trajectories* (Basingstoke, UK: Palgrave Macmillan, 2010); Jeffrey K. Olick, *The Politics of Regret: On Collective Memory and Historical Responsibility* (New York: Routledge, 2007); Gi-Wook Shin, Soon-Won Park, and Daqing Yang, eds., *Rethinking Historical Injustice and Reconciliation in Northeast Asia* (New York: Routledge, 2006); Daniel Levy and Natan Sznaider, *Holocaust and Memory in the Global Age* (Philadelphia: Temple University Press, 2006).

26 See Jan-Werner Müller, ed., *Memory and Power in Post-War Europe: Studies in the Presence of the Past* (Cambridge: Cambridge University Press, 2002).

27 Jan-Werner Müller, "Introduction: The Power of Memory, the Memory of Power and the Power over Memory," in ibid., 1–36; Herfried Münkler, "Heroische und postheroische Gesellschaften," *Merkur: Deutsche Zeitschrift für europäisches Denken* 61, nos. 8/9 (2007): 742–52; Andreas Wirsching, *Der Preis der Freiheit: Geschichte Europas in unserer Zeit* (Munich: Beck, 2012), 381; Martin Sabrow, "Die postheroische Gedächtnisgesellschaft: Bauformen des historischen Erzählens in der Gegenwart," in *Geschichtspolitik in Europa seit 1989: Deutschland, Frankreich und Politischen im internationalen Vergleich*, ed. Etienne François, Kornelia Koncal, Robert Traba, and Stefan Troebst (Göttingen: Wallstein, 2013), 311–22.

PART 1

Methodological and Theoretical Approaches

1 From Hero's Death to Suffering Victim: Reflections on the "Post-Heroic" Culture of Memory

ANDREAS WIRSCHING

In recent years, there has been much talk of a shared European culture of memory. These discussions quickly evoke the thorny topic of Europe's cultural "identity," because a sense of historical individuality is inextricably linked to such an identity.[1] However, the more history is invoked in this discussion, the more complicated it becomes. This has become particularly apparent in the wake of the rise of new populist or right-wing parties in Europe. One of their common strategies is to refer to a supposedly glorious national history in order to revive that nation's "greatness." The discussion about Europe's identity then becomes swept up a dangerous maelstrom in which the past is pushed front and centre in service of contemporary political rhetoric. Where there is no shared joint conception of one's own history, as resigned observers note, there can be no shared common identity. This seems to hold true in particular for more recent past events – that is, those of the second half of the twentieth century – which have served as particularly potent reference points in calls for "renationalization." In some Eastern European countries, this tendency has involved an inclination to "re-heroize" commemorative culture, as could recently be observed in the official pronouncement on the sixtieth anniversary of the 1956 Hungarian Uprising: "Where heroes are not forgotten, new ones will always be born."[2]

This is, however, just one side of the proverbial coin. On the other is a strong argument that a *shared* mode of viewing has emerged among Europeans. This approach is found in the common, fundamental effort of peoples to distance themselves from the dark history of the continent. This is, of course, predominantly true when it comes to the history of dictatorship, the Second World War, and mass annihilation. But, beyond that, Europeans try in numerous ways to liberate themselves from the disastrous pasts of the nineteenth and twentieth centuries and to leave those pasts behind once and for all. This is true at least for the majority of democratically minded Europeans, even though their positions are increasingly challenged by right-wing aspirations to rewrite national histories. Still, many aspects of European history serve as negative foils from which Europe distances itself both culturally and in terms of identity: the rivalry between the Great Powers, racism, colonialism and imperialism, totalitarian ideologies, world war, and genocide. In practice, the Europe of dark pasts constitutes a specific "Other," an alterity that is essentially different from the identity of the European "community of values" that has prevailed, at least until recently.[3] This "Other" is fully centred on the victim. As present-day Europe continues to liberate the victims of its past(s) from the dungeon of anonymity and forgetting, it attempts to use this opportunity for catharsis to reconstruct its current identity. It brings the victims of the past into the relevance of the present. As one observer has commented, "the victim is the hero of our times."[4]

This sustained, widely demanded distancing from their own history of injustice forms the most important shared mode of Europeans. In the process, the will and ability to identify, confront, and work through past injustices has become a key feature of European culture. Mastering the past is a ticket, as it were, required to climb aboard the European train. Thus, Turkish prospects for full membership in the European Union remain tarnished as long as the murder of Armenians in the First World War is deemed a taboo subject. The Serbian government clearly understood that the arrest of the alleged war criminal Ratko Mladić in May 2011 was a down payment to Europe on serious negotiations for Serbia's admission to the EU. Only one day after the arrest of the "butcher of Srebrenica," the Belgrade daily, *Politika,* wrote that by taking this action, Serbia had "pushed open the door to Europe."[5]

Serbia is just one recent example reflecting the fundamental change that European historical consciousness has been experiencing since the last third of the twentieth century. It is the trend toward post-heroism, where the passively suffering victim, the heroic *victima,* supplants heroic sacrifice, the *sacrificium,* as the central point of memory culture. Many scholars have observed this tendency in the dynamics of such transformation.[6] But we still lack an empirically grounded, systematic analysis of the process, one that is, above all, structured on an internationally comparative basis.[7] All too frequently, discussions about the authenticity of victims' experiences, their suffering, and their claims – political, ethical, legal, and in the realm of memory culture – remain mired in national concerns – that is, these conversations become entangled in long-felt prejudices and traumas, struggles and competition over interpretation, and modes of creating distance, all of which are reflected in national discourses. Taking a comparative approach, however, can sharpen one's view of possible commonalities among multiple national cases and for overlapping or parallel trends in similar temporal phases. As this volume demonstrates, the comparison of European and East Asian examples is particularly instructive in identifying useful similarities and differences for understanding memory culture in an international context.

The focus of this chapter is not a general comparison of the cultures of memory in Europe and Asia but, rather, a specific question: How was the role of victim constructed following the Second World War on each of these continents?[8] In exploring answers to this central question, it is necessary to ask several others: To what extent did previously ignored victim groups emerge as prominent public players? How did they legitimate their claims of authenticity regarding their experiences? What obstacles did they encounter, and what changes occurred in various perpetrator-victim relationships? Are we ultimately justified in speaking about a global trend toward a victim-centred, post-heroic memory culture?

In order to develop a systematic analysis, four sets of issues will be discussed in this chapter. First, I explore the beginning of a turn toward a post-heroic memory culture. Second, I examine attempts by states in the immediate postwar period – principally Japan and Germany – to compensate for and even whitewash their own guilt as perpetrators by constructing a victim identity. After 1945, both countries elevated the narrative of their own passive victim status into a kind of national doctrine in the culture of memory. Third, this chapter explores the motivation for and impact of this victimhood narrative's construction. It was impossible for states to conceal the fact that such a construction was an attempt to instrumentalize the past for their own contemporary purposes. Moreover, precisely that instrumentalization led true victims of Nazi or Japanese atrocities to speak out, and these voices grew louder over time. Since the 1980s and 1990s, increasing numbers of victim groups asserted the authenticity of their experience, seeking to inscribe themselves in public memory as victims of world war and dictatorship. In parallel, groups raised new, increasingly urgent demands for reparations for the aging generation who had survived the atrocities of the Second World War era. Fourth, we explore the question of whether the post-heroic memorialization of Second World War–era victims is undergoing a process of monumentalization – that is, through the creation of tangible forms of memory, such as museums – and whether perhaps this is occurring in parallel with the universalization of post-heroism.

Toward a Post-Heroic Memory Culture

The First World War constituted a watershed in Europe for the development of a heroic culture of memory. In a manner never imagined or known before then, that conflagration brought mass, violent, and anonymous death to the continent. Up until that point, it was still possible to represent death on the battlefield as something noble and heroic, something grand and almost romantic, but, above all else, highly improbable.

By contrast, after 1918, it was never again possible to think in the same way about war. On the first day of the Battle of the Somme, in 1916, twenty thousand British soldiers lost their lives, a figure almost four times as large as the total number of dead that Great Britain had suffered in the Boer War.[9] Efforts to bring about decisive battlefield encounters in fact decided nothing. Battles had to be repeatedly fought and refought, and this required fresh troops to be constantly sent into the fray. Death here was devoid of anything heroic or romantic. It had changed into an anonymous, everyday experience, introducing the dehumanization of humankind that would so disastrously come to mark the history of the twentieth century.[10]

To be sure, there was no lack of effort to "heroize" the victims of the First World War, still viewed through the lens of nineteenth-century experience. But these attempts foundered in the bloodbath of senseless mass slaughter in which victims passively suffered. Against this backdrop, a pure heroization was possible only to a very limited degree, if at all. In actuality, the First World War formed precisely the interface between the traditional, nineteenth-century construction of heroic sacrifice for the fatherland – the *sacrificium* – and the more recent experience of the victimhood of passive suffering – the *victima*. In other words, the place of honour once occupied by the hero's death now belonged to those who suffered a senseless, anonymous demise.

Walter Flex's autobiographical novella, *The Wanderer between the Two Worlds: An Experience of War* (*Der Wanderer zwischen beiden Welten: Ein Kriegserlebnis* [1916]) illustrates this transformation. The author describes how his close friend, Ernst, fell in battle at the front, leaving the author to inform Ernst's mother of her son's death. She asks, "'Before he died, did Ernst take part in a surprise attack?' I nodded. 'Yes, at Warthi.' She closed her eyes and leaned back in her chair. 'That was his greatest wish,' she said slowly, as if in her pain she was pleased he had achieved something he had long desired. A mother knows the deepest desire of her child."[11] Her son's senseless death is rendered bearable for the mother after she is assured that it had some heroic meaning, regardless of whether the affirmative nod by the narrator was truthful.

The war memorials in the states of the main parties to the Great War, primarily conceived and erected in the 1920s, display a peculiar syncretism. To be sure, the memory of those who had fallen in battle in the First World War remained in one respect fused to the traditional sense of heroism in that, like heroes, they died in service to the fatherland. The difference, however, was that they had died a victim's death – an entirely new interpretation of military sacrifice. The introduction of the victim element created a particular tension as these monuments took shape. Keeping with local tradition and the respective political relations of power, they privileged elements of a male heroism or images of sorrow and despair, ascribed to female figures, in the face of senseless death. Some soldiers' monuments emphasized the male and others focused on the female, yet they remained in competition with each other, leaving this tension unresolved.[12]

The dehumanization of humankind as mere materiel, first unleashed in the First World War, reached its highpoint in the Second World War. Especially in Central and Eastern Europe, the misery of the later conflict, intensified by the unprecedented horror of war crimes visited upon millions of largely civilian non-combatants, far surpassed the dark experiences of 1914–18. In view of the Holocaust and other mass murders, slave labour and starvation, flight and deportation, expulsion and rape, attempts to retrieve anything heroic from this unparalleled suffering were doomed to failure.[13] Instead, attention in the culture of memory after 1945 was increasingly drawn toward civilian victims, thus shifting the focus on soldiers that had prevailed in the immediate aftermath of 1918.

National Doctrine in the Culture of Memory

It was by no means self-evident after 1945 that the war's millions of victims would gain a voice. This was because, in the memory culture of the victorious powers, the death of the enemy – for many, synonymous with the conquest of evil – acquired once more an aura of heroism. The faint voices of civilian victims were simply lost. In the Soviet Union, for example, the heroizing paradigm of the "Great Patriotic War" left little place for the voices of the victims. This silencing had occurred previously with respect to the victims of the Stalinist purges, but the pattern repeated itself with Russian civilian victims in the war, such as those who perished during the starvation blockade of Leningrad by the Wehrmacht.[14] At the same time, victims of the Holocaust attracted scarcely any attention in the Soviet Union.

While the victors of the Second World War were basking in an aura of heroism, the shift to post-heroism was taking place in the memory culture of the defeated powers, principally Japan and Germany. Unable to claim victory, the vanquished powers began to view their war dead as victims, much as they did after the First World War. The relationship between victim and perpetrator shifted, however, because it was by no means always clear who belonged to the group of victims and who to the ranks of the perpetrators. Rather, in the immediate postwar period, the temptation intensified among individuals to conceal their political or military responsibility for crimes – that is, to cover up their role as perpetrators. They accomplished this by constructing a civilian victim identity for themselves. The result was a memory culture in which there was no place for the individuals who had actually suffered at the hands of these would-be victims.

West Germany and Japan initially pursued this strategy, which involved uncoupling the small number of those deemed "true perpetrators" from the majority of their nations' peoples who, now defeated, suffered a grievous fate. Germans and Japanese constructed themselves as a community of victims. In both countries, the narrative of great suffering by the civilian populations, which had paid so dearly and inequitably for war crimes, dovetailed with the view that it had been only a small clique of the military and political leadership that had unleashed the war, conducted it poorly, and ultimately abandoned or even betrayed their own people.

In Japan, this narrative was so prevalent that the memory of the war was nearly synonymous with victimhood.[15] Not least, the International Military Tribunal for the Far East kindled among many Japanese feelings of frustration or even rage against their wartime military and political leaders; this effect was similar to that generated by the Nuremberg Tribunal against Germany's main war criminals. Placing themselves in a context of personal suffering and misfortune made it easier for the Japanese to see themselves as victims of their own political and military leadership.[16] In the conservative camp, however, even those military men and politicians condemned as war criminals were honoured, including some who were ultimately executed for their crimes. The Yasukuni Shrine in Tokyo, Japan's official commemorative site for war dead since 1869, contains the names of condemned war criminals – a concrete example of the blurring of the boundary between perpetrator and victim. Conflicts over the memory culture in that country have erupted on a regular basis since at least 1975, when Prime Minister Miki Takeo visited the Yasukuni Shrine on 15 August, Japan's official day of commemoration of the war's end. Prime Minister Nakasone visited the shrine regularly in the 1980s as an official government gesture, which exacerbated tensions over memory culture, as did several visits by Prime Minister Koizumi in the early 2000s. The revival of the shrine as a place of memory, a calculated move in the politics of the past, also engendered tensions in the sphere of foreign policy.[17] Most recently, a visit by Defence Minister Inada Tomomi to the shrine in December 2016 drew disapproval from South Korea and China.[18]

From 1945, the victims of Hiroshima and Nagasaki were central to the Japanese discourse, and the survivors of those attacks banded together, demanding their rightful place in the Japanese culture of memory. In the official narrative nurtured by the government, Hiroshima and Nagasaki were, of course, at the centre of Japan's singular status as a nuclear victim. The question of Japanese war crimes and the devastation unleashed by the atomic bomb were thus intertwined in Japanese discourse on the politics of the past. No comment on the culture of memory lacked a reference to the fact that Japan was the only country ever to be attacked with a nuclear bomb. Even more extreme were efforts to compare the atomic bombing to the horrors of Auschwitz. "Hiroshima, Auschwitz: we must not forget," wrote lyric poet and Hiroshima survivor Kurihara Sadako in 1989. "Nagasaki, Auschwitz: we must not forget … the vow we made to the dead: we must not forget."[19] A sort of victim iconography took hold throughout Japan, including innumerable personal memoirs, school textbooks, and other manifestations of mass culture. This approach involved laying claim to the authenticity of the status of victim while at the same time promoting the importance of a new Japanese pacifism. Japanese suffering during the war became the basis of a new political culture that disavowed war and advocated the rejection of nuclear armament. In this way, the figure of the victim became, so to speak, a heroic figure.[20] By contrast, it was only in the shadow of this dominant victim identity that one could find affirmations of the Japanese army in the traditional, heroic sense.[21]

A similar development was observable in postwar Germany. Immediately after 1945, the Nazi regime appeared in popular imagery to be a monolithic totalitarian state led by a small clique of criminals and an all-powerful dictator who had subjugated everyone opposed to his iron will. Modern research has totally deconstructed this image, establishing that National Socialist rule had been possible only through its deep anchoring in German society and the broad mobilization of the population. But in the period immediately after 1945, it was still possible to pass on the burden of guilt for German crimes – which, in their factual basis, could not be denied – by attributing them to an omnipotent Führer and his complicit entourage. For a long time in West German discourse, National Socialist crimes, which no one dared describe with any specificity, were actions that had been taken "in the name of the German people," but without their consent or knowledge. Exogenous factors further compounded this situation. The Treaty of Versailles and the behaviour of the victorious powers after the First World War were blamed on the West; in contrast, Stalin, Poland, and Bolshevism bore guilt for the expulsion of the Germans from the eastern territories at the end of the Second World War. In a large-scale project, the German Federal Republic also exhaustively documented the voices of expulsion victims.[22] Efforts to minimize German guilt and to offset it by reference to foreign guilt meshed seamlessly with anti-communism sentiment still extant in West German society.[23]

On this basis, Germans in the early years of the Federal Republic's memory culture overwhelmingly placed themselves front and centre on the stage of victim discourse. Commemoration on 8 May memorialized suffering and destruction brought about by subjugation and control by the Allies.[24] Even a decade after the war's end, the "sea of misery and the ruins" was in the foreground of remembrance. Accordingly, collapse and capitulation, flight and expulsion, chaos and confusion characterized the "days in which a millennium sank into the depths," as historian Michael Freund put it in 1955.[25] For that reason, many Germans similarly viewed the Nuremberg Trials either as a matter that did not concern them or the unjust implementation of victors' justice. As late as 1968, a staff member in the Central Legal Protection Office in the Foreign Ministry summed matters up by noting, "the worst crimes against humanity are the so-called judgments against war criminals by individual or several adversary states." As a rule, he opined, those affected were only "innocent soldiers."[26]

So, both aggressor states, Japan and Germany, were initially quite successful in constructing a victim status for themselves in order to elude that of perpetrator. The paradox thereby created maintained its power up until the 1970s: while the civilian victims of the aggressor powers moved to the centre of memorial culture, those who had been victims of the crimes of the Second World War possessed hardly any independent voice of their own. Only gradually did that image begin to change. In the Federal Republic, memory of German suffering began to fade beginning in the 1960s. The victim status of the expellees, for example, waned to the point that other victims were able to move into the spotlight of memory. Alongside the "treks of the refugees," as Wolf Jobst Siedler formulated it in 1965, the "freight cars of the prisoners" rose from the darkness, and, in the east, not only were there "lost cities" that needed to be rediscovered but also "forgotten camps." Thoughtful individuals thus recognized that the "tyranny [of National Socialism] had not only gambled away the provinces, but also the sorrow over their loss."[27] To the same degree, the expellees from the east began to lose their special status in the Federal Republic as victims of the Second World War. In fact, the 1960s were the period when the refugees began to forfeit their privileged and dignified public aura as victims. Remembrance of the lost provinces increasingly became the special domain of the refugee associations. This sparked substantial bitterness among those who continued to consider themselves victims of the war. And that bitterness was exacerbated when, in 1970, the Willy Brandt government, in the Treaty of Warsaw, accepted the Oder-Neisse line as the border between Germany and Poland.

In Japan, the constructed image of the country's own victim status became more nuanced during the 1960s and 1970s, a process in which the context of the Vietnam War played a salient role. Japanese soldiers began to speak up, referring in their memoirs to Japanese war crimes – though, by doing so, they provoked the ire of their former comrades-in-arms who thought differently. Every attempt to have a more open debate about Japanese atrocities in the Second World War polarized the discourse on the politics of memory. This polarization also involved progressive-minded journalist Honda Katsuichi, who had been a war correspondent in Vietnam. In 1972, he published a highly controversial series of articles on the Nanjing Massacre perpetrated by Japanese soldiers, an atrocity that took the lives of at least 200,000 persons in late 1937 and early 1938. Doing so led to much hostility directed against him. He responded sharply to apologetic objections such as "war is like that. Other armies were also committing atrocities during the war" by noting that this was "the viewpoint of those who perpetrate, but not of those who suffer from aggression."[28]

The polarization of discourse on the politics of history continued in the massive debates surrounding textbooks in Japanese schools. A conservative turn in Japanese politics and society at the end of the 1970s led to a proliferation of revisionist and euphemistic statements on the war and Japanese colonial rule in government-approved textbooks, which culminated in international protests in 1982. The Japanese government came under enormous international pressure and ultimately yielded, calling for the need for understanding when it came to the sensitivities of neighbouring states. In response, resistance in right-wing circles intensified, and talk was rife about the "lie of Nanjing." But the process of pluralizing the memory culture increasingly questioned the image of the Japanese as mere victims of their own military clique and the American atomic bombing.[29]

Thus, the paradoxes of the postwar period accelerated the development of a post-heroic culture of memory. If one asks where this transition to post-heroism after 1945 can best be discerned, it is clearly in the defeated aggressor powers, Japan and Germany. Most aspects of the culture of interpretation in these countries abandoned the traditional paradigm of heroism, constructing instead – and quite successfully – an image of their own people as the suffering victim, a strategy that also served to camouflage their own atrocities and crimes.

Confrontations and Reparations: Victim Groups Emerge

The construction of an image of national victimhood can be termed the "lifelong lie" of Japanese and German memory cultures. Yet the desirable status of victim was contaminated by its apologetic function, so it was logical that, from the 1970s, the victim status of the aggressor powers increasingly began to erode. At the same time, the victims of German and Japanese atrocities achieved increasing success in inscribing their names in the culture of memory. It is not surprising that the initial success Germans and Japanese enjoyed in presenting themselves as victims of the Second World War provoked such a reaction from those who had actually suffered.

Especially from the 1980s, ever more victim groups called attention to the authenticity of their experiences and voiced demands to be accorded the status of victim of world war, dictatorship, and war crimes. Initially, this turn occurred through political means and political mobilization, since the idea that victims could assert themselves as a self-identified community in the postwar societies in Germany and Japan was by no means politically uncontroversial. On the contrary, this construction sparked confrontations over the politics of memory culture. Groups theretofore ignored by that culture discovered a field for action and an important political-moral lever in shaping views on the history of the Second World War and the events leading up to it. Their demands unfolded with increasing intensity in the context of the generational change that began in the early 1960s. One need only recall the debates over the 1959 exhibition by Reinhard Strecker, *Ungesühnte Nazijustiz* (Unpunished Nazi Justice), an exhibition that openly dealt with the Nazi past of many representatives of the legal system, as well as the confrontations over the politics of the past associated with the student protest movement of 1968 and its reverberations.[30] In addition, demands to recognize victim groups' entitlement to reparations, which emerged during détente negotiations between the Federal Republic and its European neighbours, also played an important role in precipitating this shift in memory culture.[31] In Japan, by contrast, there was no comparable moral accusation against the generation of the fathers. But, like in the Federal Republic, protest against the American war in Vietnam also played a significant role in Japan in diversifying and pluralizing the gestalt of opinion.[32]

In West Germany, an additional element in the equation was the set of legal demands made by previously unrecognized victims. This approach was a particularly important one, because framing demands for recognition in legal terms constituted the prerequisite for reparation payments, which in turn helped establish a defined victim category and further propelled a convincing victim narrative. But it would be too simplistic to view material compensation as the victim groups' paramount goal. For those affected, restoration of their personal dignity through a basic recognition of their claims to be victims of war and violence was just as important, if not more so. As remembering is the antipode of forgetting, having place within cultural memory was indispensable in assuaging the pain and injury inflicted on the lives of millions of victims and their families. Recognition, even as a symbolic measure, could perhaps mitigate their suffering. In a 1952 letter to the Federal German Ministry of Finance, a Dutch woman who had been the victim of sterilization experiments at Auschwitz expressed this sentiment directly: "We expected a 'gesture,' compensation for the great physical and moral suffering that your previous government inflicted on us. Perhaps then you would, in the eyes of the world, have taken a position of which it could have been said: Look, at least the new government understands this and is trying to mitigate what their predecessors perpetrated as criminal acts."[33] These words encapsulate the widespread struggle for recognition and legitimation of their experience that many forgotten victims waged after 1945; from the 1970s and 1980s, they intensified their efforts.

An important prerequisite for the juridical construction of victim groups was the gradual change in relevant international law. In the first several decades after 1945, restitution payments were regarded as an intergovernmental matter: if payments were effectively negotiated, it was at the state level, and individual victims had no voice in the process. Thus, beginning with Israel in 1952, the German Federal Republic took the approach of making general blanket reparation payments to its partner in a state agreement. This changed during the 1990s. In reunified Germany, owing in no small part to pressure from the United Nations, the individual gained legal relevance in the question of reparations. Involved here, along with material payments, was always the symbolic importance of recognition of the dignity of the individual victim.[34]

This change from a state-level view of collective victimhood to a juridical recognition of victims as individuals contributed decisively to the emergence and proliferation of victim groups,[35] and it had an enormous impact on the general development of the culture of memory in both Europe and Asia. Victim groups, often relying on a self-image of passively suffering victims, had struggled for decades for recognition and honouring of their experience. The fact that these groups were finally achieving success, often through judicial means, marked the culmination in memory culture of a gradual transformation from a heroic to a post-heroic mode. Several examples are worth mentioning.

For many years, victims of forced sterilization at the hands of the National Socialist regime were not included in the legal definition used by the Federal Republic for the purposes of reparations. The government justified this exclusion because sterilization was considered to be "untypical" of National Socialist persecution. Sterilization, they argued, had not been implemented for political or racist reasons and, second, it was not unique to the Nazi regime, because it had been practised in other countries as well. Not until the 1980s was there any change in this situation, despite ambitious efforts to organize by the "injured parties." In 1987, the Alliance of Victims of "Euthanasia" and Forced Sterilization (Bund der "Euthanasie"-Geschädigten und Zwangssterilisierten) was established; increasingly, its members spoke out in public. The German Bundestag in 1988 declared that judgments handed down by the Hereditary Health Courts (*Erbgesundheitsgerichte*) constituted "Nazi injustice" and revoked them. Those affected thereby obtained the status of a victim group and were then entitled to submit legal claims for reparations.[36]

In the 1990s, compensation for individuals subjected to forced labour by the Nazi regime became a much-discussed topic. The individualization of the claims vis-à-vis Germany, which had come about in part due to significant international pressure, furthered the formation of an association and the constitution of further victim groups. In practically every country occupied by Germany in the Second World War, associations emerged to represent the interests of former forced labourers. The Foundation "Memory, Responsibility, and Future" (Stiftung "Erinnerung, Verantwortung und Zukunft"), established in 2000, effectively arranged for the largely non-bureaucratic and uncomplicated distribution of compensation payments to surviving forced labourers. In so doing, the victim status of this group was elevated for the first time into the broader historical consciousness, thus enabling the entry of its members into the culture of memory.[37]

The significance of this success in achieving recognition, together with the formal recognition of the passively suffering victim *qua* category, can also be illustrated by a striking example in France, where the problematic topic of "victims in competition" attracted much public attention. Commemoration of victims in France after 1945 involved two main groups: the "heroic" fighters of the *Résistance*, in whom the older tradition of *sacrificium* was reflected, and, in the second group, French citizens who had been imprisoned in German concentration camps. By contrast, French citizens who had been subjected by Germany to forced labour were viewed after 1944/45 with greater ambivalence by France's political establishment, justice system, and public. For a long period, they were not able to fully cast off the suspicion that they had been collaborators. The consequence was that, after 1945, the large majority of the French who had been sent to Germany as forced labourers were recognized neither as deportees nor as victims. The concept of *déporté* developed as a historical designation expressing the authenticity of one's victimhood and was strongly favoured by the forced labourers themselves. However, it was soon monopolized by French concentration camp prisoners, who expressly opposed the idea that the earlier forced labourers should also be classified using this designation. Consequently, the postwar decades in French memory culture were marked by an ongoing feud between the Fédération nationale des déportés du travail and some of the concentration camp survivors' organizations over the question of the exclusivity of the "honorary designation" *déporté*.

In fact, the *déportés du travail* occupied the lowest rung in the French hierarchy of victims. In commemorative events, such as in Reims in May 1946, the victim hierarchy was clearly on display in the sequence assigned to the demonstrators in the ceremony. The forced labourers were last in line, behind the few concentration camp survivors and prisoners of war. Subsequently, the forced labourers and their association struggled in vain to be recognized as victims of the war and of National Socialism. "Pourquoi nous sommes des Victimes de la Déportation du Travail" was the despairing title of a 1961 brochure with which the Fédération nationale des déportés du travail sought to undergird its claim to an appropriate victim status.[38]

It took until 2008 for French forced labourers to achieve their long-desired equal status as victims, when the French government issued a decree according them the designation *victimes du travail forcé en Allemagne nazie*. The association welcomed this step, asking, "Is it necessary to remind people that we were the sacrificial offerings for the defeat of 1940 and the occupation of France? It is therefore imperative that our honour be preserved for future generations."[39] It is evident that these events mirror the difficulties that France experienced with the transition from the heroic to post-heroic culture of memory. Political victims from the *Résistance* and army were desirable both for contemporary political purposes and with respect to memory culture, and could be considered a heroic *sacrificium* for the motherland. Forced labourers, by contrast, perceived as purely passive victims, did not fit the image.[40]

In East Asia as well, many, if not most, of the groups representing victims of Japanese aggression did not emerge until many decades after the end of the war. Since the 1980s, at the vanguard in this respect were the surviving Korean and Chinese women who had been forced by the Japanese into sexual slavery. These "comfort women" had been seized and were confined in soldiers' brothels from late 1937 through the end of the war. They now finally spoke up, demanding compensation and recognition by Japan as the victims of sexual violence. Initially decisive was the fact that the surviving women were prepared to speak out, to present public testimony detailing their painful and degrading experiences.[41] Building on this and with further support from the international women's movement, these victims and their representatives systematically employed the tools of organization, public demonstrations, and moral pressure. The highpoint of this international action was the implementation of tribunals in The Hague and Tokyo. Ultimately, the so-called comfort women gained significant international attention and achieved the most prominent status among victims groups in the memory culture in East Asia.[42]

Other Asian victim groups began to enter the cultural field of vision in the 1980s, and evident parallels to the European analogue can be discerned. Male Korean and Chinese forced labourers, for example, who did heavy labour under inhumane conditions in mines and at construction sites in Japan, were at first barely visible in nationally oriented historiography. Western historiography was interested in the fate of British and American prisoners of war; by contrast, in Japan, the topic of prisoners of war was swept under the carpet. Major problems in accessing useful source materials, such as individual testimonies, kept research in this area limited for many years to the contexts of local action and history workshops.[43] Initially, only private initiatives such as the Japanese-Chinese Friendship Association were publicly visible representatives of former forced labourers. Already in 1951, this organization published documentation of crimes and suffering in the Japanese copper mine at Hanaoka, where many Chinese forced labourers were tortured and murdered. A few weeks before the end of the war, workers staged an uprising, with the result that over 200 of them lost their lives in the so-called Hanaoka Massacre. Only beginning in the 1980s and 1990s did former Chinese and Korean forced labourers, including the Hanaoka victims who had gained a certain relative prominence, begin to organize themselves as victim groups. For the first time, systematic interviews were conducted with the survivors, associations were established, and concrete claims for compensation were submitted through legal channels. In April 2010, a memorial was dedicated to the victims of forced labour in Hanaoka, and, in 2015, a memorial park dedicated to the Hanaoka uprising was opened in Tianjin.[44]

Significantly, the international postwar situation and its attendant political interests stood in the way of any earlier sustained commemoration of Chinese victims of Japanese war crimes. Several factors contributed to the reluctance of the People's Republic of China (PRC) to pursue commemoration of these victims. First, Mao was striving for international recognition; second, the PRC was happy to receive Japanese reconstruction assistance. Third, Mao's China, like all communist dictatorships, created a liturgy of heroes: a heroic image of history sanctioned by the Communist Party. All these factors were obstacles to free and open research on the past, and the Chinese government displayed correspondingly little interest in the civilian Chinese victims of the Second World War. Given the context of the dawning Cold War, Washington remained interested in the region, particularly in establishing Japan as an economically efficient and productive partner and, not least of all, as the most important US ally in Asia. In 1952, with these aims in mind, the United States waived demands for reparation payments from Japan and put pressure on the PRC to do the same, which was eventually achieved in a bilateral agreement between the PRC and Japan.[45]

Only following Mao's death did this begin to change, as China became a new global economic power and, in the post-communist era, sought to improve domestic ideological cohesiveness by promoting a "new nationalism." In this context, the history of civilian Chinese war victims became an important element in the memory culture and the politics of history, and regularly revised estimates of their numbers began to rise. This development also emerged as a source of political and moral leverage vis-à-vis Japan. Two elements were intertwined here. First, the heroic resistance against the Japanese acquired an aura of national dignity. Second, the growing global attractiveness of the status of victim led to this label being increasingly applied in discussions of the history of China in the war. Correspondingly, research projects and publications on Chinese victims of Japanese war crimes multiplied.[46]

One such example of this development involved the history of the Nanjing Massacre. While, in Japan, Honda Katsuichi's book on the massacre had created a great stir, in China and the West there was still relative silence about the victims of this atrocity until the 1990s. In 1997, journalist Iris Chang, an American of Chinese descent, published her sensational book, *The Rape of Nanking*, in which the perspective of the victims is narrated in great detail.[47] Since that juncture, the massacre has become a regular topic in international research.[48] This is also the case in China, where the massacre has subsequently attracted the interest of artists, resulting in numerous documentaries, film dramatizations, and literary works that give voice to the victims of the atrocity.[49]

The long list of victim groups that have organized, demanded recognition, and etched themselves into collective memory can certainly be expanded, as could the analysis of corresponding competition for recognition among different types of victims. These groups have precipitated a substantial change in international memory culture; indeed, the transition to a victim-centred post-heroism is inconceivable without them. Looking to the present and beyond, one must ask: Has this transformation influenced commemoration culture in our own day, and if so, in what ways? Are we perhaps witnessing a globalization of post-heroism?

The Universalization of Post-Heroism

Most assertions of victimhood reached their highpoint in the 1980s. It is no accident that, in the German Federal Republic, this was also the time of renewed public attention to the Holocaust, due in significant measure to the television series *Holocaust: The Story of the Family Weiss*, which aired in Germany in 1979. Consequently, the 1980s marked the beginning of an entire new phase in public remembrance of the millions of victims of the Second World War and the crimes perpetrated during the war.

The temporal rhythms of memory culture aligned with the transition from communicative memory to cultural memory, a key transformative point identified in particular by Jan Assmann.[50] Through this lens, around 1980, the memory of National Socialism, the Holocaust, and Japanese war crimes reached the point at which the communicative memory of the actors – those involved personally in the relevant traumas and atrocities – traversed the threshold into cultural memory. This critical threshold occurs approximately forty years after the relevant events, at which time personal memory begins to fade. The generation that had actually experienced these events offered itself a last chance, as it were, to inscribe its experience of victimization and victim identity in the annals of cultural memory. It then became important to render memory that could be transmitted, and handed down over generations to come.

In Germany, this transmission was manifested concretely in, among other things, the establishment of a multitude of memorial sites, and in the activities of many local initiatives, student groups, and "history workshops." These various actors worked to remove the cloak of anonymity from the victims by setting up sites of memory and documentation centres. The 1980s thus represented a new phase in memory culture in which groups and individuals sought to represent both victims and perpetrators in the tangible forms of public memory. This mode of commemorating the victims of National Socialism by concretizing their memory – encompassing, along with the Jews, the Sinti and Roma, Jehovah's Witnesses, homosexuals, military deserters, forced labourers, and others – marked the beginning of a new chapter in the reparations process, which many had already thought to have concluded.[51]

Today more than seventy years after the end of the Second World War, we have reached the turning point at which the voices of the witnesses of the time – the concrete victims of war crimes – are forever fading into silence. In other words, we are currently observing the definite transition from communicative to cultural memory described above, which, at the same time, supports the transition to post-heroism. That is because, at least in Europe, victim identity is granted a special locus in the context of memory culture. After half a century of horrific wars and crimes, post-heroic memory culture has focused its attention principally on the shattered human being, on death and violence, and on suffering and horror in history. "Victim identification" virtually becomes a European "promise of community."[52]

To what extent cultural memory in Asia is developing along comparable lines is an interesting but still unanswered question, yet certain differences are apparent. Japan, for example, continues to demonstrate reluctance in acknowledging its own role as a perpetrator of war crimes – including sexual slavery – in China, the Philippines, and elsewhere. China, on the other hand, has instrumentalized the history of war, and in particular of the Nanjing Massacre, in the framework of civic "education for patriotism." This strategy reinterprets the victim as a hero and employs these victims as an instrument within the complex of Chinese-Japanese relations, which are burdened by history's legacy. However, in recent years, ever more constructions of individual victim identities have emerged.[53]

Within the still-unfolding era of post-heroic memory culture, we can observe two dynamics of development. One centres on the process of iconizing victims and ritualizing their commemoration; the second on the universalization of that remembrance.

New museums, monuments, and other memorial sites commemorating the victims of war, violence, and terror between 1930 and 1945 have been established throughout Europe and East Asia in the past three decades.[54] Despite the diverse narratives addressed by these sites, the centrality of the victim is a striking common thread. This type of memory culture contains elements that Nietzsche described a "monumental mode" (*monumentalische Art*) of history, in that it serves, above all else, the present. Writing in an era when nations throughout Europe were erecting statues of their heroes, Nietzsche had sufficient visual material at his disposal when he described this mode that seeks to glorify the mighty and bold. He writes that, in this mode, history belongs to the "active and powerful man" who has fought a "great battle" and who therefore needs "role models, teachers, and comforters [with whom he can identify] but cannot find … among his contemporaries."[55] The function of today's post-heroic memory culture, strongly centred on the victim, is fundamentally similar to Nietzsche's *monumentalische Art* of history.

But the direction of that culture is diametrically opposed to the monumental view of history. The latter was driven by the hope "that greatness once existed, indeed that it was once *possible*, and therefore that it will be possible again."[56] The post-heroic commemoration of victims, by contrast, is guided by the political-ethical imperative of "Never again!" Yet both approaches seek to make history something vital to the present, to see continuity from the past in present life. The heroic treatment of memory rendered possible a historical lens on life in the present; today, commemoration serves the victims above all else. Both modes, the monumental mode and the post-heroic culture of memory, appropriate the past in selective ways. They promote the iconizing history and ritualizing commemoration. They extract meaning and significance from history, crafting them into a narrative that can be passed on, and, in doing so, they imbue them with the character of something mythical. All problematic aspects of a monumentalization of history oriented to the present are connected with this process.[57]

In Germany, there was a great surge of commemorative projects in the last decades of the twentieth century whose focus was centred on victims who suffered under the Nazi regime – for example, the exhibitions at the Topography of Terror and the Holocaust Memorial in Berlin, to mention but two of the most important projects, as well as the innumerable memorial sites that have been created throughout Germany.[58] Manifest here is evidence that German memorial culture has departed from any idea of a heroic memory culture, completing the transition to a post-heroic society. This shift is also discernible in the new memory culture of the Bundeswehr (German Armed Forces), which became necessary due to the increasing number of international deployments.[59]

We can observe similar trends in Japan. Through the 1990s, there was a proliferation of Japanese museums dedicated to promoting the politics of peace, and more clear-eyed examinations of the country's wartime atrocities began to emerge. The unambiguous acknowledgment and documentation of such war crimes has left only scant space for the heroization of Japanese martyrs and military figures.[60] Today's male members of the Japanese army are also torn between the tradition of wartime heroism and a post-heroic everyday life that tends more to resemble that of an office worker.[61]

Japanese memory culture thus continues to be characterized by the competition between the victim-focused, post-heroic commemorative efforts and the nationalistic elements that perpetuate a heroized image. The Hiroshima Peace Memorial Museum, reopened in 1994 after renovation, took on a new tone compared to the immediate postwar decades. The reconceptualized museum documents, along with the horror of the atomic bombing, the context of the war as a whole, including Japanese war crimes, particularly those in China. The fate of Chinese and Korean forced labourers, long neglected in official Japanese accounts, also finds a place here.[62] On the other hand, one can also discern a clear revitalization of traditional war museums following Japan's conservative turn since the 1970s. Their exhibits represent Japan's Pacific war efforts in general as honourable and the conflict as just. Moreover, the museum heroizes the memory of Japanese "martyrs" in the Second World War, while no space is allotted to commemoration of the victims of Japanese war crimes.[63]

Still, the transition between these two modes of memory culture is not always a smooth one, particularly when balancing commemoration with historical responsibility. Massive debate was sparked in 1996 when the Atomic Bomb Museum in Nagasaki was reopened after undergoing renovation and revision of its focus. A committee of experts encountered significant internal disputes about whether, and to what extent, the dropping of the atomic bomb on the city should be integrated into a comprehensive portrayal of the war's events. A majority of the committee ultimately opted for placing the bombing in a broader context, and their representation of Japanese war crimes was objective. Many local supporters of the museum, however, felt that this approach went much too far and voiced their protest in the strongest terms:

> We, residents of Nagasaki, have appealed to the world to listen to the truth about the sorrowful damages inflicted on Japan, the only nation on which the bombs were dropped, and to lead the abolition of nuclear weapons. The "atomic bomb museum," which should convey our wish to the world, however, has become a museum that approves of the dropping of the atomic bomb ... The museum that received essential funding from our taxes ... was built as a hall of "atrocities and aggression" of our nation by a small number of the city officials and indoctrinated scholars.[64]

The frustration palpable in this statement could be compared to the views of German expellees and their associations since the 1970s. In both cases, the dominant feeling was one of losing one's privileged status as a victim in an ever-changing environment shaped by shifts in memory culture and the politics of history. An extended storm of controversy raged, for example, around the German museum project "Flight, Expulsion, and Reconciliation" (*Flucht, Vertreibung und Versöhnung*), in which a similar question of the appropriate depiction of victims in the context of broader guilt was at issue.[65]

The situation appears to be different in China. Both the heroic-nationalist and the post-heroic, victim-centred renderings of the past are concretized under the umbrella of a national culture of memory. Two of the most important museums in this regard are the Memorial Museum of the Chinese People's War of Resistance against Japan, opened in Beijing in 1987, and the Memorial Museum of the Victims of the Nanjing Massacre by the Invading Japanese Military, opened in Nanjing in 1985. It is necessary to examine the two museums together in order to understand their place in the context of Chinese national memory politics. While both share the patriotic aim of civic education, the museum in Nanjing in particular links the post-heroic view of suffering civilian victims – particularly women and children – with the representation of the heroic resistance of the Chinese people. This dual motif is also clearly at the foreground of the Beijing museum.[66] Thus, a clear, government intention in utilizing the politics of history is discernible here: tropes of both victimization and heroization – the main strategies available in memory culture – have been brought together in a sort of new synthesis that serves nationalist interests.[67] As part of this, naturally, the hero-focused culture of the Communist Party and the achievements and martyrs of the Chinese military continue to be present in numerous exhibitions.[68]

The official representation of Korean victims of Japanese aggression had been overshadowed by the exigencies of broader Cold War politics that divided the state and aligned South Korea with the United States and, by association, with Japan. Only in the past few decades have the victims of Japanese crimes also found a welcome place in Korean museums. In 1988, for example, a private museum was opened in Seoul to commemorate the history and legacy of comfort women.[69]

Another dynamic observable in the creation of such museums and monuments is the proclivity toward rendering a universalized view of post-heroic memory culture. The victim discourse appears to be universally accepted as a source of legitimation, which is further enhanced by the claim to the universal validity of human rights. One can view that trend as a symptom of globalization, which has contributed to the emergence of a transnational, post-heroic culture of memory. The process of universalization began with commemoration of the Holocaust. In this process, the context of the event at hand is gradually separated from its historical nucleus, and the memory of the victims is shaped into a symbol of universal remembrance and a general appeal for preserving humanity and tolerance.[70] The Holocaust also serves an instrumentalizing function in this process in that it serves as a touchstone for other victim identities, leading them to be associated implicitly with genocide. That applies, for example, with respect to the Ukrainian concept of the Holodomor (famine). Although the term has only an accidental orthographical similarity with the Holocaust, in its interpretation as an act of "genocide against the Ukrainian people," a clear political intent to capitalize on the infamy of the Holocaust is revealed, grounded in the politics of history. And, in her 1997 book, *Rape of Nanking*, Iris Chang also placed the Nanjing Massacre in the context of the politics of history, alluding to the industrial mass murder of the Jews.[71] The memory of the victims of Hiroshima and Nagasaki is also imbued with an inherent tendency to universalize those experiences. This can be seen, for example, in the efforts of citizens of Nagasaki to utilize their victim identities to demand universal pacifism and a global abolition of nuclear weapons.[72]

Of course, such tendencies toward universalization harbour a problematic temptation for former aggressor states such as Japan and Germany. The universal, egalitarian nature of global, post-heroic memory culture offers later generations – those born after the events in question – an equal opportunity to participate. This results in the historical-empirical experience (the "historical nucleus" described above) dissolving into a more abstract concept that is uncoupled from the individuals participating in the acts of commemoration. The universal and timeless nature of exhortations to preserve humanity is undeniable, and we have seen how these emanated both from the original atrocities (e.g., those committed by Germans) and from the suffering endured by victims. Yet it would be nothing short of disastrous if such a universalization of cultural memory, centred on the victims, were to become so generalized that it overshadowed or whitewashed the responsibility and guilt of perpetrators.

Conclusion

In the trend toward a post-heroic memory culture, there remain several points of tension and ambivalence. These are created in part by the victors of the Second World War – Russia, the United States, and Great Britain – which remain committed, in part, to a heroic commemoration of that war. Probably only in Germany – a country virtually devoid of competing narratives – has post-heroism fully established itself. The sheer monstrosity of Germany's crimes closed the door to any attempts to renew heroic forms of memory. The impulse to renounce its own disastrous national history is embedded in Germany in an especially profound way that is the epitome of the general European trend creating distance between the continent's dark history and its present. The construction of victim identities is particularly suited to this trend, and, since the 1980s, a multitude of forgotten victim groups have demanded the inscription of their names into cultural memory.

This strategy has also been used in Asia, and many parallels to European examples are apparent. Nonetheless, the resulting situation in Asia is more complicated. In Japan, heroic and post-heroic elements of memory culture continue to compete with each other, whereas in China, the experience of Japanese aggression serves as a cornerstone of a heroic and nationalist commemoration of Chinese victims. By contrast, in South Korea, the legacy of comfort women dominates memory culture because they arguably can be classified most easily as pure *victimae* and thus embody post-heroism most clearly. Taking these consistencies and contradictions together, one can conclude that, although we cannot point to a uniform global trend toward post-heroism, the interpretation and representation of the memories of the Second World War have undoubtedly and fundamentally changed.

NOTES

1 One representative example is Jeffrey T. Checkel and Peter J. Katzenstein, eds., *European Identity* (Cambridge: Cambridge University Press, 2009). For a more detailed discussion of this topic, see Andreas Wirsching, *Der Preis*

der Freiheit: Geschichte Europas in unserer Zeit (Munich: C.H. Beck 2012), 348–91.

2 See "60. Jahrestag des Ungarnaufstandes," *Balaton Zeitung*, 22 October 2016, https://www.balaton-zeitung.info/3894/60-jahrestag-des-ungarnaufstandes/.

3 See Thomas Risse, *A Community of Europeans? Transnational Identities and Public Spheres* (Ithaca, NY: Cornell University Press, 2010), 53, 163. See also Pieter Lagrou, "Europa als Ort gemeinsamer Erinnerungen? Opferstatus, Identität und Emanzipation von der Vergangenheit," in *Geschichtspolitik in Europa seit 1989: Deutschland, Frankreich und Polen im internationalen Vergleich*, ed. Etienne François (Göttingen: Wallstein, 2013), 298–308. On the beginnings of a comparable tendency in Asia, see Laura Hein, "War Compensation: Claims against the Japanese Government and Japanese Corporations for War Crimes," in *Politics and the Past: On Repairing Historical Injustices*, ed. John Torpey (Lanham, MD: Rowman & Littlefield, 2003), 132.

4 Daniele Giglioli, *Die Opferfalle: Wie die Vergangenheit die Zukunft fesselt* (Berlin: Matthes & Seitz, 2016), 9.

5 Quoted in "Blick in die Presse," *Süddeutsche Zeitung*, 28/29 May 2011, 4.

6 Herfried Münkler, "Heroische und postheroische Gesellschaften," *Merkur* 61, no. 700 (2007): 742–52; Martin Sabrow, "The Post-heroic Memory Society: Models of Historical Narration in the Present," in *Clashes in European Memory: The Case of Communist Repression and the Holocaust*, ed. Muriel Blaive, Christian Gerbel, and Thomas Lindenberger (Innsbruck: Studien Verlag, 2009), 88–98.

7 See, however, K. Erik Franzen and Martin Schulze Wessel, eds., *Opfernarrative: Konkurrenzen und Deutungskämpfe in Deutschland und im östlichen Europa nach dem Zweiten Weltkrieg* (Munich: Oldenbourg, 2012), in particular the introduction by Wessel, 1–8.

8 On comparison of the cultures of memory in Europe and Asia, see the substantial volume by Christoph Cornelißen, Lutz Klinkhammer, and Wolfgang Schwentker, eds., *Erinnerungskulturen: Deutschland, Italien und Japan seit 1945* (Frankfurt: Fischer-Taschenbuch-Verlag, 2003). See also Manfred Kittel, *Nach Nürnberg und Tokio: "Vergangenheitsbewältigung" in Japan und Westdeutschland 1945 bis 1968* (Munich: Oldenbourg, 2004). On historiography, see Sebastian Conrad, *Auf der Suche nach der verlorenen Nation: Geschichtsschreibung in Westdeutschland und Japan 1945–1960* (Göttingen: Vandenhoeck & Ruprecht, 1999).

9 For a good analysis of how traditional heroism shifted into the pure and anonymous battle of materiel, see Martin Gilbert, *The Battle of the Somme: The Heroism and Horror of War* (Toronto: McClelland & Stewart, 2007).

10 This was, however, only the experience at the Western Front. One can wonder whether on the Eastern Front, where the war was more one of

tactical movement, the idea of heroism was more strongly preserved. This hypothesis and the history of the Eastern Front generally deserve more attention by researchers than they have been afforded to date.

11 Quoted translation from Walter Flex, *The Wanderer between the Two Worlds*, trans. Brian Murdoch ([England]: Rott Publishing, 2014), 35.

12 Antoine Prost, "Les monuments aux morts," in *Les lieux de mémoire*, ed. Pierre Nora (Paris: Gallimard, 1997), 199–226, esp. 201ff. on the iconographic motifs in the monuments. See also Annette Becker, *Les monuments aux morts: Patrimoine et mémoire de la Grande Guerre* (Paris: Éditions Errance, 1988) and Andreas Wirsching, "Umstrittene Erinnerung: Die französischen monuments aux morts nach dem Ersten Weltkrieg. Das Beispiel Levallois-Perret," in *Nationale Mythen – kollektive Symbole: Funktionen, Konstruktionen und Medien der Erinnerung*, ed. Klaudia Knabel, Dietmar Rieger, and Stephanie Wodianka (Göttingen: Vandenhoeck & Ruprecht, 2005), 127–43.

13 This is also the dominant chord in Timothy Snyder, *Bloodlands: Europe between Hitler and Stalin* (New York: Basic Books, 2010).

14 See the chapter by Tatiana Voronina in this volume. See also Voronina, "Vom Krieg auf Russisch: Die Erinnerung an die Leningrader Blockade in den Verbänden der Blockadeteilnehmer," in Franzen and Wessel, *Opfernarrative*, 191–215.

15 The literature on this is extensive and difficult to survey. Representative here, for example, is James J. Orr, *The Victim as Hero: Ideologies of Peace and National Identity in Postwar Japan* (Honolulu: University of Hawai'i Press, 2001) and Orr, "Victims and Perpetrators in National Memory: Lessons from Post–World War Two Japan," *Schweizerische Zeitschrift für Geschichte* 57, no. 1 (2007): 42–57. For a differentiated and comparative treatment, see Thomas U. Berger, *War, Guilt, and World Politics after World War II* (Cambridge: Cambridge University Press, 2012), 123–229 and Wolfgang Schwentker, "Täter oder Opfer? Schuldfrage, atomarer Schrecken und nationale Identität in Japan 1945–1995," in *Sieger und Besiegte: Materielle und ideelle Neuorientierung nach 1945*, ed. Holger Afflerbach and Christoph Cornelißen (Tübingen: Francke, 1997), 141–63.

16 Madoka Futamura, "Japanese Societal Attitudes towards the Tokyo Trial: A Contemporary Perspective," *Asia-Pacific Journal* 9, issue 29, no. 5 (July 2011): 1–19.

17 For an excellent and nuanced summary, see Sven Saaler, "Ein Ersatz für den Yasakuni-Schrein? Die Diskussion um eine neue Gedenkstätte für Japans Kriegsopfer," *Nachrichten der Gesellschaft für Natur- und Völkerkunde Ostasiens* 175/176 (2004): 59–91, esp. 62–72. On religious aspects, see Kunichika Yagyû, "Der Yasukuni-Schrein im Japan der Nachkriegszeit: Zu den Nachwirkungen des Staatsshintô," in Cornelißen, Klinkhammer,

and Schwentker, *Erinnerungskulturen*, 243–53. The "Yasukuni problem" is comparable in some ways to the 1985 West German "Bitburg scandal," when Chancellor Helmut Kohl arranged a commemoration of war dead at the military cemetery in Bitburg, where members of the Waffen-SS are also buried. In both cases, the blurring of the lines between perpetrator and victim caused anger and resentment.

18 See Nobuhiro Kubo, "Japan Minister Visits Controversial Shrine Honoring War Dead after Pearl Harbor Trip," *Reuters*, 29 December 2016, http://www.reuters.com/article/us-japan-shrine-inada-idUSKBN14I025.

19 Kurihara Sadako, *Black Eggs* (Ann Arbor: University of Michigan Press, 1994), 292. A morally grounded anti-Americanism is a common thread running through these poems.

20 For a detailed treatment, see Orr, *Victim as Hero*.

21 Ibid., 38ff.

22 Theodor Schieder, ed., *Dokumentation der Vertreibung der Deutschen aus Ost-Mitteleuropa* (1953–62; reprint, Munich: Deutscher Taschenbuch Verlag, 1984). On this, see Mathias Beer, "Im Spannungsfeld von Politik und Zeitgeschichte: Das Großforschungsprojekt 'Dokumentation der Vertreibung der Deutschen aus Ost-Mitteleuropa,'" *Vierteljahrshefte für Zeitgeschichte* 46, no. 8 (1998): 345–89.

23 See Andreas Wirsching, "Antikommunismus als Querschnittsphänomen politischer Kultur, 1917–1945," in *"Geistige Gefahr" und "Immunisierung der Gesellschaft": Antikommunismus und politische Kultur in der frühen Bundesrepublik*, ed. Stefan Creuzberger and Dierk Hoffmann (Munich: Oldenbourg de Gruyter, 2014), 15–28.

24 Erich Dombrowski, "8. Mai 1945," *Frankfurter Allgemeine Zeitung*, 7 May 1955, 1.

25 Michael Freund, "Die Wochen, die ein Jahrtausend zerstörten," *Die Zeit*, 5 August 1955, 2. See more generally, Robert G. Moeller, "Germans as Victims? Thoughts on a Post–Cold War History of World War II's Legacies," *History and Memory* 17 (2005): 147–94; Gilad Margalit, *Guilt, Suffering, and Memory: Germany Remembers Its Dead of World War II* (Bloomington: Indiana University Press, 2010).

26 Letter from Dr. Steinmann, 28 August 1968, B 83 (Ref. V 4), vol. 574, Politisches Archiv des Auswärtigen Amtes.

27 Wolf Jobst Siedler, "Trauer über den verlorenen Schmerz," *Die Welt*, 8 May 1965.

28 Quoted in Takashi Yoshida, "A Battle over History: The Nanjing Massacre in Japan," in *The Nanjing Massacre in History and Historiography*, ed. Joshua A. Fogel (Berkeley: University of California Press, 2000), 80.

29 For a detailed discussion of the representation of the war in Japanese textbooks, see Orr, *Victim as Hero*, 71–105 and Mark Selden and Yoshiko

Nozai, "Japanese Textbook Controversies, Nationalism, and Historical Memory: Intra- and International Conflicts," *Asia-Pacific Journal* 7, issue 24, no. 5 (15 June 2009): 1–24. See also Ishida Yuji, "Das Massaker von Nanking und die japanische Öffentlichkeit," in Cornelißen, Klinkhammer, and Schwentker, *Erinnerungskulturen*, 233–42.

30 See Gottfried Oy and Christoph Schneider, *Die Schärfe der Konkretion: Reinhard Strecker, 1968 und der Nationalsozialismus in der bundesdeutschen Historiografie* (Münster: Westfälisches Dampfboot, 2014) and Wilfried Mausbach, "Wende um 360 Grad? Nationalsozialismus und Judenvernichtung in der 'zweiten Gründungsphase' der Bundesrepublik," in *Wo "1968" liegt, Reform und Revolte in der Geschichte der Bundesrepublik*, ed. Christina von Hodenberg and Detlef Siegfried (Göttingen: Vandenhoeck & Ruprecht, 2006), 15–46.

31 For a summary, see Constantin Goschler, *Schuld und Schulden: Die Politik der Wiedergutmachung für NS-Verfolgte seit 1945* (Göttingen: Wallstein, 2005) and articles in *Grenzen der Wiedergutmachung: Die Entschädigung für NS-Verfolgte in West- und Osteuropa 1945–2000*, ed. Hans Günter Hockerts, Claudia Moisel, and Tobias Winstel (Göttingen: Wallstein, 2006).

32 Orr, *Victim as Hero*, 3–4; Berger, *War, Guilt, and World Politics*, 162. For a comprehensive treatment, see Thomas Havens, *Fire across the Sea: The Vietnam War and Japan, 1965–1975* (Princeton, NJ: Princeton University Press, 1987).

33 Quoted in Stefanie Michaela Baumann, "Opfer von Menschenversuchen als Sonderfall der Wiedergutmachung," in Hockerts, Moisel, and Winstel, *Grenzen der Wiedergutmachung*, 147; see also Baumann, *Menschenversuche und Wiedergutmachung: Der lange Streit um die Entschädigung und Anerkennung der Opfer nationalsozialistischer Humanexperimente* (Munich: Oldenbourg 2009).

34 Henning Borggräfe, *Zwangsarbeiterentschädigung: Vom Streit um "vergessene Opfer" zur Selbstaussöhnung der Deutschen* (Göttingen: Wallstein, 2014), 207ff.

35 See Laura Hein, "War Compensation: Claims against the Japanese Government and Japanese Corporations for War Crimes," in *Politics and the Past: On Repairing Historical Injustices*, ed. John Torpey (Lanham, MD: Rowman and Littlefield, 2003), 133–6.

36 Svea Luise Hermann and Kathrin Braun, "Systematisches Unrecht oder individuelles Schicksal? Die Kämpfe der Opfer staatlicher Sterilisationspolitiken in Deutschland und Tschechien um Anerkennung, Wiedergutmachung und moralische Rehabilitation," in Franzen and Wessel, *Opfernarrative*, 101–25.

37 See Katrin Schröder, "Der Opferstatus der ehemaligen NS-Zwangsarbeiter in den Debatten zu den Leistungsgesetzen für NS-Opfer der 1990er Jahre in Tschechien und Polen," in Franzen and Wessel, *Opfernarrative*, 127–50;

Krzysztof Ruchniewicz, "Die Bemühungen um Entschädigungszahlungen an die ehemaligen polnischen Zwangsarbeiter," in *Zwangsarbeit als Kriegsressource*, ed. Kerstin von Lingen and Klaus Gestwa (Paderborn: Schöningh, 2014), 447–61. See also Constantin Goschler, "Die Auseinandersetzung um die Entschädigung der Zwangsarbeiter zwischen Kaltem Krieg und Globalisierung," in *Zwangsarbeit im Europa des 20. Jahrhunderts: Bewältigung und vergleichende Aspekte*, ed. Hans Christoph Seidel and Klaus Tenfelde (Essen: Klartext-Verlag, 2007), 115–30, as well as the legal study by Jörg Hagen Hennies, *Entschädigung für Zwangsarbeit vor und unter der Geltung des Stiftungsgesetzes vom 2.8.2000* (Baden-Baden: Nomos, 2006).

38 It is telling, for example, that the Fédération does not appear in a list of associations active in memory politics in Danièle Déon Bessière, *1940–1945: Résistances et Déportations. Cette mémoire, comment la transmettre?* (Paris: Harmattan, 2010). Here I sum up some of the findings of a master's thesis by Andreas Löns, "Französische Arbeitskräfte in Deutschland während des Zweiten Weltkrieges: Geschichte und Nachwirkungen" (Eberhard-Karls-University, Tübingen, 1998).

39 "Faut-il rappeler que nous avons été les victimes expiatoires de la défaite de 1940, de l'occupation de la France, il est donc impératif que notre Honneur soit conservé pour les générations futures." See "Après 57 ans de combat," Histoire d'une période noire, http://www.requis-deportes-sto.com/index.php/histoire/aujourd-hui/apres-57-ans-de-combat.

40 For a comprehensive description of memory culture in France, see Henning Meyer, *L'évolution de la "culture de mémoire" française par rapport à la Seconde Guerre mondiale* (Nice: Editions Bénévent, 2007).

41 For such a collection of personal testimonies, see Keith Howard, ed., *True Stories of the Korean Comfort Women* (London: Cassell, 1995).

42 There is now extensive literature on the subject. The most important work, which collects and makes heard the voices of many former forced prostitutes, is C. Sarah Soh, *The Comfort Women: Sexual Violence and Postcolonial Memory in Korea and Japan* (Chicago: University of Chicago Press, 2008). For details on the legal argumentation of the comfort women and their legal representatives, see Hein, "War Compensation," 133–8. See also Chin-Sung Chung, "The Origin and Development of Military Sexual Slavery in Imperial Japan," in *Asian Labor in the Wartime Japanese Empire: Unknown Histories*, ed. Peter H. Kratoska (New York: Sharpe 2005), 303–25, esp. 317–24. For a view by a Japanese author, see Yoshimi Yoshiaki, *Comfort Women: Sexual Slavery in the Japanese Military during World War II* (New York: Columbia University Press, 2000).

43 Franziska Seraphim, "Chinesische Zwangsarbeit in Japan: Der Fall Hanaoka," in von Lingen and Gestwa, *Zwangsarbeit als Kriegsressource*, 357.

44 Ibid., 367ff. On the broader context, see also Paul H. Kratoska, "Labor Mobilization in Japan and the Japanese Empire," in Kratoska, *Asian Labor*, 3–21.
45 Hein, "War Compensation," 132.
46 Peter Hays Gries, *China's New Nationalism: Pride, Politics, and Diplomacy* (Berkeley: University of California Press, 2004); Parks M. Coble, "China's 'New Remembering' of the Anti-Japanese War of Resistance, 1937–1945," *China Quarterly* 190 (2007): 394–410.
47 Iris Chang, *The Rape of Nanking: The Forgotten Holocaust of World War II* (New York: Basic Books, 1997), 81–104.
48 See Fogel, *Nanjing Massacre*.
49 Michael Berry, *A History of Pain: Trauma in Modern Chinese Literature and Film* (New York: Columbia University Press, 2008), 108–78.
50 Jan Assmann, *Das kulturelle Gedächtnis: Schrift, Erinnerung und politische Identität in frühen Hochkulturen* (Munich: C.H. Beck, 1992), 50–4. See also Assmann, "Communicative and Cultural Memory," in *Cultural Memory Studies: An International and Interdisciplinary Handbook*, ed. Astrid Erll and Ansgar Nünning (Berlin: de Gruyter, 2008), 109–18.
51 Hockerts, Moisel, and Winstel, *Grenzen der Wiedergutmachung*.
52 Ulrike Jureit and Christian Schneider, *Gefühlte Opfer: Illusionen der Vergangenheitsbewältigung* (Stuttgart: Klett-Cotta, 2010), 86.
53 For more on this point, see the chapter by Daqing Yang in this volume.
54 For Eastern Europe, see the articles in *Krieg im Museum: Präsentationen des Zweiten Weltkriegs in Museen und Gedenkstätten des östlichen Europa*, ed. Ekaterina Makhotina, Ekaterina Keding, Włodzimierz Borodziej, Etienne François, and Martin Schulze Wessel (Göttingen: Vandenhoeck & Ruprecht, 2015).
55 Adapted and translated from Friedrich Nietzsche, "Vom Nutzen und Nachteil der Historie für das Leben" (On the use and abuse of history for life) in *Unzeitgemäße Betrachtungen* (Leipzig: Alfred Kröner Verlag, 1930), 112.
56 Ibid., 14.
57 On this, see in particular Giglioli, *Opferfalle*.
58 As early as 1987, the Federal Agency for Civic Education published an extensive list of such sites. *Gedenkstätten für die Opfer des Nationalsozialismus: Eine Dokumentation* (Bonn: Bundeszentrale für politische Bildung, 1987). See also a more recent compilation, Constanze Werner, ed., *KZ-Friedhöfe und -Gedenkstätten in Bayern: "Wenn das neue Geschlecht erkennt, was das alte verschuldet…"* Bayerische Verwaltung der staatlichen Schlösser, Gärten und Seen (Regensburg: Schnell & Steiner, 2011).
59 Herfried Münkler, "Militärisches Totengedenken in der postheroischen Gesellschaft," in *Bedingt erinnerungsbereit: Soldatengedenken in der Bundesrepublik*, ed. Manfred Hettling (Göttingen: Vandenhoeck & Ruprecht,

2008), 22–30. On the broader context of the military and post-heroism, see Gerhard Kümmel, "Tod, wo ist dein Stachel? Die Deutschen, die Bundeswehr und militärische Einsätze in postheroischen Zeiten," in *Krieg und Zivilgesellschaft*, ed. Dierk Spreen and Trutz von Trotha (Berlin: Duncker & Humblot, 2012), 189–217.

60 Takashi Yoshida, *From Cultures of War to Cultures of Peace: War and Peace Museums in Japan, China, and South Korea* (Portland, ME: MerwinAsia, 2014), 48–111.

61 Sabine Frühstück, "After Heroism: Must Real Soldiers Die?" in *Recreating Japanese Men*, ed. Frühstück and Anne Walthall (Berkeley: University of California Press, 2011), 91–111.

62 Yoshida, *From Cultures of War*, 81.

63 Ibid., 144, 149.

64 Ibid., 170. For a similar statement, see also "Citizens Group That Seeks to Correct Atomic Exhibitions in Nagasaki," *Korede iinoka: Nagasaki genbaku shiryōkan* (This Isn't Right! The Nagasaki Atomic Bomb Museum) (Nagasaki, 1996).

65 For a collection of press material from 1998 to 2008 related to this debate, see "Materialien zur Debatte um das "Zentrum gegen Vertreibungen," http://www.zeitgeschichte-online.de/thema/materialien-zur-debatte-um-das-zentrum-gegen-vertreibungen. For more current press coverage, see the collection of Spiegel-online, http://www.spiegel.de/thema/zentrum_gegen_vertreibungen/.

66 Yoshida, *From Cultures of War*, 200–15.

67 On this, see also Kirk A. Denton, *Exhibiting the Past: Historical Memory and the Politics of Museums in Postsocialist China* (Honolulu: University of Hawai'i Press, 2014), 31–52.

68 Ibid., 95–132.

69 Yoshida, *From Cultures of War*, 224–9.

70 On this, see Jan Eckel and Claudia Moisel, eds., *Universalisierung des Holocaust? Erinnerungskultur und Geschichtspolitik in internationaler Perspektive* (Göttingen: Wallstein, 2008).

71 Chang, *Rape of Nanking*.

72 Yoshida, *From Cultures of War*, 170.

2 Victim Identities and the Dynamics of "Authentication": Patterns of Shaping, Ranking, and Reassessment

MICHAEL SCHWARTZ

The Social Construction of Victimhood: Public Authentication

"Are victims actually 'authentic'?" This unsettling question is posed by media scholar Ophelia Lindemann in an essay on victim stories and their "paradoxes of recognition." What does being "authentic" mean if we accept Lindemann's assumption that all victim narratives are in competition for social recognition – that the genuineness of victims is bound by conditions of narrative, discursive, and socio-political competition, and finally by gradated social approval? A precondition for the fact that the suffering speaks from the victim almost undisguised seems to be the passivity of the victim at the moment of atrocity, Lindemann notes, observing that victim narratives accordingly often try to pre-empt allegations of the victims' own complicity. "This points out the normative margins of the 'successful,' 'authentic' victim narrative," that is, the diagnosis of social conditionality of each narrative from which Lindemann's conclusion derives: to narrate one's own experience, as a victim or as a perpetrator, is never unmediated or "authentic."[1]

In his study on "triumph and trauma," sociologist Bernhard Giesen asserts that all authenticity – including the authenticity of victims – is constructed; he points out that truth and authenticity are claimed by the victim-narrator and are recognized or rejected by the audience. Giesen cites Primo Levi and Elie Wiesel as examples that embody true victim authenticity.[2] But social attribution of such qualities can also go astray, Giesen notes, as became obvious in a scandal surrounding the autobiography of a supposed survivor of the Majdanek extermination camp who was later proved to be neither a concentration camp survivor nor a Jew – but not before the fraudulent work was celebrated as a moving, authentic testimony and translated into thirteen languages.[3] Here, according to Giesen, it was the public's willingness to believe as well as its basic longing for authenticity that led to a (in this case, misguided) construction of sacred authenticity. The background to this error is the fact that the moral authority of the surviving Jewish victims of Nazism is so overwhelming that it normally would not be questioned by anyone.[4] A literary critic who had been an early sceptic of potentially false victim memoirs compared the author of this narrative to people who in earlier centuries had claimed to be descendants of kings. Like medieval kings, survivors of the Holocaust are now surrounded by an aura of sanctity and protected by the taboo of questioning that status. Their memories are treated like sacred texts, and any criticism is therefore profane, if not sacrilegious.[5]

The construction of a passive, helpless victim image creates, as Giesen also points out, a contradiction between this sacrificial picture and the apparent socio-political power involved in representing the victim's interests. The representation of the victim by advocacy associations, for example, contradicts this sacralized public image, which is imagined as powerless and incapable of fighting for its own interests. But in Giesen's view, real victims would always need some form of help – from publishers, media, therapists, lawyers, humanitarian organizations, or other representatives – in order to be heard. Victims thus, in principle, need *mediation*. The subsequent professionalization of such representation is not regarded by Giesen as a problem but instead as enhanced efficiency in the pursuit of the victim's interests, namely, the parallel moderation of the often intense emotions that arise in public discourse, which thus enhances the likelihood of compromise. If, as Giesen emphasizes, all forms of authenticity are necessarily "mediated and constructed,"[6] then these activities of organized victim advocacy groups and associations become a constitutive part of authentication processes and thus of the social construction of victim authenticity. To what extent such a function can lead to a problematic *mediatization* of genuine victim experiences will be examined below.

Scholars such as Lindemann and Giesen recognize the extent to which social handling of victim narratives was and is dependent on how perpetrator narratives were and are dealt with simultaneously. "Are victims actually 'authentic'? And culprits 'false'? Do victims endure a story while perpetrators just tell stories?" asks Lindemann, highlighting the fact that the story of a suspected perpetrator from the outset appears suspicious, as being "made" (in the sense of being fabricated) because one suspects the ulterior motive of self-interest.[7]

This is an apt description of how these narratives are currently viewed, but it cannot be generalized for the entire history of intertwined victim and perpetrator discourses in Germany since 1945. On the contrary: we can observe significant changes over time in the power relations between these groups, if we use Klaus Günther's paradigm of "the zero-sum game between perpetrator and victim" in which "each gain for the offender" is regarded as "a loss for the victim – and vice versa."[8] The substance of these discourses involves not only conflicting authenticity claims of different victim groups and associations but also changes of generations and opinions within German societies – and, subsequently, a significant change in what was considered "speakable." The social assignment of victim authenticity has been undergoing a "structural change of recognition" for over seven decades, but this transformation has required corresponding structural changes in society and public opinion in general.

Postwar Beginnings: German Self-Victimization and Selective Authentication

In the three-stage model of remembrance formulated by historian Martin Schulze Wessel, the memories of individuals constitute the most basic level but are nonetheless "part of a communicative memory." This model is most concerned with the macro level of official state policy of remembrance as well as the middle level represented by the self-organized commemoration of victim associations.[9] Such associations distinguish, as does much state legislation, between victims who are deemed to be entitled to public recognition and financial compensation and the "unworthy." The statutes of the French association of Holocaust survivors, Amicale des déportés d'Auschwitz, explicitly stated that racially persecuted persons – that is, former Jewish inmates of the extermination camp – should be admitted only if their conduct in the camp had served the honour of France.[10] The German Democratic Republic (GDR) determined in 1950 that so-called Gypsies could be recognized as "persons persecuted by the Nazi regime" (*Verfolgte des Naziregimes*, or VdN), only if (1) they could demonstrate that they had been "imprisoned due to their ethnic origins" and not based on a charge of "asociality"; (2) they had been registered after 1945 as willing to work (which would support a claim that they were not "asocial"); and (3) they had also "maintained antifascist-democratic attitudes."[11] As a result of these restrictions, the state recognized only 122 Sinti as VdN in the whole GDR up until 1954.[12] These examples demonstrate how groups of victims that had secured public recognition opposed the recognition of "questionable" groups of victims in order to avoid the public perception that all inmates of the concentration camps had been criminals – a perception that had prevailed both before and after 1945.

According to Constantin Goschler, Jews and former political prisoners therefore attached great importance to excluding all those "unworthy of [state] support" (*die zur Betreuung Unwürdigen*) from the circle of recognized Nazi victims: "Specifically, this meant, for example, that people who had been persecuted as 'asocials,' 'Gypsies,' or homosexuals met similar difficulties in West and East [after 1945] and were usually excluded from [state] care. The concern of former persecutees for their own reputation often clashed with the interests of frugal-minded authorities."[13] This was exactly what Klaus Günther has called the defence of the authenticity of experiences of the "pure victims" – a marked distinction "especially against the 'false victims,' who merely assume the status of victims because of secondary recognition gains."[14]

Much of the postwar German-speaking world – the German Democratic Republic, the Federal Republic of Germany (FRG), and also the special case of Austria – found it difficult to recognize true victims of the Nazi past. In the 1950s, Germans in both of the republics, and Austrians to an even greater extent, regarded *themselves* as victims, as Gilad Margalit has shown: as victims of Hitler, as victims of the Second World War, and as victims of the brutal warfare or expulsion policies of the Allies. The then-influential "shapers and agents of Germany's postwar memorial culture," as Margalit calls it, were primarily concerned with public commemoration of fallen German soldiers, who, of course, were included in the "victims of fascism and militarism" (as they were called in the GDR) or the "victims of war and tyranny" (in the FRG). Even the main committee of the Victims of Fascism, an organization formed in occupied Berlin in July 1945, from which the Union of Persecutees of the Nazi Regime (Vereinigung der Verfolgten des Naziregimes) would later emerge, justified its original decision to recognize only active "fighters against fascism" – that is, victims of political persecution – with the remarkable statement that this category of recognized and socially privileged victims should not get out of hand. Without some sort of restrictions, the number of the Nazis' victims would have to be counted by the millions and would include all those who lost their homes and property as well as those who were forced to join Hitler's war as soldiers, were persecuted and murdered as Jews, or were punished as Jehovah's Witnesses or as those who refused to work.[15] In a speech introducing the first official observance of the "People's Day of Mourning" in 1952, the president of the FRG, Theodor Heuss, mentioned civilian deaths in Allied air raids in the same breath as concentration camp inmates and other Jewish Nazi victims. "There will be those who will resent my calling these victims the victims of a single evil policy," he said. "But I know that the sincere soldier is at my side." This moral equation shocked Jewish victims, but they did not have the power to force a public apology.[16]

Postwar West German society permitted not only that implicit equation of Jewish Nazi victims with German civilian war victims but also a fairly clear underestimation of the Nazis' victims within the early hierarchies of victimhood. During this era of "German self-victimization" (*Selbstviktimisierung*),[17] a 1951 opinion poll of German citizens afforded "the greatest entitlement to [financial] help" first to "war widows and war orphans," then to victims of aerial bombing, followed by German expellees from the east and then, only at the end of this long line of victim groups, to the "resistance fighters of 20 July." Surviving Jewish victims existed only toward the bottom of this hierarchy of victims, which comprised the majority of German society.[18] Those who wanted to receive public recognition and assistance had to prevail against this background of complex hierarchization and contradictory claims. Micha Brumlik rightfully criticized the Charter of Expellees – "expellees" being the self-assigned term for twelve million surviving German (or ethnic German) victims of flight, expulsion, and forced resettlement in Central and Eastern Europe since 1944/45.[19] Various organizations representing Germans displaced from pre-war eastern Germany and Central and Eastern Europe produced the charter in 1950 to support their public demand for recognition, basing their claims on a collective self-definition as "the most affected by the suffering of this time." Brumlik interprets this as an unacceptable effort by German expellees to compete with victims of the Nazis.[20] The composition of these self-described victim groups in 1950, however, was far more diverse than Brumlik would admit – it included not only expellees but also victims of aerial bombing, war injured, and former prisoners of war. Yet, while Germans struggled against each other for recognition, the true victims of the Nazis were barely noticed at all.[21]

A similar yet distinct struggle for a place in the hierarchy of victims took place in the Soviet zone of occupation and later the GDR. In 1947, a Liberal member of Saxony's parliament (*Landtag*) – who herself had been imprisoned in Ravensbrück concentration camp – demanded tax reductions for expellees, arguing that, to "a certain extent," even these "resettlers" (*Umsiedler*, the official term in East Germany for expellees) might be considered "victims of fascism." This assertion provoked outrage among members of the Socialist Unity Party (SED). Olga Körner, a Communist who had also been imprisoned at Ravensbrück, resented that equation and observed that, in contrast to true Nazi victims, "there existed a huge percentage [among the resettlers] who had been willing followers of Hitler's fascism." The prevailing consensus in the

Communist-dominated Central Administration for Resettlers in 1947 was that – unlike the recognized "victims of fascism" – "resettlers" and victims of Allied bombing raids "had not been disadvantaged by Nazi actions, but rather by the consequences of Nazi actions." Apart from that important distinction, in the postwar era, even the SED leadership considered these German victims of "resettlement" to be victims of the "criminal, imperialistic Nazi robbery politics" and among "the most damaged" by that regime. This assessment entitled them to special social assistance that lasted until 1952/53.[22]

After 1945, survivors of Nazi persecution faced both new and continued forms of exclusion and rejection, if not continued persecution per se, as Jewish survivors in Poland did. Regula Ludi has described this situation in the broader European context, observing that a legal victim status became not only a precondition for financial assistance but also a crucial component of moral authority and of a recognized identity.[23] In June 1945, the chairman of the main committee of the Victims of Fascism in Berlin stated that, although the Jews clearly had been persecuted by the Nazis, they were not real "victims of fascism" in the sense of the new legal category because they had not been actively engaged in fighting the Third Reich. These criteria meant that the only officially recognized victims of Nazism in the Soviet zone were Communists who had been persecuted as political enemies, in addition to a few Social Democrats and even fewer bourgeois individuals. The main committee's decision to exclude Jews was eventually rescinded in September 1945, following vehement protests by representatives of Jewish victims who were supported by prominent Protestant victims of the Nazis, but the prejudice they faced never entirely disappeared.

A hierarchy later emerged in the GDR that clearly prioritized (communist) "fighters" over mere "victims."[24] In 1947, the government of Saxony, then part of the Soviet zone and later of the GDR, defined political "fighters against fascism" as "persons who had fought, based on democratic motivation, a deliberate struggle against fascism on an organized basis and consequently had been subjected to persecution of the Nazi regime," whereas "victims of fascism" were defined as "persons who had rebelled against the Nazi regime as political loners or had been persecuted because of their racial affiliation or religious conviction." The Saxon government criticized the first victim welfare measures implemented in September 1945 because the term "OdF" (*Opfer des Faschismus*, or victims of fascism) was insufficiently clear and did not adequately address the militant aspect ("das kämpferische Moment"). Nevertheless, that government declared that both groups, fighters as well as victims, would receive the same welfare benefits in 1947, acknowledging that 18,629 persons belonged to this overall category at that time. The vast majority of them – over 14,000 – were male. Following the distinction above, 8,169 of them were recognized as political "fighters" and the remaining 10,460 as "victims." The social structure of the group also indicated the dominance of political activists from workers' movements: 13,763 were identified as employees, whereas only 976 were independent entrepreneurs or self-employed. Prior to the Nazi seizure of power, 10,827 of them had been members of the Communist Party (KPD) and 2,853 had been members of the Social Democratic Party (SPD). Only 145 had belonged to the German Democratic Party (DDP, the leftist liberals) and 50 to the conservative German National People's Party (DNVP); 3,002 had had no party affiliation. Only 904 persons were indicated as belonging to a "religious community," most of whom were probably German Jews.[25] In the Western occupation zones, the initial focus was also on political victims of Nazi persecution, clearly relegating victims persecuted for religious or racial reasons to the second or third places in the government-defined hierarchy.[26]

This was not a specifically German development. As late as 1993, Simone Veil expressed her frustration that postwar French society viewed Jews as mere victims and not as heroes, particularly when compared to French Resistance fighters. Some may argue that Veil made this statement at a time when the Holocaust had already been recognized in global memory politics as the ultimate evil,[27] but in the immediate postwar period, this tendency to diminish the Jewish experience undoubtedly felt painfully prejudicial.

Survivors of Nazi persecution initially tried to escape the stigma of victimization by overemphasizing their apparent successes in the struggle against National Socialism. They sought to form an identity by integrating into the prevailing anti-fascist ethos. It was only much later that the dominant myth of the "fighters" was replaced by a new narrative of victim sacrifice, which turned the characteristics of passivity and helplessness from a liability into an asset.[28] This turn developed gradually in the West from the 1960s and in the Eastern Bloc mainly as a result of the upheaval of 1989–91.

Ongoing Competition of Victims and Shifts in Authentication Strategies

The history of public recognition for various victims of the National Socialist dictatorship is thus a history of unequal treatment. It is a history of recognizing authentic – that is, rightful and legitimate – victim groups as well as one of exclusion, injury, and sometimes even continuing discrimination. Some of these groups have experienced relegation in status over time, as happened with German expellees in the Federal Republic since the 1960s or as was the case with Communist victims of the Nazi regime, once hailed as heroes in the GDR but later downgraded in the reunified Germany after 1990. Affected victim groups have fought against such losses of status in a provocative manner, by ramping up their rhetoric: in 1994, for example, there was talk of an alleged "West German final solution of anti-fascism on the territory of the former GDR."[29] Similarly, representatives of the German expellees reacted to their temporary loss of public recognition by describing the flight and expulsion they had endured as "genocide," "another Holocaust," or an "expulsion Holocaust."[30] It is worth noting that such counter-strategies no longer called into question the place held by the Nazi's Jewish victims atop the hierarchy of recognition but, instead, claimed for themselves the categories recognized for Jewish victims. In addition, demands made by Sudeten Germans from the 1990s clearly remained "in the shadow" of Jewish claims for compensation.[31]

Equating other victim experiences with the Holocaust became an increasingly important strategy among groups that had initially been excluded from recognition in the hierarchy of victims following 1945. Some groups, such as homosexual men or Roma and Sinti, continued to be prosecuted under various laws even in the postwar period. By the 1970s, some self-organized gay-rights advocates claimed that homosexual men in the Third Reich had been targeted by as part of another "final solution," and they often made exaggerated estimates of up to 1.5 million murdered in order to frame such persecution as a "homocaust."[32] Activists within the gay movement itself soon revised these distorted estimates with substantiated data. Similar demands by Roma and Sinti organizations for recognition of their murdered peoples as victims of genocide were much more soundly justified, and Chancellor Helmut Schmidt recognized their experience as such in 1982.[33] Roma and Sinti activists received notable support in their fight for recognition from prominent representatives of Jewish victim groups such as Simone Veil and Simon Wiesenthal, which effectively "authenticated" their claims as victims. A heated scholarly debate nonetheless arose in the 1980s over the question of whether the Shoah was a singular historical occurrence or if it was comparable to the *Porajmos* (the Romani term for genocide of their peoples).[34]

These significant changes in victim hierarchies have been the result of fierce competition. Belgian social scientist Jean-Michel Chaumont's pioneering work has described this "competition of victims" as a quest for identity and recognition.[35] Historian Berthold Unfried has astutely observed that views of the Nazis' victims have been shaped by a highly complicated "history of inclusion and exclusion and the hierarchization of different groups" and that these hierarchies have undergone major changes since 1945. Since the 1970s, there has been a transnational appreciation, which began in the United States, that situated the Holocaust as a point of reference for the politics of memory (*Holocaust als erinnerungspolitischer Bezugspunkt*).[36] Persecuted Jewish survivors at this time experienced a significant "role reversal," which transformed their original "degradation" and resulting "time of shame" into an unexpected "time of glory" at the top of transnational victim hierarchies. As Chaumont has shown, using the example of Simone Veil, what had been "the source of shame" suddenly became not only acceptable but the basis for explaining the singularity of the Jewish genocide.[37] The victim was no longer blamed for passivity, which was then transformed into positive evidence of innocence and purity (*Makellosigkeit*). Iris Nachum has observed that this construction of the "pure" Nazi victim stood in contrast to other groups that could not claim such purity due to their (at least partial) complicity with the Nazis, which relegated them to a lower rung in the victim hierarchy. Moreover, Nachum notes that some victim groups, such as homosexuals, continued to bear a stigma after 1945, a stain that apparently justified the continued denial of reparation payments. Even the transformed hierarchy of victims continued to construct groups of "unworthy," or at least subordinate, victims.[38]

However, the global political momentum of the 1968 protests brought about the transnational politicization of hitherto invisible group interests and brought into view new social movements that reversed this trend over the long term. According to Gilad Margalit, as the Jewish victim narrative gained force in the 1980s and became more widely represented in memorials, the public slowly became receptive to the victim narratives of other groups, such as Sinti and Roma and gay men.[39] But the majority of society did not open up to these groups of its own volition. Instead, numerous self-organized actors were needed to bring about a structural change in victim recognition through a corresponding structural change in the public, including sensational new forms of protest.[40] The cultural and socio-political "ascent of minorities" since the 1960s, therefore, was an essential precondition to the restructuring of victim hierarchies that began in the 1980s.[41]

It is interesting to note that new associations of victims selected "authentic locations" – that is, sites at which Nazi crimes had been committed – as a means to claim recognition. Since the late 1970s, the emerging "memorial movement" has been closely associated with the recognition of previously excluded victim groups.[42] In the case of the

Roma and Sinti, a younger generation of victims first protested at the Bergen-Belsen Memorial in 1979 against their exclusion from the forms of remembrance practised there. A hunger strike followed in 1980 at the Dachau Memorial before the Federal Republic recognized the extermination of these groups as genocide in 1982. Memorial sites in the GDR had also made little mention of the Nazi persecution of "Gypsies," with the exception of an exhibition panel in the Buchenwald Museum installed in 1985.[43] This was preceded by a gradual relaxation of East German commemorative policies that had originally been focused almost exclusively on communist resistance fighters. By the mid-1970s, however, even the state's central party newspaper, *Neues Deutschland* (*New Germany*), was beginning to mention Christian and Jewish victims of the Nazis, and in 1985, even Nazi-persecuted criminals were added as a side note.[44]

As early as 1983, groups of lesbians attempted to place bouquets in commemoration of murdered homosexual victims of the Nazis at the former Sachsenhausen and Buchenwald concentration camps but were prevented from doing so by state authorities. They subsequently expressed their outrage in an open letter to state and party leader Erich Honecker that was reprinted in the leftist West Berlin newspaper *taz*: "[To think] that in the GDR the homosexual victims of fascism are still discriminated against like this!"[45] In East German Protestant church newspapers in the mid-1980s, the homosexual victims of the Nazis gained sudden recognition – again a result of self-organization by gay activists, in this case within the churches.[46] Public criticism seems to have altered the SED regime's attitude. In subsequent years, singular commemorative acts by West or East German gay and lesbian activists became possible at official sites of memory, such as the GDR memorial at Sachsenhausen in 1985. Only one year earlier, an attempt by East German Protestant homosexual activists to do the same had been prevented by the GDR State Security (the Stasi). Coincidentally, in 1985, the Comité International de Dachau, the international organization of former prisoners of that Nazi concentration camp, refused to support the installation of a plaque dedicated to the camp's homosexual victims; it was eventually installed ten years later.[47]

Young activists also sought out sites of Nazi crimes to commemorate disabled persons who had been euthanized by the Nazi regime. A commemorative relief had existed since 1953 in the hospital at Hadamar, a prominent site in the Nazis' T4 "euthanasia" program, but in 1983, a student initiative successfully lobbied for public access to the former gas chamber in the hospital and for a provisional memorial exhibition. An official memorial at Hadamar was established in 1989, and a newly designed permanent exhibition was opened in 1991. According to historian Georg Lilienthal, the student activists' main goal was "to open up the crime scene – in the truest sense of the word" – in order to commemorate the victims.[48]

In a speech on the fortieth anniversary of the end of the Second World War, FRG president Richard von Weizsäcker commemorated the defeat of the Third Reich as a liberation for all Germans, an interpretation that became paradigmatic for widening the circle of officially recognized victim groups. In addition to commemorating the war dead, Weizsäcker emphasized the suffering of the Nazis' victims, especially the six million murdered Jews. But he also mentioned other groups greatly affected by the regime that had previously been neglected in commemorative exercises, including Soviet and Polish citizens, homosexuals, disabled individuals, and those killed because of their political or religious convictions.[49] This was a response to the "controversy over 'forgotten victims,'" which had been sparked by various new social movements since 1980. By 1984, there was wide public support for the "political and material compensation of all Nazi victims," fuelled to a significant extent by the left-liberal press. Another important consequence of this growing public attention was the self-organization of various advocacy groups. The Central Council of German Roma and Sinti was founded in 1982, followed by the Federation of Victims of Euthanasia and Forced Sterilization as well as the Federal Association of Homosexuality in 1986, and the Federal Coalition of Victims of Nazi Military Justice in 1990.[50] In the case of foreign forced labourers of the Nazi regime, such mobilization for advocacy extended even beyond Germany's borders. One notable category of victims who did not self-organize in this way was the group once persecuted as "asocials."[51] The absence of advocacy on this group's behalf undoubtedly had a negative effect on the extent to which it was recognized by the public, and, as a result, there remained a persisting lack of public understanding of this heterogeneous and widely stigmatized group of Nazi victims.

The Latest Trends in Competitive Commemoration

The enlargement of the hierarchy of victims, carried out by increasingly diverse new actors with a critical view of the past, might be referred to as a reform phase of victim authentication. The growing prominence of physical memorials in German commemorative culture in this period, particularly since the 1990s, can be regarded as a testament to the successful recognition and integration of new victim groups as they have been admitted into the hierarchy of "authentic victims." This physical memorialization has built on the trend in the 1980s of viewing sites of Nazi crimes as places of authenticity. On the other hand, it has deviated from that trend through the increased emphasis of establishing a symbolic presence in the political centre of twenty-first-century German society: the capital of Berlin. No sooner had discussions begun regarding a Holocaust memorial, to be constructed in the former Nazi government district, than a conflict emerged as to whether this memorial was to be dedicated exclusively to the Jewish victims or whether it would recognize other groups as well. The chairman of the Central Council of German Sinti and Roma, Romani Rose, advocated for an inclusive solution. Despite such efforts, however, the result focused exclusively on Jewish victims, and the Memorial to the Murdered Jews of Europe was dedicated in 2005.[52] But Jewish activist groups also felt a certain ambivalence regarding the monument. Even before it was constructed, the chairman of the Central Council of Jews in Germany, Ignatz Bubis, criticized the plans because the monument lacked the authenticity embodied by memorials established at original sites of Nazi crimes.[53] Eventually, a "memorial portal" component was added to the monument's exhibit, which informed visitors of other sites of Nazi persecution.[54]

This Holocaust memorial remains the largest and most famous in the heart of Berlin, but it is hardly alone. Since its inception, activists have sought to pay tribute to other victims of National Socialism by establishing commemorative sites in the capital, often with the active support of the Central Council of Jews in Germany. In 2008, the Monument to Homosexuals Persecuted under National Socialism was built, followed in 2012 by the Monument to the Sinti and Roma of Europe Murdered under National Socialism. Thus, two groups of victims – both of which had been persecuted long after 1945 and were only recently recognized as victims of Nazi aggression – successfully advanced within two decades to the top ranks of the current victim hierarchy. Even more remarkable are the internal debates that occurred among the victim groups and their representatives who wished to establish these memorials. These sometimes pointed disputes represent important stages in the processes of authentication, and they have significantly redefined the boundaries of authenticity.

As early as 1992, a civil society initiative sought to establish a gay memorial in Berlin, which received further support starting in 2000 from the Lesbian and Gay Federation in Germany (Lesben- und Schwulenverband in Deutschland, or LSVD) in its political lobbying efforts. This national memorial was approved by the German Bundestag (federal Parliament) in 2003 and was erected in Berlin's Tiergarten in 2008, not far from the other memorial sites for Nazi victim groups.

The symbolism of this great political success, however, was accompanied by a vehement dispute between lesbian and gay advocates over memory politics. At the core of this disagreement was whether the central element of the memorial – a video, played on loop, showing two men kissing – left visitors with the impression that only homosexual male victims should be memorialized, even though it was men who, between 1933 and 1945, faced the threat of criminal prosecution and secret police persecution for homosexual behaviour. The conflict arose based on the suggestion that lesbians – who had not been targeted by the Nazi regime in the same ways – might also have suffered persecution or discrimination, albeit in less visible forms, and should therefore be included in the monument.[55] Lesbian advocates had long criticized such commemoration for its almost exclusive focus on Nazi-persecuted homosexual males. At the beginning of this debate, the concentration camp symbol of the pink triangle for persecuted male homosexuals seemed to be an adequate symbol for authentication,[56] but a compromise was eventually reached among these groups by agreement that the video would be changed every two years to show, respectively, a male couple and a female couple kissing.

There is undoubtedly a history of discrimination suffered by lesbians under National Socialism that must not be ignored. At the same time, it is important to heed the criticism of historian Magdalena Beljan that "the gay victim community was institutionally expanded to become a gay-lesbian community of victims" that has little to do with the Nazi period or the emancipation movements of the 1970s.[57] There is indeed a delicate balance between, on the one hand, the desire to create inclusive victim groups with flexible boundaries and, on the other hand, the levelling of important historical differences with the aim of claiming the greatest possible number of self-identified victims.[58]

The authenticity of another planned Berlin memorial became the subject of further conflict around the year 2000, this time within the Central Council of German Sinti and Roma. Beginning in the 1980s, the prevailing appellations of "Gypsies" (*Zigeuner*) and "travellers" (*Landfahrer*) were replaced with "Sinti and Roma" in common usage, but this label was also criticized as inadequate because it elided other groups that had been persecuted under Nazi rule, such as the Yenish (*Jenische*) people. In fact, the Sinti Alliance of Germany (Sinti Allianz Deutschland e.V.) argued in its criticism of the Central Council's position that the former *Zigeuner* label would be more inclusive of all those persecuted. The Central Council countered by saying that this term would perpetuate the category assigned by the Nazi perpetrators. Subsequent attempts by politicians at mediation proved unsuccessful. The president of the

Bundestag, Wolfgang Thierse, proposed that the broader term *Zigeuner* be used, but that it always be put in quotation marks because of its historical contamination. The Federal commissioner for culture and media, Christina Weiss, tried to escape these problems of terminology by suggesting use of the English word "Gypsies." The stalemate was ultimately resolved by the decision in 2006 to design the memorial without any inscription.[59] Practicality dictated, however, that the monument could not remain nameless, so the label "Sinti and Roma" eventually prevailed in common usage, despite objections that some victims with legitimate claims of having been persecuted would be excluded by that limiting term.[60]

Claims and assertions of authenticity seem to have essential ties to successful advocacy, lobbying, and networking. Despite the boom in memorial sites and monuments in Germany, there is still "a narrowing in the general public's view of history … from which essential parts are hidden," as Peter Jahn observed in 2003.[61] Jahn found it striking that most recognized victim groups represented victims from (or at least perceived to be from) Germany, and that this focus excluded numerically significant groups of Slavic victims, especially Soviet prisoners of war and the many civilian casualties resulting from the German occupation of Eastern Europe. In Jahn's view, a monument in the centre of Berlin for these Soviet Nazi victims would be historically justified, yet "it depends on political will, whether such a project … could be implemented."[62]

As we know, this political will has not emerged so far, which is undoubtedly a result of insufficient representation of such victims in the public space. The same is true for more recent differentiations in the historiography, whereby national or religious categories like Polish, Ukrainian, Belorussian, or Jewish are preferable to a broader "Soviet" label, which might misleadingly imply Russian origins.[63] Historian Timothy Snyder observed in 2010 that, outside of Poland, the extent of Polish suffering under Nazi rule is often underestimated.[64] In fact, there have been recent calls to establish a Berlin memorial for all Polish victims of National Socialism, though the impact of this campaign remains to be seen.[65] Nonetheless, some progress is being made in official recognition of victim groups. For example, surviving Eastern European forced labourers were recognized by the German federal government in the year 2000 as victims of the Nazi regime and were subsequently compensated, with payments distributed by a federal foundation funded partially by German companies. This Foundation "Remembrance, Responsibility, and Future" (Stiftung "Erinnerung Verantwortung Zukunft") made reparation payments to former inmates of concentration camps, residents of Jewish ghettos, prisoners in forced-labour camps and other places of internment, and, finally, former forced labourers who had worked in industry.[66]

Thus, the era of competition among victims for authentication and preferential spots in victim hierarchies is not over. These hierarchies have been upended and expanded, but the dynamics of the zero-sum game between rising and sinking victim groups have not yet been overcome. "Today," Stefanie Kowitz-Harms noted recently, "not only Jews but also Sinti and Roma, homosexuals [and] resistance fighters claim to belong to the victims of the Nazi regime and insist on their due recognition." The competition among such claims for public recognition of victim groups that suffered distinct but similar injustices or atrocities takes place not only in Germany but also in other national and even transnational contexts. This includes, for example, the Soviet Great Terror and the Armenian genocide.[67] Especially at European or global levels, such struggles for recognition are becoming more diverse and often more heated. In Germany itself, there has been a renewed evaluation since the dawn of the twenty-first century of the hierarchical relations between war victims and groups persecuted under Nazi rule. Gilad Margalit has sharply criticized this new round of debates because, in his view, those focusing on "German suffering" during the Second World War and thereafter continue to downplay German guilt and responsibility for Nazi crimes. The result is seen as a dangerous false equivalency because the new wave of interest in German victims – particularly German refugees and expellees, but also victims of aerial bombing – comes at the expense of recognizing victims of the Third Reich.[68] Such alarmism might be exaggerated, but the many intertwined problems of reorienting victim hierarchies cannot be ignored.

Conclusion: Competition for Authentication and Authorizing "Deputy" Lobbyists

The history of public memory of the diverse victims of the Nazi dictatorship is a history of unequal treatment. It is not only a history of acknowledgment but also of segregation, abuse, and lasting discrimination. Some groups of victims experienced a demotion from their original postwar status – for example, Nazi-persecuted communists lost their privileged top position in the hierarchy following German reunification. By contrast, Jewish victims experienced a reversal of fortune, from being largely disregarded initially – the "time of shame" – to experiencing a "time of glory" at the peak of transnational global victim hierarchies.[69] But for other groups of victims, the period of being disregarded or undervalued lasted much longer, and the debasement of their experiences ran even deeper, sometimes to the point of entirely denying them status as victims. Moreover, in some cases, this indignity was exacerbated for decades after 1945 by persistent discrimination that echoed Nazi persecution. Though they serve as only one example, individuals persecuted by the Nazis on the basis of homosexuality experienced this dark side of public policy for a very long time after the regime's defeat. The same is true regarding Sinti and Roma, sterilization victims, and other groups. These examples support Berthold Unfried's observation, discussed above, that this process has been defined by a highly complicated "history of inclusion and exclusion and the hierarchization between different groups" that have undergone major changes since 1945.[70] These transformations of public perceptions of victims, shown in the processes of subsequent hierarchization and re-hierachization, have been the consequence of a massive and multifaceted "competition of victims" about "identity and recognition."[71] As we have seen, the dialectic between these two factors has resulted in significant changes in group identities.

Observers should not overlook the important role that victim organizations have played in these conflicts. They competed against each other in order to establish a hierarchy of claims and recognition, but they also successfully established patterns of inclusion or exclusion even among the victims they represented. Thus, the self-organizing by victims cannot be said to have resulted in an all-inclusive memory policy. These advocacy associations have sought to differentiate between victims considered worthy of recognition and compensation and those deemed not worthy of the same, and the state has sought to make the same distinctions through legislative means.[72] Moreover, victim associations sometime marginalized individual memories even within the accepted groups of "worthy" victims if those memories were considered incompatible with the collective image that the group wished to promote for political or public purposes. The Communist-dominated Vereinigung der Verfolgten des Naziregimes (Union of Persecutees of the Nazi Regime) not only denied recognition to other groups of victims from the very start but also aimed to establish a specific internal hierarchy that would privilege or subordinate specific victim experiences and testimonies.[73]

Alongside these uneven memory policies, a power play took place between majorities and minorities. The majority of German society initially tended to place its own war victims at the top of any conceivable hierarchy and thus prioritized those victims' entitlement to social assistance. Consequently, this "self-victimization" of the majority gained priority over any acknowledgment of the Nazis' victims.[74] Those disabled by the war and surviving dependants clearly ranked ahead of victims of aerial bombing raids, while the latter, in turn, were prioritized over refugees and expellees, who were considered foreign and undesirable in postwar German society. The more these refugees opposed discrimination, the more they were pushed aside in the hierarchy. This development began in the 1960s, but, after the caesura of 1989, it led to ever more competition between victim groups.[75]

The early, post-1945 hierarchies of victims of National Socialism were characterized by a basic preference for not passive, helpless victims but, rather, active opponents of Nazi rule. This "heroic concept of victimhood" emerged in the late 1940s and into the 1950s and was incompatible with merely passive victim experiences as well as with "deviant" social behaviour (e.g., homosexuality).[76] In West Germany, this conceptualization focused on members of the abortive 20 July 1944 conspiracy against Hitler, elevating these mainly conservative military figures above persecuted Jews and other political victims of lower social standing.[77] A similar discrepancy was seen in postwar France, where apparently active political opponents of the Nazi occupation were accorded a privileged status as compared to persecuted Jews.[78]

Communists persecuted under National Socialism – who had been publicly acknowledged in the early years after 1945, even in West Germany – were made outcasts anew in the Cold War–era FRG, and to some extent were persecuted again following that state's banning of the Communist Party of Germany in 1956.[79] Homosexual victims, socially marginalized persons (*Asoziale*), and the Sinti and Roma were not part of the official hierarchy of victims at all in either German state but continued to be considered criminals and were prosecuted as such until gradual reforms began circa 1970.

In the East German state, Communists persecuted under Nazi rule were placed at the top of the hierarchy as active and politically conscious "fighters against fascism" (the official designation), distinctly above the passive "victims of fascism," who were assigned the second rung of public recognition. Social Democrats and bourgeois members of the anti-Nazi resistance were afforded even less recognition. Jewish victims were acknowledged in the GDR as well as in the Federal Republic, but they endured a rather ambivalent situation, ranging from Stalin's anti-Jewish actions in the early 1950s to Honecker's politically symbolic restoration of the Berlin synagogue in the Oranienburger Straße in the 1980s. Homosexuals, "asocials," and Sinti and Roma in the GDR faced patterns of oppression similar to those in West German society, although the GDR dictatorship relaxed and later abolished the legal persecution of homosexuals years earlier than did the FRG. On the other hand, the pluralistic media of West Berlin was a necessary factor in creating public pressure on the SED regime to relent, as shown by the example of the lesbian activists' attempt to lay a wreath at the memorial at Sachsenhausen. Change was dependent to some extent on the pluralistic channels of expression unavailable in East Germany, but open expressions such as these constituted meaningful change in the GDR.

The basic competition of victims (following Chaumont) was the means not only for establishing specific hierarchies of victimhood but also for destabilizing and reshaping those hierarchies. Since the 1970s, we can observe a transnational global revalorization of the "Holocaust as a focal point for the policy of commemoration."[80] That upgrading of the status of Jewish victims resulted in a basic transformation of victim identities and hierarchies in general. The paradigm of the passive victim of Nazi rule, previously disparaged and disregarded, underwent a significant re-evaluation. The very lack of resistance that had long been a "cause for shame" suddenly became not only acceptable but even formed the basis for the now-established singularity of the Holocaust.[81] The passive Jewish victim was no longer guilty of passivity; to the contrary, that very passivity transformed into proof of innocence.[82] This new public construction of innocent, blameless victims resulted not only in the relegation of various groups of war victims who had a possible connection to the Nazi regime (e.g., refugees and expellees) but also in continued discrimination against other groups, such as homosexuals, who still had a more ambiguous place in society. The "imperfections" in the victimhood of these groups prevented them from being included among whose claims for financial indemnification were accepted. The stain of guilt stemming from pre-1945 political attitudes – as well as from both pre- and post-1945 attitudes toward sexuality – continued to render certain groups of victims as "unworthy," or at least marginalized them on the fringes of the reshaped official hierarchies of victimhood.[83]

The rise in status of Jewish Holocaust victims, however, subsequently triggered a dynamic that led to expanded inclusivity in the new hierarchy of so-called passive victims. In the past twenty years, this process has not replaced the hierarchy (still dominated by the Holocaust victims), but it has increasingly enabled the admission of formerly neglected groups of victims into the inner circle of acknowledged victimhood. This is evidenced perhaps most obviously in the growing array of memorials in Berlin. This process, based on previous societal changes, might be summarized by the notion of the global socio-political "ascent of minorities" since the 1960s within a society that was increasingly transformed by the values and consequences of individualism.[84]

These results – the primacy of Jewish victims and the inclusion of formerly neglected groups – undoubtedly marked real and important progress. Nevertheless, we have to ask: Does the construction of a victim identity based on the notion of innocence and blameless purity represent the authentic experiences of millions of victims? Historians could easily deconstruct such hermetic patterns of commemorative identities. In fact, many groups of Nazi victims were composed of inevitably ambivalent, even dubious, members. Examples such as the Jewish kapos (prisoners who were given certain guard duties) in Nazi concentration camps or "gay Nazis," who suffered persecution as homosexuals but were nevertheless complicit in other Nazi crimes, demonstrate the sometimes complex nature of such identities.[85] Consequently, the task of historical science should not be restricted to the (basically completed) deconstruction of the heroic concept of victimhood. Indeed, there should also be a critical examination of the present concept of the blameless victim.

Moreover, what should we think when listening to the historical diagnoses made today? "Everybody likes to be a victim, and this wish leads to reconstructions of memory, animated and accompanied by experts of commemoration."[86] Should we not stop and ask: Where in this complex public representation of victimhood is the place for authentic experiences of victims? Where is the place for victims who would prefer *not* to be victims but had to experience the basic existential situation of any victimhood – being in a helpless, humiliating, and threatening situation? Where is the place for experiences that, at least superficially, appear to contradict each other – for example, one refugee being raped by a Soviet soldier and another being protected by a Soviet soldier? When considering these questions, it is worth recalling, for instance, that only about half of the thirteen members of the first board of the Union of German Expellees (Bund der Vertriebenen), formed in 1958, had personally experienced flight and expulsion. All of these men nonetheless continued, for years and decades thereafter, to represent the individuals who *had* experienced these forced migrations.[87] The simple reason for this was that all of the board members were men who had been soldiers and, later, prisoners of war, whereas most of the actual victims of this ethnic cleansing experience had been women and children.

A decade ago, Ulrike Jureit and Christian Schneider pointed to the general problem, far greater than any one example, of the eventual disappearance of authentic victims, as those generations begin to die. As soon as those victims are no longer able to speak for themselves with their "authentic moral legitimacy," the authors warned, subsequent generations of advocates and lobbyists – the "remembrance functionaries and mourning administrators," as they put it – would "determine what works and what does not work." This inevitable shift sees a transfer of agency from authentic – or, perhaps more accurately, publicly authenticated – eyewitnesses and victims to a new generation of bureaucrats who speak on their behalf but who lack those direct victim experiences. Jureit and Schneider nonetheless question the attendant loosening of membership criteria for victim groups: "genealogy" – that is, being children or grandchildren of actual victims – constitutes just one of many qualifications in the "fight for memory." Concepts such as "secondary testimony" that seek to preserve the authenticity of (actual) victim perspectives beyond death, they would argue, point to an "expansion of the combat zone." The "transgenerational transmission of experienced history" could function, or claim to function, only through the emotional reliving of the narrated traumatic experiences of others. In other words, dying Holocaust survivors are able to "legitimize [i.e., appoint] their own successors or, more accurately, the representatives who are permitted to speak for them in the future." From the point of view of the authors, this "concept of secondary testimony" stands for the younger generation's self-empowerment strategy as they take up the narratives of their predecessors' direct, lived victim experiences.[88]

This current development is evident not only among Holocaust survivors but across the whole spectrum of victim groups. The successive extinction of the "generations of experience" has led, for example, to their replacement by "confessional expellees," some of whom never experienced the expulsion first-hand in any way. "What a perverted terminological creation," the expellee and author Horst Bienek commented in 1985, filled with contempt for this new practice of legitimizing rising functionaries: "This is not a satire; this is a farce!"[89] It may be a farce, but, in any case, it will be a significant part of the future of the authentication of victimhood. In the future, as in the past, the authentication of victims and their competitions with each other cannot be left solely to politicians and lobbyists.

That is only one of many reasons why, finally, we should emphasize the critical task of historical discourses. For scholars of contemporary history, there exists a strong temptation to be part of the public establishment of commemorative industries. But such industries serve to sustain existing patterns of memory rather than to question them. The main difference between historical science and any politics of memory is the fundamental ability to ask questions that might undermine present certainties or the apparent rules of victim memories. In dealing seriously with the past, history cannot be merely an agent representing present power constellations of knowledge; it must also act as an agent for improving a still unknown but undoubtedly different future.

NOTES

1 Ophelia Lindemann, "Opfergeschichten: Paradoxien der Anerkennung zwischen Erzählen und Zuhören," in *Strukturwandel der Anerkennung: Paradoxien der sozialen Integration in der Gegenwart*, ed. Axel Honneth, Ophelia Lindemann, and Stephan Voswinkel (Frankfurt: Campus, 2013), 249–73, esp. 267 and 270ff. "Sind Opfer eigentlich 'echt'? ... Sich selbst – als 'Opfer,' als 'Täter' – erzählen, ist nie unvermittelt, ist nie 'echt.'"
2 Bernhard Giesen, *Triumph and Trauma* (London: Routledge, 2016), 67.
3 Binjamin Wilkomirski, *Fragments: Memories of a Wartime Childhood*, trans. Carol Brown Janeway (New York: Schocken Books, 1996).
4 Giesen, *Triumph and Trauma*, 67.
5 See Regula Ludi, *Reparations for Nazi Victims in Postwar Europe* (Cambridge: Cambridge University Press, 2012), 247.
6 Giesen, *Triumph and Trauma*, 69.
7 Lindemann, "Opfergeschichten," 270: "Sind eigentlich Opfer 'echt'? Und Täter 'falsch'? Erleiden Opfer eine Geschichte, während Täter Geschichten erzählen?"
8 Klaus Günther, "Ein Modell legitimen Scheiterns: Der Kampf um Anerkennung als Opfer," in Honneth, Lindemann, and Voswinkel, *Strukturwandel der Anerkennung*, 235.
9 Martin Schulze Wessel, "Einleitung," in *Opfernarrative: Konkurrenzen und Deutungskämpfe in Deutschland und im östlichen Europa nach dem Zweiten Weltkrieg*, ed. K. Erik Franzen and Martin Schulze Wessel (Munich: Oldenbourg, 2012), 1–8, esp. 2.
10 Jean-Michel Chaumont, *Die Konkurrenz der Opfer: Genozid, Identität, Anerkennung*, trans. Thomas Laugstien (Lüneburg: zu Klampen, 2001), 36. Originally published as *La concurrence des victimes: Génocide, identité, reconnaissance* (Paris: Éditions la Découverte, 1997).
11 Constantin Goschler, "Wiedergutmachung," in *Geschichte der Sozialpolitik in Deutschland seit 1945*, vol. 8, *1949–1961 – Deutsche Demokratische Republik: Im Zeichen des Aufbaus des Sozialismus*, ed. Dierk Hoffmann and Michael Schwartz (Baden-Baden: Nomos, 2004), 645.
12 Peter Widmann, "Fortwirkende Zerrbilder: Sinti und Roma im Nationalsozialismus und im Nachkriegsdeutschland," in *Dimensionen der Verfolgung: Opfer und Opfergruppen im Nationalsozialismus*, ed. Sibylle Quack (Munich: Deutsche Verlags-Anstalt, 2003), 218.

13 Constantin Goschler, "Wiedergutmachung," in *Geschichte der Sozialpolitik in Deutschland seit 1945*, vol. 2, bk. 1, *1945–1949 – Die Zeit der Besatzungszonen: Sozialpolitik zwischen Kriegsende und der Gründung zweier deutscher Staaten*, ed. Udo Wengst (Baden-Baden: Nomos, 2001), 799ff.
14 Günther, "Ein Modell legitimen Scheiterns," 235.
15 Gilad Margalit, *Guilt, Suffering, and Memory: Germany Remembers Its Dead of World War II* (Bloomington, IN: Bloomsbury Academic, 2010), 3, 52, and 80ff.
16 Ibid., 136.
17 Arnd Bauerkämper, *Das umstrittene Gedächtnis: Die Erinnerung an Nationalsozialismus, Faschismus und Krieg in Europa seit 1945* (Paderborn: Schöningh, 2012), 298.
18 Rolf Wiggershaus, *Die Frankfurter Schule: Geschichte – theoretische Entwicklung – politische Bedeutung* (Munich: Deutscher Taschenbuch-Verlag, 1988), 496.
19 For German expellees and the political struggle of "correct terminology," see Michael Schwartz, *Vertriebene und "Umsiedlerpolitik": Integrationskonflikte in den deutschen Nachkriegs-Gesellschaften und die Assimilationsstrategien in der SBZ/DDR 1945–1961* (Munich: Oldenbourg, 2004), 3–6. See also Michael Schwartz, "Assimilation versus Incorporation: Expellee Integration Policies in East and West Germany after 1945," in *Vertriebene and Pieds-Noirs in Postwar Germany and France: Comparative Perspectives*, ed. Manuel Borutta and Jan C. Jansen (Basingstoke, UK: Palgrave Macmillan 2016), 73–94.
20 Micha Brumlik, *Wer Sturm sät: Die Vertreibung der Deutschen* (Berlin: Aufbau-Verlag, 2005), 98.
21 On the topic of compromises made among groups of German expellees, see Michael Schwartz, *Funktionäre mit Vergangenheit: Das Gründungspräsidium des "Bundes der Vertriebenen" und das Dritte Reich* (Munich: Oldenbourg, 2013), 19–26.
22 Schwartz, *Vertriebene und "Umsiedlerpolitik,"* 233.
23 Ludi, *Reparations for Nazi Victims*, 197–9.
24 Margalit, *Guilt, Suffering, and Memory*, 88ff.
25 Report for the Soviet Military Administration, 7 October 1947, Landesregierung Sachsen, Ministerium für Arbeit [Saxony Ministry of Labour, Dept. for Victims of Fascism], 921, Bl. 48–54, Sächsisches Hauptstaatsarchiv, Dresden.
26 See Wengst, *Geschichte der Sozialpolitik in Deutschland*, vol. 2, bk. 2, 110, 120.
27 Ludi, *Reparations for Nazi Victims*, 73ff.
28 Ibid., 197–9.
29 This draws on the title of Monika Zorn, ed., *Hitlers zweimal getötete Opfer: Westdeutsche Endlösung des Antifaschismus auf dem Gebiet der DDR* (Freiburg: Ahriman, 1994).

30 *50 Jahre Vertreibung: Der Völkermord an den Deutschen – Ostdeutschland und das Sudetenland – Rückgabe statt Verzicht*, ed. Rolf-Josef Eibicht (Tübingen: Hohenrain-Verlag, 1995); Rolf-Josef Eibicht and Anne Hipp, *Der Vertreibungs-Holocaust: Politik zur Wiedergutmachung eines Jahrtausendverbrechens* (Riesa: DS-Verlag, 2000); Karsten Kriwat, *Der andere Holocaust: Die Vertreibung der Deutschen 1944–1949* (Munich: FZ-Verlag, ca. 2004); Henryk M. Broder, "Der Holocaustneid: Die Sudetendeutschen wollen auch Opfer eines Völkermordes sein," *Der Tagesspiegel*, 31 May 2006.

31 Iris Nachum, "Im Schatten der Juden: Sudetendeutsche Wiedergutmachungsforderungen nach 1989," in *Die Globalisierung der Wiedergutmachung: Politik, Moral, Moralpolitik*, ed. José Brunner, Constantin Goschler, and Norbert Frei (Göttingen: Wallstein, 2013), 228–90.

32 Günter Grau, "Terror gegen Homosexuelle: Zu den Zielen der nationalsozialistischen Homosexuellenpolitik – ein Resumee," in Quack, *Dimensionen der Verfolgung*, 121–3.

33 Widmann, "Fortwirkende Zerrbilder," 221.

34 Torben Fischer and Matthias N. Lorenz, eds., *Lexikon der "Vergangenheitsbewältigung" in Deutschland: Debatten- und Diskursgeschichte des Nationalsozialismus nach 1945*, 3rd ed. (Bielefeld: Transcript, 2015), 330, 333.

35 Chaumont, *Die Konkurrenz der Opfer*.

36 Berthold Unfried, *Vergangenes Unrecht: Entschädigung und Restitution in einer globalen Perspektive* (Göttingen: Wallstein, 2014), 255–7 and 278.

37 Chaumont, *Die Konkurrenz der Opfer*, 30, 41.

38 Nachum, "Im Schatten der Juden," 283, 288.

39 Margalit, *Guilt, Suffering, and Memory*, 143, 146. On the transformation of social and political discrimination of homosexual men between the 1960s and 1990s, see Michael Schwartz, *Homosexuelle, Seilschaften, Verräter: Ein transnationales Stereotyp im 20. Jahrhundert* (Berlin: De Gruyter Oldenbourg, 2019), 237–322.

40 See Sven Reichardt, *Authentizität und Gemeinschaft: Linksalternatives Leben in den siebziger und frühen achtziger Jahren* (Berlin: Suhrkamp, 2014).

41 Bodo Mrozek, *Jugend Pop Kultur: Eine transnationale Geschichte* (Berlin: Suhrkamp, 2019), 717–25.

42 Thomas Lutz, "Gedächtniskultur, Erinnerungspolitik und gemeinsame europäische Zukunft," in *Vertreibungen europäisch erinnern: Historische Erfahrungen – Vergangenheitspolitik – Zukunftskonzeptionen*, ed. Dieter Bingen (Wiesbaden: Harassowitz, 2003), 253.

43 Widmann, "Fortwirkende Zerrbilder," 219ff.

44 Anne-Kathleen Tillack, *Erinnerungspolitik der DDR: Dargestellt an der Berichterstattung der Tageszeitung "Neues Deutschland" über die nationalen Mahn- und Gedenkstätten Buchenwald, Ravensbrück und Sachsenhausen* (Frankfurt: Peter Lang, 2012), 83–90.

45 "Offener Brief an Erich Honecker: Homosexuelle in der DDR" (copy of letter from the editorials of the West Berlin lesbian newspaper, *Unsere kleine Zeitung*, 20 October 1983), in *tageszeitung* (*taz*) 23 November 1983, 55.5/194, Evangelisches Landeskirchliches Archiv Berlin (ELAB). For the general context of East–West German gay relations, see Teresa Tammer, "Schwul bis über die Mauer: Die Westkontakte der Ost-Berliner Schwulenbewegung in den 1970er und 1980er Jahren," in *Konformitäten und Konfrontationen: Homosexuelle in der DDR*, ed. Rainer Marbach and Volker Weiß (Hamburg: Männerschwarm Verlag, 2017), 70–88.

46 Gerhard Thomas, "Eine Minderheit sucht das Gespräch," *Mecklenburgische Kirchenzeitung*, 21 April 1985, 55.5/194, ELAB.

47 See "Tot geschlagen – Tot geschwiegen – den homosexuellen Opfern des Nationalsozialismus," available at: https://www.advent-zachaeus.de/gemeindeleben/gespraechskreis-homosexualitaet/gedenken-an-die-homosexuellen-opfer-des-nationalsozialismus.html.

48 Georg Lilienthal, "NS-'Euthanasie'-Opfer und Wege des Gedenkens," in Quack, *Dimensionen der Verfolgung*, 270–3.

49 Margalit, *Guilt, Suffering, and Memory*, 144, 226.

50 The German names of these organizations are, respectively, Zentralrat Deutscher Sinti und Roma, Arbeitsgemeinschaft Bund der "Euthanasie"-Geschädigte und Zwangssterilisierten, Bundesverband Homosexualität, and Bundesvereinigung Opfer der NS-Militärjustiz.

51 Fischer and Lorenz, *Lexikon der "Vergangenheitsbewältigung,"* 263ff.

52 Ibid., 315.

53 Bubis was obviously not ready to accept the site of the Nazi perpetrators' former offices in the centre of Berlin as a place equally important to Auschwitz or Dachau. Ernst Benda, "Ignatz Bubis in der deutschen Politik," in *Ignatz Bubis: Ein jüdisches Leben in Deutschland*, ed. Fritz Backhaus, Raphael Gross, and Michael Lenarz (Frankfurt: Suhrkamp, 2007), 134–7, esp. 136.

54 Cornelia Geißler, *Individuum und Masse: Zur Vermittlung des Holocaust in deutschen Gedenkstättenausstellungen* (Bielefeld: Transcript, 2015), 109.

55 Fischer and Lorenz, *Lexikon der "Vergangenheitsbewältigung,"* 214ff.

56 Hans Scherer, "Rosa Winkel: Eine Berliner Diskussion über das Homosexuellen-Mahnmal," *Frankfurter Allgemeine Zeitung*, 12 December 1996, 55.5/0739, ELAB.

57 Magdalena Beljan, *Rosa Zeiten? Eine Geschichte der Subjektivierung männlicher Homosexualität in den 1970er und 1980er Jahren der BRD* (Bielefeld: Transcript, 2014), 81.

58 See Ulrike Jureit and Christian Schneider, *Gefühlte Opfer: Illusionen der Vergangenheitsbewältigung* (Stuttgart: Klett-Cotta, 2010). Our criticism must not be restricted to the inclusion of lesbian victims but should

also include the generalization that assumes that all male homosexuals were Nazi victims. In reality, only the *threat* of persecution between 1934 and 1945 applied to the homosexual population as a whole, but the actually persecuted homosexual men were a quantitative minority of that population: about 50,000 were convicted and imprisoned and about 5,000 were sent to (and mostly murdered in) concentration camps. See Michael Schwartz, "Über Verfolgung – und darüber hinaus: Zur Vielfalt von Lebenssituationen homosexueller Menschen in Deutschland aus zeithistorischer Sicht," in *Späte Aufarbeitung: LSBTTIQ-Lebenswelten im deutschen Südwesten*, ed. Martin Cüppers and Norman Domeier (Stuttgart: Landeszentrale für Politische Bildung Baden-Württemberg, 2018), 39–90.

59 Fischer and Lorenz, "*Lexikon der Vergangenheitsbewältigung*," 334.

60 For the terminological problems of self-designations and foreign denominations, see Karola Fings, *Sinti und Roma: Geschichte einer Minderheit* (Munich: C.H. Beck, 2016), 11–15. For discussion of groups, such as the Lalleri, not represented by "Sinti and Roma" terminology in the context of Nazi genocide, see Mark Levene, *The Crisis of Genocide*, vol. 2, *Annihilation: The European Rimlands, 1939–1953* (Oxford: Oxford University Press, 2013), 132–9.

61 Peter Jahn, "Sowjetische Kriegsgefangene und die Zivilbevölkerung der Sowjetunion als Opfer des NS-Vernichtungskrieges," in Quack, *Dimensionen der Verfolgung*, 146–7.

62 Ibid., 165–6.

63 Timothy Snyder, *Bloodlands: Europa zwischen Hitler und Stalin* (Munich: C.H. Beck, 2011), 403–10; originally published as *Bloodlands: Europe between Hitler and Stalin* (New York: Basic Books, 2010).

64 Ibid., 407.

65 Jacek Lepiarz, "Polen-Denkmal in Berlin?" *Deutsche Welle*, 16 December 2019, https://www.dw.com/de/polen-denkmal-in-berlin/a-49455956.

66 Cord Pagenstecher, "Der lange Weg zur Entschädigung," Bundeszentrale für Politische Bildung (bpb), Dossier NS-Zwangsarbeit: Lernen mit Interviews, 2 June 2016, https://www.bpb.de/geschichte/nationalsozialismus/ns-zwangsarbeit/227273/der-lange-weg-zur-entschaedigung.

67 Stefanie Kowitz-Harms, *Die Shoah im Spiegel öffentlicher Konflikte in Polen: Zwischen Opfermythos und Schuldfrage (1985–2001)* (Berlin: De Gruyter, 2014), 12.

68 Margalit, *Guilt, Suffering, and Memory*, 292.

69 Chaumont, *Die Konkurrenz der Opfer*, 23 and 89.

70 Unfried, *Vergangenes Unrecht*, 255ff.

71 Chaumont, *Die Konkurrenz der Opfer*, 287–318; Unfried, *Vergangenes Unrecht*, 257.

72 Chaumont, *Die Konkurrenz der Opfer*, 36, with reference to the French Amicale des déportés d'Auschwitz.

73 Heidrun Kämper, *Der Schulddiskurs in der frühen Nachkriegszeit: Ein Beitrag zur Geschichte des sprachlichen Umbruchs nach 1945* (Berlin: De Gruyter, 2005), 125ff.

74 Arnd Bauerkämper, *Das umstrittene Gedächtnis: Die Erinnerung an Nationalsozialismus, Faschismus und Krieg in Europa seit 1945* (Paderborn: Schöningh, 2012), 298.

75 Alexander von Plato, "Zweiter Weltkrieg und Holocaust – Realgeschichte und Erinnerung," in *Krieg – Erinnerung – Geschichtswissenschaft*, ed. Siegfried Mattl (Vienna: Böhlau, 2009), 275–300, esp. 285; Michael Schwartz, "Dürfen Vertriebene Opfer sein? Zeitgeschichtliche Überlegungen zu einem Problem deutscher und europäischer Identität," *Deutschland Archiv* 38, no. 3 (2005): 494–505.

76 Wessel, "Einleitung," 6ff.; Michael Schwartz, "Welcher NS-Opfer gedenken wir? An welche NS-Opfer soll ein Homosexuellen-Mahnmal erinnern?" in *Zu spät? Dimensionen des Gedenkens an homosexuelle und transgender Opfer des Nationalsozialismus*, ed. QWIEN Zentrum für schwul/lesbische Kultur und Geschichte und WASt (Wiener Antidiskriminierungsstelle für gleichgeschlechtliche und transgender Lebensweisen) (Vienna: Zaglossus, 2015), 206–31; Nachum, "Im Schatten der Juden," 287.

77 The military figures were placed clearly ahead of those who suffered injury or damage in bombing raids, expellees, resistance fighters, and persecuted Jews. On the results of a US survey in West Germany in 1951, see Wiggershaus, *Die Frankfurter Schule*, 496.

78 Chaumont, *Die Konkurrenz der Opfer*, 23–87.

79 Boris Spernol, "Die 'Kommunistenklausel': Wiedergutmachungspraxis als Instrument des Antikommunismus," in *"Geistige Gefahr" und "Immunisierung der Gesellschaft": Antikommunismus und politische Kultur in der frühen Bundesrepublik*, ed. Stefan Creuzberger and Dierk Hoffmann (Berlin: De Gruyter Oldenbourg, 2014), 251–73; Michael Schwartz, ed., *Ernst Schumacher – ein bayerischer Kommunist im doppelten Deutschland: Aufzeichnungen des Brechtforschers und Theaterkritikers in der DDR 1945–1991* (Munich: Oldenbourg, 2007).

80 Unfried, *Vergangenes Unrecht*, 278.

81 Chaumont, *Die Konkurrenz der Opfer*, 30, 41.

82 Nachum, "Im Schatten der Juden," 283ff.

83 Ibid., 288.

84 Mrozek, *Jugend Pop Kultur*, 717.

85 On the kapos, see, for example, Holger Hintzen, *Paul Raphaelson und Hans Jonas: Ein jüdischer Kapo und ein bewaffneter Philosoph im Holocaust* (Cologne: Greven, 2012). On Nazis homosexuals, see Andreas Pretzel, "Schwule Nazis: Narrative und Desiderate," in *Homosexuelle im Nationalsozialismus*, ed. Michael Schwartz (Munich: De Gruyter Oldenbourg, 2014), 69–76 and

Alexander Zinn, *"Aus dem Volkskörper entfernt"? Homosexuelle Männer im Nationalsozialismus* (Frankfurt: Campus, 2018).

86 Unfried, *Vergangenes Unrecht*, 258.

87 See Schwartz, *Funktionäre mit Vergangenheit*, 559–84. Six of the thirteen board members had belonged to the Wehrmacht or SS and became prisoners of war in 1945. Only four experienced the flight during the winter of 1944/45. One was subjected to the expulsion of spring 1945, and another was subjected to forced resettlement in 1946. The remaining board member lived in exile in Great Britain and was allowed to migrate to West Germany in 1949.

88 Jureit and Schneider, *Gefühlte Opfer*, 86ff, 154.

89 Horst Bienek, "Schlesien – aber wo liegt es?" *Die Zeit*, 8 February 1985, http://www.zeit.de/1985/07/schlesien-aber-wo-liegt-es.

PART 2

Victims of Genocide and Massacres

3 Eastern European Shoah Victims and the Problem of Group Identity

INGO LOOSE

Survival, Identity, and Migration

In the first years after the Holocaust, Jewish survivors throughout Europe found themselves in a miserable and disorienting position. Although they had survived the abyss of the Shoah, most of their hometowns had been totally destroyed, and their families, friends, and Jewish neighbours had been decimated. Under these circumstances, the vast majority of Jewish survivors had no sense of how and where they should live.[1] In addition, postwar societies in Central and Eastern Europe, which had been devastated by the war, often showed re-emergent, or ongoing, tendencies toward anti-Semitism. This chapter uses this backdrop as well as specific examples from Poland, the Soviet Union, and Germany to outline the sources and development of Jewish identity among Holocaust survivors. It also describes the impact of that identity on the ways in which survivors in Europe thought about the Holocaust and takes into account the turning point of Israel's independence in 1948. These examples will illustrate the long and exhausting struggle between narratives of the authentic experience of Jews as victims and those that sought recognition by non-Jewish populations, including political entities, in the first postwar years of this specifically Jewish example of suffering.

In 1945, as information emerged regarding the unprecedented crimes that had been committed against European Jews, Yiddish poet Kadia Molodowsky wrote one of her most famous poems, entitled "El khanun" (God of Mercy):

O God of Mercy
For the time being
Choose another people.
We are tired of death and corpses,

> We have no more prayers.
> For the time being
> Choose another people.
> We have run out of blood
> To be victims.
> Our houses have been turned into desert,
> The earth lacks space for tombstones,
> There are no more lamentations
> Nor songs of woe
> In the ancient texts.[2]

Molodowsky, who had immigrated from Belarus to the United States in 1935, remained a close and engaged observer of the post-Holocaust remnants of Jewish settlement in Eastern Europe. In the following years, the Holocaust and its impact on Jews and their commemorative culture remained one of her major poetic themes.[3] She was among millions of Jews who struggled to define what Jewishness and Jewish life meant in the postwar era.

In place of elaborate theories of identity, this chapter follows the older sociological approach of Alphons Silbermann about the Jewish spirit and the question of identity.[4] Silbermann's work – as well as that of Steven T. Katz, Michael A. Mayer, and other scholars[5] – identifies three main sources of what is often referred to as a Jewish identity, and memory plays a decisive role in each of these sources: religion and faith, culture, and anti-Semitism.

With respect to the first of these sources, religion and faith, the Holocaust powerfully disrupted the faith of many survivors who wondered – like Kadia Molodowsky in the poem above – how the God of Abraham and David could allow such a catastrophe to befall the Jewish people. As Bejnisz Berkowicz from the small town of Nowogródek (today, Navahrudak, Belarus; at the time, located in the Reichskommissariat Ostland) wrote in his diary in January 1943:

> Everything is destroyed, and there will not be any remembrance for us. It is meaningless what will happen after this bloodshed, for whom will new land be created, new life? The entire hope and pride were built on the Eastern Jewry, and it does not exist any longer. I beg you, American brothers: Do not compile a book with lamentations about our destruction, just a book with anathemas, or more precisely: with one strong curse over all of humankind and its culture.[6]

In contrast to this disillusionment, others redoubled their commitment to Judaism following the Holocaust. Yet the questions facing both groups were the same: How was the Holocaust to be understood in terms of the Abrahamic covenant, the special relationship between God and the Jewish people? And how could the Shoah be understood? As a punishment? For what? Was it some sort of divine trial?

The second source of Jewish identity is culture. This aggregate term is understood in this context to embrace diverse concepts such as common history, fate, language, and traditions, including Zionism since the end of the nineteenth century. Most Jewish survivors from Eastern Europe had been totally uprooted, wiping out the histories of countless shtetls and making culture an even more abstract and intangible concept centred on memory and remembrance. Although Zionism should be considered part of Jewish culture and Jewish heritage (especially among Jews from Eastern Europe), the link between the Holocaust and immigration to Palestine – and from 1948, to the State of Israel – was in fact less obvious than it might seem. Emigration from Europe prior to Israel's founding meant something more than just migrating to other countries, such as the United States. In fact, the first *aliyah* (migration of Jews to Israel) took place many years before the Shoah. In addition, building a new Jewish homeland in Palestine left little time for the survivor *olim* (migrants on *aliyah*) to form an identity that encompassed Holocaust memory in general and the many stories of personal loss in particular.[7] The State of Israel may have been regarded as a victory of the Jewish people, but not as redemption for the Shoah.

Finally, anti-Semitism had been a source of Jewish self-definition and counter-strategies before the Holocaust and long before German-Jewish historian Heinrich Graetz identified the themes of "learning and suffering" as being central to the Jewish people's fate since ancient times.[8] Although the Holocaust itself was certainly not explainable as a mere outburst of anti-Semitism, Jewish survivors were persistently shocked at the anti-Semitism that remained strong among non-Jewish populations in Europe even in the postwar years. In some instances, such sentiment led to new pogroms and anti-Jewish violence in Eastern and Central Europe.

Jewish identity was, and of course still is, closely intertwined with and overlapped by other identities, since we mostly understand identities as products of complex social interactions. That said, the situation of Jewish survivors was peculiar, because the existing aspects of their identity were based in a world and on social structure that no longer existed after the Holocaust. Consequently, of all these aspects, only religion and culture (including history and traditions) turned out to be what one could call "mobile" or "transferable identity." The lack of structure in Jewish life meant that the remnants of Jewish identity and Jewishness pointed directly toward emigration, and hundreds of thousands of Jews followed precisely that path.

The world of Jews in Central and Eastern Europe prior to 1939 was destroyed by the end of the Second World War, but there is nonetheless an abundance of authentic sources – even if scattered across the world in many archives and libraries – for research on Jewish identity. Even during the Holocaust, many Jewish eyewitness reports addressed the necessity of creating authentic documentation of the crimes being committed against their people. The following examples can be considered pieces of what we might call the broader puzzle of identity. Assembling these pieces properly can provide a clearer, even if incomplete, picture of Jewish identity as it emerged among Holocaust survivors in the first years after the Second World War.

Journeys: Early Jewish Accounts from a Ruined Garden

There were many early accounts of the Holocaust as well as numerous *Yizkor-bikher* (books of remembrance) published later in Israel, the United States, and South America.[9] Another important source is the considerable number of early diaries and reports written by Jewish travellers, some members of the Allied forces, who passed through the devastated landscapes of Poland in the early postwar period.[10] Most of these authors came from the United States or South America, many of them with Eastern European Jewish heritage, and, immediately after the liberation, they began to undertake research on what had been the centre of Jewish faith, culture, and life. Their publications were aimed exclusively at Jewish readers abroad, which was evident in the fact that they were written in Yiddish or Hebrew, and they did not seek to avoid bias in their accounts. Authenticity and credibility emerged not from neutrality but from their personal impressions and their conviction that they had a historical mission to report to the world what they had seen on the killing fields of Eastern Europe. All of them began their journey in Warsaw in order to pay tribute to the Jewish resistance during the ghetto uprising in April 1943. As Jacob Pat, a prominent Yiddish author who had emigrated from Poland in 1938, wrote: "The brain, the thoughts, the heart, they all swim in an endless ocean of destruction. I saw the biggest Jewish drama since Jews began writing history. I saw thousands of Jews, each of them was either a shivering tragedy or an unbelievable miracle."[11]

The reality was hard to imagine. The Jewish travellers from abroad (some of whom had emigrated in the 1930s), like the survivors themselves, returned to Poland and found no one left of their friends, neighbours, and relatives. In addition, their belongings and all of their property were also gone, scattered, divided, destroyed, or taken over by non-Jews who were resolutely reluctant to give back what in the meantime they had grown to regard as their property.[12] Already in 1942, the Polish resistance stated in its reports to the Polish government in exile in London that it was certain that former Jewish property would be appropriated completely by non-Jews after the surrender of Germany and the rebirth of an independent Polish state.

It is thus unsurprising that well-known authors and journalists such as Mordechai Tsanin did not see anything but a desert where an oasis of Jewish settlement once had stood. "When I go through the town," Tsanin wrote of Polish-Jewish coexistence in his book *Of Stones and Ruins: A Journey through One Hundred Destroyed Communities in Poland* in 1952, "there are only wastelands, where there was recently a world, a whole world with small streets, prayer houses, synagogues. Now it seems to be just a dream, a dream of six hundred years [of Jewish settlement in Poland]."[13]

Aside from the supposedly peaceful world of Jewish pre-war life in the shtetls, these travel reports painted a particular picture of postwar Poland, especially in the minds of their American readers, and it was not a pretty one. The texts were a mixture of shock, grief, and stereotypes that undoubtedly contributed to a stronger sense of solidarity between Jewish survivors in Europe and Jews in the New World. This sense of alienation and despondency was exacerbated by several pogroms, the best-known examples of which include Krakow in August 1945 and Kielce in July 1946.[14] As far as the survivors were concerned, these and other anti-Semitic incidents accelerated the process of hasty emigration and flight to the West, where they would be under the protection of the western Allies.

Displaced Persons Camps and the Identity of a Common Jewish Fate

A second important source of Jewish post-Holocaust identity centred on the camps erected for roughly 200,000 Jewish displaced persons (DPs) after the war, some of them in western Germany, especially in the American and British zones (around 50,000 Jews), where they were under the watch of Allied forces. These Jews referred to themselves as *Sh'erit ha-Pletah* (Hebrew for "the surviving remnant"). Most Jewish DPs did not intend to stay in Western Europe, nor did they wish to return to their former homes in Eastern Europe, where the reign of Stalinism had already been established.[15] Survivors continued to pour into the camps, in the main from Poland and the Soviet Union, because they no longer saw any future in the east. Holocaust survivors were welcome practically nowhere, and their suffering and loss were rarely acknowledged by non-Jews. "Every road," wrote Jonas Turkow, a well-known actor and survivor of the Warsaw Ghetto uprising, "every way that led to the free world, was overcrowded with the hardly rescued, half-naked shadows of those who once had been called human beings."[16]

From the very beginning, Zionist convictions were widespread among Jewish DPs in western Germany who were active in a wide range of activities seeking to help Jews cope with the atrocities they had just endured. Their efforts also included reuniting families torn apart during the Holocaust, documenting atrocities against Jews, collecting personal testimonies and other materials, prosecuting Jewish collaboration in "honour courts," and, finally, assisting the Allies in bringing perpetrators to justice.[17] Yiddish periodicals such as *Fun letstn khurbn*, published in Munich between 1946 and 1948, provided striking accounts of these initiatives. The early dissemination of these authentic stories influenced how the truth became widely known, but this unfortunately remained an almost exclusively Jewish dialogue.[18] Yet this lack of contact with the surrounding German population helped form strong bonds among Jewish DPs, who connected with each other based not only on a shared experience of persecution, suffering, and resistance, but also on their hopes and plans for the future.[19]

It was also in these DP camps where the topic of Jewish resistance during the Holocaust was first raised. These discussions had many implications for the ways in which the State of Israel later defined itself, first in the 1948 War of Independence, and later, in the early 1960s, following the Eichmann trial. In these contexts, "resistance" came to mean almost exclusively armed resistance against the Nazi perpetrators. Meanwhile, memories of suffering, including the many shared experiences of Jewish victims as they were dragged across the killing fields of Europe, ceased to be part of the discourse.

Another issue strongly contributing to the feeling of a common Jewish fate was the ignorance, especially of the British authorities, with regard to emigration to Palestine and the poor, sometimes harrowing, conditions under which DPs lived in the camps. In August 1945, a report compiled by a representative of the United States, Earl Grant Harrison, criticized the Allied DP policy in blunt terms: "We appear to be treating the Jews as the Nazis treated them except that we do not exterminate them. They are in concentration camps in large numbers under our military guard instead of S.S. troops. One is led to wonder whether the German people, seeing this, are not supposing that we are following or at least condoning Nazi policy … Refusal to recognize the Jews as such has the effect, in this situation, of closing one's eyes to their former and more barbaric persecution."[20]

The Harrison report documented the inadequacy of survivors' living conditions and recognized their other needs as well as the baffling situation of Jews being housed side by side with Germans. With such treatment by their liberators and with few prospects, it was no wonder that the DPs (and, with them, several Jewish institutions) began to fend for themselves by building up their own social and intellectual infrastructure and their own organizations, all of which would later prove useful in Israel. Not least of these efforts was the creation of their own authentic historical narrative of the Holocaust. For the vast majority of Jewish DPs, emigration to Israel was the one and only aim, which can be seen clearly in the astounding wave of immigration experienced by the fledgling state during the late 1940s and early 1950s. Israel doubled its population within only two years, with roughly 700,000 Jews from some seventy countries arriving between 14 May 1948 and the end of 1951, more than 20 per cent of them survivors from DP camps in Germany, Austria, and Cyprus.[21] For them, the Holocaust and the attendant shared experience of victimhood created a strong tie of Jewishness associated not only with the past but also, in the new State of Israel, with the future. Different emigration strategies in Eastern European countries provided a preview of those states' future relationship with Israel. Czechoslovakia, for example, allowed 20,000 Jewish survivors to leave the country per year. Although reluctant to allow Jewish emigration, Poland eventually allowed 28,000 Jews to leave for Israel, and Romania permitted some 88,000 to depart.[22]

The Black Book: The Soviet Case

In more than one respect, the fate of the Jews in the Soviet Union was unique. The 1920s in the Soviet Union had been, in some respects, a promising era for the Jewish population, which saw the flourishing of Yiddish literature and culture on an unprecedented scale as well as the creation of Jewish agricultural settlements in Crimea – all this despite official government policy banning Judaism itself, along with all other religions. However, Jews were increasingly targeted, and, by 1929, the topic of anti-Semitism was addressed in several publications.[23] The problem continued to grow, especially in the western Soviet republics among the working class. The 1930s saw Stalin's political purges and show trials, often marked with open displays of anti-Semitism, as well as a drastic decline of Jewish institutions, including Jewish segments of the Communist Party and several Yiddish scientific institutions in Belorussia and Ukraine.

During the war, the USSR suffered the greatest civilian casualties of the Allies, but it was Jews who fell victim to the worst atrocities committed by the German *Einsatzgruppen*. The most widely known response to these horrors, especially the mass killings of Soviet Jews after June 1941, was undoubtedly the founding of the Jewish Anti-fascist Committee by Ilya Ehrenburg and Vasily Grossman in August 1941. They also planned to publish a "black book" documenting Nazi crimes and Jewish resistance, not only in the Soviet Union but throughout Eastern Europe.[24] However, *The Black Book of Soviet Jewry*, as it was eventually titled, was first published only in the United States and in abridged form. In the Soviet Union, publication of the book's full contents was banned by Stalin himself, and the unabridged volume did not see the light of day until it was published in Israel in 1970. Other Soviet publications chronicled the fates of Jewish victims not as civil and military dead of the Great Patriotic War: they were killed not because they were "normal" Soviet citizens but, rather, because they were Jews. Yet even in the narratives presented in these early Soviet publications, Jews served as a sort of training ground for Nazis to hone their plans for further forms of annihilation. Those plans would soon engulf all Soviet peoples, the Slavs, and other groups, as expressed in Ilya Ehrenburg's 1944 book, *Murderer of Nations*.[25]

This denial of a special status was key in Soviet authorities' attempts to regulate memory of the fates of "Soviet people of Jewish nationality." The ways in which Stalin and the Soviet Union dealt with the Holocaust can be described as a competition of victims or a "memory war" over the authenticity of different narratives, many of which distinguished between heroic Soviet citizens and unarmed Jewish victims. Soviet Jews very soon understood that communist heroism was by no means compatible with Holocaust remembrance.

It is therefore surprising that the Soviet Union in the early postwar years demonstrated greater enthusiasm for an independent Israel than was discernible elsewhere. Golda Meir, the first Israeli ambassador to the Soviet Union and later prime minister of Israel, recalled, "I desperately wanted to make contact with the Jews [in the USSR] … What had remained of their Jewishness after so many years of life under a regime that had proclaimed war not only against all religions as such, but also specifically against Judaism, and regarded Zionism as a crime for which the only appropriate punishment were penal servitude in a forced-labour camp or exile to Soviet Asia."[26] After a cold reception by Soviet officials, Meir was overwhelmed by the warm welcome given to her by Soviet Jews themselves:

> Now, the street [in front of the synagogue] was filled with people, packed together like sardines, hundreds and hundreds of them, of all ages,

> including Red Army officers, soldiers, teenagers and babies carried in their parents' arms. Instead of the 2,000-odd Jews who usually came to synagogue on High Holiday, a crowd of close to 50,000 people was waiting for us. For a minute, I couldn't grasp what had happened – or even who they were. And then it dawned on me. They had come – those good, brave Jews – in order to be with us, to demonstrate their sense of kinship and to celebrate the establishment of the State of Israel.[27]

The more than 50,000 Soviet Jews who enthusiastically greeted Meir in the streets around the Israeli Embassy in Moscow faced severe consequences in many cases, particularly under the so-called anti-cosmopolitan campaign run by Andrei Zhdanov. It was an irony of history that, in September 1948, one of Meir's first official duties was to express her condolences on the occasion of Zhdanov's death. The reaction to Meir's short stay in Moscow demonstrates clearly that neither the Holocaust nor the relentless anti-religion policy of Soviet authorities in the preceding twenty-five years had destroyed a sense of common identity and solidarity among Jews.

Although Soviet anti-religion policy, with its decades long propaganda against Judaism and everything Jewish, undoubtedly had a greater impact on Jewish identity, the Holocaust was also a major factor, as it resulted in more than 2.5 million Jewish victims on Soviet territory alone (including occupied Polish territories after 17 September 1939). Despite the horror of the Shoah, anyone in the postwar Soviet Union who espoused the "exclusiveness" of Jewish suffering became a target of Stalin's regime. Soviet Jews paid a heavy price for this alleged treachery, which supposedly undermined Soviet-Communist ideals. In 1948, Solomon Michoëls, the legendary theatre director and one of the leading figures of the USSR's Jewish intelligentsia, was killed in an automobile accident in Minsk that was believed to have been arranged by the secret police. Everything linked to the commemoration of Jewish suffering and death during the Holocaust was rooted out, the Yiddish theatre was closed, and the Emes (Yiddish for "truth") publishing house was shuttered. In the first half of 1949, hardly a single Jewish organization was left in the Soviet Union, and discussions of Jewish issues, including Holocaust remembrance, ceased entirely. The final blow came in August 1952, when the entire Jewish-Yiddish literary elite as well as activists of the Jewish Anti-Fascist Committee were murdered; twenty-six of them were killed after a short and clandestine military trial, in the style of the 1930s purges, in which they were accused of espionage and other anti-Soviet activity.[28] Shortly before Stalin's death in March 1953, the Soviet Jews faced the further threat of mass deportations to the Soviet Far East. The only remaining space was Birobidzhan, a Jewish town on the Soviet-Chinese border.[29] Only hardcore Jewish communists, however, could have perceived the town as an authentic Soviet Zion or as a new Jewish homeland superior to Palestine, especially after May 1948.[30]

A Socialist Zion in Former German Silesia

Even the emerging communist regimes in Eastern Europe understood the great attraction that the promise of a new Zion would have for uprooted Jewish survivors. Poland supported a quasi-Zionist project by giving an entire swathe of Lower Silesia to Jewish Holocaust survivors and Jewish resettlers from the Soviet Union. Many Jews, led by Jewish Soviet soldier Jakub Egit, had gathered in the vicinity of Reichenbach im Eulengebirge (now Dzierżoniów), not far from the former Groß-Rosen concentration camp with its numerous labour camps. In 1945, Egit proposed creating a Jewish settlement or commune of 50,000 survivors on former German territory as a sort of retribution. Egit received not only permission from the authorities but, in the beginning, even the assistance of the Red Army in realizing his plans.

The regime pursued this plan based on two considerations. First, a specifically Jewish settlement seemed necessary in creating a postwar social peace that resolved both the catastrophic living conditions of Holocaust survivors and the strong currents of anti-Semitism within the non-Jewish population. The second goal was a geopolitical one, since Lower Silesia had been given to Poland as a form of reparation. The former German territory had been evacuated but needed to be repopulated and developed – with Jewish survivors and Polish settlers from the ceded Polish eastern territories.

According to the official plans, some 50,000 Jews were to be settled in Lower Silesia. This seemed to be a manageable task, since Silesia was the main gathering point of Jewish survivors in Poland anyway.[31] And indeed, by the early summer of 1946, about 100,000 Jews were already residing in more than forty Silesian towns. The development of these Jewish settlements was impressive, given the extent of devastation faced by Poland. These efforts, even if limited, allowed for some shift in perspective from postwar violence and mass migration to the topic of reconstruction. Although they are almost forgotten today, new social and cultural institutions flourished, including Jewish publishing houses, Jewish newspapers in Yiddish (*Nidershlezye* [Lower Silesia]) and Polish (*Nowe Życie* [New Life]), and Yiddish schools and theatres.

The goal of engaging Jews in occupations beyond their traditional roles in trade was an integral part of the project's espoused social planning, and the region subsequently saw new Jewish businesses, farming collectives, and small factories.

This settlement could have been a promising starting point for new Jewish life in Eastern Europe and for Polish-Jewish coexistence, but hopes were short-lived. Postwar pogroms in Poland led to mass emigration of Jewish survivors, and, by 1947, there were only about 50,000 Jews still living in the country. Particularly in the context of the founding of Israel, the project turned out to be a grand illusion, as Egit himself put it many years later.[32] The Polish government allowed emigration, although reluctantly, and, by 1951, more than 50 per cent of the aforementioned Jewish population of Silesia had left Poland. The uncertainty of the Israeli fledgling state turned out to be far more attractive than the equal uncertainty of life behind the Iron Curtain built on the ruins of a destroyed Jewish world.

Conclusion

How do these few puzzle pieces fit together to form a picture of Jewish identity among Holocaust survivors? In questions of post-Holocaust Jewish identity, Zionism, Judaism, and socialism provide many, but not all, of the answers.

The clearest turning point in the development of this identity, particularly that of Holocaust survivors, was undoubtedly the founding of the State of Israel in 1948. Later on, it becomes harder to distinguish post-Holocaust identity from pro-Zionist or, more precisely, a pro-Israel identity (which did not necessarily indicate a personal desire to emigrate to the Promised Land). In the late 1940s and the 1950s, Jewish populations were preoccupied by their efforts to establish a new homeland and defend it against the surrounding enemies. It was not until the Eichmann trial in 1961 that Holocaust remembrance became a prominent feature in Israeli identity.

Prior to May 1948, the picture of Jewish identity in Eastern Europe was less clear: Jewish suffering was non-heroic and remembrance highly fragmentized and painful. In addition, the surrounding societies and political systems tended to ignore the fate of the Jewish victims and were eager to silence any form of authentic Jewish remembrance – first in the Soviet Union, then throughout Eastern Europe. Alternatively, Jewish identity was forced to become just one participant in a competition among various victims groups that had suffered under Nazism or Stalinism (or both). The commemoration of the Shoah, a non-heroic understanding of history among Jews, became what the Polish scholar Zofia Wóycicka has very aptly described as "arrested mourning."[33]

Despite impediments to that mourning, one cannot speak of total silence within the Jewish community, as there was no shortage of accounts of the Holocaust that emerged directly after the war. The first Yiddish eyewitness accounts, the efforts of activists within the numerous DP camps, and commemorative efforts of Soviet Jews (though later brutally beat down) were the first elements of a postwar Jewish memory culture, even if that culture remained a completely internal Jewish discourse for many years. A shift toward a European perspective in dealing with and remembering the Holocaust did not occur until decades later, and it occurred without any significant input from Jewish survivors or expressions of authenticity through their first-hand experiences.[34]

Given the wealth of source material generated in the early postwar years, one could argue that the passing away of the last survivors will not constitute the major shift portended by some. Although it is important to record the last voices in order to document their experiences, it is also crucial that historians re-evaluate the very first voices as well. Already in the 1960s, Yad Vashem in Jerusalem and the YIVO Institute for Jewish Research in New York had started to register bibliographical details of all testimonies published in Yiddish; there are several thousands of these narratives, plus several more thousand authentic reports held in the Jewish Historical Institute in Warsaw, including the Oneg Shabbat archive of Emanuel Ringelblum from the Warsaw Ghetto.[35] Historians seeking to discover something new – new information, new approaches, new forms of integrating the actual victims' perspective – should venture back a few decades and start anew in analysing and evaluating the authenticity of these numerous testimonies. This will help ensure that these accounts serve the purpose intended by their authors: understanding and acknowledgment of what those victims experienced.

NOTES

1 See Zorach Warhaftig and Jacob Freid, *Uprooted: Jewish Refugees and Displaced Persons after Liberation* (New York: Institute of Jewish Affairs of the American Jewish Congress and World Jewish Congress, 1946), 219. Russian-born Zorach Warhaftig immigrated to Palestine/Israel in 1947, was a signatory to Israel's Declaration of Independence, and was co-founder of Bar-Ilan University as well as a member of the Knesset from 1949 to 1981.

2 English translation from Milton Teichman and Sharon Leder, eds., *Truth and Lamentation: Stories and Poems on the Holocaust* (Champaign: University of Illinois Press, 1994), 427–8. Originally published in Kadia Molodowsky, *Der meylekh dovid aleyn iz geblibn: Lider un poemes* (New York: Papirene brik, 1946), 3–4. See also Kadia Molodowsky, *Fun lublin biz niu york: Tog-bukh fun rivke zilberg* (New York: Papirene brik, 1942); Mates Olitski, *In fremdn land lider* (Eschwege: Farlag Ibergang, 1948); Frieda W. Aaron, *Bearing the Unbearable: Yiddish and Polish Poetry in the Ghettos and Concentration Camps* (New York: SUNY Press, 2012), 6–8; Kathryn Hellerstein, "Gender and Nation in the 1945 Poems of Kadya Molodowsky and Malka Heifetz Tussmann," in *Women Writers of Yiddish Literature: Critical Essays*, ed. Rosemary Horowitz (Jefferson, IA: McFarland, 2015), 175–207.

3 Not later than 1942/43, the US public was rather well informed about the Holocaust in general and about the fate of Polish Jews in particular. See Jacob Apenszlak, ed., *The Black Book of Polish Jewry: An Account of the Martyrdom of Polish Jewry under the Nazi Occupation* (New York: American Federation for Polish Jews, 1943).

4 Alphons Silbermann, *Was ist jüdischer Geist? Zur Identität der Juden* (Osnabrück: Edition Interfrom, 1984).

5 Steven T. Katz, Shlomo Biderman, and Gershon Greenberg, eds., *Wrestling with God: Jewish Theological Responses during and after the Holocaust* (Oxford: Oxford University Press, 2007); Steven T. Katz, ed., *The Impact of the Holocaust on Jewish Theology* (New York: NYU Press, 2005); Michael A. Meyer, *Jewish Identity in the Modern World* (Seattle: University of Washington Press, 1990).

6 Quoted in Bert Hoppe, ed., *Die Verfolgung und Ermordung der europäischen Juden durch das nationalsozialistische Deutschland 1933–1945*, vol. 8, *Sowjetunion mit annektierten Gebieten II* (Munich: de Gruyter Oldenbourg, 2015), 578 (document no. 238). Unless otherwise attributed, translations are my own. The original Hebrew manuscript is held in the archives of the Jewish Historical Institute in Warsaw (302/192).

7 Shmuel N. Eisenstadt, *The Transformation of Israeli Society* (London: Weidenfeld and Nicolson 1985); Tom Segev, *1949: The First Israelis* (New York: Free Press, 1986).

8 Heinrich Graetz, Geschichte der Juden von den ältesten Zeiten bis auf die Gegenwart (Leipzig: Leiner, 1990).

9 On this, see Frank Beer, Wolfgang Benz, and Barbara Distel, eds., *Nach dem Untergang: Die ersten Zeugnisse der Shoah in Polen, 1944–1947: Berichte der Zentralen Jüdischen Historischen Kommission* (Berlin: Metropol-Verlag, 2014); Zofia Wóycicka, *Arrested Mourning: Memory of the Nazi Camps in Poland, 1944–1950* (Frankfurt: Peter Lang, 2013).

10 Marcin Urynowicz, "Wokół stacji gdzie przejeżdża pociąg, mieszkają dzicy ludzie – Pamięć o Polsce i Polakach w żydowskojęzycznych reportażach

pierwszych lat powojennych. Przyczynek do badań," in *Zagłada Żydów na polskiej prowincji*, ed. Adam Sitarek, Michał Trębacza, and Ewa Wiatr (Łódź: Instytut Pamięci Narodowej, 2012), 441–52.

11 Jacob Pat, *Ash un fayer: Iber di khurves fun poyln* (New York: Cyco, 1946), 8. Pat was also the long-time executive secretary of the Jewish Labor Committee in the United States.

12 An early, if not the first, account on that topic is M. Farshtendig, *Di yidishe farmegens in poyln: Dekret un komentar* (Munich: Ibergang-federatsye fun yidn in poyln, 1947). See also Jan Grabowski and Dariusz Libionka, eds., *Klucze i kasa: O mieniu żydowskim w Polsce pod okupacją niemiecką i we wczesnych latach powojennych 1939–1950* (Warsaw: Stowarzyszenie Centrum Badań nad Zagładą Żydów, 2014).

13 Mordechai Tsanin, *Iber shteyn un shtok: A rayze iber hundert khorev-gevorene kehiles in poyln* (Tel Aviv: Letste Nayes, 1952), 30.

14 Jan Tomasz Gross, *Fear: Anti-Semitism in Poland after Auschwitz. An Essay in Historical Interpretation* (Princeton, NJ: Princeton University Press, 2006); Marcin Zaremba, *Die große Angst: Polen 1944–1947. Leben im Ausnahmezustand* (Paderborn: Schöningh, 2016); Anna Cichopek-Gajraj, *Beyond Violence: Jewish Survivors in Poland and Slovakia, 1944–48* (Cambridge: Cambridge University Press, 2014).

15 Donald L. Niewyk, ed., *Fresh Wounds: Early Narratives of Holocaust Survival* (Chapel Hill: University of North Carolina Press, 1998). For a unique, photo-illustrated documentary history of Jewish DPs and DP camps, see Nathan Baruch, *Pictorial Review* (Munich: Vaad Hatzala, 1948). See also Irmela von der Lühe, Axel Schildt, and Stefanie Schüler-Springorum, eds., *"Auch in Deutschland waren wir nicht wirklich zu Hause": Jüdische Remigration nach 1945* (Göttingen: Wallstein, 2008).

16 Jonas Turkow, *Nokh der bafrayung (zikhroynes)*, vol. 2 (Buenos Aires: Dos poylishe yidntum, 1959), 65.

17 On examples from Poland of honour courts, see Andrzej Żbikowski, *Sąd Społeczny przy CKŻP: Wojenne rozliczenia społeczności żydowskiej w Polsce* (Warsaw: Jewish Historical Institute, 2014).

18 See the overview in Anne-Katrin Henkel and Thomas Rahe, eds., *Publizistik in jüdischen Displaced-Persons-Camps: Charakteristika, Medien und bibliothekarische Überlieferung* (Frankfurt: Vittorio Klostermann, 2014).

19 The topic of Jewish women and their influence on the emergence of Jewish post-Holocaust identity has not yet been adequately investigated and should be a topic of further research.

20 Earl Grant Harrison, *The Plight of the Displaced Jews in Europe: A Report to President Truman* (New York: Jewish Joint Distribution Committee, 1945).

21 Golda Meir, *My Life* (London: Weidenfeld & Nicolson, 1975), chapter "Minister to Moscow," 212.

22 Ibid., 213.
23 The most prominent of these publications was the comprehensive study by Jurij Larin, *Antisemitizm v SSSR* (Moscow: Gosizdat, 1929).
24 Shimon Redlich, *Propaganda and Nationalism in Wartime Russia: The Jewish Antifascist Committee in the USSR, 1941–1948* (Boulder, CO: East European Monographs, 1982); Arno Lustiger, *Rotbuch: Stalin und die Juden. Die tragische Geschichte des Jüdischen Antifaschistischen Komitees und der sowjetischen Juden* (Berlin: Aufbau, 1998); Markus Nesselrodt, *Dem Holocaust entkommen: Polnische Juden in der Sowjetunion, 1939–1946* (Berlin: De Gruyter, 2019).
25 Il'ja Ėrenburg, *Merder fun felker*, vol. 1 (Moscow: Der emes, 1944), 3.
26 Meir, *My Life*, 203.
27 Ibid., 205.
28 Joshua Rubenstein and Vladimir P. Naumov, eds., *Stalin's Secret Pogrom: The Postwar Inquisition of the Jewish Anti-Fascist Committee* (New Haven, CT: Yale University Press, 2001). It is telling that the origin of the archival materials used in this collection is not revealed, which is a clear hint that they likely stem from the former KGB (now FSB) Archive.
29 Robert Weinberg, *Stalin's Forgotten Zion: Birobidzhan and the Making of a Soviet Jewish Homeland – An Illustrated History, 1928–1996* (Berkeley: University of California Press, 1998); Antje Kuchenbecker, *Zionismus ohne Zion: Birobidžan: Idee und Geschichte eines jüdischen Staates in Sowjet-Fernost* (Berlin: Metropol, 2000).
30 Peter Brod, *Die Antizionismus- und Israelpolitik der UdSSR: Voraussetzung und Entwicklung bis 1956* (Baden-Baden: Nomos, 1980).
31 Jakub Egit, *Tsu a nay leben: Tsvey yor yidisher yishev in nidershlezye* (Wrocław: Farlag Nidershlezye, 1947); Shlomo Strauss-Marko, *Di geshikhte fun yidishn yishuv in nokhmilkhomedikn poyln* (Tel Aviv, 1987).
32 See Jacob Egit, *Grand Illusion* (Toronto: Lugus Productions, 1991). Egit was imprisoned for a period before immigrating to Canada.
33 Wóycicka, *Arrested Mourning*.
34 See Lawrence L. Langer, "What More Can Be Said about the Holocaust?" in *Admitting the Holocaust: Collected Essays*, ed. Lawrence L. Langer (Oxford: Oxford University Press, 1995), 179–93; Daniel Levy and Natan Sznaider, *Erinnerung im globalen Zeitalter: Der Holocaust* (Frankfurt: Suhrkamp, 2001).
35 Philip Friedman and Joseph Gar, eds., *Bibliography of Yiddish Books on the Catastrophe and Heroism* (New York: Marstin Press, 1962); Joseph Gar, ed., *Bibliography of Articles on the Catastrophe and Heroism in Yiddish Periodicals*, vol. 1 (New York: Marstin Press, 1966); vol. 2 (New York: Marstin Printing, 1969); Bolesław Woszczyński and Violetta Urbaniak, eds., *Źródła archiwalne do dziejów Żydów w Polsce* (Warsaw: Wydawnictwo DIG, 2001).

4 History on Trial before the Social Welfare Courts: Holocaust Survivors, German Judges, and the Struggle for "Ghetto Pensions"

JÜRGEN ZARUSKY

In June 1997, a Jewish Holocaust survivor won a lawsuit before the German Federal Social Welfare Court (*Bundessozialgericht*) and was awarded a pension for the time she had lived and worked in the ghetto of Łódź. She argued that she had found employment on her own initiative and had received payment for it. Under such conditions, the German Social Security Law (*Reichsversicherungsordnung*), which at that time applied to the territories of Poland that had been annexed by the Third Reich, provided the right to receive a worker's pension. The basis for the court's decision turned on a very important distinction: although the claimant had been forced to live in the ghetto, she had needed to seek work by herself. Thus, work in a ghetto was not the same as forced labour, although one might hesitate to call it "free labour."

This decision set a precedent and demanded a reaction – not so much on the part of the social courts but by German pension funds and, in the end, by lawmakers. It was, of course, hardly imaginable that Holocaust survivors from the Łódź Ghetto would receive pensions, while those who, for instance, had worked in the Warsaw Ghetto would not be entitled to such payments simply because German social security legislation applied only to areas of Polish territory that had been formally annexed and not those under the jurisdiction of the General Government, as was the case in Warsaw.[1] Thus, after some discussion, the Law Regarding Conditions for Making Pensions Payable on the Basis of Employment in a Ghetto (*Gesetz zur Zahlbarmachung von Renten aus Beschäftigungen in einem Ghetto*, or ZRBG), more popularly known as the Law on Ghetto Pensions, was passed unanimously by the German Bundestag in June 2002.[2] It opened up the possibility for every Holocaust survivor who had worked in a ghetto under German occupation to receive such a pension, with the proviso that the person had chosen their work by their own free will and had received payment for it.[3]

One of the initial problems with the implementation of the law was the lack of knowledge about Jewish labour in the ghettos, which itself resulted from two underlying problems. On the one hand, the pension funds drew on findings established only by administrative and legal procedures, without consulting expert historians. On the other hand, the real effects of the politics of ghettoization and exploitation – more than 1,000 ghettos in Eastern Europe and the use of their workforces for various German war needs – were not known at that juncture even to these historians. Important reference works – for example, *The Yad Vashem Encyclopedia of the Ghettos during the Holocaust* or the specific volumes of the *Encyclopedia of Camps and Ghettos, 1933–1945*, published by the United States Holocaust Memorial Museum – had not yet appeared.[4]

The pension funds, and consequently the German federal government, estimated the number of potential applicants at approximately 6,000.[5] Surprisingly, the real number of applicants turned out to be nearly twelve times greater – some 70,000 thousand – thanks not least to the intensive activities of supporters of Nazi victims in spreading the word about the new law worldwide. But, after the German pension funds evaluated the applications, the number actually granted turned out to be closer to the initial estimates, since more than 90 per cent of the applications were turned down.[6] What followed was a wave of lawsuits before the social welfare courts, some 20,000 in total. Since most of the applicants lived either in Israel or the United States, these matters were heard by courts in North Rhine–Westphalia and Hamburg, the German federal states responsible for pensioners resident in these countries. In most cases, the social courts affirmed the pension funds' decisions, although there were significant differences between the more generous court in Hamburg and its more restrictive counterpart in North Rhine–Westphalia. Similarly, pension fund decisions were more likely to be favourable in Hamburg than in the North Rhine. More than once, applicants living in the United States were granted a pension, while, in nearly identical cases (e.g., same ghetto, same type of work), applications of Israeli citizens were turned down. These problems indicate a lack of precise criteria in the implementation of the law.[7]

It is, of course, difficult, if not impossible, to establish precise criteria when the historical context is unclear. Paying pensions to Holocaust survivors was not entirely new for the German pension funds, but the cases they had dealt with previously had often concerned former German civil servants. Although the careers of the latter had usually been ended abruptly by the anti-Semitic measures of the Nazi regime, the social courts and pension funds were always able to find a suitable point of reference within existing laws and rules. The same is true with regard to those belonging to the so-called German language and cultural sphere, as a regulation exists that allows the granting of pensions for expellees or late repatriates of ethnic German origin from Eastern Europe, and it has been applied to Holocaust survivors since 1963.[8]

The ZRBG, however, posed far more difficult problems. The basic question was how working conditions in the ghettos could be described using terms of German social welfare and security law, especially in cases where they did not neatly fit the law's categories, as was true of the 1997 court decision. Yet no one asked this question explicitly. When the federal government reported to the Bundestag in 2006 on problems that had arisen in the law's implementation, it pointed to the complexity of the law, which was not correctly understood by Holocaust survivors.[9] This seemed to be an elegant, political way to deal with the problem, but it was far from being satisfactory for the former ghetto workers, who felt that *they* were not being understood, or, even worse, that they were regarded as liars out for monetary gain.

Why was it so difficult to achieve understanding with respect to pensions for those who worked in the ghettos? I see four main reasons:

1. the difficulty of applying the regulations and the terminology of the German social welfare law to the complex reality of the ghettos;
2. procedural deficiencies – above all, the physical absence of the applicants themselves from the trials;
3. the lack of historical knowledge available to the German authorities compounded by the lack of appreciation for historians' expertise, which could have facilitated proper administration of the ghetto pension cases; and
4. the general inadequacy of historical knowledge about the ghettos available at the time of the disputes over ghetto pensions.

In regard to the first point, the two key questions for those making decisions on ghetto pension applications were whether the applicant had received payment for labour performed, and whether the applicant had taken up work voluntarily. Both questions are closely linked: a free decision to engage in a certain kind of work is always linked to some kind of consideration given in return (*Gegenleistung*). But, under German social welfare law, not all types of consideration can be regarded as payment. To qualify as payment, the amount would have to have been at least one-sixth of the wage normally paid to unskilled workers in the locality concerned. If the worker were paid not with money but instead received in-kind benefits, especially food, the amount of these benefits had to exceed that of simple sustenance – in German juridicial terminology, *freier Unterhalt* (rougly, "free subsistence"). If these minimums were not exceeded, then the benefit would not count as payment.[10]

Theoretically, these critieria should not have constituted an obstacle. The German occupation authorities in Poland, and later also in the occupied parts of the Soviet Union, issued regulations on wages with special rules for Jews, who were to receive 80 per cent of the wages earned by non-Jews for the same work.[11] But in practice, in every one of the more than one thousand ghettos created during the war, private and state enterprises exploited the Jewish workers and did not pay these wages. Very often, they were simply given some amount of food. Under the extreme conditions of a ghetto economy, characterized by hunger and black markets, food was of much greater value than some small amount of cash that would be insufficient to purchase anything useful. Moreover, it was also a common practice in the ghetto to pay wages – if they were paid at all – not directly to the workers but to the Jewish councils (*Judenräte*), the self-governing bodies of the ghettos, for distribution to the workers. The councils were required to provide the workforce for German use and to oversee the ghettos' supplies, particularly food. To do so, they depended to a great degree on wage payments, which were heavily taxed.[12] German social welfare and labour legislation did not account for such unique circumstances. The relevant measure was of the in-kind benefits received by the worker, which were, in many cases, regarded as insufficient to qualify as payment for work and, thus, to warrant a ghetto pension.

The problem of distinguishing between so-called free or forced labour should, in principle, have been less complicated, because basically it had already been solved by the Federal Social Court in 1997. But here the bureaucratic reconstruction of reality took its toll. In a large number of the cases, in the process of evaluating applications, the pension funds and the social courts turned to the archives and consulted the case law regarding the German Federal Indemnification Law of 1952.[13] Significantly, the relevant proceedings had taken place mainly in the 1950s and 1960s. At that time, the differentiation made by the Federal Social Court in 1997 between forced labour and "free" ghetto labour did not yet exist. Nevertheless, numerous applications were turned down by judges or pension-fund employees for only one key reason: the term "forced labour" had appeared in the applicants' statements. In some cases, the authorities even interpreted the fact that an applicant had *not* mentioned free labour in their statement as a reason to deny a ghetto pension. In plain language, this means that Holocaust survivors were denied such benefits because, in the 1950s and 1960s, they had not answered questions that in actuality had never been put to them, and they had not used a legal terminology that, in fact, was not even created until the late 1990s.[14] It would seem that the pension funds and social courts took a rather Kafkaesque approach in their role as gatekeepers before the law.

Moreover, only in a very few cases were the applicants themselves able to appear before the courts to tell their stories directly. Most of them were too old or did not wish to travel to Germany. As a result, communication occurred via questionnaires and lawyers in an abstract, highly formalized, and partially biased manner. The filings from the indemnification proceedings are a very interesting source with regard to the problem of recognition of victimhood. Since the German Federal Indemnification Law applied only to Germans and persons belonging to the German language and cultural sphere, there were two stages of recognition. First, the applicant had to prove that they had suffered harm to their liberty and/or health. Of course, any biography of a Holocaust survivor contains a plethora of such damages and injuries suffered, often accompanied by a claim to a solatium, but one does not find much of such testimony in the indemnification files. Neither the applicants nor the German authorities were interested in an extended dialogue regarding the victims' life stories. During a court hearing in Tel Aviv in 2008, one applicant for a ghetto pension remembered the words of his lawyer when he had applied for the indemnification: "*Ein Sach sog!*" (Say one thing!) – in other words, provide just one fact sufficient for fulfilling the requirements of the indemnification law.[15] Such preferences resulted in very short descriptions of dramatic and tragic life stories, the average length being about a half page.

Matters take a different turn when it comes to the question of the German language and cultural sphere. Here, one finds detailed interviews, transcripts of language tests, and extensive discussions on their interpretation, with an especially wary ear trained on anything that might sound more Yiddish than German. Without any doubt, these files are sources that demand careful historical critique. Instead, in assessing claims for ghetto pensions, the evaluators read these documents with an incredible degree of insensitivity.

Not only were the methodological approaches questionable, but the sources of historical knowledge were, in many cases, extremely modest. At one hearing in the North Rhine–Westphalian Higher Social Welfare Court in October 2007, a representative of that state's pension fund responded proudly to the question about which historical information he and his colleagues had drawn on in their decision making: they were in possession, he noted, of a library of five books and had watched a documentary film in order to prepare for this task. A very important but questionable role was played by an internet project developed since the

1990s, "Deutschland – Ein Denkmal" (Germany – A Memorial), which features an interactive map showing sites of National Socialist crimes, especially camps and ghettos. This database enjoyed great popularity because it was readily accessible, notwithstanding criticism by historians that it cited outdated literature.[16]

Although this state of research did not seem to pose any difficulty or cause for concern for most social court judges and civil servants working with the pension funds, things were beginning to change. In April 2008, the conference "Ghetto Pensions and Historical Research" was held at the Institute of Contemporary History in Munich, attended mostly by lawyers and legal scholars, among them several judges of social welfare courts. By that time, Jan-Robert von Renesse, a judge on the State Social Welfare Court of North Rhine–Westphalia, had already begun to tread new paths in the handling of ghetto pension cases. Not only had he found new ways to organize official hearings with applicants in Israel, but he also drew extensively on expert opinions from historians, psychologists, and sociologists. Once the established system dominated by the courts and the self-interested pension funds began to include the voices of the applicants – and, probably still more important, those of the experts – the discourse on ghetto pensions began to change.[17] This change was gradual and certainly not without resistance on the part of the people and institutions who saw their routine practices being challenged. Representatives of the North Rhine–Westphalian pension funds boycotted the first hearings, organized by von Renesse and his colleague Matthias Röhl, for former ghetto workers who had settled in Israel. The pension-fund representatives argued that such interviews would not yield any valuable information and that the elderly Holocaust victims might well be retraumatized by the ordeal.

"Can the victims speak?" This question, which Svenja Goltermann choose as the title for her paper at the December 2014 Berlin conference on authenticity and victimhood that served as a basis for this volume, is a very important one. And the answer is an unqualified yes. Although a wrenching emotional experience for them, the former ghetto workers, at dozens of hearings, provided valuable and precise information that matched, often perfectly, historical scholarship of which they would have been unaware. Many of those interviewed thanked the judges as well as the experts for having listened to them. When Judge von Renesse compelled representatives of the pension funds to attend hearings in Israel by imposing financial penalties for non-participation, the consequence was a significantly higher rate of approval of ghetto pensions than usual.[18]

In June 2009, the history of the ghetto pensions took a decisive turn when the Federal Social Welfare Court made fundamental decisions that changed the interpretation of the relevant law. Most important was the acknowledgment that any kind of benefits received on the basis of work performed now constituted payment. "Only on this basis can the intent and purpose of the ZRBG [Law on Ghetto Pensions] be fulfilled," reads the judgment.[19] This decision corresponded to one of the central demands of the "Historians' Appeal," published by thirteen historians who, in their work as expert witnesses, possessed detailed knowledge of the problems in the implementation of the Law on Ghetto Pensions. The historians implored the court to take their expertise into account, noting that fair "decisions on ghetto pensions may not be taken by overlooking historical reality."[20] The decision by the Federal Social Welfare Court in 2009 led to the reopening of nearly 57,000 cases in which ghetto pension applications had been rejected. Two and a half years later, according to statistics provided by the Conference on Jewish Material Claims against Germany (the Claims Conference), 25,153 of those cases had resulted in approvals and 14,322 in rejections; 375 applications had been withdrawn; and 16,903 cases could not be resolved.[21]

Historians played an important role in attaining recognition for the claims of the former ghetto workers, but the fate of those workers had not been a topic of major historical research before the debate surrounding the ZRBG emerged. The intensification of research on the history of the ghettos took place more or less at the same time as the disputes over the ghetto pensions, but most of the results came too late to be of much help in resolving those cases. Ghetto labour had been almost completely ignored by historians, with the exception of Isaiah Trunk's study on the Jewish Councils.[22] It became a research topic among academics only in the wake of the Law on Ghetto Pensions disputes and, therefore, after much research had been done in support of the expert opinions.[23]

This case study points to the significance of material claims, courts, and politics for the culture of remembrance. In view of this history of ghetto pension litigation, it seems erroneous to assume that the activists in the sphere of cultural memory – be they lobbyists, intellectuals, or politicians – are always advocates of the victims. The most significant public symbol of remembrance of the Holocaust in Germany, the Memorial to the Murdered Jews of Europe, was (nota bene) initially a project of German non-Jews. The erection of the monument in 2005 was preceded by an intense public debate.[24] The discussion of the proposal seemed to take on a life of its own, at times almost overshadowing the planned memorial itself. Documentation of this discussion was published in 1999, the year the German Bundestag took the decision to construct the monument, in a massive volume of 1,300 pages.[25] Both before and after the opening of the monument, several other books dedicated to the subject were also published. The disputes over ghetto pensions were taking place at virtually the same time, but the German public hardly took any notice. To the author's knowledge, only two journalists, Robert Probst of the *Süddeutsche Zeitung* and the late Christian Semler of the *taz*, covered the topic on a regular basis, but even those efforts did not result in more than a handful of articles annually. The situation changed a bit after 2009, but, by then, the basic problems had already been solved – albeit not the problems that Jan-Robert von Renesse encountered with the colleagues in his court and elsewhere.[26]

Historians were latecomers to the pensions question, and, without von Renesse's efforts, they probably would not have been involved at all. To my knowledge, the first historical conference on the topic took place in 2008, and the first article on the topic written by a historian appeared that same year.[27] One could argue that being a latecomer is inherent to the historian's profession, because the task of that profession is to analyse the past, not to intervene in current disputes. But what was at stake here was the history of the Holocaust and the distortion that resulted from the bureaucratic handling of historical realities, which led to severe disadvantages for a great number of Holocaust survivors.

Most important was the fact that Holocaust survivors themselves fought for their own interests, especially the woman who achieved the 1997 judgment mentioned at the outset, which had a significant effect in getting the ball rolling. It would have been a step backwards had lawmakers chosen to react to this precedent with a solution created within the framework of reparations legislation.[28] German authorities have always declared that reparations for victims of Nazi persecution represented voluntary benefits (i.e., benefits paid voluntarily by the state), whereas the ghetto pensions were based on a legal obligation. "Ghetto pensioners" are not recipients of voluntary benefits: rather, they receive the pension they have earned with their work, just as any German worker would. For some of them at least, this is the most important aspect of recognition.

NOTES

1 Stephan Lehnstaedt, "Wiedergutmachung im 21. Jahrhundert: Das Arbeitsministerium und die Ghettorenten," *Vierteljahrshefte für Zeitgeschichte* 61 (2013): 369–71.

2 Jan Robert von Renesse, "Wiedergutmachtung fünf vor zwölf: Das Gesetz zur Zahlbarmachung von Renten aus Beschäftigungen in einem Ghetto,"

in *Ghettorenten: Entschädigungspolitik, Rechtsprechung und historische Forschung*, ed. Jürgen Zarusky (Munich: Oldenbourg Verlag, 2010), 14.

3 Gesetz zur Zahlbarmachung von Renten aus Beschäftigungen in einem Ghetto, 20 June 2002, http://www.gesetze-im-internet.de/zrbg/.

4 Guy Miron, ed., *The Yad Vashem Encyclopedia of the Ghettos during the Holocaust*, 2 vols. (Jerusalem: Yad Vashem, 2009). See also Geoffrey P. Megargee, ed., *Encyclopedia of Camps and Ghettos, 1933–1945*, vol. 2, parts A and B. (Bloomington: University of Indiana Press, 2012); Ilya Altman, ed., *Cholokost na territorii SSSR: Ėnciklopedija* (Moscow: ROSSPĖN, 2009).

5 Lehnstaedt, "Wiedergutmachung im 21. Jahrhundert," 371.

6 Renesse, "Wiedergutmachung fünf vor zwölf," 15.

7 Ibid.; Jürgen Zarusky, "Hindernislauf für Holocaust-Überlebende: Das 'Ghettorentengesetz' und seine Anwendung," *Tribüne: Zeitschrift zum Verständnis des Judentums* 47, no. 187 (2008): 156–7.

8 Renesse, "Wiedergutmachung fünf vor zwölf," 13.

9 German Bundestag, "Überarbeitung des Gesetzes zur Zahlbarmachung von Renten aus Beschäftigungen in einem Ghetto," Drucksache 16/1955, 20 June 2006, http://dipbt.bundestag.de/doc/btd/16/019/1601955.pdf.

10 Renesse, "Wiedergutmachung fünf vor zwölf," 22. For an example, see decision of North Rhine–Westphalia Social Court, L 8 R 257/05, 5 March 2008, http://openjur.de/u/133765.html.

11 Bogdan Musial, *Deutsche Zivilverwaltung und Judenverfolgung im Generalgouvernement: Eine Fallstudie zum Distrikt Lublin 1939–1944* (Wiesbaden: Harrassowitz Verlag, 1999), 165, 169.

12 Stephan Lehnstaedt, *Geschichte und Gesetzesauslegung: Zu Kontinuität und Wandel des bundesdeutschen Wiedergutmachungsdiskurses am Beispiel der Ghettorenten* (Osnabrück: fibre Verlag, 2011), 55.

13 Bundesentschädigungsgesetz. As noted on the website of the Conference on Jewish Material Claims against Germany, the compensation "was referred to by the German government as *Wiedergutmachung*, which literally means 'making good again.' However, this term was not accepted by the Claims Conference and is generally no longer used in recognition of the fact that the suffering of Nazi victims cannot be 'made up for' by any amount of material compensation." See "West German Federal Indemnification Law – BEG," http://www.claimscon.org/what-we-do/compensation/germany-payments/beg/.

14 Observations made by the author in the course of his work as an expert for the State Social Court of North Rhine–Westphalia. See also Eva Dwertmann, "Zeitspiele: Zur späten Entschädigung ehemaliger Ghettoarbeiter," in *Die Praxis der Wiedergutmachung: Geschichte, Erfahrung und Wirkung in Deutschland und Israel*, ed. Norbert Frei, José Brunner, and Constantin Goschler (Göttingen: Wallstein Verlag, 2009), 643–9, 657.

15 The author attended the hearing as an expert.

16 On the development of the project, see Bettina Sarnes and Holger Sarnes, "1996 bis 2009: Entstehung des Projekts," http://www.deutschland-ein-denkmal.de/ded/information/texts?textName=text-002.

17 Lehnstaedt, *Geschichte und Gesetzesauslegung*, 89.

18 Stephan Lehnstaedt, "Der Deutungsstreit um die 'Ghettorenten': Anmerkungen zur Diskurspraxis des Landessozialgerichts Nordrhein-Westfalen," *Vierteljahrshefte für Zeitgeschichte* 63 (2016): 109–18, 113. For a detailed examination of the hearings, see Kristin Platt, *Bezweifelte Erinnerung, verweigerte Glaubhaftigkeit: Überlebende des Holocaust in den Ghettorentenverfahren* (Munich: Wilhelm Fink, 2012), 181–207.

19 Bundessozialgericht, B 13 R 139/08, 2 June 2008, reproduced in Lehnstaedt, *Geschichte und Gesetzesauslegung*, 271.

20 Lehnstaedt, *Geschichte und Gesetzesauslegung*, 264–5.

21 "Status of Re-Opened Applications for German Social Security Payments for Work in Ghettos," Conference on Jewish Material Claims against Germany, http://www.claimscon.org/what-we-do/compensation/germany-payments/zrbg/. Statistics represent totals as of 12 January 2012. The "cannot be resolved" category includes decision deferrals and claims closed after contact with claimants or legal successors failed.

22 Isaiah Trunk, *Judenrat: The Jewish Councils in Eastern Europe under Nazi Occupation* (New York: Macmillan, 1972).

23 See Stephan Lehnstaedt and Jürgen Hensel, eds., *Arbeit in den nationalsozialistischen Ghettos* (Osnabrück: Fibre, 2013); Jürgen Zarusky, "Das Ghettorentengesetz und die Zeitgeschichtsforschung: Einige bilanzierende Überlegungen," in ibid., 407–20.

24 See the chapter by Michael Schwartz in this volume.

25 Ute Heimrod, ed., *Der Denkmalstreit – das Denkmal? Die Debatte um das "Denkmal für die ermordeten Juden Europas": Eine Dokumentation* (Berlin and Vienna: Philo Verlagsgesellschaft, 1999).

26 Stephan Lehnstaedt, "'Causa Renesse': Die Sozialgerichtsbarkeit NRW und die Ghettorenten," *Mitteilungen der Deutsch-Israelischen Juristenvereinigung* 4 (2013): 86–91; Julia Smilga, "A Mentsh: Jan-Robert von Renesse," *Jewish Voice from Germany*, 25 March 2013.

27 Zarusky, "Hindernislauf für Holocaust-Überlebende."

28 Ulrich Freudenberg, presiding judge of the State Social Welfare Court of North Rhine–Westphalia, indicated a preference for such a solution. See Ulrich Freudenberg, "Beschäftigung gegen Entgelt im Rahmen von Ghetto-Renten," in *Aktuelle Fragen des Sozialrechts: Erste rechtspolitische Gespräche zum Arbeits- und Sozialrecht*, ed. Ralf Thomas Baus, Günter Krings, and Rainer Schlegel (Sankt Augustin: Konrad-Adenauer-Stiftung e.V., 2010), 146.

5 Construction of Victimhood in Contemporary China: Toward a Post-Heroic Representation of History?

DAQING YANG

In January 2010, the results of a nationwide contest for the Achievement Awards for Urban Sculpture in the New China were announced in Beijing. Sponsored by the Chinese Ministry of Housing and Urban Development as well as the Ministry of Culture, the contest drew over nine hundred entries, out of which six received Achievement Awards. Topping the list of awardees is the Monument to the People's Heroes in the middle of Tiananmen Square. A tall, modified obelisk, the monument features at its base eight large marble reliefs portraying Chinese "people's struggles" ranging from the Opium War of 1840 to the War of Liberation of the late 1940s. Built in the early 1950s, shortly after the founding of the People's Republic of China (PRC), the monument was situated at the very centre of China's most sacred political space and represented the new regime's self-proclamation of legitimacy on the basis of history. It took no one by surprise that it received the top honour.

Second place was awarded to something of a much more recent vintage and in a somewhat unlikely location: a group of sculptures of human figures at the Memorial Hall of the Victims of the Nanjing Massacre by Japanese Invaders (hereafter, Nanjing Massacre Memorial) in the capital of Jiangsu Province.[1] Created by a local Nanjing artist, the sculptures were added to an existing memorial during its massive expansion in 2007. Grouped under titles such as "Broken Family, Lost Lives," "Seeking Refuge," "Calls of Grieved Souls," and "Peace," the sculptures represent the suffering endured by ordinary Chinese citizens during the war, particularly as a result of the atrocities committed by the invading Japanese forces in the winter of 1937 in what was then China's capital.

The contrast between the imagery of these top two recipients of the urban sculpture competition cannot be more stark: the former has human figures standing erect, mostly muscular men (and a few women), commanding respect and admiration of hundreds of millions of citizens of the New China; the latter depicts mostly unmistakable objects of sympathy, such as the old and weak, often in different stages of falling. As one Chinese newspaper put it:

> The Monument to the People's Heroes, standing in Tiananmen Square, captured the great revolutionary historical events in various artistic relief carved in white marble. They not only became a classic in the history of urban sculpture in the New China, they also serve as the spiritual symbol of Chinese people's unbent resistance and readiness to self-sacrifice. The large sculptures at the Memorial to the Compatriot Victims of the Nanjing Massacre created heart-wrenching artistic figures with sadness, hatred and strong emotions. They have left a memory of bitter suffering of an entire nation; they also fully represent the timely desire for never forgetting national humiliation and for striving for peace.[2]

The juxtaposition of these two highly acclaimed urban sculptures, created half a century apart, seems to point to an obvious conclusion: in contrast to celebrating the revolutionary heroes in domestic and external struggles in the early decades of the PRC, the zeitgeist of the country now seems to have turned to nurturing its sufferings at the hands of foreign aggressors in recent history.

This development seems to fit in a larger trend toward a post-heroic narrative of history that has also been emerging in other parts of the world in recent times. It has been widely noted that contemporary Western society is increasingly concerned, even obsessed, with victims. In her book, *The Violence of Victimhood*, Diane Enns identifies several factors that have contributed to this phenomenon: Freudian psychiatry, soldiers returning from war, the discovery and popularization of trauma as a clinical concept, the Nazi Holocaust and the establishment of Jewish victims as standards for victims, and feminist intervention against rape. This proliferation of victim narratives in recent decades has led some to ponder why countries or ethnic groups seem to derive more pride from their victim status than from their past achievements.[3] In the meantime, given the high stakes in the age of memory politics, the proliferation of victim narratives inevitably raises questions about their authenticity.

This chapter examines the rise of victimhood narratives in China in recent decades, with a focus on "sites of memory" such as memorials and commemorations related to China's war with Japan between 1937 and 1945. After placing this development in the larger context of memory culture in the People's Republic of China, I highlight the dynamic forces at play in the designation and implementation of China's first National Memorial Day of the Nanjing Massacre in 2014. My goal is to unpack this construction of victimhood in contemporary China by examining its historical roots and agencies as well as by placing it in a broader context. Why did the PRC seem to have moved in recent decades from a heroic narrative of modern history to that of victimhood? Who are the architects of such narratives, aside from the party state? To what extent has this transformation in China been influenced by the broader trends emphasizing victimhood? How do the Chinese deal with the question of authenticity? Drawing from official political statements as well as visual representations, this chapter examines the interplay of structural shifts and human agency behind the changing representations of the past in contemporary China.

Heroes and Victims as Tropes in Chinese Memory Culture since 1949

The Monument to the People's Heroes in the centre of Tiananmen Square is a good starting point for our discussion, as it represents an official view of modern history in the early PRC era. The historical narratives featured in those reliefs were carefully selected by highly regarded historians at the Institute of History in the newly established Chinese Academy of Sciences, and final approval was given by China's top political leaders. They included "people's struggles" against foreign aggressors (British imperialism and Japanese invasion) as well as the corrupt domestic regimes (the Manchu dynasty and the Nationalist government). This combination neatly dovetails with the words spoken by Mao Zedong when he proclaimed the founding of the PRC on 1 October 1949 at the nearby Tiananmen Gate: "The Chinese people have stood up." In Communist vocabulary, this meant the overthrow of the "three great mountains" on the people's backs – imperialism, feudalism, and bureaucratic capitalism of the past – and the dawn of a New China.

Echoing Mao's speech and bearing the slogan "Long Live People's Heroes!" in Mao's own calligraphy, the monument emphasizes the efforts of and sacrifice by these nameless peoples' heroes and their ultimate victory. The New China, consisting of diverse political forces under the leadership of the Chinese Communist Party, thus traced its genesis to the spirit of these people's heroes from the mid-nineteenth century.

In addition to the monument to people's heroes on Tiananmen Square, those who entered the pantheon of Communist revolutionary martyrdom were honoured with various memorials throughout the country. Interestingly, perhaps the largest such memorial complex is in the outskirt of Nanjing, the former capital of the overthrown Nationalist government. The Yuhuatai Cemetery of Revolutionary Martyrs was built to commemorate those Communists and other revolutionaries who had been executed by previous regimes. The site's museum documents the lives of revolutionary martyrs both collectively and as individuals, emphasizing their ultimate sacrifice for the cause of revolution.

In addition, the Chinese government produced another series of individual heroes who distinguished themselves in war or peacetime and who were to serve as role models for the entire population. Most were soldiers of the People's Liberation Army, such as Lei Feng, who died in an accident in early 1962. Mao himself posthumously elevated Lei to the status of national hero. Although most of these heroes were soldiers killed in battle or accidents, a few civilians received this status for their outstanding contribution to the socialist reconstruction. Dubbed the "Iron Man," a worker named Wang Jinxi became such a model for the country for his role in overcoming the difficulties in establishing operations in the Daqing Oil Field.[4]

Although the founding of the PRC was the major victory of Chinese Communists and is thus written in a heroic narrative – represented, above all, in the monument in Tiananmen Square – accounts of victimization also played important roles in rallying popular support in the new regime's early decades. In fact, much of Chinese Communists' success in mobilizing the masses was through their public denunciation of alleged exploitation and abuse caused by the "three great mountains." Although Chinese victims of foreign imperialists are not entirely missing from these narratives, far greater attention was devoted to victims of domestic class enemies. In particular, the suffering of the peasant class at the hands of landlords and rich peasants served to justify Communist land-reform policy and even the physical liquidation of abusive landlords and their families.

The public denunciation of old class enemies by alleged victims and others reached an apex during the Cultural Revolution. One manifestation was the spread of the so-called Rent-Collection Courtyard, a series of life-size clay sculptures depicting peasants enduring the abuse of evil landlords. Originally the creation of local artists in Sichuan Province, it soon was reproduced throughout the country, serving as the nucleus of an intense public education campaign to highlight the contrast between the pre-Communist "Old Society" and the Communist-led "New Society." One feature of the "recall bitterness, reflect upon sweetness" campaign of the late 1960s and early 1970s was to have young children and teenagers eat coarse grain so that they could literally "taste" the bitter suffering of the oppressed masses before the PRC was established. Together with the influential power of school education and mass media, the Communist regime succeeded in legitimizing the New Society in the eyes of the generation born after the revolution.[5]

A major shift took place in China's memory culture after the death of Mao Zedong in 1976. As the country emerged from decades of incessant and brutal internal ideological campaigns and political struggles, it was finally time to address the victims of internal political persecution. Although the devastation of the Cultural Revolution was officially recognized and some "thin reconciliation" was carried out – such as rehabilitation of political victims – the Communist leaders sought to move on without dwelling too much on the internal victimhood of recent times. Deeply cognizant of how much China was falling behind advanced industrialized countries in the West as well as Japan, Deng Xiaoping, the new leader from 1978, reoriented China away from revolutionary politics and launched the ambitiously termed "Four Modernizations." History was important to Deng, who wanted education and propaganda to emphasize China's modern history in order to motivate citizens to devote their energy to strengthening the motherland through economic modernization instead of continuing class struggle against imagined enemies within. This modern history began with the Opium War of 1840, the start of the "century of humiliation," which was marked by unequal treaties and foreign invasions. Deng's successor, Jiang Zemin, later offered a succinct lesson to be drawn from that history: "Being backward leads to being bullied." After the Tiananmen protest of 1989, Jiang launched new "patriotic education" in which "never forget national humiliation" became a dominant theme in school curriculum, government propaganda, and public media.[6] It is against this background that the Second World War took on new significance in China.

Remembering the Second World War: From Old to New

The War of Resistance against Japan, as the Second World War has been known in China since before the PRC years, has always been represented by a mix of heroic and victimization narratives. In the so-called Shanghai Incident of 1932, the Chinese Nationalist Nineteenth Army engaged in urban warfare with Japanese forces and subsequently earned a reputation as national heroes. This stood in contrast to the lack of resistance by the Chinese army during Japan's takeover of northeastern China. However, as the Japanese dropped bombs and cities like Nanjing were "sacked" after full-scale war broke out in 1937, the Chinese government and its foreign sympathizers adroitly used reports of Japanese atrocities to garner international sympathy and support for China while painting Japan as a barbaric aggressor that must be stopped.[7] However, not everyone was happy with the portrayal of Chinese as passive victims, like "innocent lambs waiting to be slaughtered." One astute Chinese observer lamented during the war that the widespread stories of Japanese atrocities against Chinese victims would dampen Chinese resolve to fight back against the formidable foreign invader. He felt that more heroic narratives would better serve China's goal of victory. As historian Parks Coble has recently noted, this fear of the effects of victimhood was a common phenomenon in wartime Chinese writings about Japanese atrocities. Passive victimhood carries with it negative connotations.[8]

Heroic narratives of the war against Japan came to be emphasized in the early decades of the PRC. Communist-led forces – the Eighth Route Army and the New Fourth Army – as well as Communist-led guerrillas and their supporters were all considered heroes. One of the eight panels of the Monument to the People's Heroes was given the title "Anti-Japanese Guerrilla Warfare behind Enemy Lines." It portrays half a dozen Chinese fighters in forward postures while others stand erect and composed. Yet the inscriptions on the monument did not mention the war against Japan by name, even while they listed the recent Wars of People's Liberation (the civil war against the Nationalists, 1946–9) as well as the People's Revolution (since the May Fourth Movement in 1919) and the broader "people's struggle" all the way back to the Opium War in 1840.

Popular culture in Mao's time featured several films devoted exclusively to Communist-led guerrilla warfare and its success against the Japanese invaders. Both landmine and underground tunnel warfare demonstrated how Communist-led forces, though poorly equipped compared to the Japanese, managed to outwit and defeat the Japanese and the Chinese puppet forces allied with them. Though most of the heroes in these films were fictional or anonymous, they occasionally depicted extraordinary individual heroism based on reality. One such example, the so-called Five Heroes of Mount Langya (*Langyashan wu zhuangshi*), drew on soldiers in an Eighth Route Army unit that fought against a much larger Japanese force on a mountain in northern China. The last five surviving soldiers retreated to a mountain cliff and, after destroying their weapons, allegedly jumped off in order to avoid capture by the enemy. Only one survived, after being saved by nearby villagers.[9]

In the early decades of the PRC, narratives of victimization of Chinese people during the Japanese invasion were kept largely at an abstract level. Some examples of collective suffering were common knowledge, such as the "ten-thousand-person pits" containing corpses of abused Chinese workers at Japanese-operated coal mines in China and the "Three Alls" ("kill all, burn all, loot all") campaign by the Japanese army against Communist forces in northern China. However, specific details of other Japanese war atrocities, especially those committed in areas controlled by Nationalist forces – such as the Nanjing Massacre in 1937 – were largely absent.[10]

But there were exceptions. Mei Ru'ao, the former judge at the Tokyo Trial appointed by the Nationalist government, stayed on in the PRC as an adviser to the foreign ministry. Around 1960, Mei wrote about the conviction of the top Japanese general responsible for the Nanjing Massacre. Aware of new publications on the Holocaust abroad, he called for studies of the atrocities in Nanjing. His call did not gain any traction, and for good reason. When the official Chinese line was that the Japanese people were victims of their militaristic rulers, accounts of Japanese atrocities in China sometimes resulted in fanning hatred against *all* Japanese, including the civilian population.[11]

As a number of scholars have noted, it was not until the early 1980s that PRC representations of the Second World War embraced what Arthur Waldron and others have termed "new remembering."[12] For the first time, official narratives embraced non-Communist resistance fighters active during the war. This coincided with Beijing's reaching out to its arch-rival, the Nationalist regime in Taiwan, with the goal of national reunification. Another important aspect of this new remembering is the increasing emphasis on China's victimhood during the war. In addition to frequent references to Japanese war atrocities in China, Chinese official statements and media regularly began to deploy the term "the largest victim country." In a speech delivered in 1995, the fiftieth anniversary of the end of the war, then-president Jiang Zemin cited concrete numbers of thirty-five million Chinese casualties and economic losses totalling six hundred billion US dollars in that war, thus making China the largest victim country.[13] Not only was the enormity of the Chinese victimhood emphasized, but new categories of suffering emerged. Foremost among them were victims of Japan's systematized sexual violence. Although wartime mass rape had been widely known, the so-called comfort women system was recognized only in the 1990s. Lastly, Chinese victimhood was not limited to the time of war. Civilians in certain parts of China continued to be affected by the chemical artillery shells left behind by the Japanese military after war's end.

Several additional factors helped shape China's new remembering, with its particular emphasis on victimhood. Internally, as China adopted the policy of market-oriented reform after the late 1970s, the masses gained some voice. Loosening the state's grip on society produced multiple effects. Whereas the top-down hero worship under Mao was becoming increasingly unsustainable, supporting victims of Japanese aggression seems to unite both society and the state. The human suffering during the war, sustained by tens of millions, many of whom were still alive, seemed to find a receptive audience in China. Some survivors of Japanese atrocities became public advocates and speakers at home and abroad and achieved minor celebrity status.[14]

A new factor in this development has been the idea of victims' rights, as seen in the lawsuits seeking compensation from the Japanese government or companies since the 1980s. With permission from the government, many Chinese victims brought lawsuits against the Japanese government (or, in instances of forced labour, corporations). Shaping victim narratives in these cases were what James Reilly has called "history activists" – a loosely connected group of individuals who run internet portals, conduct surveys, and offer legal support – rather than the Chinese government.[15] The non-governmental movement to seek compensation from Japan was spearheaded by Tong Zeng, a former mid-level government employee, in Beijing in 1990. He helped many former Chinese forced labourers to file lawsuits in Japanese courts with the help of Japanese activists. Another activist was Wang Xuan, a Chinese woman living in Japan who has worked tirelessly to unearth evidence and gather oral testimonies from victims of Japan's chemical warfare in China. Wang gained so much coverage in the Chinese media that she was voted one of the ten individuals with the greatest influence on the Chinese public. In many locations, people have taken up wartime suffering as part of local identity and demanded greater recognition. Victims of Japanese aerial bombing in China's wartime capital, Chongqing, have become particularly outspoken.

Developments outside China, particularly elsewhere in East Asia, have been just as important in exerting influence on Chinese government and society, as international travel and greater flows of information have become possible. First, from the early 1980s, Japanese historical revisionism with respect to the Second World War, which downplayed atrocities and presented the war as one of anti-colonial liberation, provided a timely justification for strong Chinese countermeasures. Those who questioned the authenticity of both China's national grand narrative of victimhood as well as individual survivor-victims were branded as deniers and condemned in the harshest language.[16] Many Chinese therefore cite the "struggle with Japan" (*dui-Ri douzheng*) in justifying their publications as well as museum projects focusing on victimization.

Greater attention to global victims of the Second World War has also affected Chinese discourse. Su Zhiliang, a Chinese history professor, was first alerted to the issue of sexual slavery perpetrated by the Japanese military when he witnessed protests by Korean "comfort women" and their supporters in Tokyo in 1992. Upon returning to China, Su started visiting sites and victims in order to investigate this history. Within a few years, Su and his collaborator had become the foremost authorities on sexual violence of the Japanese military during the Second World War and had founded the Research Center for Chinese "Comfort Women." Su described the dilemma in his investigation: "there is nothing more cruel than uncovering the history of how the female population of one's own people was humiliated ... The new discovery and recording of evidence did not make me excited; rather each step forward increased my pain and bitterness." Su declared that it consequently was his duty as a Chinese historian to reveal such Japanese military atrocities against "hundreds of thousands of Chinese compatriot comfort women."[17]

Of the many instances of victimization of the Chinese people at the hands of the Japanese, the Nanjing Massacre emerged from obscurity to become, since the 1980s, the ultimate symbol of wartime suffering. The establishment of the Nanjing Massacre Memorial in 1985 marked the beginning of a new memory culture of collective suffering. It followed in the wake of the "textbook controversy" that occurred in 1982, when Japanese newspapers reported that the Japanese Ministry of Education had recommended changing the verb "invaded" to "advanced into" in school textbook discussions of the Japanese invasion of northern China. The reaction across Asia was vitriolic.

The Nanjing memorial was endorsed by China's supreme leader, Deng Xiaoping, whose calligraphy graces its entrance. In the early 2000s, the memorial underwent a massive expansion and renovation, at the cost of ¥540 million (US$64 million, using 2004 rates). The size of the memorial increased nearly threefold. At the time, it claimed to be the largest museum in China. Given its wide exposure in Chinese media and education, the Nanjing Massacre became the prime symbol of Chinese victimhood during the Second World War. Numerous polls in China have consistently shown that the incident tops the list of all events Chinese respondents associate with Japan.

The Nanjing Massacre Memorial portrays Chinese suffering in both symbolic and direct ways. Among the examples of the former is a giant figure of a human half buried near a brick wall in the shape of a bayonet and smeared with blood. The latter approach includes a display of numerous mangled skeletal remains in glass cases in close proximity to the viewer. The memorial was eventually expanded to include an excavation site displaying half-exposed human bones with markers indicating the results of scientific dating of the remains.

This public display of victims' remains, which some may find to be disrespectful of the dead, presumably serves as iron-clad proof of the Nanjing Massacre. Other additions have included large sculptures of ordinary victims, as described at the beginning of this chapter, as well as handprints of survivors displayed in public next to their names, in a format jarringly reminiscent of Hollywood Walk of Fame. Together with other objects and photographs from the war period, the remains of the victims offer a potent response to those who would challenge the site's authenticity.[18] Statements by some Japanese politicians and others seeking to deny the atrocities in Nanjing continue to fuel China's fervent efforts to defend the authenticity of its victimhood narratives. For example, historians based in Nanjing received generous state funding to compile a seventy-five-volume set of documentation that would serve to refute any deniers.[19] This extensive archival documentation played a pivotal role in earning the Nanjing Massacre a coveted place in the UNESCO Memory of the World register in 2015.[20]

The strategies of using historical narratives to promote national cohesion and labelling all Chinese as victims of Japanese aggression in the Second World War has had many consequences. Portraying the Chinese people collectively as victims disguises the truth about those who collaborated with the Japanese, either actively or passively. Moreover, such narratives have driven other, more recent victims in Chinese history out of the country's memory culture. First and foremost among the forgotten were victims of domestic political conflict, both from the Nationalist era before 1949 and certainly those from the PRC era after 1949. The victims of the Cultural Revolution – tens of thousands of intellectuals and others who were killed, as well as the Red Guards who died in armed conflict in the mid- to late 1960s – are a strikingly representative example of this omission. Ba Jin, a well-known Chinese writer and translator who personally faced persecution and lost his wife in the Cultural Revolution, called for a museum to commemorate those lost in that period. But, unlike the numerous museums dedicated to Chinese victims of the war with Japan, the museum envisioned by Ba Jin was never built.[21]

National Commemoration of Wartime Suffering

In February 2014, the Standing Committee of the National People's Congress met for its seventh session and adopted two resolutions concerning anniversaries of the Second World War. First, a resolution declared that Victory over Japan Day would be observed on 3 September. The Chinese V-J Day has a long history dating back to the immediate aftermath of Japan's surrender. The Nationalist government designated 3 September – the date on which Japan signed the instrument of surrender aboard the USS *Missouri* – as the Day of Victory. The People's Congress decision in 2014 thus revived a date established by the previous regime that had fallen into oblivion under the PRC.

The second resolution called for a national memorial ceremony of the Nanjing Massacre to be held for the first time on 13 December 2014.[22] This decision constituted a major landmark in China's memory culture. Zhu Chengshan, then director of the Nanjing Massacre Memorial, observed at the time, "This is the first time in the history of the Chinese nation that common people are commemorated in the name of the state."[23]

An examination of the background of the establishment of China's first Public Memorial Day reveals a confluence of multiple influences. To begin with, it is not simply a top-down "manipulation" of the past by the government in Beijing. Indeed, much credit should be given to mid-level or even local actors. The newfound emphasis on wartime suffering, discussed above, was no doubt the key background factor, but national as well as global trends also played roles in legitimizing the move. Finally, the new leadership of Xi Jinping as well as tensions in China-Japan relations clearly also influenced the decision to establish the holiday.

The decision to institute a national commemoration of the Nanjing Massacre has a history that goes back at least two decades. In the mid-1990s, a member of the Standing Committee of the National People's Congress suggested to the Jiangsu provincial government (located in the city of Nanjing) that a special date be set aside to commemorate the 1937 massacre. Unable to decide on the date himself, he asked the officials in Nanjing to do so. He soon received a reply from the provincial officials, informing him that they had chosen 13 December – the day Nanjing fell – and that a number of commemorative activities were planned, including the sounding of a siren at noon.

There was also a strong push from below – from the local level in Nanjing – for greater national recognition of the city's victimhood. Commemorating the Nanjing Massacre just at the provincial level was not satisfactory to some, including the long-time director of the Nanjing Memorial, Zhu Chengshan, who led efforts to accord greater importance to the commemorations. Zhu, who was himself born in Nanjing, took up his post as director of the memorial in the 1990s after being discharged from the People's Liberation Army. A prolific writer of several dozen books, he set up the Society of Nanjing Massacre Studies and publishes a history journal devoted to the history of the massacre. Making Nanjing the centre of a national commemoration was reported to be Zhu's "lifetime wish."

Zhu would later cite a visit he had made to Japan as part of a Chinese delegation in 1978 as his inspiration. In addition to being impressed by Japan's economic success, evident in its advanced urban infrastructure and high living standards, Zhu also took note of the "strong national identity" of the Japanese people. "They never forgot the victims in the two atomic bombings. Each year in Hiroshima and Nagasaki they hold a large, solemn commemorations. Heads of state and other national leaders attend them to pay tribute to the deceased. It was very touching." Zhu felt that the suffering in China, and not only Nanjing, eclipsed that in the bombed Japanese cities, yet the Chinese had remained silent for decades. "As China becomes more modern and living stands improve," he reasoned, "future generations would gradually forget the national humiliation, which would in turn weaken national identity and create a sense of crisis about the future. This would be very dangerous."[24] Such justification was widely echoed.[25]

An energetic traveller and avid reader, Zhu paid close attention to international trends while contributing to the crafting of memory culture in China. In the 1990s, for instance, he installed a "wailing wall" at the Nanjing Massacre Memorial inscribed with the names of known victims. Before the memorial underwent expansion and renovation in 2004, he launched an international competition for its design and incorporated elements found in memorials outside China, including an emphasis on dark colours to convey a sense of mourning. The newly expanded hall of the memorial bears a close resemblance to part of Yad Vashem, the World Holocaust Remembrance Centre in Israel. Such symbolic appropriation, for Zhu, serves not only to bring international attention to China's past sufferings but also to build international allies for China's memorialization. Citing the examples of Auschwitz Liberation Day and Pearl Harbor Day in the United States, Zhu argued that the country's leaders should mark the Nanjing Massacre – representing China's single worst case of suffering, in his view – by instituting a national day of commemoration.[26]

As the expansion of the Nanjing Massacre Memorial was nearing completion, Zhao Long, a member of the Standing Committee of the National People's Congress and vice-director of the Jiangsu Provincial Political Consultative Committee, visited the memorial and had a long discussion with Zhu about his wishes. Subsequently, in 2005, Zhao and forty-nine deputies from China's Political Consultative Committee proposed setting 13 December as a day of national commemoration that would include the participation of top Chinese leaders as well as greater prominence of the Nanjing Massacre Memorial. Although their proposal was not adopted at the time, it was widely reported in the mass media. Seven years later, another deputy from Nanjing made a renewed proposal. At the end of that year, his proposal received a response: the Jiangsu Provincial Government and Communist Party were to send the proposal to the national leadership in Beijing.[27]

Since the beginning of the new millennium, there have been calls to institute various days of national commemoration for the purpose of building national solidarity. Suggestions have included, for example, a holiday in honour of the Yellow Emperor, who is thought of as the mythical ancestor of the Chinese people. While recognizing the important public function of such cohesiveness, one Chinese sociologist has alluded to a debate within China on the appropriateness of state sponsorship in commemorating mythical figures.[28] Others, including deputies of the People's Congress, suggested as early as 2007 a national commemoration of martyrs of the revolution by proposing a National People's Martyrs' Day. A national commemoration of the Nanjing Massacre was certainly influenced by China's new memory culture. The global commemorative culture of victims provided inspiration for designating a memorial day. In designating China's first National Memorial Day for the Nanjing Massacre, the People's Congress working group reportedly compared proposals with the regulation and practice of Holocaust Day by the United Nations, the United States, Israel, and some thirty countries.

The timing of the official designation was influenced by both domestic and international politics. At home, it coincided with the inauguration of new top leadership under Xi Jinping in early 2013. The leadership in Beijing warmed to the idea of a national day of commemoration, and it was finally approved in early 2014. Many in China wondered, though, whether the commemorations would be accepted or recognized by other countries, given that new tensions had arisen between China and Japan over the Diaoyu/Senkaku Islands in 2012.[29] Although an analysis of the precise decision-making process will have to until records are unsealed decades from now, it seems plausible that China's new leadership signed on to some of these national commemorative events partly in responses to local initiatives. There is no doubt that provincial functionaries such as Zhu leveraged history to gain greater attention for the Nanjing Massacre and may even have influenced the most powerful man in China.

One important area of ambiguity in the 2014 decision was whether 13 December was meant as a day to memorialize Chinese victims in the Second World War or if it was in remembrance of Chinese victims of Japanese aggression in all past conflicts. Given the fact that the designation of a National Memorial Ceremony in December was to commemorate *all* victims of the Japanese invasion throughout China, a leading party newspaper organized, on the Nanjing Massacre National Memorial Day, a ten-city rally with its regional counterparts in nine cities where Japanese troops had committed atrocities. Zhu, on the hand, offers his more expansive interpretation that all Chinese casualties of Japanese military action – from its expedition to Taiwan in 1874 through the Second World War – are included in the commemorations observed on that 13 December.[30]

President Xi Jinping Goes to Nanjing

On 13 December 2014, all eyes in China were fixed on Nanjing. That morning, hundreds of people filed past the prize-winning sculptures of the Nanjing Memorial to take part in the first-ever National Memorial Ceremony of the Nanjing Massacre. This was understandably a carefully orchestrated event. The president of China, Xi Jinping, attended the ceremony accompanied by other members of the Politburo. One highlight of the event was the unveiling of a monument of the national memorial ceremony in the shape of an ancient Chinese bronze vessel, thus inscribing the 1937 massacre in the annals of Chinese history that span thousands of years. Xi was flanked by two other individuals selected to unveil the monument together. One was an eighty-five-year-old survivor, thus providing an authentic link to the victims of the 1937 Japanese atrocity. The other was a teenager, symbolizing the transmission of the memory of China's suffering to new generations. Whether the selection of the teenager to be part of the trio also represents a continuation of the identity of a victim remained ambiguous.

Some clarity, however, might be found in the speech delivered by Xi. He declared that the commemoration served to "cherish the memory of innocent compatriot victims in the Nanjing Massacre" as well as "all victims slaughtered by the Japanese invaders." The commemoration was also intended to "mourn revolutionary martyrs and national heroes who had given their lives for the victory of [the] Chinese people's war of resistance against Japan." And it was to "express the noble wish of the Chinese people to firmly follow the path of peaceful development, and to proclaim the firm stance of the Chinese people to firmly remember history, never forget the past, cherish peace, and open the future."[31] After reiterating the standard official characterization of the Nanjing Massacre, Xi changed his emphasis:

> [The] Chinese people and Chinese nation always possess a heroic attitude [*taidu*]. Faced with the extremely barbaric and brutal Japanese invaders, the Chinese people, with the great patriotic spirit, did not capitulate, but instead consolidated their unprecedented resolve to fight the invaders ferociously to the bitter end, and strengthened their belief in the ultimate victory of resisting Japan and saving the nation. Under the call and leadership of the Chinese Communist Party, and with the joint action of all positive forces of the entire Chinese nation, sons and daughters of China were united, never wavered in front of death; they steadily went to the front line and together fought against the foreign enemy.[32]

Here on display was the latest effort, by the head of the state, to balance carefully the conflicting messages of victimhood and heroism, suffering and resistance, past and future.

In fact, Xi had already emphasized the "spirit of the war of resistance" on many other occasions. On 7 July 2014, he spoke at the Museum of Chinese People's War of Resistance outside Beijing to mark the outbreak of the full-scale war between Japan and China in 1937, and used that phrase to call for unity among all Chinese, regardless of political affiliation. He also referred to the war generation's willingness for self-sacrifice, determination to weather setbacks, and belief in final victory. On 3 September, speaking on the occasion of the newly designated Victory Day, Xi again stressed the spirit of the war of resistance.

In fact, the heroic spirit of the war of resistance was not entirely absent from the Nanjing Massacre Memorial even before Xi took office. It became a crucial antecedent to two other concepts that were emphasized in the 2007 expansion and renovation: victory and peace. After witnessing panel after panel depicting scenes of Japanese atrocities in Nanjing, the visitor is directed through a darkened hall of mourning, which leads to an area designated as Peace Park. Standing at its end is a tall monument featuring a mother holding a baby and releasing a white pigeon, and the word "peace" is inscribed on the monument in Chinese and English. The visitor, having just seen a graphic portrayal of Chinese suffering and abuse at the hands of Japanese invaders, is led to contemplate the importance of peace. Between the main exhibition halls and the monument to peace is a long wall featuring reliefs of Chinese fighting in the war of resistance. Imposed across the relief is a large V, at the centre of which stands a Chinese soldier blowing a bugle. A closer look reveals that he is wearing the uniform of the Communist-led force. Resistance, victory, and peace are now meant to be inseparable.

In 2015, a vast, outdoor park-like Peace Square was added to the memorial in the third major expansion since its founding in 1985. A major component of its exhibition space was devoted to a key phrase coined by Xi himself: "Justice is destined to triumph; [the] people are destined to triumph; peace is destined to triumph." The square features scenes of China's victory celebration and Japan's surrender in 1945 and also displays a variety of military memorabilia from the war.[33] Although this new addition was planned before Xi's visit, the emphasis on peace was reflected in Xi's speech in Nanjing as well as at China's first victory parade later, in 2015. On the latter occasion, which constituted China's largest military parade ever, Xi repeated the word "peace" over twenty times in his speech![34] There is a surprising resonance with victims in Hiroshima and Nagasaki and the war generation in Japan as a whole: our suffering during the war stiffened our resolve to preserve peace.

Conclusion

Since the early 1980s, Chinese narratives dealing with the country's modern history have been dominated by an emphasis on "national humiliation" at the hands of foreign imperialists starting in the mid-nineteenth century. In particular, Chinese narratives of the Second World War shifted from a focus on Communist-led heroic resistance to Chinese sufferings and Japanese atrocities. In this context, the Nanjing Massacre has become a major theme in China's collective memory of the Second World War.

This chapter argues that a broader ideological reorientation away from class-based revolution and a gradual loosening of societal control, as well as international trends in memory culture, have all helped shape this new construction of victim identities in post-reform China. The phenomenal economic rise of China since the 1980s also tipped the psychological balance in favour of claiming victimhood without the sense of shame often associated with suffering. Although the Chinese party state no doubt continues to play a huge role in shaping and setting the tone of views expressed in educational resources and media, not every initiative in this reorientation came from Beijing. Instead, academics, local authorities, and other "history activists" in China are creating individual or local victim identities through compensation lawsuits or claiming new categories such as victims of systemic sexual violence. External factors have also shaped changes in historical representation in China. These have included the broader, global re-examination of memories of the Second World War, particularly the newfound emphasis on its victims, as well as challenges to the authenticity of China's victimhood by Japanese "revisionists" and deniers. The construction of the Nanjing Massacre Memorial and the recent designation of the Nanjing Massacre National Memorial Day seem to indicate that multiple influences are at work in these processes. The continued use at the memorial of victims' remains as well as survivors' testimonies and handprints, along with the publication of multiple volumes of documentary evidence, signifies a desire by China to shore up the authenticity of its claimed victimhood.

The rise of victimhood narratives in China has not displaced the tales of heroism. Both categories – heroes and victims – have been expanded to embrace the entire Chinese nation instead of being limited to those affiliated with Chinese Communists. As Kirk Denton has confirmed in his studies of Chinese museums devoted to the Second World War, Chinese curators must carefully balance representations of atrocities and victimization with those of heroic resistance. This trend can also be observed in the new addition to the Nanjing Memorial dedicated to the theme of peace and China's victory.

Since Xi came to power in 2012, there has been a concerted effort to revive the theme of heroism in official discourse, even though it has become more difficult for the regime to promote or revive individual heroes as it once did during Mao's time.[35] On 30 September 2014, Xi and the entire Politburo attended China's first-ever Martyrs Commemoration Day, held in front of the Monument to the People's Heroes on Tiananmen Square.[36] The date had been adopted by the National People's Congress barely a month before. In justifying the designation, committee members of the People's Congress claimed that "China has always been a country respecting heroes" and that, "without heroes, a country has no future."[37] In this sense, although the last several decades have witnessed considerable changes in China's representation of its modern history and the Second World War in particular, both heroes and victims have secured their places in sites of collective memory.

NOTES

1 The literal translation of the Chinese name, *Qin-Hua Rijun Nanjing datusha yünan tongbao jinianguan*, is the Memorial to the Compatriot Victims of the Nanjing Massacre by the Invading Japanese Army.

2 "Xinzhongguo chengshi diaoshu 60 nian" [Sixty years of urban sculpture in New China], *Zhongguo wenhua bao*, 30 December 2009.

3 Diane Enns, *The Violence of Victimhood* (University Park, PA: Penn State University Press, 2012). For a recent attempt at theorizing, see Tami Amanda Jacoby, "A Theory of Victimhood: Politics, Conflict and the Construction of Victim-based Identity," *Millennium* 43, no. 2 (2015): 511–30. For a critique of victimhood-centred history, see Ian Buruma, "The Joy and Peril of Victimhood," *New York Review of Books*, 8 April 1999.

4 On the making of Lei Feng and other socialist heroes in the PRC, see James Alan Schnell, "A Historical Interpretation of Lei Feng: Government Subsidized Role Model in the People's Republic of China," *China Media Research* 9, no. 2 (2013): 59–63 and L. Edwards, "Military Celebrity in China: The Evolution of Heroic and Model Servicemen," in *Celebrity in China*, ed. Elaine Jeffreys and Louise Edwards (Hong Kong: Hong Kong University Press, 2010), 21–44.

5 For a recent study, see Xinmei Ge, "A Tale of 'Ku' (Bitter) vs. 'Tian' (Sweet): Understanding China's 'Yiku Sitian' Movement in the 1960s and 1970s from the Perspective of Cultural Discourse Analysis" (PhD diss., University of Massachusetts, 2016), https://scholarworks.umass.edu/dissertations_2/573/.

6 Many have written about the topic of national humiliation before and after 1949. See, for example, William A. Callahan, "National Insecurities: Humiliation, Salvation, and Chinese Nationalism," *Alternatives: Global, Local, Political* 29, no. 2 (2004): 199–218 and Wang Zheng, *Never Forget National Humiliation: Historical Memory in Chinese Politics and Foreign Relations* (New York: Columbia University Press, 2012).

7 For an early assessment of the atrocities in war propaganda, see Bruno Lasker and Agnes Roman, *Propaganda from China and Japan: A Case Study in Propaganda Analysis* (New York: American Council Institute of Pacific Relations, 1938).

8 This instance of wartime Chinese concern over the depiction of passive victimization is discussed in Daqing Yang, "The Malleable and the Contested: The Nanjing Massacre in Postwar Japan and China," in *Perilous Memories: The Asia-Pacific War(s)*, ed. T. Fujitani, Geoffrey M. White, and Lisa Yoneyama (Durham, NC: Duke University Press, 2001), 50–86 and Parks Coble, "Writing about Atrocity: Wartime Accounts and Their Contemporary Uses," *Modern Asian Studies* 45, no. 2 (2011): 379–98.

9 For a new report on the current controversy about this incident, see "Chinese Court Orders Apology over Challenge to Tale of Wartime Heroes," *New York Times*, 29 June 2016.

10 Kirk A. Denton, "Heroic Resistance and Victims of Atrocity: Negotiating the Memory of Japanese Imperialism in Chinese Museums," *Japan Focus* 5, no. 10 (2007): 1–29. For a discussion of the few instances when the Nanjing Massacre was mentioned in the press before the 1980s, see Yang, "Malleable and Contested."

11 Yang, "Malleable and Contested."

12 Parks Coble, "China's 'New Remembering' of the Anti-Japanese War," *China Quarterly* 190 (2007): 394–410.

13 This casualty figure was significantly higher than those released by the Nationalist government shortly after the war and has raised some questions outside China. Starting in 2004, the Chinese Communist Party History Office began a nationwide project to produce a three-hundred-volume book series documenting the loss of life and property in China during the Second World War. *Kang-Ri zhanzheng shiqi Zhongguo renkou shangwang he caican sunshi congshu* (Beijing: Zhonggong Dangshi Chubanshe, 2015).

14 On China's victim-redress movement, see Yukiko Koga, "Accounting for Silence: Inheritance, Debt, and the Moral Economy of Legal Redress in China and Japan," *American Ethnologist* 40, no. 3 (2013): 494–507.

15 On the role of non-government actors in redressing past suffering, see James Reilly, "Remember History, Not Hatred: Collective Remembrance of China's War of Resistance to Japan," *Modern Asian Studies* 45 (2011): 463–90 and Reilly, *Strong Society, Smart State: The Rise of Public Opinion in China's Japan Policy* (New York: Columbia University Press, 2012).

16 For a review of some of the revisionist claims regarding the Nanjing Massacre, see Daqing Yang, "Revisionism and the Nanjing Atrocity," *Critical Asian Studies* 43, no. 3 (December 2011): 625–48.

17 Su Zhiliang, *Wei'anfu yanjiu* [A study of the comfort women] (Shanghai: Shanghai shudian, 1999). A revised English version was published as Peipei Qiu, Su Zhiliang, and Chen Lifei, *Chinese Comfort Women: Testimonies from Imperial Japan's Sex Slaves* (Oxford: Oxford University Press, 2014).

18 On the Nanjing Massacre Memorial, see Yang, "Malleable and Contested," 50–86; Takashi Yoshida, *The Making of the "Rape of Nanking": History and Memory in China, Japan, and the United States* (New York: Columbia University Press, 2004); Kirk Denton, "Heroic Resistance."

19 Zhang Xianwen, ed., *Nanjing da tusha shiliaoji* [Collected documents on Nanjing Massacre] (Nanjing: Jiangsu renmin chubanshe, 2005–10).

20 See the chapter by Lori Watt in this volume.

21 Concerning Chinese memories of the Maoist era and especially of the Cultural Revolution, see Chris Berry, Patricia M. Thornton, and Peidong Sun, "The Cultural Revolution: Memories and Legacies 50 Years On," *China Quarterly* 227 (September 2016): 604–12 and Sebastian Veg, ed., *Popular Memories of the Mao Era: From Critical Debate to Reassessing History* (Hong Kong: Hong Kong University Press, 2019).

22 *Quanguo renmin daibiao dahui changwu weiyuanhui gongbao* [Gazette of the standing committee of the National People's Congress], February 2014.

23 Zhu Chengshan, "Qianshi buwang houshi zhishi" [Past not forgotten is guide for the future], *Zhongguo shehui kexue bao*, 12 December 2014.

24 Zhu Xiangyuan, "Huiyi 20nianqian de yijian zhengxie ti'an" [Recollection of a proposal at the Political Consultation Committee twenty years ago], *Beijing ribao*, 22 December 2014.

25 "Guojia gongji shi guoji guanli, buneng jiandande rang datusha chengwei lishi yiwang" [National memorialization is international custom; massacres cannot be allowed to be history and forgotten], *Jihua shibao*, 8 December 2014.

26 Zhu Chengshan, "12.13 heyi chengwei guojia gongjiri" [How did 13 December become the National Memorial Day], *Nanjing ribao*, 1 March 2014. Prior to this, a 2010 editorial in local newspaper in the southern China city of Zhuhai (adjacent to Macau), called for a national memorial day for martyrs, citing precedents in the United States, Russia, the United Kingdom, and France. "Jianyi zheli 'guojia gongji ri'" [A proposal for a National Memorial Day], *Zhuhao tequ bao*, 30 March 2010.

27 "Meiti shuli zheli guojia gongjiri lailong qumai" [Media presents background to establishment of National Memorial Day], *Renmin Ribao*, 8 December 2014.

28 Li Xiangping, "Guojia gongji yu guojia xiandaixing zhonggou de queshi" [National public memorialization and shortcomings of restructuring national modernity], *Zhongguo minzu bao*, 3 April 2009.

29 Zhu, "Huiyi 20nianqian de yijian zhengxie ti'an."

30 Liao Hui, "Shi cheng tong ji: Ran guojia jiyi chengwei guomin jiyi [Joint memorialization in 10 cities: Let state memory become public memory], *Xinhua ribao*, 12 December 2014.

31 Xi Jinping, "Zai Nanjing datusha sinanzhe guojia gongji yishi shang de jianghua" (speech at the National Public Memorial of Victims of the Nanjing Massacre), *Renmin ribao*, 14 December 2014.

32 Ibid.

33 For more information, see the memorial's official website: www.nj1937.org.

34 For a detailed analysis of China's commemoration of the seventieth anniversary of the end of the Second World War, see Daqing Yang, "China: Meanings and Contradictions of Victory," in *Memory, Identity,*

and Commemorations of World War II: Anniversary Politics in Asia Pacific, ed. Daqing Yang and Mike Mochizuki (Lanham, MD: Lexington Books, 2018), 29–46.

35 See, for example, Andrew Jacobs, "Chinese Heroism Effort Is Met with Cynicism," New York Times, 5 March 2012, A7. Recently, the Chinese government has taken countermeasures by banning "nihilist tendencies" – that is, questioning established heroic icons as such the "Five Heroes of Mount Langya." "Chinese Court Orders Apology over Challenge to Tale of Wartime Heroes," *New York Times*, 29 June 2016.

36 The attendance by Xi and the Politiburo was repeated in 2015 and 2016. In contrast, Xi did not return to Nanjing after 2014.

37 "Woguo sheli lieshi jinianri zhengdang qishi" [It is time for China to establish a Martyrs Commemoration Day], *Zhongguo renda xinwen*, 30 August 2014.

6 The "Death of Manila" in the Second World War and Its Postwar Commemoration

NAKANO SATOSHI

The Battle of Manila, which took place from 3 February to 3 March 1945, was the most devastating instance of urban warfare fought between the United States and Japan in the Asia-Pacific Theatre of the Second World War. The battle transformed a plan to liberate the city and its inhabitants from Japanese tyranny into a massive slaughter of non-combatant civilians and caused the total devastation of downtown area. The US strategy of carpet shelling the centre of Manila has come under increasing criticism in recent years as a major cause of the city's destruction and associated civilian casualties. However, scholars and journalists attribute primary blame for both the bulk of civilian deaths there – allegedly amounting to one hundred thousand – and the emotional trauma of the survivors and the bereaved to atrocities and indiscriminate massacres by Japanese Imperial Army and Navy forces remaining in Manila. The victims and those who commemorate them have remembered the battle as the "Death of Manila," a loss from which they have not fully recovered despite the city's postwar physical reconstruction.[1]

Japanese war crimes in the Philippines, particularly during the Battle of Manila, were once given considerable publicity in the early postwar years, both internationally and even in Japan. The Philippine government assumed the role of a main critic of Japan's return to the international community, and the deep animosity felt among the Filipino people toward Japan prevented the two countries from normalizing diplomatic relations for more than a decade. By the end of 1980s, however, Japanese war crimes and atrocities in the Philippines had been almost completely erased from Japanese collective memory; currently, the Japanese government views the Philippines as one of the most "Japan-friendly" countries in the world. Multiple factors that have brought about this remarkable and bewildering transformation will be discussed later in this chapter.

The fiftieth anniversary of the battle, in February 1995, signified a shift against this trend toward forgetting and was marked by the dedication of the monument erected by Memorare–Manila 1945, a small but influential group of the battle's survivors and the bereaved. This group could have become a vocal opponent of the Philippines-Japan diplomacy of mutual forgetting. Indeed, it was poised to become such in the first decade of the twenty-first century, but perspectives shifted. Japan's preventive diplomacy, Memorare's attitude of restraint toward Japan, and a growing recognition of the battle – not only in the Philippines but also in Japan – have all helped to prevent another history war in Asia. The state visit of Japan's emperor and empress to the Philippines in January 2016 perpetuated the unique Filipino-Japanese pattern of reconciliation, which differentiates its bilateral relations from the troubled ones among Northeast Asian nations.[2]

The Battle of Manila

Manila had been the capital of the Philippines since its establishment as a colony under Spain in the late sixteenth century. The United States occupied the city in 1898 during the Spanish-American War and later annexed the remaining islands of the Philippines. Facing the South China Sea and developed along the northern and southern banks of the Pasig River, the city had a population of 623,492 according to the 1939 census.[3] On the southern bank of the Pasig River lies Intramuros, the oldest historic district, which originally constituted the walled city of Manila. Located further south are the Ermita and Malate districts, which rapidly grew to become the city's urban centre during the world wars. At the time, these three districts were home to the city's most affluent residents.

In 1935, the Commonwealth of the Philippines was established as an autonomous government in preparation for full-fledged independence, which was to be granted in 1946. Thus, during the Second World War, the country remained under US sovereignty. As the threat of war between Japan and the United States grew, President Franklin D. Roosevelt called the Philippine Commonwealth Army into service in July 1941 as part of the US Army Forces in the Far East (USAFFE), commanded by Douglas MacArthur. Japanese bombers effectively neutralized US air power based in the Philippines within hours of the Pearl Harbor attack in Hawaii in December 1941. MacArthur ordered all USAFFE forces in Luzon to retreat to the Bataan peninsula, and he himself evacuated to the fortified island of Corregidor at the south end of the peninsula, declaring Manila an "open city" in order to save it from destruction. MacArthur left the Philippines entirely – making the famous pledge "I shall return" – and arrived in Australia in March 1942. The remaining USAFFE forces in Bataan and Corregidor surrendered in the following months.[4] On 20 October 1944, the Allied Forces in the Southwest Pacific Area (SWPA) led by MacArthur landed on the beaches of Leyte as he had promised, and the battle for the liberation of the Philippines began.

Throughout the war, the Philippines was the most hostile territory to Japan in Southeast Asia. Because the country was already planning for its official independence in 1946, Japan's war propaganda depicting Japanese rule of Asians as liberation from Caucasians was pointless. The Japanese occupation, it seemed, precipitated only economic collapse and misery. The occupiers became increasingly intolerant of the guerrilla insurgency and the other resistance activities. In Manila itself, the Japanese Kempeitai (Military Police) and other forces tried to maintain a tight grip, taking the lives of both resistance fighters and innocent civilians. US air raids starting in September 1944 killed a small number of civilians. During the last months of Japanese occupation, the influx of refugees from outside Manila bloated the city's population to almost one million. Meanwhile, the collapse of the rice market and the rationing system, exacerbated by confiscations by the departing Japanese forces, made the food shortage so serious that the Allied press reported that hundreds were dying of starvation daily in Manila in late January 1945.[5]

By then, most of the approximately 270,000 troops of the Imperial Japanese Forces had left the city and headed north to Baguio and Mountain Province in Northern Luzon, while more than 80,000 forces remained in Central and Southern Luzon, including Manila. In postwar military tribunals, General Yamashita Tomoyuki, the supreme commander of the Imperial Japanese forces in the Philippines, and other commanding generals insisted that they had considered the city indefensible and directed the forces under their command to abandon Manila in order to fight in the eastern mountainous area. There are, however, conflicting accounts of what exactly the Japanese defence forces in the city were ordered to do or what they understood those orders to mean. After all, the Japanese did not declare Manila an "open city," and the approximately 20,000 Japanese troops deployed as Manila Defence Forces in the city were determined to fight to the last against US forces.[6] Some of the city's non-combatant civilians, sensing the danger of urban battle, evacuated the city. The bulk of downtown residents, however, chose to stay, partly because they did not expect the battle would become so deadly and partly because they thought it would be safer to stay within the inner city where there were many fireproof buildings and large residences in which they could take shelter.

The Battle of Manila began on 3 February 1945, when US forces liberated some 3,700 Allied civilian internees, mostly Americans, from the Santo Tomas Internment Camp in the northern part of the city. The almost bloodless liberation was made possible through careful negotiation between the Americans and a Japanese unit that took 200 internees as hostages. This would stand in stark contrast to the near-total neglect of civilian lives in the subsequent month-long urban battle. Japanese forces torched the Tondo district, blasted the North Harbor facilities, and destroyed bridges in their chaotic retreat to the south of the Pasig River, which then became the major battle zone between the two forces. By 12 February 1945, the US forces led by the Thirty-Seventh Infantry, First Cavalry, and Eleventh Airborne Division completely besieged the downtown areas south of the Pasig – specifically, the Intramuros, Ermita, and Malate districts – which became fierce battlegrounds and horrendous scenes of Japanese war crimes. American heavy artillery barrages launched from the outskirts of the city wiped out most of the flammable structures in the area, while Japanese forces continued to hold major buildings of solid construction until they were eventually annihilated by shelling or neutralized through close combat. Intramuros remained a nightmarish battle zone, and residents and refugees endured a seemingly never-ending hostage crisis, atrocities at the hands of the Japanese, and sustained US shelling. The governmental buildings between the Intramuros and Ermita districts became the last strongholds of the Japanese forces, but the structures were shelled to ruins by US artillery fire. On 3 March 1945, US troops took the Finance Building after neutralizing all the Japanese soldiers remaining inside and thus effectively ending the Battle of Manila.[7]

The body count of Japanese soldiers resulting from the battle was recorded as 16,665; American forces counted 1,010 killed and 5,565 wounded. There were no official statistics for the loss of civilian lives, but the postwar Philippine government estimated 100,000 non-combatant civilian deaths.[8] The Philippine National Artist Nick Joaquin used the words "by sword and fire" in the last lines of his play, *A Portrait of the Artist as Filipino* (1966), to describe how the battle brought about "the death" of "the old Manila."[9] "Sword" signifies the Japanese soldiers' bayonets, used to kill so many civilians during the battle, whereas "fire" represents Japanese machine guns, grenades, and mines and, even more poignantly, the destruction caused by US shelling. Military historians estimate the shelling might have been responsible for as much as 40 per cent of civilian deaths,[10] arguing that MacArthur's politically motivated impatience for victory and the field officers' urge to use heavier artillery in order to minimize US casualties was to blame for the massive and unnecessary collateral damage to the civilians, who "stoically and philosophically accepted decimation" of their families by the American artillery.[11] In one case, at the Remedios Hospital in Malate on 12 and 13 February 1945, apparently misdirected shelling killed almost four hundred civilians.[12]

Despite the horror unleashed by these US tactics, the mass killings and other atrocities committed by Japanese forces constituted the primary cause of the civilian casualties. In order to secure operational positions against US forces and to eliminate the hostile population that certainly would have assisted the Americans in the coming battle, Japan's Manila Defence Forces indiscriminately killed people with bayonets, machine guns, and grenades as well as by setting fires. Japanese defendants on trial for war crimes as well as surviving veterans all acknowledged the tactical difficulties in distinguishing guerrillas from civilians. The magnitude of atrocities committed by the Japanese forces during the battle, however, could hardly be justified or explained by such claims. The surviving records of telegrams exchanged between the Tokyo Imperial General Headquarters and the army and naval forces in Manila suggest that some of the Japanese units, unable to reach the front lines to engage in close combat with US forces, deemed it appropriate to report the slaughter of civilians as military achievements.[13]

Authenticity of Victimhood in the Battle of Manila

The victims of the Battle of Manila in particular and of military action in the Philippines in general had good reason to believe that the question of authenticity of their victimhood was beyond controversy. Details of their victimization had been well established through war crimes investigations conducted immediately after liberation and through subsequent military tribunals. The resulting reports detailing war crimes committed by the Japanese forces during the Battle of Manila might well be counted among the most extensive and accurate of all the war crimes investigation reports from Second World War that were based largely on victims' perspectives. This is partly because the atrocities took place exactly during the time that US forces in each combat theatre were busy organizing war crimes investigation units in preparation for future prosecution. Following the establishment of the United Nations War Crime Commission in 1943, the Judge Advocate General (JAG) of the US Army established the War Crimes Office in Washington, DC, in October 1944 and ordered the commander of each theatre, including SWPA, to establish a war crimes branch at the JAG section of each headquarters.[14]

The atrocities also took place precisely in locations being approached by US forces and where liberation was therefore imminent. As early as 25 February 1945 and into the first week of March, the Fourteenth Army Corps Inspector General's Office conducted a preliminary investigation into the alleged Japanese atrocities in Manila. Colonel Emil Krause, the officer in charge, conducted multiple rounds of interviews at hospitals including the Insular Psychopathic Hospital, Quezon, San Lazaro Hospital, and Chinese General Hospital as well as at the University of Santo Tomas, where the survivors received care immediately after liberation. Testimonies were compiled into a report dated 9 April 1945 that was submitted to the commanding general of the Fourteenth Corps,[15] which would later conduct full-scale investigations in order to identify all instances of Japanese war crimes in the Philippines.

One important example is that of the De La Salle College massacre, which occurred between 7 and 14 February 1945 and was one of the best-known cases of Japanese atrocities during the Battle of Manila. Colonel Krause recorded testimonies as early as 2 March 1945, at San Lazaro Hospital, and 7 March, at Santo Tomas University.[16] A full investigation by the Manila Branch followed and resulted in "Report No. 27," dated 4 July 1945, which gathered numerous documents, including twenty-three duly sworn statements and thirty-three photo exhibits. The report concluded that fifteen brothers, of German and other nationalities, were murdered, as were sixteen Filipino civilians and five Spanish refugees and college employees. The college's president, an Irish national named Brother Xavier, as well as four other Filipino civilian refugees and college employees were presumed killed. The report concluded that "the brutal and savage manner in which the wholesale execution was conducted is revealed by the indiscriminate bayonetting and killing of women and children and the later attempt to violate wounded and dead victims" and that the perpetrators, if and when identified and apprehended, would be tried and the Imperial Japanese Government held responsible for the crimes.[17]

These investigations enabled officers to obtain detailed and first-hand accounts from the surviving victims and witnesses of mass killings and rapes. The war crimes investigation report (Manila Report No. 94) concluded that, in Intramuros alone, 132 Spanish nationals, despite being citizens of a neutral country, were killed, as were 104 Dutch, American, English, Spanish, Chinese, and Filipino nationals who were patients and members of the medical staff at San Juan de Dios Hospital. In addition, approximately 50 female and 2,000 male Filipino civilians in the district were presumed to have been killed by Japanese forces.[18] The investigation also exposed numerous cases of atrocities in the Ermita and Malate districts, including the Red Cross Building (more than 50 murdered victims), St. Paul's college (432 victims), Paco (400 victims), German Club (500 victims), Price House (100 victims), Rubio Residence (29 victims), and other fire-resistant buildings and residences in those districts.[19] Rapes were rampant and well organized. Especially in the case of the Bay View Hotel in Ermita district, at least 40 women were systematically gang-raped; girls of apparently Caucasian appearance were disproportionately targeted.[20]

These reports were compiled by the prosecution in preparation for the public trial of General Yamashita, which was held in Manila from 29 October to 7 December 1945. Yamashita was accused of "wilful disregard and failure to discharge his duty" to take control as commander in preventing his subordinates from committing war crimes.[21] The trial opened at "the shell-scarred ballroom at the High Commissioner's Residence on Dewey Boulevard,"[22] only a few blocks from the scenes of horrendous war crimes in Ermita. During the first week of the public trial, many witnesses testified: movie star Corazon Noble (Patricia Abad), whose ten-month-old daughter was bayoneted three times and slowly died in her arms at the Red Cross Building; Father Francis J. Cosgrave, a survivor of the De La Salle Massacre; victims of the Bay View Hotel rapes; and the inhabitants of Ermita/Malate districts who lost their friends and families.[23] After five weeks, the military commission found Yamashita guilty and sentenced him to death. The Supreme Court of the United States refused the defendant's appeal in a five-to-two decision, and Yamashita was hanged on 23 February 1946.

Since then, the trial has been criticized as unfair and hastily arranged, and even as an act of personal revenge by Douglas MacArthur. The argument supporting this view is that Yamashita was hanged not for what he did but for what he failed to prevent – that is, the war crimes committed by his subordinates.[24] US Supreme Court Justice Frank Murphy reflected this criticism in his dissenting opinion, writing, "The recorded annals of warfare and the established principles of international law afford not the slightest precedent for such a charge."[25] It should be noted, however, that even Yamashita's defence counsel accepted most of the prosecution's evidence establishing that war crimes were committed by the Japanese forces under his command. Of the 123 war crime case reports submitted to the military commission, 42 were related to the Battle of Manila, which found that "over 8,000 men, women and children, all unarmed, non-combatant civilians were killed and over 7,000 mistreated, maimed and wounded without cause or trial." Yamashita was also accused of other war crimes committed under his command throughout the Philippines but especially in the area surrounding Manila. These included the killing of more than 16,000 people in the Province of Batangas as well as the murder of hundreds in Bulacan, 3,000 in Laguna, and 750 in La Union. The Battle of Manila was just the tip of the iceberg.[26]

In total, the Manila Branch compiled more than 350 official investigation reports, plus thousands of closed-case reports, by the beginning of 1947. An undated memorandum prepared by the JAG War Crimes Office suggests that the grand total of the Filipino civilian victims reported in these investigation reports amounted to more than 91,000.[27] It was usually very difficult, however, to identify the individual perpetrators on the ground, especially in the Manila atrocity cases, because most witnesses encountered the perpetrators for the first time in the midst of the chaotic battle, and most of the perpetrators were presumed to have been killed by the time the investigation took place. Many cases were thus eventually closed without having apprehended the actual perpetrators of the crimes.

Urban Elite as Victims

Another reason that Japanese atrocities during the Battle of Manila became one of the most accurately recorded war crimes was because the survivors of the month-long battle included affluent urban elites, both Filipino and foreign. Warfare in general tends to victimize the less privileged because the affluent have greater means to save themselves. In Manila, however, the privileged and the affluent – including European foreign nationals, even Germans and neutral Spanish – could not escape the chaos and, indeed, were targeted by the Japanese soldiers.

The photograph reproduced here may be of some help in understanding what happened to urban elite families during the battle. The picture was taken on 19 February 2011 at the annual memorial service held by Memorare–Manila 1945, an event that will be discussed more fully later in this chapter. Ambassador Miguel Perez-Rubio ("1" in photo) was the only member of his family not killed by the "Imperial Japanese Marines" during the Perez-Rubio Residence Massacre on 12 February 1945 (Miguel was fighting in the outskirts of Manila as a guerrilla at the time).[28] Ambassador Juan Jose Rocha (2) lost his mother to US shelling and eleven members of his family during the Japanese massacre. Lourdes R. Montinola (3), the daughter of Far Eastern University Founder Dr. Nicanor Reyes, lost her parents and two siblings during the Japanese attack on their residence, which she describes in

A photo taken at the annual Memorial Service held by Memorare–Manila 1945 at Plazuela de Santa Isabel, Intramuros, Manila, 19 February 2011.

a 1996 memoir.[29] Ambassador Isabel Caro Wilson (4), fourteen years old at the time of the battle, barely escaped being raped by Japanese officers at the Bay View Hotel. Gemma Cruz Araneta (5), who was Miss International 1964, lost her father, grandfather, and many other relatives in the battle.

These members of Manila's urban elite, who were affluent and thus able to afford better education, were deemed more reliable witnesses in the context of both investigations and trials for war crimes. They also have had more opportunities, especially since the mid-1990s, to share their experiences of the postwar years through newspaper columns, memoirs, novels, poems, theatrical plays, and so on.[30] Such efforts try to convey their sense that the Battle of Manila not only physically destroyed the city but left its inhabitants with incurable trauma from a massacre that nearly destroyed their culture and way of life. Indeed, the survivors and the bereaved did not have the enthusiasm to rebuild their lives at the site of their traumatic experience. By the end of the 1960s, the bulk of the city's affluent had fled the city in favour of the new, fortified gated communities in suburban Makati. Meanwhile, Ermita and Malate became one of Asia's largest red-light districts, attracting foreign tourists, including Japanese, for sex tourism.

Reconciliation and Forgetting

Japanese people in the early postwar years had plenty of opportunities to learn the history of Japanese atrocities during the Battle of Manila. The public trial of Yamashita received much publicity in Japan because of the general's popularity as a war hero. During the International Military Tribunal for the Far East (1946–8), prosecution of Japanese war crimes in Manila and the Philippines in general (the "Philippine phase" of the trials) was given a five-day session, which one Japanese observer present at the proceedings described as "the most disturbing scene for me at the tribunal."[31]

Another focal point of Japanese historical memory regarding Manila grew out of Nagai Takashi's important book *The Bells of Nagasaki* (*Nagasaki no Kane*). This moving account, authored by a Christian radiologist involved in rescue efforts after the atomic bombing of Nagasaki, despite being severely wounded himself, was published in 1949 and became the first bestselling book in postwar Japan. The publication, however, was allowed by the General Headquarters of the Supreme Commander of the Allied Powers (GHQ/SCAP) on the condition that the book include an appendix entitled "The Tragedy of Manila," a compilation of affidavits that had been gathered by Colonel Emil Krause during his preliminary investigations and were translated into Japanese.[32]

Given the depth of the pain that the Philippines suffered during the Japanese occupation and the war, it was only natural for the Filipino people to harbour deep animosity toward Japan for decades afterwards. The degree of bilateral exchange was kept to a minimum for more than a decade after the war. Yukawa Morio, the first postwar Japanese ambassador to the Philippine Republic, recalled that, when he was assigned there in 1957, "although I had prepared, I was so surprised at the depth of the bad feeling towards Japan."[33]

Given this deep-seated resentment, it might seem to be a diplomatic miracle that the Japanese government portrayed the Philippines in press materials in 2016 as the country that is "most friendly towards Japan, having overcome the obstacles connected with the past tragedy."[34] On the other hand, the Battle of Manila in particular and the Battle of the Philippines in general has gradually but steadily disappeared not only from Japanese collective memory but also from the narratives shared by the two nations, and the wartime past has seldom been mentioned by government officials in the context of bilateral issues. In other words, Japan's recent relations with the Philippines can be characterized as "amity through amnesia," which contrasts greatly with the discord or *rekishi mondai* (history issues) that exist between Japan and its Northeast Asian neighbours. The latter set of relations forces Japan to confront its history of colonial rule in Korea (1910–45) as well as the Second Sino-Japanese War (1937–45). Unsettled issues stemming from these periods have arisen in various contexts, such as debates over history textbooks and controversies involving comfort women, conscripted workers, the Nanjing Massacre, and the Yasukuni Shrine.[35]

Conditions of Reconciliation: Victory and Punishment

Several factors have likely enabled the Philippines and the Filipino people to move gradually from amnesia toward forgiveness in more recent times. Above all, there is no room to suggest that the relationship between Japan and the Philippines during the Second World War was anything other than one of perpetrator and victim. While US responsibility for indiscriminate shelling and bombing has certainly been debated, it has not at all changed the victimizer/victimized relationship between Japan and the Philippines. Ironically, the unquestionable roles in this relationship may have made it easier for the Japanese to position themselves as apologizers asking for forgiveness from Filipinos, as compared to Japan's posture toward Korea and China. The act (and repetition) of apologizing to these countries has been viewed as a much more divisive issue in Japanese contemporary politics.[36]

Second, the Philippines and the Filipino people defeated the enemy and liberated their people by fighting shoulder to shoulder with the Americans. The subsequent war crimes trials, first conducted by the United States and later handed off to the Philippine government,[37] gave Filipinos the opportunity not only to punish Japanese war criminals but also to show mercy by commuting sentences, repatriating the accused, and, finally, granting them clemency under President Elpidio Quirino in December 1953. It was a well-known fact in the Philippines and even in Japan that Quirino had lost his wife and three of his five children during the battle.[38] The fact that Filipinos were able to exert agency through these experiences of victory, punishment, and clemency might well have made it psychologically more acceptable for the nation to move gradually forward toward reconciliation.

Victimhood as a Diplomatic Weapon

Despite the experiences of pain and resentment, the geopolitical situation of the Cold War meant that the Philippines could not afford to overlook the importance of Japan as a potential ally that belonged to the US-led anti-communist bloc. The San Francisco Peace Conference in September 1951 offered an opportunity for the Philippines to accept this reality. At the same time, the country was able to use its victimhood as a powerful diplomatic weapon. During the pre-conference negotiations, the Philippine government strongly objected to the American proposal that Japan not be required to pay reparations to the victimized countries, including the Philippines, and it succeeded in having the clauses pertaining to reparations retained in the treaty.[39] Even so, the terms on reparations in the Peace Treaty were, in the Philippine government's view, still too generous to Japan. Secretary of Foreign Affairs Carlos P. Romulo voiced serious reservations about the provisions, stating, "We do not pretend that the attitude of the Filipino people towards Japan has been completely untouched by emotion. We would be less than human to make such a claim."[40] Nishimura Kumao, then the director of the Japanese Foreign Ministry's Treaty Division, recalled it being painful to witness Filipinos "showing how deep their hatred and distrust of Japan was."[41]

The Philippines signed the peace treaty but declared that it would postpone ratification pending the conclusion of a reparation agreement. After difficult but necessary negotiations, the agreement was finally concluded in May 1956 and was ratified along with the peace treaty; normalization of diplomatic relations occurred in July of the same year. The amount of reparations, equivalent to US$550 million plus a payment of US$250 million over twenty years, was the largest reparation package to result from the treaty.[42]

During consideration of the reparation agreement in Japan's National Diet, the opposition Socialist Party criticized the proposed amount as "excessive." Kotaki Akira, a councillor representing the governing party, testified before the Foreign Relations Committee that "even 8 billion U.S. dollars [the initial claim by the Philippine government] was not baseless. We should express our respect for their statesmanship reaching a compromise with this moderate amount of reparation."[43] In the decades after the war, it was not uncommon to find individuals like Councillor Kotaki in key positions in the Japanese government who were sensitive enough, based on their own contemporary knowledge and experiences, to accept the victimhood narrative asserted by the Philippine government. The reparation agreement paved the way for the two countries to forge stable and mutually beneficial economic relations that continue to today. The Philippines has been ranked the fifth among recipients of Japanese official development assistance (ODA) programs in terms of the accumulated total amount of bilateral assistance, and Japan has long been both the greatest ODA donor and one of the Philippines' top trading partners.[44]

With bilateral relations gradually improving, more Japanese tourists began to visit the Philippines, especially after the Japanese government liberalized foreign travel in 1964. Interestingly, the Philippine government and the Filipino people as a whole would soon find that demonstrating forgiveness and kindness to Japanese visitors *without* referring to the horrific past could prove effective in establishing positive relations. One of the most publicized path-breaking experiences was the visit of Prince Akihito and Princess Michiko in 1962. The royal couple and the embedded Japanese press corps were fully prepared for demonstrations of animosity by Filipinos but were instead greeted with a warm welcome and few visible signs of protest. This very much impressed the royal visitors as well as the press, who, in return, expressed deep gratitude for their hosts' generosity.[45]

The royal couple's experience was not a privileged exception but, rather, was shared widely by Japanese visitors, especially by surviving Japanese veterans and bereaved families of dead Japanese troops. Because of the vast number of Japanese who died in the Philippines during the war – some 518,000, combatants and non-combatants combined[46] – Japanese people held more commemorative events in the Philippines than in any other country outside Japan. The Japanese built more than four hundred memorials to their war dead throughout the Philippines.[47] Many also visited the country on government-sponsored missions to recover remains (*ikotsu-shushu*, literally meaning "bone collecting") and "pilgrimage tours" to former battle sites. The visitors were generally aware, or were told to be aware, that they should be sensitive, well behaved, and apologetic about the harm that Japan as a nation – if not their dead loved ones in particular – had inflicted on the Philippines. Local Filipino communities were and continue to be mostly welcoming and to accept Japanese visitors, showing forgiveness and astonishing levels of hospitality. Japanese visitors often tried to show their gratitude by bringing gifts, offering support to local communities, for example, through donations to elementary schools. Not all interactions between the tourists and their hosts were so positive. There were occasional displays of arrogance by tourists as well as instances in which the locals retrieved remains (possibly, or possibly not, of dead Japanese soldiers) in anticipation of selling them to Japanese visitors. Nonetheless, efforts to maintain good will developed, in many cases, into important grassroots, non-governmental civic exchange.[48]

As early as the 1980s, the pattern that could be called "a virtuous circle of apology and forgiveness" was established at the national level: the Japanese side would demonstrate remorse, and the Philippine side would accept it in good faith. When Prime Minister Nakasone Yasuhiro visited the Philippines in May 1983, he was so moved by the welcoming crowds – apparently mobilized by then-dictator Ferdinand E. Marcos – that he personally redrafted his banquet speech, in which he said, "Our country deeply regrets and repents having caused your country and people such trouble in the past war. The more you treat us with warm friendliness and generosity, the deeper should we repent and castigate ourselves."[49] Another noteworthy event occurred during President Corazon Aquino's state visit to Japan in November 1986, when Emperor Hirohito allegedly "kept apologizing for what the Japanese caused the Philippines," while President Aquino told the emperor "to forget about this."[50]

Another important actor in maintaining these positive relations has been the Nippon Izokukai (Japan War Bereaved Association, hereafter JWBA), Japan's largest association for bereaved families of war dead. At a 1977 memorial ceremony held at the Memorial for the War Dead in Carilaya Memorial Park in the Philippines – which, in 1973, became the first such memorial built by Japanese government on foreign soil – JWBA secretary general Itagaki Tadashi summarized the state of these relations:

> Sincerity and truthfulness of the war-bereaved families has opened a way to heart-to-heart exchange between our two nations, transcending love and hate and leading to the establishment of amicable relationships due to the efforts of people in both countries. This is ample proof of the fact that *EI'REI* [those who died heroically] on both sides will live forever as the foundations of peace.[51]

This gesture by a top JWBA official, who was later elected to the House of Councillors as a Liberal Democratic Party (LDP) politician and who advocated for prime ministers' official visits to the Yasukuni Shrine – a Shinto shrine to the war dead commemorating, among millions of others, Class A war criminals – and other conservative nationalist causes, had a significant political implication in light of the deep relationship between JWBA and LDP politicians. Although many LDP politicians expressed strong resentment concerning the Japanese "diplomacy of apology" toward China and Korea, it was – and is – rare for the same politicians to criticize the Japanese-Filipino apologizer-forgiver relationship, most possibly because they understood how satisfied JWBA has been in its amicable relations with the Philippines. The absence of such antagonism with respect to the past is significant because it has resulted in a relationship with the Philippines that is far less strained than those with China and Korea.

There is, however, a flip side to this story of reconciliation. The virtuous circle of apology and forgiveness may have worked very well among those who lived through the war. Yet the effect of this relationship was not so much to preserve war memories as to hasten their erasure, thus preventing any institutionalized memory from being transferred to subsequent generations. Consequently, Japanese public memory of the war in the Philippines has dwindled to dangerous levels – to the point of near-total amnesia among the younger population. In the short term, the suppression of ugly memories may have fostered the relaxation of tensions and the creation of mutual amity between the two countries. In the long run, it may have undermined the foundations of their mutual understanding of the past.

Commemoration and Protest against Forgetting

From the perspective of Filipino victims, the master narrative of Filipino-Japanese reconciliation seems to have had a twofold effect. On one hand, the authenticity of their victimhood has remained intact because it has rarely encountered challenges from Japanese right-wing revisionists. On the other hand, the lack of controversy and absence of public acts of remembrance have allowed Japan and the world to forget the tragedy. By the 1990s, it became apparent in the eyes of the survivors and the bereaved that the memory of the Battle of Manila had almost completely vanished.

The fiftieth anniversary of the battle, in February 1995, marked the beginning of the protest against forgetting. Memorare–Manila 1945, a private, non-profit organization founded by the battle's survivors and the bereaved – erected a monument that commemorates the non-combatant victims of the battle. Memorare had been created in October 1993 with the aim of "the gathering of the names of the non-combatant who died in the battle for the liberation of Manila, the erection of a monument in Intramuros for those victims, and the offering of a Requiem Mass for them." Many of the Memorare's sponsors were the urban elite survivors of the battle included in the photo reproduced in this chapter, as well as Victoria Quirino Delgado, Elpidio Quirino's surviving daughter, and Jaime Zobel de Ayala, then the chairman of Ayala Corporation, a real estate giant and the Philippines' largest corporation. Major media corporations and industries also joined the list of sponsors.[52]

For its first project, Memorare was able to gather thousands of victims' names, including much specific information on how they were killed (whether by Japanese massacre or by US fire, for example), often supported by diaries and personal accounts of the battle. These materials are now stored and available for the public and researchers at the Filipinas Heritage Library in Makati, Metro Manila.

Memorare's most ambitious goal was to build a monument in Intramuros, which was unveiled on 18 February 1995 at Plazuela de Santa Isabel. The monument, created by sculptor Peter de Guzman, features eight figures: a hooded woman weeping over a dead child in her arms, surrounded by six other figures, each expressing the anguish and pain of innocent victims of war. The monument's inscription, composed by Nick Joaquin, reads:

> This memorial is dedicated to all these innocent victims of war, many of whom went nameless and unknown to a common grave, or never even knew a grave at all, their bodies having been consumed by fire or crushed to dust beneath the rubble of ruins.
>
> Let this monument be the gravestone for each and every one of the over 100,000 men, women, children and infants killed in Manila during its Battle of Liberation, February 3–March 3, 1945. We have not forgotten them, nor shall we ever forget.
>
> May they rest in peace as part now of the sacred ground of this city: the Manila of our affections.

The dedication of the monument was followed by a requiem mass at the nearby Manila Cathedral "to honor the non-combatants who perished in the Battle for Manila." Mozart's *Requiem* was sung with the Philippine Philharmonic Orchestra, and Jaime Cardinal Sin served as main celebrant. One of the Prayers of the Faithful, apparently directed at the Japanese perpetrators, was read by Fernando Vasquez-Prada, who was five years old at the time of the De La Salle College Massacre and the sole survivor of his family of six:

> For those who killed and
> Raped and slaughtered that
> they may acknowledge
> their guilt and seek forgiveness
> let us pray to the Lord[53]

Media coverage in the Philippines of these commemorative events was extensive and seemed to mark the beginning of restoring the battle's place in the collective memory. In Japan, there was no coverage of these events, nor would there be any for more than a decade to come.

Ever since the dedication of the monument, Memorare has tried to influence the public and the government by sponsoring events such as annual commemorative gatherings and public lectures, publishing books and newspaper columns, and making appearances on the news and in documentary films. The group and its sympathizers had the prominence to become vocal opponents of the diplomacy of mutual forgetting established by the two countries, and their opposition to the status quo came to a head on the occasion of the sixtieth anniversary of the Battle of Manila in 2005.

Maria Isabel Ongpin, one of Memorare's founders, lamented in a February 2005 newspaper column that no officials from the Philippine government showed up at the organization's memorial gathering, although the diplomatic corps from the United States and the European Union did attend. Ongpin stressed the importance of remembrance as a part of the "universal awakening that has risen all over the world affected by World War II."[54] The *Manila Bulletin* published a letter to the editor from a person orphaned during the Battle for Manila who protested the observance of Philippines-Japan Friendship Month in February.[55] Bambi L. Harper, a cultural writer and a columnist for the *Philippine Daily Inquirer*, claimed in a November 2005 column that the Japanese government had made no official apology for past aggression,[56] which was, in fact, not correct but nonetheless represented the displeasure among Filipino intellectuals about insufficient Japanese attention to the Philippines regarding memory of the war.

Although these columns rarely sought to rouse antagonism – indeed, they frequently demonstrated objectivity and tolerance – they nevertheless pointed to gathering clouds with the potential for developing into a storm. In the end, protests against forgetting did not lead to any greater conflicts between the two countries, mostly thanks to the preventive diplomacy launched in late 2005 by the Japanese embassy. Yamazaki Ryuichiro, then the Japanese ambassador, had not participated in the sixtieth-anniversary events but attended every major memorial gathering of the sixty-first anniversary and expressed words of sincere apology beginning with the marking of General MacArthur's famous Leyte Landing.[57] Shortly thereafter, Bambi L. Harper, almost certainly having been approached and informed by the Embassy of Japan about the government's official position of apology, published a column in January 2006 that focused on the brighter side of postwar Filipino-Japanese relations, referring to the remarks made by both Prime Minister Koizumi Junichiro and Ambassador Yamazaki, who on several occasions acknowledged "the misery brought about by Japan's colonial rule and aggression on the people of Southeast Asia."[58]

In February 2006, Memorare marked the sixty-first anniversary with a commemorative event, which Ambassador Yamazaki attended – the first for a Japanese ambassador to the Philippines. In his speech, Yamazaki remarked, "I would like to express my heartfelt apologies and deep sense of remorse over the tragic fate of Manila. Let me also reiterate the Japanese Government's determination not to allow the lessons of that horrible World War II to erode, and to contribute to the peace and prosperity of the world without ever waging a war."[59] Bambi L. Harper, who was in attendance, offered the following observation: "There was hardly a dry eye in the audience when Ambassador Juan Rocha, who lost his mother in that holocaust, remarked that it had been difficult to forgive when there was no contrition. Yamazaki's sincere regrets may go a long way in healing those festering wounds."[60] Japanese diplomacy thus successfully rescued the virtuous circle of apology and forgiveness, at least for the time being, and did so with the involvement of Memorare. It should also be noted, however, that the ambassador's apology was not given much coverage in Japanese media, which was perhaps a missed opportunity to remedy the declining state of memory in Japan regarding the war in the Philippines.

As the seventieth anniversary of the Battle of Manila approached, signs of a significant shift in historical amnesia, especially in Japan, gradually emerged. In August 2007, the NHK (Japan Broadcasting Corporation) produced and broadcast the first-ever major Japanese TV documentary on the battle, titled *Shogen Kiroku Manila Shigaisen* (Testimonies: The Urban Warfare of Manila). Additional NHK documentaries on the topic followed and might have contributed moderately to awareness among the Japanese public of the battle, once largely forgotten in Japan.

Another noteworthy development was that Memorare found its Japanese counterpart in Bridge for Peace (BFP), a small, non-profit peace advocacy group led by individuals mostly in their twenties and thirties. The group was organized in August 2004 by Jin Naoko (6 in the photo on page 133), then a twenty-six-year-old Japanese woman, who launched the project by bringing video messages from ex-Japanese soldiers, including many who admitted their guilt and sought forgiveness, to Filipino survivors and the bereaved. The group, though small, has attracted considerable attention from Japanese media, mainly because of its uniquely non-partisan and youthful character.[61] Through this author's mediation, Jin Naoko and BFP received an invitation from Memorare to attend its annual commemoration ceremony on 19 February 2011. These were the first Japanese invitees to attend since Ambassador Yamazaki. Dr. Benito Legarda Jr describes in his article on the event that some of the Memorare members in attendance even felt consoled by the Japanese visitors' presence.[62] The BFP has been invited to every annual commemoration gathering since then.

Numerous events including exhibitions, public lectures, and film screenings were held throughout February 2015 in Manila to mark the seventieth anniversary, and the Philippine government launched the first official website commemorating the Battle of Manila.[63] It seemed that recognition of the battle as a national tragedy had finally reached the level long sought by Memorare. On 14 February of that year, Memorare held a ceremony that, for the very first time, was covered by major Japanese news media and was broadcast on primetime news programs.[64]

Further unexpected developments followed. From 2 to 5 June 2015, Philippine president Benigno Aquino III made a state visit to Japan and, in turn, invited Emperor Akihito and Empress Michiko for a state visit to the Philippines. The visit, which was realized in an unusually short interval, took place from 26 to 30 January 2016. Prime Minister Abe Shinzo issued a statement announcing that the purpose of the visit was to "further strengthen the intimate relations of friendship and goodwill" with the Philippines on the occasion of the sixtieth anniversary of the normalization of diplomatic relations between the two countries.[65] Japanese media widely reported that the emperor wished to commemorate the war dead not only of Japan but also of the Philippines. Upon his departure from the Haneda International Airport, the emperor made a televised address, officially referred to as "His Majesty's words" (*okotoba*), in the presence of the prime minister and others: "During World War II, countless Filipino, American, and Japanese lives were lost in the Philippines. A great many innocent Filipino civilians became casualties of the fierce battles fought in the city of Manila. This history will always be in our hearts as we make this visit to the Philippines."[66]

The emperor's mention of the Battle of Manila was entirely unexpected, since it was unprecedented for him to refer directly to a particular event in the war in a public address. The Battle of Manila was thus retrieved from the decades of amnesia to receive definitive recognition in the records of "His Majesty's words," although critics still could say his words stopped short of making apology.

In the Philippines, the emperor and empress reinforced their words with careful and deliberate body language. The couple bowed on the stairs of the airplane, which they had not done, for example, on their

1992 state visit to China. They also bowed deeply in front of the National Tomb of the Unknown Soldier at Libingan ng mga Bayani (Hero's Cemetery) for more than a full minute, thus showing their sense of remorse without uttering a word. The Philippine media warmly embraced the aged imperial couple, who had returned to the Philippines after fifty-six years to a very warm welcome.[67] In August 2016, Emperor Akihito made a televised address to the nation, hinting that he wanted to retire; he consequently abdicated in April 2019, making his state visit to the Philippines the culmination of his "pilgrimage tours."[68]

Conclusion

It may be fair to say that Memorare's protest against forgetting and its efforts to commemorate victimhood have been largely successful in mobilizing the media and scholars both in the Philippines and abroad (including myself – I attended the dedication of the monument and the Requiem Mass in 1995) to devote more attention to the battle of Manila and its historical significance. Akihito's 2016 *okotoba* and state visit to the Philippines might have offered an opportunity to bring the two nations a step closer to sustainable reconciliation through remembrance.

Yet caution should be taken in labelling the postwar Filipino-Japanese reconciliation and recent increased awareness among the Japanese public as simply a success story. The growing media attention to the Battle of Manila, the Philippines, and the emperor's state visit requires careful examination of the broader context of East Asia's memory politics. This context entails differentiated bilateral relations between Japan and, respectively, the Philippines, China, and Korea. These relationships each involve intertwined issues of regional security, border disputes, and economic rivalry. The growing presence of Chinese and Korean capital and the resulting soft power could reshape memory politics in a way that challenges the established narrative of Filipino-Japanese binational reconciliation.

One should also remember that the Filipino-Japanese pattern of reconciliation found in the forgiver-apologizer relationship has worked most effectively among the "generation of war," while that same pattern, lacking significant institutionalized public memory, had the effect of promoting Japanese public amnesia of the topic. Even a seemingly absolute recognition by the emperor in 2016 did not change the basic structure of Japanese national war memory, which has been criticized for unduly focusing on Japan's own victimhood and encouraging national amnesia with respect to its wartime aggression.[69] Perhaps ironically, the amity achieved by those who lived through the war threatens to forestall a continued conversation among subsequent generations of Japanese and Filipinos. This conversation is necessary to preserve, deepen, and cement reconciliation worthy of the name.

NOTES

1 For an overall history of the battle, see Richard Connaughton, John Pimlott, and Duncan Anderson, *The Battle for Manila* (London: Bloomsbury, 1995); Alfonso J. Aluit, *By Sword and Fire: The Destruction of Manila in World War II, 3 February–3 March 1945* (Manila: National Commission for Culture and Arts, 1994); and James M. Scott, *Rampage: MacArthur, Yamashita and the Battle of Manila* (New York: W.W. Norton, 2018).
2 The observation of recent developments surrounding the seventieth anniversary and the imperial state visit in this chapter may be somewhat biased by my own participation. I have been actively involved in the campaign for raising awareness of the Battle of Manila in Japan as an adviser to the NHK (Japan Broadcasting Corporation) and various journalists and have served as a mediator between Bridge for Peace and Memorare–Manila 1945.
3 Bureau of the Census, Commonwealth of the Philippines, *Census of the Philippine Islands, 1939* (Manila: Bureau of Printing, 1940–3).
4 The American and Filipino prisoners of war then faced the ordeal of the "Bataan Death March," a forced transfer by foot in brutal heat that cost the lives of hundreds of American and thousands of Filipino POWs. General Homma Masaharu, the supreme commander of invading Japanese forces, was later tried by a US military tribunal for violating international rule of war and was executed in April 1946. On Japanese war crimes trials, see Yuma Totani, *Justice in Asia and the Pacific Region, 1945–1952* (New York: Cambridge University Press, 2015). For Japanese-language accounts, see Hayashi Yoshifumi, *BC-kyu Senpan Saiban* [Trials of BC Class War Criminals] (Tokyo: Iwanami Shoten, 2005) and Nagai Hitoshi, *Firipin to Tainichi Senpan Saiban: 1945–1953* [The War Crimes Trials and Japan-Philippines Relations, 1945–1953] (Tokyo: Iwanami Shoten, 2010).
5 "Starvation in Manila," *Sydney Morning Herald,* 26 January 1945, 1.
6 Connaughton, Pimlott, and Anderson, *Battle for Manila*, 70–1; Maehara Toru, *Manira Bo'eisen: Nihongun no Toshi no Tatatakai* [The Battle of Manila Defence: The Japanese Forces Urban Combat] (Tokyo: Boei Kenshujo [National Defence Institute], 1982), 59–133.
7 On detailed accounts and chronology of the battle, see Aluit, *By Sword and Fire*; Connaughton, Pimlott, and Anderson, *Battle for Manila*; and Scott, *Rampage*.

8 Robert Ross Smith, *United States Army in World War II: The War in the Pacific: Triumph in the Philippines* (Washington, DC: Office of the Chief of Military History, Dept. of the Army, 1963), 306–7.
9 Nick Joaquin, *A Portrait of the Artist as Filipino: An Elegy in Three Scenes* (Manila: MCS Enterprises, 1966), 116.
10 Connaughton, Pimlott, and Anderson, *Battle for Manila*, 121.
11 Ibid., 174.
12 Ibid., 145. See also Pedro M. Picornell, *The Remedios Hospital, 1942–1945: A Saga of Malate* (Manila: De La Salle University, 1995).
13 Some of the after-action reports of sneak attacks (*kirikomi*) found in the Japanese army and navy telegrams seem to support this theory. See Hayashi Yoshifumi, "Shiryo Shokai: Nihongun no Meirei Denpo ni miru Manira-sen" [Introduction of documents: Battle of Manila as seen in Japanese forces orders and telegrams]," *Shizen-Ningen-Shakai* 48 (2010): 69–95.
14 Greg Bradsher, "The Exploitation of Captured and Seized Japanese Records Relating to War Crimes, 1942–1945," in *Researching Japanese War Crimes Records: Introductory Essays*, ed. Edward Drea, Greg Bradsher, Robert Hanyok, James Lide, Michael Petersen, and Daqing Yang (Washington, DC: National Archives and Records Administration, 2006); "Establishment of War Crimes Office," 25 December 1944, RG153: Records of the Judge Advocate General (Army), entry 145, box 73l, US National Archives at College Park (hereafter NACP).
15 "Report of Investigation of Alleged Atrocities by Members of the Japanese Imperial Forces in Manila and Other Parts of Luzon, Philippine Islands Made by Colonel Emil Krause, IGD, and Lieutenant Colonel R. Graham Bosworth, IGD, Headquarters, XIV Corps," 9 April 1945, RG 331: Records of Allied Operational and Occupation Headquarters, World War II, entry 1358, box 1993, NACP.
16 "Report of Investigation of Alleged Atrocities by Members of the Japanese Imperial Forces in Manila," exhibit 35, "Testimony of Miss Emiliana Gonzaga taken at San Lazaro Hospital, Manila, on 2 March 1945" and exhibits 69–70, "Testimony of Father Francis J. Cosgrave, Redemptorist [sic] Monastery, taken at Santo Tomas University, Manila, on 7 March 1945."
17 "Manila Report No. 27: Investigation of the Massacre of 41 Civilians; Attempted Murder of 15 Civilians, All of Various Nationalities; Rape and Attempted Rape of 4 Filipinos at De La Salle College, 1501 Taft Avenue, Manila, Philippine Islands, between 7 and 14 February 1945," 4 July 1945, RG 331, entry 1214, box 1110, NACP.
18 "Manila Report No. 94: Atrocities Committed by Japanese at Intramuros, Manila, P.I., during February 1945," 30 October 1945, RG 331, entry 1214, box 1118, NACP.

19 The numbers of murder victims are found, respectively, in Reports 11, 53, 59, 66, 70, and 13.

20 Scott, *Rampage*, 261–8; Hayashi Hirofumi, "Manira-sen to Beibyu Hoteru Jiken" [The Battle of Manila and Bay View Hotel Case], *Shizen-Ningen-Shakai* 52 (2012): 49–83.

21 On the Yamashita trial, see Richard L. Lael, *The Yamashita Precedent: War Crimes and Command Responsibility* (Wilmington, DE: Scholarly Resources, 1982).

22 "Yamashita Charged with 123 Crimes as Trial Begins Today," *Manila Times*, 29 October 1945, 1.

23 *United States v Tomoyuki Yamashita*, Public Trial Proceedings, vols. 2–8, 29 October to 3 November 1945, RG 331, entry 1327, box 1720, NACP.

24 One early and important criticism was made by Yamashita's own government-appointed defence counsel. A. Frank Reel, *The Case of General Yamashita* (Chicago: University of Chicago Press, 1949).

25 *In re Yamashita*, 327 U.S. 1 (1946).

26 General Headquarters, US Army Forces, Pacific, Office of the Theater Judge Advocate, "Review of the Record of Trial by a Military Commission of Tomoyuki Yamashita, General, Imperial Japanese Army," 26 December 1945, RG 331, entry 1327, box 1720, NACP.

27 This total represented 89,818 murdered, 1,258 tortured, 7 subjected to starvation and neglect, and 101 subjected to other mistreatment and assault. War Crimes Office, "Inf. Re Statistical Reports and Post Trial Activities (general)," 116–20, undated, RG 153, entry 145, box 111, NACP.

28 "Manila Report No.13: Alleged Shooting, Bayonetting and Burning of Civilians at the Perez Rubio Residence, 150 Vito Cruz Street, Singalong, Manila, Philippine Islands, on 12 February 1945," RG 331, entry 1214, box 1109, NACP; Miguel A. Perez-Rubio, *Nine Lives: The Reminiscences of Miguel A. Perez-Rubio* (Manila: Vibal Foundation, 2017).

29 Lourdes R. Montinola, *Breaking the Silence* (Quezon City: University of the Philippines Press, 1996).

30 One early and outstanding example of victims who spoke out about their experience is Carmen Guerrero Nakpil, who survived the battle as a pregnant woman with an infant daughter, Gemma (5). See Nakano Satoshi, "Methods to Avoid Speaking the Unspeakable: Carmen Guerrero Nakpil, the Death of Manila, and Post–World War II Filipino Memory and Mourning," *Hitotsubashi Journal of Social Studies* 48, no. 1 (January 2017): 27–41.

31 Quotations by Takigawa Masajiro, in Nagai Hitoshi, "The Tokyo War Crimes Trial," in *Philippines-Japan Relations*, ed. Ikehata Setsuho and Lydia N. Yu Jose (Quezon City: Ateneo de Manila University Press, 2003), 280.

32 Nagai Takashi, *Nagasaki no Kane: Manila no Higeki* (Tokyo: Hibiya Shuppan, 1949); published in English as *The Bells of Nagasaki: A Message of Hope from a Witness, a Doctor*, trans. William Johnston (Tokyo: Kodansha, 1984).
33 Tsuchitani Naotoshi, ed., *Yamayukaba Kusamusu Kabane* [Corpses among the weeds on the hill] (Tokyo: Nippon Izokukai, 1965), 91.
34 Gaimusho Nanto Ajia 2-ka (Foreign Ministry Second Southeast Asian Division), "Firipin Kyowakoku no Gaiyo" [Outline of the Republic of the Philippines], January 2016. This is press briefing material distributed to Japanese media in connection with the emperor and the empress's state visit to the Philippines.
35 On the East Asia's recent *rekishi mondai* (history issues) in general, see Tsuyoshi Hasegawa and Kazuhiko Togo, eds., *East Asia's Haunted Present: Historical Memories and Resurgence of Nationalism* (Santa Barbara, CA: ABC-CLIO, 2008) and Thomas Berger, *War, Guilt, and World Politics after World War II* (New York: Cambridge University Press, 2012).
36 See Berger, *War, Guilt, and World Politics*, 175–229.
37 The US military tribunals held in Manila tried 215 alleged Japanese war criminals, 195 of whom were found guilty, 92 were sentenced to death, and 69 were executed. The Philippines military tribunals tried 151; 137 were found guilty, 79 were sentenced to death, and 17 were executed. Eventually, 108 Japanese war criminals were granted amnesty and repatriated to Japan in 1953. Hayashi, *BC-kyu Senpan Saiban*, 61, 83; Nagai, *Firipin to Tainichi Senpan Saiban*, 8.
38 On the Quirino family's ordeal, see Aluit, *By Sword and Fire*, 217–18.
39 Takushi Ohno, *War Reparations and Peace Settlement: Philippines-Japan Relations, 1945–1956* (Manila: Solidaridad Publishing House, 1986).
40 "Excerpts of Speeches Delivered by Delegates at the Japanese Peace Treaty Conference," *New York Times*, 8 September 1951.
41 Nishimura Kumao, *Nihon Gaiko-shi 27: San Francisco Heiwa Jouyaku* [Japan's Diplomatic History, Vol. 27: San Francisco Peace Treaty] (Tokyo: Kashima Kenkyusho Shuppankai, 1971), 267.
42 The reparations included US$200 million for Burma (concluded in November 1955), $223 million for Indonesia (January 1958), and $39 million for Vietnam (May 1959). Miki Y. Ishikida, *Toward Peace: War Responsibility, Postwar Compensation, and Peace Movements and Education in Japan* (New York: iUniverse, 2005), 27.
43 Minutes of Sangi'in Gaiko I'inkai (House of Councillors, Foreign Relations Committee), 3 June 1956, http://kokkai.ndl.go.jp/.
44 Gaimusho, "Firipin Kyowakoku Kihon Deta" (basic information on the Republic of the Philippines), http://www.mofa.go.jp/mofaj/area/philippines/data.html#section6.

45 *Mainichi Shimbun*, 13 November 1962, evening edition, 2; Shoji Junichiro, "Philippine Visit by Emperor Emeritus and Empress Emerita as the Culmination of Their Journey to Pay Tribute to the War Dead," National Institute for Defense Studies (NIDS), *NIDS Commentary* no. 98 (23 December 2019): 2–3, http://www.nids.mod.go.jp/english/publication/commentary/pdf/commentary98e.pdf

46 Koseisho Shakai Engo Kyoku (Ministry of Health and Welfare Bureau of Social Welfare and War Victim's Relief Bureau), ed., *Engo 50 nenshi* [Fifty Years of War Victim Relief] (Tokyo: Gyosei, 1997), 578–9.

47 See the website of the Philippine War Memorial Preservation Association, at http://www.pwmemorial.gr.jp/index3.htm.

48 For more details on Japanese commemorative practices in the Philippines, see Nakano Satoshi, "Politics of Mourning," in Ikehata and Jose, *Philippines-Japan Relations*, 337–76.

49 *Asahi Shimbun*, 5 May 1983, morning edition, 1.

50 *Washington Post*, 11 November 1986, A23. There have been conflicting accounts on what exactly Hirohito said to Aquino at the meeting. Shoji, "Philippine Visit," 1–2.

51 *Nippon Izoku Tsushin* (journal of the JWBA), no. 313 (February 1977).

52 Brochure dated 1995, Memorare–Manila 1945 Papers, Filipinas Heritage Library, Makati, Metro Manila (hereafter Memorare Papers).

53 Requiem Mass program leaflet with lyrics, 18 February 1995, Memorare Papers.

54 Maria Isabel Ongpin, "Ambient Voices," *Today*, 19 February 2005.

55 "Not in February!" *Manila Bulletin*, 22 February 2005. Since 2006, the Friendship Month events have taken place in July. See Lydia N. Yu Jose, "Japan's Soft Power Viewed through the Lens of the Philippines' Commemoration of Historical Events," *Philippine Political Science Journal* 33, no. 2 (2012): 146–60.

56 Bambi L. Harper, "Resentments," *Philippine Daily Inquirer*, 8 November 2005.

57 "Japanese Envoy Expresses Remorse over WWII," *Philippine Daily Inquirer*, 21 October 2005, section 7.

58 Bambi L. Harper, "That Time of Year," *Philippine Daily Inquirer*, 25 January 2006.

59 Remarks by H.E. Ambassador Yamazaki Ryuichiro on the occasion of the 61st Anniversary of the Battle for the Liberation of Manila at Plazuela de Santa Isabel, Intramuros, Manila, 18 February 2006, quoted in Yamazaki Ryuichiro, "Opening Remarks," Yuchengco Institute of Philippines-Japan Relations, *Proceedings of the Symposium: The Philippines-Japan Relationship in an Evolving Paradigm* (Manila: Yuchengco Center, 2006), 3.

60 Bambi L. Harper, "Closure," *Philippine Daily Inquirer*, 21 February 2006.

61 See the media page of the Bridge for Peace website, http://bridgeforpeace.jp/aboutus/english/.

62 Benito Legarda Jr., "A Remarkable 66th," *Philippine Free Press*, 5 March 2011, 18, 33.

63 "Battle of Manila," Malacañan Presidential Museum and Library website, http://malacanang.gov.ph/battle-of-manila/.

64 Including *Umoreta Manira Shigaisen: Shinjitsu wo* [Forgotten Battle of Manila: seeking the truth], *Kokusai Hodo*, NHK-BS1, 4 March 2015, https://www.nhk.or.jp/archives/chronicle/index.html.

65 "Statement by Prime Minister Shinzo Abe on Their Majesties' Visit to the Philippines," 4 December 2015, http://www.mofa.go.jp/press/release/press4e_000950.html.

66 "Remarks by His Majesty the Emperor at the Time of Their Majesties' Departure for the Republic of the Philippines," 26 January 2016, Ministry of Foreign Affairs of Japan, https://www.kunaicho.go.jp/page/okotoba/showEn/3#6.

67 *Asahi Shimbun* reported they bowed for "nearly two minutes." *Asahi Shimbun*, 27 January 2016. As an example of the favorable coverage by the Philippines media, see "Emperor Urges Youth to Learn from WWII," *Philippine Daily Inquirer*, 28 January 2016, http://globalnation.inquirer.net/135733/emperor-urges-youth-to-learn-from-wwii.

68 Shoji, "Philippine Visit," 6–8.

69 James J. Orr, *The Victim as Hero: Ideologies of Peace and National Identity in Postwar Japan* (Honolulu: University of Hawai'i Press, 2001).

PART 3

War Victims

7 Air Raid Victims in Japan's Collective Remembrance of War

JAMES ORR

In the early 1980s, I taught English at an elite boys' secondary school located in the foothills on the west side of Hiroshima. A large bank of windows lined the east side of the teachers' room, affording a clear panoptic view of the city, especially when lit by the late-winter afternoon sun. The historical significance of Hiroshima became a point of discussion on one such afternoon, when I interviewed one of my students as part of his final exam. Until that point, the student had been cheerful, but he turned unexpectedly sullen and resentful. His family was from Tokyo and had experienced the firebombings there, which he told me were every bit as horrific as the atomic bombings in Hiroshima that received so much attention.

I had known about the Tokyo firebombings, of course, but living in Hiroshima I did not hear much about them, as that particular incidence of wartime Japanese suffering was overshadowed by memories and commemoration of the atomic bombings. I had become familiar with the normal Cold War construction of the *hibakusha* (atomic-bomb victim) experience as a form of Japanese national condemnation of nuclear weapons that reflected a determination to avoid becoming embroiled in any war again. I had also encountered an occasional native Hiroshima sentiment of mild resentment over outsiders appropriating the personal local histories of victims to support progressive, anti-government objectives they might not agree with, which one might term a challenge to the authenticity of the public and nationalist discourse in favour of the personal and local. But this first-year high school student's dissent from the Hiroshima narrative was on a different discursive axis, not so much against pacifist objectives as it was against Hiroshima's privilege of place in the national imagination. I have since come to understand such one-upmanship among victims as a kind of competition over commemorative status in what I have elsewhere called a "hierarchy of horror," a competition that has its cousins in Europe and other parts of the world.[1]

This chapter offers a first step toward a comparative genealogy of victim narratives of the Hiroshima and Nagasaki atomic bombings, on the one hand, and the Tokyo and other city fire and air bombings, on the other. For a variety of reasons I discuss below, Hiroshima came to the fore of the national consciousness in the mid-1950s, whereas aerial bombings of Tokyo and more than sixty other cities came to be fully commemorated beginning only in the early 1970s. The contemporary political context then influenced the logic informing the respective atomic and firebomb victim commemorations. In the 1950s, when Japan was a passive participant in the Cold War, the nuclear bombings contributed to a victim discourse that elided Japan's agency for conventional war perpetrations. Collective remembrance and recollection movements of the firebombing and air raid experiences, on the other hand, emerged at the height of the Japanese government's support for the US war in Vietnam in the late 1960s and early 1970s. Popular opposition to this war accordingly encouraged a commemoration of the Second World War that exhibited fuller consciousness of Japanese aggression and therefore partial complicity for the conditions that led to the raids. This consciousness in firebombing remembrance of Japan's responsibility for the war suggests significant comparative differences with German war-victim narratives. Finally, I offer a few observations on human agency and the nature of heroes and victims, and what it means to speak of the victim as hero in a Japanese context that differs considerably from the German.

Hiroshima Becomes an Icon in the Construction of a Pacifist National Ethos

The year 1954 was critical in the emergence of Hiroshima as a central icon for the nation and of atomic bomb victims as symbolic "heroes" of a postwar pacifist Japan. *Hibakusha* became heroes, if you will, not in the conventional sense of soldiers giving their "last full measure of devotion" to the patria but rather in the mythic sense of individuals who symbolized an essential community value. As such, they were deserving of special recognition both at home, in the form of state healthcare and livelihood assistance, and abroad, in the form of formal though circumscribed diplomatic rhetoric against nuclear weapons and their testing. But before that fateful year, although Hiroshima was understood to have been a critical event in the national experience, its prominence in national war remembrance was tempered by several factors.[2]

First, a social stigma surrounded the *hibakusha*. Ignorance of the nature of radiation poisoning, fear of contamination through contact, and a sense of inevitability that an A-bomb survivor might fall ill at any moment despite apparent health: all these encouraged silence and even concealment of one's exposure to the bomb's radiation, lest one be socially ostracized and disadvantaged in work and business. In addition to self-censorship, official Occupation-era censorship suppressed anything – in this case, the reality of horrific human suffering in Hiroshima – thought to be detrimental to the Allied powers' interests.[3] In the early postwar years, Hiroshima was situated in a discourse of competing Cold War ideologies that linked anti-nuclear activism to a communist agenda, which limited the appeal of that activism from the perspective of other points on the political spectrum. At one point, even the Socialist Party avoided anti-nuclear rhetoric out of fear of being labelled "red." Furthermore, the atomic bombing of Hiroshima competed for national attention on a more or less equal footing with the firebombings in Tokyo, Nagoya, Osaka, and other major cities, and with other nationally experienced war privations. Hiroshima's pacifist import was often overshadowed by a Janus-faced discourse over nuclear energy's potential for global salvation or destruction. Finally, the idea that Japan was the only country to be attacked with atomic bombs was contingent, in the face of uncertainty during the Korean War that other nations might also be bombed with nuclear weapons.

All these realities constrained Hiroshima's prominence as a national icon and limited the political and social potential for *hibakusha* to receive state recognition, let alone commemoration, beyond the local level. Or rather, viewed from afar, Hiroshima's global significance transcended the national. There are several episodes that illustrate this, but especially symbolic was the outcome of what is known as the Epitaph Dispute over the meaning of the poem on the Memorial Cenotaph erected in Hiroshima's Peace Park in 1952. The epitaph, translated literally as, "Rest in peace, for the mistake shall not be repeated," appears to leave open the questions of precisely what mistake was being atoned for, and who was doing the atoning. Japanese often omits the grammatical subjects of sentences, so the ambiguity was likely not intended to confuse. On visiting the recently constructed cenotaph, Rabindranath Pal, the sole dissenting judge who had rejected guilty verdicts at the International Military Tribunal for the Far East, interpreted the poem to mean that the Japanese had made the mistake and therefore needed to atone. In characteristic fashion, Pal insisted that the Americans also ought to acknowledge their mistake in bombing Hiroshima and commit to atonement. In reaction to Pal's view, which was rooted in a world view that reified nation states as primary agents, the mayor of Hiroshima as well as the epitaph's author insisted that the implied "we" was whoever stood in front of the cenotaph reading. The main point, however, is that the mayor and the author insisted on a transcendent and globally inclusive vision of Hiroshima as an event equally important to all humanity. This idealist vision seems to have been predominant at the time and is generally characteristic of postwar Japanese pacifism.[4]

Soon after the Occupation ended in 1952, though, conservative forces embarked on their first attempt to revise the postwar peace and civil liberties settlement in order to revive both state-centred nationalist sentiments and more conventional state policies regarding the military. In addition to the famous Article 9 of Japan's postwar constitution, which rejected using military force as an instrument of foreign policy, US Occupation authorities had disbanded the military and also forbade special treatment for veterans, including veteran pensions and solatia for bereaved families. Although the postwar constitution, including Article 9, was still in effect when the Occupation ended, the Japanese government successfully began the process of reinstating these benefits. Even before then, the United States had shifted to pressuring the Japanese to re-establish its military. Prime Minister Yoshida, who until then had resisted a strong remilitarization in favour of policies that supported economic recovery, was also under pressure from his conservative political rivals to re-establish the military services. A National Police Reserve force was founded in the early Korean War years, and, on 1 July 1954, the Japanese military was inaugurated in its current guise, the Self-Defence Forces, or SDF. One of Yoshida's rivals and successor as prime minister, Hatoyama Ichirō, indicated in December 1954 his view that nuclear deterrence made sense if one accepted the logic of peace based on strength.

The remilitarization of Japan did not encounter great resistance, but, in March 1954, a Japanese tuna trawler named the *Lucky Dragon #5* was exposed to radioactive fallout from a hydrogen bomb test at Eniwetok Atoll. The boat was outside the declared danger zone, but the explosion was more powerful than anticipated, and weather patterns had shifted. On return to port, the crew was showing signs of radiation exposure – hair falling out and subcutaneous bleeding – and their catch was radioactive. Ocean-caught fish was a major protein source for Japan in those days, and, with the closure of fish markets nationwide, the Japanese people experienced in a quotidian and nationally constructed manner a shared nuclear vulnerability. Although residual radioactivity in the atmosphere was a global phenomenon, the fact that the *Lucky Dragon* crew was Japanese called attention to the issue of Japanese susceptibility to radioactivity. A petition movement against nuclear weapons testing arose throughout the country, sometimes organized by pre-existing political entities such as local politicians and political arms of labour unions but also, in many cases, by grassroots efforts of concerned citizens such as fishmongers and housewives.

The petition movement found national leadership in a particularly active community centre in Tokyo, Suginami, where a community council was formed to coordinate efforts. The leaders decided to follow a strategy that focused on Japanese nuclear victimhood and avoided Cold War partisanship so as to appeal to Japanese national sympathies across the political spectrum. They encouraged representations of the *Lucky Dragon* incident as the third instance of Japanese nuclear exposure, with the Hiroshima bombing having been the nation's nuclear baptism. What emerged from the movement was a hybrid nationalist movement that rejected ultranationalism and war – explicitly nuclear war, but implicitly any war.

The renewed attention to Hiroshima and Nagasaki privileged Japanese nuclear victimhood over responsibility for Japan's conventional wartime predations and, abetted by the appeal to victim memories in general,[5] led to a tendency to ignore sordid memories of Japanese perpetrations abroad. At home, the *Lucky Dragon* episode and ensuing nationwide anti-nuclear movements raised the *hibakusha* above other domestic victim groups in Japan's hierarchy of war victims. Although *hibakusha* and their advocates had earlier lobbied for state support, it was not until after the *Lucky Dragon* incident that a consensus on their special status emerged, leading to legislation in 1957 that provided them with nationally funded healthcare and livelihood support beyond the general level of welfare available to all Japanese citizens. By the end of the decade, Socialist-sponsored amendments aimed to accord *hibakusha* the same level of support that wounded veterans and bereaved families had received since 1952.[6] Socialist activists for *hibakusha*, at least, attempted in effect to validate anti-nuclear pacifism with state support that implicitly challenged the privileges of war veterans and subverted the conventional notions of a war hero.

We can make three observations about contemporary realities that help explain the timing of Hiroshima's emergence in national remembrance of the Second World War. First, several developments following the Korean War armistice produced a period of relative calm in Cold War tensions and made it seem that perhaps Japan would remain the only country to become a nuclear victim. This status quo was shaped in part by the Geneva meetings regarding French Indochina, Khrushchev's post-Stalin reforms and his policy of "peaceful coexistence," and the early, broad political appeal of Prime Minister Hatoyama's "autonomous diplomacy" (*jiritsu gaikō*) in pursuing rapprochement with the Soviet Union and a foreign policy independent of US hegemony. Second, this period of lessened antagonisms and distrust at either end of the Cold War ideological spectrum also contributed to an environment in which the nationalist construction of nuclear victimhood became more feasible. Third, coming as it did at a time when the Japanese conservative establishment was beginning its first attempt to revise the postwar pacifist settlement, the *Lucky Dragon* incident altered the terrain of remembrance. It refocused attention on feelings of victimhood, which inhibited a return to the more conventional or, as one later advocate of Japanese nuclear arming called it, "normal" state embrace of military power. The shift in focus also hindered a return to more conventional "heroic" narratives involving proactive identification with, and subordination of self to, state interest. Political necessity led all of Hatoyama's conservative political successors to adopt the rhetoric of Japanese exceptional nuclear victimhood, issuing pro-forma protests against nuclear tests even when otherwise they were committed to the security arrangement under the US nuclear umbrella.

Firebombing Recollection Movements

It could be argued that the firebombings and other conventional air raids, which affected over sixty of Japan's major cities, were more truly a shared national, although purely urban, experience than Hiroshima. Early investigation by the Japanese Economic Stabilization Agency in 1949 estimated the firebombings killed 187,000 people, injured 214,000, and made 9 million people homeless.[7] The Tokyo firebombing of 9–10 March alone killed about 100,000 and destroyed the homes of a million people.

Air raids, of course, were routine in Europe, so, in that sense, they were not a uniquely Japanese experience. By all accounts, the firebombings did not gain their place in the narrative of national victimhood until the late 1960s and 1970s, when the war-victim discourse was itself undergoing a second transformation.[8] Why did they emerge only in the late 1960s, and how did this timing affect the character of firebombing remembrance?

One highly significant development was that, by the 1960s, the culture of war-victim commemoration had established itself as legitimate public practice. State commemoration of the war in Japan was, and is still, limited by anxieties over re-establishment of the wartime ethos of subordination and sacrifice to the needs of the state. But in the run-up to the 1964 Tokyo Olympics, there was more openness to nationalist sentiment, as evidenced by a state ceremony commemorating the war's end that subsequently became standard tradition. In 1963 at Hibiya Hall in Tokyo, the emperor read a message expressing regret, condolence for bereaved families, and appreciation to the dead. Due to strong pacifist sentiment among the public, government officials were careful to emphasize in the announcements and interviews leading up to the ceremony that all Japanese victims of the war, military and civilian, were to be memorialized. Reflecting the emerging era of prosperity and high growth in Japan, Chief Cabinet Secretary Kurogane Yasumi told the press on 14 August, "Deeply reflecting that because of the revered sacrifice of over three million we have been given today's peace and development (*heiwa to hatten*), [the service reflects] the whole nation's wish to offer our sincere tribute to their memory."[9]

The notion that war victims had contributed to postwar peace and development reflects an intriguing shift from the ubiquitous early postwar focus on building a nation of peace and culture. In those early postwar years, culture writ large, including engineering and the sciences as well as the arts, was promoted as the proper venue for Japanese aspirations to peace, replacing military-led expansion as the best means to rebuild the nation.[10] Kurogane's statement thus signifies an emergent commemorative culture that valorized war-victim experiences as service to the economically resurgent postwar nation. This commemorative practice was further institutionalized in the mid-1960s, when two major groups of war victims, dispossessed landlords from the early postwar land reform and repatriates (forced returnees) managed to gain state payments in 1965 and 1967, respectively. In both instances, the rationale for the payments valorized the war-victim experience as service to postwar national development.[11] In an era of increasing national pride in economic success, and strong pacifist sentiment that prevented outright glorification of military sacrifice, civilian war victimhood was given rhetorical status within the parameters of conventional, albeit non-military, notions of sacrifice and heroism in service to the state and nation.

A second critical development in the 1960s was the Japanese reaction to the United States' escalation of the war in Vietnam, especially as it concerned the bombing of Hanoi that began in February 1965. *Hokubaku*, as the policy of aerial bombing is called in Japanese, received exceedingly negative reporting in the mainstream Japanese press, and it soured generally favourable views toward America. Discussions of *hokubaku* resonated with Japanese memories of the Second World War aerial bombing of Japanese cities and led to a sympathetic identification with the Vietnamese people as fellow victims of American technological warfare. Beyond the obvious mutual experience of civilian populations being bombed by US air forces, several other coincidences encouraged this identification. First, the twentieth anniversary of the great Tokyo firebombing was in 1965, one month after the US began its aerial bombing of Vietnam. The anniversary received greater journalistic coverage that year than ever before, probably due to a combination of its coincidence with the bombing campaign in Vietnam, the new commemorative culture of war-victim experiences that had emerged in the 1960s, and the possibility that two decades represented a potent latency period for remembrance to occur.[12]

The first substantive article on the recollection movement related to the firebombing is journalist and political commentator Matsuura Sōzō's March 1968 essay in the prominent general interest magazine *Bungei shunjū*. After a heart-rending vignette of one family's loss in the firebombings, Matsuura begins his narrative by noting that, in 1944, American forces retook the Mariana Islands, located latitudinally south of Japan proper, which became the base for US bombing of Japanese cities. Having thus situated the directionality of the US air raids, he refers to the bombing as a *hokubaku* bombing of the north, meaning Tokyo instead of Hanoi, self-consciously applying the Vietnam War term to the Japanese experience. At the end of his essay, Matsuura drives home the linkage. He writes that he was shocked when he learned in December 1964 that the Japanese government had awarded US Air Force General Curtis LeMay – the man responsible for bringing carpet firebombing to Japan after he had been reassigned from the European bombing campaigns in 1945 – the Grand Cordon of the Rising Sun for postwar contributions to building Japan's Air Self-Defence Force. "When I saw this article, I felt as if I had become a Vietnamese." He then references *hokubaku* again after briefly mentioning the "Reischauer incident" of May 1965, in which the foreign editor of the national daily *Mainichi shinbun* newspaper was forced to resign after the US ambassador criticized his reporting of civilian bombing victims in a Hanoi leper hospital. Matsuura pointedly ends his essay with a rhetorical question: "Are the Americans so afraid that the Japanese will, 23 years after the fact, oppose the Vietnam *hokubaku* by linking it to the Tokyo firebombings and air raids on the Japanese homeland?"[13]

The rhetoric of *hokubaku* created a discursive space for a community of pan-Asian war victimhood to emerge, leading a new generation of Japanese peace activists in the 1960s to adopt a more self-aware victim consciousness that energized Japanese pacifist praxis. A central figure in this new generation of political activists was Oda Makoto, who had been a boy of thirteen when his city of Osaka was bombed in 1945. Oda often connected his wartime-victim experiences in firebombed Osaka with the *hokubaku* in Vietnam, and how Japanese government support for the latter made him aware of the interwoven responsibilities of the individual and the state as victim and victimizer in modern warfare. And through his involvement in *Beheiren*, an anti–Vietnam War citizens' movement in Japan, Oda's insight influenced his whole generation. As one compatriot remarked years later, "As a result of visiting Hanoi [under Oda's lead], we self-conscious victims realized that we were victimizers as well."[14] The late 1960s and early 1970s were a time when peace activists and, to some extent, other segments of the Japanese population began to re-examine their myopic tendencies with respect to victim consciousness. But this was also a time when Japanese citizens scrutinized their state's accountability for its own victims. As editor Mori Kyōzō, a veteran of the wartime naval press corps in Southeast Asia, commented in the 3 January 1973 *Asahi shinbun*, "The Japanese people became conscious of their own responsibility for aggression in the Pacific War with the bombing of North Vietnam. It was an awareness that the Japanese military had once prosecuted evil of the same character as the American military."[15] In the language of the day, the discourse on victimhood and war remembrance had gone from one of "war responsibility" to one of "postwar responsibility." Postwar responsibility included acknowledgment of multiple mechanisms of victimhood and perpetration as well as political action forcing Japan's government to take postwar responsibility for wartime crimes against other Asian peoples.

In 1970, years into this transformation of Japan's victim consciousness, a group of air raid survivors and public intellectuals in Tokyo centred on Saotome Katsumoto organized the Society for Recording the Tokyo Air Raids. The next year, Saotome published some of these recollections, and soon similar citizen groups formed in forty other Japanese cities.[16] Over sixty cities were bombed in the war, and, although each city's movements are in some ways unique, they seem to share a common awareness of the complexity of war responsibilities. For example, the Kita Kyushu group, formed in 1972, was careful from the beginning to assert the need to recognize air raid victims' own responsibility for the war's prosecution. Kita Kyushu's case is notable because, by whim of weather, it escaped being subjected to the atomic bomb that found its way instead to Nagasaki. In his 1972 essay "War Responsibility on the 'Home Front,'" Imamura Osamu recounts how war industries were active in the city, employing large numbers of Koreans who were being used as forced labourers in factories. He asserts that, in Kita Kyushu's air raid recollection movement, there was an awareness of these facts as well as reflection on the dangers of seeking peace through military action.[17]

Beyond the collection of personal testimonies, these air raid recollection movements have achieved mixed results in establishing official institutional support for maintaining public memory of the bombings. Although Japan possesses a vibrant citizen-activist community, conservative forces in government have not always embraced their cause. In Tokyo in the 1990s, for example, city and the national governments remained unresponsive to citizen groups' demands for official recognition in the form of a Tokyo Peace Museum. Some fifty years after war's end, city authorities had recorded only 3,930 names of air raid victims. Both financial and political vagaries stymied efforts, but, by the time a Tokyo memorial to the air raid victims was built in 2001 – instead of a more substantial Tokyo Peace Museum – municipal authorities had recorded 68,072 names. The air raid victim memorial ended up being placed in Yokoami Park, the location of the Tokyo charnel house put up originally for the remains of victims of the 1923 Great Kanto earthquake. The memorial, called the Dwelling of Remembrance, does not mention the Asia-Pacific War in its text, much to the chagrin of peace activists. Instead, it situates victimhood in the standard state-sanctioned rhetoric of mourning reminiscent of the inaugural ceremony commemorating war victims in August 1963 – to wit, "to remind succeeding generations that today's peace and prosperity was built on the sacrifices of many precious lives."[18]

Observations on War Victimhood in Japan

This volume problematizes two ideas: (1) what the editors term "authenticity" in regard to self-proclaimed victimhood, and (2) the political ramifications of such claims in potentially post-heroic societies. It could be argued that "authenticity" is not a question historians should try to answer because it is a subjective pursuit that begs normative questions, which, in efforts to escape bias and achieve dispassionate analysis, the discipline of history tends to avoid. Examining the underlying logic of such questions does, however, seem to be fair game. A claim to victimhood may be seen as authentic within the context of one discourse if it is in line with that discourse's starting premises and yet may be viewed as inauthentic in another discourse with other defining concerns. Again, as the editors posit, "by creating new narratives about the past, those events are ascribed a sense of validity and legitimacy."

In the broader discourse of global human rights that emerged at the turn of the twenty-first century, any claim to victimhood that disrespects and diminishes any other victim experience makes such a claim inauthentic. If the underlying motivation of a war-perpetrator group's claim to victimhood – for example, of the civilian German or Japanese air raid victim population – is to oppose the inhumanity of war in principle and to express repugnance toward such inhumanity, then it would seem authentic. It would constitute what Levy and Sznaider, in analysing the controversies surrounding the creation of a European Centre against Expulsions to memorialize postwar forced migration of ethnic German "expellees," would call a form of "cosmopolitanization of memories."[19] But if such a group's aim is ultimately to elicit not just recognition but also exculpation of war guilt by asserting some level of equivalency to its own victims – say, German expellees invoking the language of "ethnic cleansing" to suggest equivalency with Holocaust victims, or victims of Anglo-American air raid campaigns similarly indulging in the language of the Holocaust – it becomes suspect and open to being labelled inauthentic. As a strategy for exculpation of German predations, such efforts would constitute, again following Levy and Sznaider, a form of "renationalization" of collective remembrance.[20] And, to the extent that it diminishes the opprobrium against the original perpetrations, it might abet a return to a more heroic as opposed to post-heroic society. During the Cold War, the East German state's equation of the Dresden bombings with Nazi barbarity served an ideological, as opposed to nationalist, agenda, intended to besmirch the Anglo-American capitalist order – and, not inconsequentially, to obscure Soviet misdeeds. To the degree the claim of victimhood was self-serving, however, it lost authenticity.[21]

Japanese authors' conflation of the United States' bombing of North Vietnam in the late 1960s with the firebombing of Japanese cities in 1945 seems to echo the Cold War East German state's equation of American bombings in either context with Nazi barbarity. But the difference is that the advocates of this view in Japan were generally of the progressive political camp, who usually stood in opposition to the perennially ruling conservative Liberal Democratic Party (LDP) and the state it controlled. Although the postwar constitution's Article 9 peace clause has remained extremely popular, the LDP leadership has shown itself reluctant to acknowledge Japanese culpability for wartime predations. This was perhaps not surprising, given that some of the men in that leadership were also powerful figures during the war. Such leaders included Kishi Nobusuke, who had been arrested as a Class-A war criminal before going on to serve as prime minister in the late 1950s. His half-brother, Sato Eisaku, who also served as prime minister, fully supported the US war in Vietnam during the mid- to late 1960s.

In other words, the discursive aim of claiming a fellowship of air raid victimhood included both a democratic demand that the postwar Japanese state acknowledge wartime predations and address its postwar responsibilities to atone for that guilt and, in addition, a highly political criticism of that very same state for complicity in repeating those predations. This fellowship claim was explicit in speaking truth to power in regard to the state's complicity abroad in North Vietnam, and it was implicit in its criticism of the government's inattentiveness to progressive political demands for moral redress at home. In Germany, where the establishment had more or less accepted the reality of Nazi criminality, the notion of a community of victims is suspect because it threatens to belittle those thought to be more authentically victims. In Japan, however, such transnational empathy played a role in their affirmation.[22]

Postwar Japan's political system is a constitutional monarchy. It was designed by US Occupation reformers to foster a democratic society that safeguarded civil liberties and averted a return of militarism. While there is a strong and persistent conservative revisionist community in postwar Japan, the country's social and political orders present many of the characteristics of Jan-Werner Müller's "post-heroic" age. Postwar Japanese society fits Eyal Lewin's formulation of Müller's post-heroic construct, which applies to a society that "had gone through its violent history of blood and passion, eventually settling its politics and ideologies on the foundation of prosperity and individualism."[23] It also conforms to Herfried Münkler's observation that, "particularly in Europe willingness to kill or to die for one's political community was no longer positively viewed; rather it was referred to as reactionary fanaticism of an archaic nationalistic or religious nature." One thinks most immediately of Japanese peace activist Oda Makoto's famous observation that defeat in the Second World War had turned the "glorious shattering of the jewel," as the wartime phrase termed death in battle, into a "dog's death."[24]

This chapter has contrasted the timing and character of collective Japanese remembrance of the atomic bomb victims and the victims of firebombings and air raids in the Second World War. In both instances, victim consciousness has accommodated itself to the postwar liberal society, though firebomb victim remembrance has, from the beginning, been more conscious of postwar responsibilities to remember Japanese national complicity in the debacle of war making. Remembrance of atomic bomb victims has reflected this raised consciousness from the 1970s as well, and has had an impact in the inclusive policy repercussions for Korean *hibakusha* litigation from that decade.[25] And the rejection of war inherent to the remembrance of war victims has challenged the conventional statist patriotism, the "unquestioned pride and linear or homogeneous national [war] narratives of heroes and victories."[26] This occurred soon after war's end, when the ethic of total devotion to emperor and state was rejected along with faith in the probity of the wartime state's leadership. In ideal-typical form, the "post-traditional culture" posited by Jan-Werner Müller would "indeed also [be] a post-heroic one." Japan's national constitutional culture also "remains not only based on, but also permeable to, national (and subnational) experiences, and in particular narratives of troubling pasts, of oppression and oppression overcome."[27] But Japan's remembrance culture, like most, remains contested.

Elsewhere I have used the phrase "victim as hero" to indicate simply that the war victim became the main trope for remembering the Japanese national war experience, and that advocates of the Japanese war victim strove for equivalence with traditional heroes. Victim groups have been able to situate their experiences in the national imagination so that they could be considered deserving of treatment accorded to war heroes of the more conventional sort – say, those fallen in battle or simply during war mobilization, veterans, and bereaved families. Furthermore, the notion of what constituted "heroism" has been stretched, at least in Japan, to support in contradiction a rejection both of war making and of subordination of the individual's interest to the state – indeed, of sacrifice itself in the rhetoric of that very same sacrifice.

In arguing for state recognition of war victims, progressive advocates in Japan often seek treatment equal to war veterans and their bereaved; this is especially evident in efforts to gain monetary payments. The conventional state levels of recognition have served as the standard for war-victim advocates, and while this strategy is implicitly a challenge to the conventional state valorization of war heroism, this leads, as we have seen, to a national and local government co-optation of rhetoric that compromises the antiheroic position of war victims. This is evident in the language of sacrifice, of deaths serving postwar peace and prosperity, a rhetoric with slippage that permits both a resolution for peace and a potential for return to conventional state patriotism. The former "peace" trope for the moment symbolizes the pacifist heritage of victim consciousness emerging from the tragedy of the war as well as the postwar civil liberty society. The "prosperity" trope reflects economic nationalism and the potential for a return to patriotism as well as a continuation of a peaceful and orderly society, with which civil liberties overlap. After all, in official ceremonies and memorial language, the authoritative city and national government representatives have resisted any intimation that traditional military service was any less heroic because, to channel Münkler, it was archaic, reactionary, or fanatic.

If we have entered a new "post-heroic" age, then it makes sense that such terms in the popular arena should accrue new meanings suitable to the dominant ideologies of our day. The end of the twentieth century witnessed the rise of a global human rights ideology that insists on recognizing victims of all sorts and compels societies to act responsibly to make amends for past mistreatment. This ideology insists fundamentally on the dignity of victims and the necessity of according them some agency. Yet it seems clear from state co-optation of victim remembrance, as seen in the Tokyo Yokoami Park memorial cited above, that the older trope of heroism, of service and sacrifice to possibly questionable state interests, remains strong in Japan. This is so even as the rejection of the older trope is a strong motivation in peace activists' programs to gain recognition of victim suffering.

So, in the end, perhaps a reformulation of our definition of "heroic" is in order, granting human agency in resisting one's own victimization in ways that are socially constructive. In the old and persistent order, fighting back and seeking revenge have been seen as one heroic method of asserting agency and overcoming victimhood. The recurring anti-Japanese protests by angry Chinese students in 2006 and 2012, full of condemnation of Japan for its wartime predations against China, righteously conflate the personal with the interests of the nation state. Protestors seek agency through reversing the victim dynamic, asserting the authenticity of their own victimhood – or, at any rate, that of their collective ancestors – at the hands of the Japanese. Yet the twentieth century has provided other examples of overcoming victim experiences through transcendence of divisive, vengeance-seeking identities, along the lines of Gandhi or Mandela. Japanese A-bomb and firebomb victims, and their progressive activists, are decidedly not apologists for Japan's war actions. Rather, they seek to remember their nation's troubling past, they seek to transcend disparate interests that attend competing identities, and they seek that transcendence responsibly, in ways that respect their obligations to their own victims. The efforts to commemorate the war-victim experience, and to define the character of the victim as hero, nonetheless remain contested.

NOTES

1 James J. Orr, review of *The Nanjing Massacre in History and Historiography*, ed. Joshua A. Fogel (Berkeley: University of California Press, 2000), *Journal of World History* 14, no. 3 (2003): 423–5.
2 For an early treatment of this process, see James J. Orr, *The Victim as Hero: Ideologies of Peace and National Identity in Postwar Japan* (Honolulu: University of Hawai'i Press, 2001): 36–70.
3 Similar horrors were, of course, also unleashed on Nagasaki. References to Hiroshima in this chapter generally refer to the experiences of both cities attacked with atomic bombs.
4 Hiro Saito, "Reiterated Commemoration: Hiroshima as National Trauma," *Sociological Theory* 24, no. 4 (December 2006): 366–7.
5 See the chapter by Andreas Wirsching in this volume.
6 See Orr, *Victim as Hero*, 142–8.
7 Bret Fisk and Cary Karacas, "The Firebombing of Tokyo and Its Legacy: Introduction," *Asia-Pacific Journal* 9, issue 3, no. 1 (January 2011), http://apjjf.org/2011/9/3/Bret-Fisk/3469/article.html.
8 Karacas argues that the delay in returning the firebombing experiences to a prominent place in this discourse was due to Occupation censorship, the postwar fixation on high growth (which diverted attention), a fear among Japanese conservatives of alienating their US alliance partners, and the fact that the firebombing was not an exclusively Japanese experience. Cary Karacas, "Place, Public Memory, and the Tokyo Air Raids," *Geographical Review* 100, no. 4 (2010): 524, 528. In school textbooks, one does find marginally increased treatment of the air raids and evacuation of schoolchildren, and certainly Tokyo Shoseki's 2017 edition of its major elementary school textbook, *Atarashii shakai* (*shakai* 631), presents a vivid two-page spread on fire-ravaged cities.
9 *Asahi Evening Edition*, 14 August 1963. The annual ceremony was held at the Yasukuni Shrine in 1964 but has been held every year since in the Nippon Budōkan.
10 Orr, *Victim as Hero*, 77ff.
11 Ibid., 137–72.
12 A keyword search on the news corporation Yomiuri's *Yomidasu rekishikan* database of articles reveals an increase in the number of related articles beginning with the 10 March 1965 morning edition of the flagship *Yomiuri shinbun*.
13 Matsuura Sōzō, "Kakarezaru Tōkyō daikūshū," *Bungei shunjū* 46, no. 3 (1968): 147, 156. The *Mainichi* foreign editor was Ōmori Minoru. George R. Packard, *Edwin O. Reischauer and the American Discovery of Japan* (New York: Columbia University Press, 2010), 224. See also Tsuruki Makoto,

"Surveillance Function of Mass Media and Frames of International Events," *Journal of Mass Communication Studies* 55 (1999): 99–103. This "Reischauer incident" should not be confused with the March 1964 assassination attempt on the same person.

14 Konaka Yōtarō, "Oda Makoto: Hanoi kara minami Taiheiyō e'nanshi' to 'kyōsei,'" in *Sengo bungaku to Ajia*, ed. Nihon Ajia and Afurika Sakka Kaigi (Tokyo: Mainichi Shinbunsha, 1978), 105, as quoted in Orr, *Victim as Hero*, 4.

15 As quoted by Ubukata Naokichi, "Tōkyō saiban o meguru shoronten: 'jindō ni tai suru tsumi' to jikō," *Shisō* 719 (May 1984): 106.

16 Karacas, "Place," 525–6.

17 Imamura Osamu, "Kakusho: 'kengo' no senso sekinin – Kūshū taiken no undo no naka de," *Shiso no kagaku* 10 (November 1972): 101–5.

18 Karacas "Place," 533.

19 Daniel Levy and Natan Sznaider, "Memories of Universal Victimhood: The Case of Ethnic German Expellees," *German Politics and Society* 23, no. 2 (75) (2005): 1–27.

20 Ibid. See also Annette Seidel Arpaci, "Lost in Translations? The Discourse of 'German Suffering' and W.G. Sebald's *Luftkrieg und Literatur*," in *A Nation of Victims: Representations of German Wartime Suffering from 1945 to the Present*, ed. Helmut Schmitz (Amsterdam: Brill, 2007): 161–79.

21 Thomas C. Fox, "East Germany and the Bombing War," in *Bombs Away: Representing the Air War over Europe and Japan*, ed. Wilfried Wilm and William Rasch (Amsterdam: Brill, 2006), 113–30; Gilad Margalit, "Dresden and Hamburg: Official Memory and Commemoration of the Victim of Allied Air Raids in the Two Germanies" in Schmitz, *Nation of Victims*, 125–40.

22 For a related discussion of victim consciousness in Asia, see James J. Orr, "Victims and Perpetrators in National Memory: Lessons from Post–World War Two Japan," *Schweizerische Zeitschrift für Geschichte* 57 (2007): 42–57.

23 Eyal Lewin, *Ethos Clash in Israeli Society* (Lanham, MD: Lexington Books, 2013), 46.

24 Oda has used this phrasing in several of his writings. See *"Nanshi" no shiso* [The philosophy of the "Dog's Death"] (Tokyo: Iwanami Shoten, 1991). In English, see Oda Makoto, *The Breaking Jewel*, trans. Donald Keene (New York: Columbia University Press, 2003).

25 See, for example, Toyonaga Keisaburō, "Colonialism and Atom Bombs: About Survivors of Hiroshima Living in Korea," in *Perilous Memories: The Asia-Pacific War(s)*, ed. T. Fujitani, Geoffrey M. White, and Lisa Yoneyama (Durham, NC: Duke University Press, 2001), 378–94.

26 Jan-Werner Müller, *Constitutional Patriotism* (Princeton, NJ: Princeton University Press, 2007), 63.

27 Ibid.

8 Between Memory and Policy: How Societies of Leningrad Siege Survivors Remember the War

TATIANA VORONINA

In his book on the history of veterans' organizations in Australia, Alistair Thomson wrote: "Our memories are risky and painful if they do not conform with the public norms or versions of the past. We compose our memories so that they will fit with what is publicly acceptable, or, if we have been excluded from general public acceptance, we seek out particular publics which affirm our identities and the way we want to remember our lives."[1] Thomson was writing about Australian veterans who had served in the First World War, the legacy of which played a crucial role in the construction of Australian national identity. As an oral historian, he was interested in how veterans interpreted legends of the Great War in their individual narratives.

When considering how popular official, heroic narratives of the past were perceived among veterans, Thomson referred to the concept of "popular memory." By this, he meant that the memories and stories of eyewitnesses are complex combinations of both their own experiences and subsequent interpretations of that experience. Thomson wrote:

> We compose our memories to make sense of our past and present lives. "Composure" is the aptly ambiguous term used by the Popular Memory Group [a research network of oral historians at the University of Birmingham] to describe the process of memory making. In one sense we "compose" or construct memories using the public language and meanings of our culture. In another sense we "compose" memories, which help us to feel relatively comfortable with our lives, which gives us a feeling of composure. We remake or repress memories of experiences which are still painful and "unsafe" because they do not easily accord with our present identity, or because their inherent traumas or tensions have never been resolved. We seek composure, an alignment of our past, present and future lives.[2]

This observation also holds true with regard to the memories of those who survived the Leningrad Blockade, and the similarities are not limited to the way in which popular memories are composed. The memories of both the First World War and the Siege of Leningrad are traumatic ones. There are also similarities in the way that personal experiences from each event became represented in the "legend," as Thomson called it, or the particular image of the events reproduced in national culture and used as a basis of national pride. Survivors of the Siege of Leningrad, like the Australian veterans, have been both subjects and exponents of the process of myth building, and, consequently, they have become both beneficiaries of and hostages to those myths.

Aleida Assmann describes four major kinds of memories that are determined by the "space-time range" involved, the group's size, and the consistency or stability of the memories. For her examination, Assmann establishes as her levels of analysis the individual, the social group, the nation, and culture.[3] She argues that the "social" category of memory belongs to a whole generation: "Every generation creates its own attitude towards its past, denying attempts of the previous generation to impose another point of view. Frictions inside the social memory are obvious; they're triggered by values and needs that are typical for different generations and set certain frames for memories, however temporary."[4]

For Assmann, "collective memory" differs from individual and social memory, in that it is embodied in symbols. These symbols become the focal points for future memories and ensure the continuity of those memories for the next generation. Monuments, memorials, anniversaries, and rituals strengthen commemoration from one generation to the next through material signs and repetition. They enable subsequent generations that did not directly experience an event to take part in the common memory of it. The memories articulated by organizations of Leningrad siege survivors are typical of this type of collective memory, although they originated as a kind of social memory.

Why do groups of witnesses who belong to different cultural contexts describe and evaluate the same event so differently? Is the difference due primarily to cultural variations in how they remember? A further example might shed light on these questions. In July 2008, the German government agreed to the demands of the "Claims Conference" – the shorthand name of the Conference on Jewish Material Claims against Germany, which was founded in 1951 to ensure compensation and restitution to Holocaust survivors – to accord Jewish survivors of the Leningrad Blockade the same status as Holocaust survivors and pay €2,556 to each of them. This entitlement was given to

Jews then living in Israel and in other Western countries who had been present in Leningrad between 8 September 1941 and 27 January 1944 or who had been evacuated during the siege. This agreement was barely covered by Russian media. The few observers who did take notice of it criticized the German government for distinguishing between Jewish and non-Jewish victims of the Siege of Leningrad, a decision that overlooked the majority of victims. Such criticism, however, ignored the fact that Russian survivors' organizations had raised no claims with the commission.

It is somewhat puzzling why Russian survivors who actually had inhabited the besieged city, and later came together in social organizations, did not seize the opportunity to request compensation from Germany for their suffering. An explanation can be found through an analysis of the policies regarding memory of the siege as it is embedded in the social organization of the witnesses.

According to Assmann, the foundation of national memory is composed of the historical images that belong to the witnesses and participants of an event. She suggests that the survivors of a tragedy interpret their own historic roles in a variety of ways, depending on their specific culture. Some groups perceive their experience as a sacred, and therefore meaningful, sacrifice for ideals, their future, their homeland, family, and so on. Such sacrifices are integrated in official historical narratives and become a basis of pride and of a positive identity. Other groups of witnesses may consider themselves as purely "victimized" and therefore fail to see anything positive in the past event, either for the state or for themselves. For them, the traumatic experience of suffering and shame can hardly find its way into memory, since this experience cannot be integrated into a positive notion of a person or a nation about itself.[5]

Assmann contends that the sacralization of victimhood represents the first step that a nation takes when healing from historical trauma. The second step is to reconsider the trauma, using categories of humanistic discourse, such as labelling it a crime against humanity, thereby taking the event out of the context of specific national laws and treating it more broadly. This linear scheme, however, seems artificial when one considers the fact that Holocaust survivors have effected not only a reappraisal of the Second World War in Europe but also a rejection of heroically oriented nationalist histories. In this way, Holocaust survivors have moved past the "heroization" stage: victims of concentration camps have never been considered sacred sacrifices made in the name of victory. Meanwhile, groups of war veterans – be they in Australia, Russia, the United States, or other countries – have never become "senseless victims," as Holocaust survivors have.[6] Both groups – war heroes and victims – emphasize the authenticity of their versions of the past in order to legitimize their positions. This happens in both cases despite the connection between the conceptualization of authenticity and the process of self-victimization.[7] In Russian social studies, this phenomenon is reminiscent of Irina Kaspe's concept of documentation.[8]

The authenticity of the witness has played an important role in the formation of public memory in the Soviet Union, but the witnesses have not always participated in this process as active subjects. In the case of the blockade, the authenticity of the witness narrative was important in legitimizing the official interpretation of the past. However, authenticity in narratives of the blockade took different forms at different points in the past. During the war, authenticity was ascribed to the testimony of writers and poets who saw and described the blockade from the point of view of socialist realism. As a result, one of the main authors who wrote about the blockade was the chairman of the Union of Writers of the USSR, Alexander Fadeyev. Fadeyev did not experience the blockade personally, but he created works that were incorporated into the canon of siege literature as an authentic description of the event.[9] Perhaps even more drastic was the fact that many Leningrad poets and writers who were present inside the city during the blockade were forced to abandon their memories for the sake of the new, officially authenticated version of the Soviet past. This version upheld a personal story of heroism, but not of catastrophe. Other, alternative memory narratives, even those created during the blockade, did not become a source of public knowledge on the history of the event.

During the 1960s, notions of authenticity were ascribed not to the memories of military commanders and party leaders, as had been the case earlier, but to the experiences of ordinary people. Associations of survivors of the Leningrad Blockade – also formed in the 1960s, after having obtained permission from the state to create such organized communities – acted to legitimize this new version of the past. These associations could not change the canonical image of the event that had existed up until that point, but they could supplement it with references to personalized subjects and memories such as the history of childhood during the blockade.

However, the most acute questions about the authentic history of the blockade arose only during perestroika, when struggles for the legalization and domination of past memories intensified. Against the backdrop of a crisis in Soviet historiography and widespread mistrust in Russian society, the championing of authentic siege history, as remembered by witnesses, seemed like a panacea for the lies of Soviet interpretations. The survivors who wrote memoirs during those years contributed to this perspective, asking, "For whom is history written if not for us, soldiers of the war university?"[10] Becoming more and more influential agents of memory, blockade societies actively assumed the role of the only honest, authentic interpreters of the past, closing their eyes to the fact that their own memories were composed using social and public memories in addition to their individual ones. Thus, their way of interpreting the past was quite consistent with those versions already in existence. As a result, the "authentic" history of the blockade in late Soviet society became associated not so much with the experience of a particular person but with their chosen method of representation. If the story was built with the Soviet narrative in mind, it was considered authentic and legitimate.[11] If not, it was ignored and remained unnoticed in the public space.

Therefore, social group memory is not just an outgrowth of ideas generated by a community of people about their experiences. It is also a site of political battles and arguments within a community, especially with regard to economic, political, or symbolic resources. As Paul Ricœur has noted, those who tell history through their own power are active agents who shape collective ideas.[12] They often tell or write the history in a specific way that reflects their own interests or the interests of groups they represent. Pierre Bourdieu's concept of social fields of cultural production offers a key to understanding their behaviour. In light of Bourdieu's framework, I suggest that public representations of collective notions or versions of the past are, in part, the manifestations of agents of various social fields who are working to strengthen their position within their own realms. I see memory of the past as part of cultural production as well as a means for certain agents to dominate and legitimize their positions.

At the end of the twentieth century, fields of cultural production in different countries had their own specific features and unique rules regarding the regulation of access to resources. Some of them, including those in Russia, cultivated heroism and a sacral understanding of past deeds of heroes, while others, like those in Germany, tended to emphasize the helplessness and defencelessness of victims. In both cases, group memories were closely connected to cultural, economic, and political processes in the society, and cannot be explained solely based on the witnesses' own views of their past trauma. The societies of survivors of the Siege of Leningrad provide some of the clearest evidence for this view.

The Origins of Siege-Survivor Societies in Leningrad

For much of the Soviet period, politicians, along with well-connected historians and writers, defined the policies regarding memory of the Second World War and laid the foundation for future narratives about the conflict. After the change in political leadership following Stalin's death in 1953, artistic and historical works became less dependent on state decisions. Moreover, the earlier taboo against discussing the blockade was lifted. That taboo had dated from the Leningrad Affair – the political repression of prominent politicians and leaders of wartime Leningrad that was initiated in 1946 during the postwar power play among Stalin's political favourites and that peaked between 1949 and 1952. Things changed in 1956, when the new general secretary, Nikita Khrushchev, delivered an address to the Twentieth Congress of the Communist Party of the Soviet Union entitled "On the Cult of Personality and Its Consequences," and subsequently launched a specific attack on the role of the late leader. He effectively removed the Stalin cult from public discourse and, in the process, reinterpreted the victory in the Second World War as an achievement of the Soviet nation and the Communist Party, not of Stalin. In the years following the address, Khrushchev's stance was adopted and developed by historians, journalists, and a variety of other public figures. The memory of the war emerged as one means through which to educate youth about Soviet patriotism.[13]

By the 1960s, various fields of Soviet cultural production (literature, law, science, and the like) contributed new features to the memory of the war, especially as new agents entered the playing field. One such agent was the Lenin Komsomol (Communist Youth Organization). Leaders of Komsomol frequently made speeches about the connections between generations – the current, young one and the older, heroic one of wartime – and often used (typically preapproved) witness testimonies as a source of didactic material about the past. Through these speeches, they encouraged average citizens to talk about their war experience and thus to re-examine – along with party leaders, professional historians, and writers – the wartime past. These speeches, however, rarely reached a wide audience. Komsomol leaders of the 1960s were not the first to rely on oral and written memoirs recounting the heroic past of the country. This was an old technique of political education. Even in the 1930s, Soviet schoolchildren regularly met individuals who had participated in the revolution of 1917 and studied their versions of the past. For instance, the most widely known association, which existed from 1921 to 1935, was the Society of Former Political

Prisoners and Deportees, which was led by top members of the Soviet bureaucracy. Felix Dzerzhinsky was among its founding members. In 1924, the society was transformed into a nationwide organization with dozens of branches all over the USSR. It united Bolsheviks who had been active prior to the revolution. It also was designed to provide former political prisoners and deportees with material assistance; organize lectures and reports; and collect, store, and publish materials on tsarist prisons, penal servitude, and internal exile.[14] The participation of top Soviet politicians was not a coincidence: they were present in order to control both the society's activities and the image of the past that it disseminated. It is obvious that the majority of works that the society published were heavily censored. The state, therefore, used old revolutionaries to articulate its truths and to reinforce its own legitimacy. To participate in such a society was considered a demonstration of loyalty toward the authorities and included many privileges.

The first society of survivors of the Siege of Leningrad was nothing like the earlier society of tsarist political prisoners, especially given past taboos against discussion of the blockade. But, eventually, the interests of siege survivors started to coincide with those of Soviet propagandists, and the survivors came to represent a social group with growing self-awareness and public recognition. Valery Selivanov was one of the founders of the organization, which originally was part of Leningrad's regional committee of the Komsomol. He described the establishment of the first society of siege survivors in his memoir, explaining that, in the 1960s, he was one of the founders of two societies: The Union of Orphans of Besieged Leningrad and The Union of Young Participants in the Defence of Leningrad. The latter organization was organized in Leningrad in 1968 as the result of an event, arranged by the Leningrad Komsomol committee, to honour those who were schoolchildren during the blockade and to award them the For the Defence of Leningrad medal. They were invited to take part in a ceremony for the erection of a monument called the Flower of Life, which was located on the "Road of Life."[15] This monument was dedicated to the children of the besieged city.

At the first meetings of this newly formed group, elections were held for a leadership board that would oversee the administration and tasks of the union. The Museum of the History of St. Petersburg hosted the meetings and played an influential role in the early growth of the siege-survivor movement. Hence, one of the current memorial exhibitions dedicated to the siege is housed in a branch of this museum.[16] The board met twice per month and initially was called *Poisk* (Search), since one of its main tasks was to locate and contact former schoolchildren who survived the siege and were awarded the For the Defence of Leningrad medal.[17] Its second major task was to educate current youth: members of the union volunteered to visit schools and share their experiences of the siege with the younger generation. The board mainly included people who were teaching in city high schools or universities. This is how Valery Selivanov, a history teacher in the Nakhimov Naval Academy and then a member of the regional committee of Leningrad Komsomol, became involved. He later became a deputy of the Legislative Assembly of St. Petersburg and one of the authors of several bills regarding siege survivors. Other founding members of the organization were also active members of the party and Komsomol, and some held chairs in Communist Party history at city universities.

The memoirs written by members of the administrative board of the Young Participants in the Defence of Leningrad show that they arranged talks with Leningrad schoolchildren. Some members told stories of having attended music school during the war, and others recalled various remarkable and peculiar incidents of their lives during the siege. We can be quite certain that the status of participants and the objective of the meetings (what new things about the siege can one share with schoolchildren?) together determined in advance the range of subjects that were discussed. The storytellers were well educated and well grounded ideologically; they did not, however, always demonstrate great sensitivity in choosing themes to be shared with their young audiences. One of the members of the society described her meetings with schoolchildren in the following way:

> I've told them, you see, how people studied, how we studied. How much heroism is there in that? There is nothing heroic about it, but everyone carried out their duties. And when … if people stopped carrying out their duties, the city would have simply lost everything, because there were justifications for panic about every awful thing that might come as a result of the war. Everyone was busy and everyone somehow expected the best, hoping for victory. Everyone had hope, though why should they? I don't get this … When you talk to older ones, you put it in a more serious way … You start talking about – in particular, I always start by saying I'm no heroine, that I was afraid throughout the whole siege. Though my award is the same as soldiers' and generals', I don't consider myself a heroine. A true heroine … a hero, it was the whole city. The city's heroism was in the lack of panic, in the lack of chaos, in everyone doing … doing their own task. This is our city's wonder. It's our city's miracle.[18]

The fact that these history lessons revolved around civilian heroes of the siege, rather than soldiers, was an important symptom of social changes. Although their personal narratives were shaped to coincide with the usual siege themes – for example, the heroism or uniqueness of Leningrad as a city – there was still a place for the uniqueness of individual experience. As a result, the notion of heroism expanded. From then on, it included description of daily routines of "typical schoolchildren under siege." The topic of "siege childhood" became for a unifying theme for members of the first societies of siege survivors. Over time, it did not fade into obscurity but rather became one of major themes in collections of articles written in the 1980s, when some siege survivors began taking an academic approach to the topic.[19]

It is notable that the initiative for creating the first organizations of siege survivors came from the regional committee of the Komsomol. At that time, the activists in the Young Participants in the Defence of Leningrad were approximately forty years old. It is also notable that the board of administrators was elected from people working in Leningrad's educational system, many of whom were also members of the Communist Party. At this early stage in the society's existence, therefore, it was assumed that its members would educate Leningrad's younger generation in a way that would foster patriotism as well as pride in their city and country. This desire is evidenced by one of the formal requirements for joining the newly created society: prospective members must have received the For the Defence of Leningrad medal. One of the obligations of medal recipients was to impart to younger generations why they had received this decoration. This requirement partially guaranteed that siege survivors would heavily incorporate notions of victory and heroism in their memories, which was in line with the siege narratives disseminated by the media and cinema.[20]

The founding society members performed specific rituals each year on Victory Day, observed in Russia on 9 May to celebrate the victory over Nazi Germany, in order to strengthen connections between the generations. One such annual ritual, as described by a board member, began with a joint procession of Pioneers (Soviet Scouts) and siege survivors from the nearest railway station, Rzhevka, to the Flower of Life monument, where they then held a meeting. The final stage of the event was tying the Pioneers' scarves around birches of the memorial alley and placing a floral wreath on the monument: putting "flowers for the Flower."[21] Thirty years later, this ritual is still performed, though the young participants are regular schoolchildren of St. Petersburg instead of Soviet Pioneers.

Another ritual connected to the memorial, starting in January 1970, was a winter marathon dedicated to the memory of the siege. The distance of the race was first chosen by athletes who were siege survivors.

It started at the *Razorvannoe koltso* (Broken Ring) monument and followed the route between Lake Ladoga and Leningrad; the final metres led through the memorial alley of the Flower of Life complex.[22] This athletic event better established the memorial, which was far from Leningrad and not as popular as the other tourist sites in the city. In addition, it emphasized the importance of the monument and the connection between generations, since the race has been traditionally open to athletes of all ages.

The opening of the Flower of Life monument was timed to coincide with the fiftieth anniversary of the Komsomol's founding, celebrated in October 1968. The related festivities included several patriotic events including, for example, a skiing trip called the Heroes' Ski Run, routed through battle sites of the Leningradsky and Volkhovsky fronts. The events also included storytelling about "heroes and feats" and meetings with veterans, which were advertised in the Leningrad Komsomol's official newspaper of the Leningrad Komsomol, *Smena* (Shift or Successors).[23] One announcement invited "former partisans of the Komsomol detachment of the Second Partisan Brigade" to the newspaper's editorial office to meet "tourists from 'Volna' (Wave) and 'Saturn'" clubs from the Moscow region before their departure on a twenty-day skiing trip around the territory where partisans had been active during the war. The newspaper urged "all comrades who were fighting in the Komsomol detachment to come to meet the pathfinders."[24] Another announcement invited former soldiers and officers of the Komsomol firefighting regiment.[25] The reunion of former schoolchildren of the siege had many analogues in Soviet commemorative culture. They all created a channel for dialogue between generations, in which youth were supposed to learn from the example of older comrades. Nevertheless, only the former schoolchildren were able to establish a sustainable society of united like-minded participants.

It is remarkable that the siege-survivor movement was spearheaded by relatively young people, who had been children, not adults, during the blockade. The reason these individuals formed the first siege-survivor society is that they were eager to relate the history of the siege from the point of view of children, which had not yet been represented in literature, film, or scholarship. Members of the older generation were already portrayed in official depictions as heroes participating in battles and defending the city, but the younger generation of survivors felt the need to legitimize their status as heroic participants in these events. One individual who had survived the siege as a child articulated this common sentiment: "[The adults] were victorious, they were the generation of winners; we, the children, were behind this generation. They did not have to compete for anything, literally nothing, they got a green light everywhere."[26] The conflict between different generations of survivors reminds us of Assmann's thoughts on the social – that is, generational – memory of witnesses. According to her observations, the young generation's version of the past contradicts the "older" one.[27] The overall situation creates tensions and makes society seek a range of symbols and meanings for the event that are acceptable to all sides of this intergenerational discussion. In 1968, the younger generation was still forming its collective identity, so the process of interacting with that of the older generation was still new. The newer identity transformed especially during *perestroika*, when arguments between siege survivors of different generations and societies became a common feature of life in the city.

It is worth mentioning that one's status as an older or original member of a survivor's society – a "true hero" – later became a sort of capital that could be used to gain importance and administrative authority within that society. For example, in 1990, many societies of siege survivors typically appointed or elected the oldest member as their leader, as he or she had the For the Defence of Leningrad medal, while the younger members, often people without that medal, did the actual work of the organization.[28] The younger generation often created these societies in response to the widespread conception of siege heroism that presumed that the elder generations who had worked at city factories had been more heroic than the child survivors.[29] The aim of these organizations was to fight for rights and privileges of younger siege survivors not yet officially recognized by the state as heroes.

During and just after the war, the heroism of siege survivors was defined narrowly as having fulfilled one's duty to the state either by having fought in the Red Army or by having worked in city factories. As for the war years, the notion of heroism was reserved almost exclusively for those involved in the military defence of Leningrad. The For the Defence of Leningrad medal was established on 22 December 1942 by decree of the Presidium of the Supreme Soviet of the USSR and was awarded first to professional soldiers and conscripts in the Red Army and then to civilians who had worked to strengthen the city's defence lines, volunteers in local air defence brigades, and employees of local defence factories.[30] The dominant versions of the siege narrative emphasized working adults as heroes. People who, as children, had served in the Russian navy's Baltic Fleet during the siege had been decorated for their service, so it was not a coincidence that a society called the Sea Cadets of the Baltic Navy emerged not long after the Young Participants of the Defence of Leningrad appeared.

There is, however, another explanation for the official emphasis on children. The theme of children's participation in the Great Patriotic War was adopted early on by Soviet propagandists and then perpetuated by writers. It resonated with the cult of heroic Pioneers, which developed between the late 1940s and early 1950s and was captured in Alexander Fadeev's novel *Molodaya Gvardiya* (*The Young Guard*), which focused on high school students from Volgodonsk who fought against the Nazi occupiers. The major themes of this work were the Soviet teenagers' heroic battle against fascism and their courage, fortitude, and sacrifice for victory. The novel became extremely popular, and school athletic teams, ships, and city streets were named after its characters. Leningraders not only reproduced the novel's heroic narratives about Komsomol heroes from Volgodonsk but also created new, local ones. For example, a monument to young heroes of the defence of Leningrad was built in 1962 in Tavrichesky Garden at the initiative of the Leningrad regional committee of the Komsomol. The sandstone stela depicted a half-destroyed wall with the figures of four Pioneers carved into it. Above the figures is the dedication "To young heroes of the defence of Lenin's city." On the rear of the monument, another inscription reads "This monument was built to the courage and will of the brave, their selfless feats, all heroes-pioneers, by the young hands of Leninists."[31]

The image of children in wartime occupied an ambivalent place in Soviet culture. It represented, on the one hand, the readiness of all Soviet people, regardless of age, to sacrifice their lives for the victory and salvation of their motherland, but at the same time, wartime literature and posters used figures of children as symbols of innocent victims of Nazism. Soviet literature on the siege, written both by and for adults, portrayed children as less politically conscious survivors, given their tender age. It was acceptable to portray children of the siege as suffering or helpless, whereas adults were uniformly and obligatorily depicted as optimistic heroes. In this way, authors were able to convey the harsh reality without violating the boundaries of the socialist-realist canon. It made their depictions more realistic and closer to the images of the blockade described in children's diaries of the siege.[32] The younger generation of siege survivors accordingly crafted their biographies with attention to heroes of Soviet artistic works. Their social memory included a more tragic view of the siege, even given the parameters of official Soviet narratives, which they enriched with new details and plots.

As a result, by the late 1960s, there was a basis to form a society of heroic Pioneers who had survived the Leningrad Blockade. As they organized themselves, the existing interpretations that stressed the heroism of working adults, not children, gradually weakened. The status of the siege heroes changed even more during the perestroika of the late 1980s and early 1990s, for two reasons. First, the older generation of siege survivors had largely passed away. Second, in 1994, the state recognized almost the entire population of the besieged city as heroes. The first society of survivors, created by the Komsomol and former schoolchildren, was already oriented toward this broader view of heroism. The heroes of the siege, like war veterans, had their own society that enabled them to perpetuate memories of the siege from the perspective of former schoolchildren and to communicate this to younger generations. At first, the Young Participants in the Defence of Leningrad focused on this objective and not on their rights as a labour union lobbying for benefits.

Perestroika and the Institutionalization of Siege-Survivor Societies

Perestroika set several political and economic changes in motion that influenced questions of historical memory. Politicians and public activists engaged in a fight for the past, and they justified their goals by linking them to historical developments and revisionist interpretations. The historical symbolism of Leningrad turned out to be a powerful rallying point both among those in favour of perestroika, because they saw Leningrad as a stronghold of independence and democracy, and among conservative communists who still adhered to Soviet ideology. The siege became a matter of utmost importance for social activists who were becoming engaged in politics at this time. Since the 1990s, hailing from St. Petersburg was itself a badge of honour. At that time, the city was considered not only the "cradle of the Revolution" but also the "cradle of Russian democracy." The Russian democrats of the 1990s believed that the authorities in Leningrad had pursued politics independent from the Kremlin, that Leningrad had always (even in Soviet times) had more potential for democracy than elsewhere in the country, and that the Siege of Leningrad had demonstrated the city's capacity for independence.[33] The communists, on the other hand, regarded the siege as an event that had revealed the power of communist ideas and ideals. They emphasized the fact that the city's leadership during the siege represented the Communist Party. On both sides, politicians recognized the siege as a crucial event that could be used to support the arguments of very different ideologies and people.[34] The siege was a frequent topic, not only among politicians but also among civil activists and, of course, among siege survivors themselves.

The identity of the siege survivor held considerable social value both before and after the collapse of the USSR. It could be used to one's advantage in certain situations – for example, in negotiations with state authorities for better housing or in resolving social disputes.[35] Still, the heroization of siege survivors remained incomplete, particularly with respect to material benefits from the state, which were more generous for war veterans than for other categories of pensioners. This changed during the 1970s and 1980s, when Brezhnev's "cult of victory" policy led to an expansion of benefits for veterans of the Great Patriotic War, such as special health care benefits, significant housing subsidies, free passes for public transportation, and so on. This development fuelled siege survivors' expectations for greater recognition and more extensive benefits on the basis of the special role that they and Leningrad as a city played in the official heroic narrative of the war.

The survivors' expectations were partially met in 1985. On 14 May, shortly after the fortieth anniversary of victory over Germany, the Central Committee of the Communist Party of the Soviet Union and the Council of Ministers of the USSR issued Bill No. 416. This decree extended the benefits already being received by civilian volunteers of the Red Army to all people who had laboured in besieged Leningrad; it also awarded them the For the Defence of Leningrad medal.[36] Residents of the city who had been employed in industry and specific organizations would receive slightly greater benefits than other categories of pensioners. This group of siege survivors was the first to receive social benefits – in addition to the existing honours for defence – on the basis of their experience.

The bill had been prepared without input from the authorities in Leningrad, and local activists and city council members soon started to question why benefits were being afforded to only one category of survivors. The city councillors successfully argued that the scope of the law was too narrow and left out many people who had made significant contributions during the blockade.[37] Many activists who by then had joined together to form advocacy organizations gained the support of the city council, which itself had emerged as a forum of democracy during the era of perestroika.

In the 1980s and 1990s, Leningrad's siege-survivor societies were also active, along with other organizations, in distributing humanitarian aid. Poor and elderly survivors joined such groups during these years of economic crisis in order to improve their quality of life. Membership in these organizations consequently expanded well beyond their initial core. Russian pensioners were receiving payments that were well under a living wage at the time, and participation in political life through these sorts of organizations seemed to offer an opportunity to improve their financial situation. In other words, financial hardship encouraged siege survivors to take a clear stance on whether they were victims or heroes so that they could clearly articulate their demands for legislative change and explain why they required special compensation or benefits from the state. The resulting increased awareness of these groups was due not to the historical narratives they promoted but rather to the poor living conditions of most siege survivors, most of whom were elderly by that point.

Siege-survivor societies attracted members in different ways. Some invited all people who had worked in Leningrad during the siege to join their organizations; others focused on those who had been students or orphans at the time. One group called 900 Days accepted only those who had remained in Leningrad for the duration of siege, in distinction to those who had been evacuated. Many of the first siege-survivor societies admitted only recipients of the For the Defence of Leningrad medal, which indicated that the person had actually been in the city and that their contributions were recognized by the state.

An issue associated with soliciting new members for these societies was deliberation over who the "real" siege survivors were and what constituted evidence of their heroism. Activists within these groups criticized state authorities, arguing that the whole population of besieged Leningrad deserved compensation, even those who were not workers or had not received a medal of recognition. Leningrad's *Lensovet* (city parliament) shared this opinion and therefore, on 23 January 1989, created a new designation (*znak*), "To the Citizen of Besieged Leningrad," for those who had not received the For the Defence of Leningrad medal. This designation, which entitled the recipient to certain benefits, was granted to those who could provide documentary proof that they had resided in Leningrad during the siege, thus expanding the number of individuals recognized for their experience. Citizens of Besieged Leningrad immediately became a category of local importance.

The creation of this designation had a fundamental effect on the future development of survivors' societies and their activities. It inspired them to seek out and assist tens of thousands of people who identified themselves as siege survivors but who lacked legal recognition of that status because they had not received a medal. In everyday language, people used the term *blokadnik* (siege survivor or blockade survivor) to describe anyone who had spent a significant amount of time in Leningrad during the siege. The formation of different groups and their demand for legal recognition resulted in a narrower application of the term. The "To the Citizen of Besieged Leningrad" designation from the *Lensovet* stated that the term would be applied only to recipients of the For the Defence of Leningrad medal, as established by the governmental decree of 1985, or to individuals who had spent four months or more in Leningrad but had not received that honour.[38] The threshold of four months seems to have been established in consideration of the severe winter of 1941–2,[39] which lawmakers recognized as the "quintessence of the siege." This period was the hardest time for the city's population: food rations were at their lowest levels (decreased from 400 to 125 grams of bread per day), heating and electricity were non-existent, the transportation system had ceased to operate, and temperatures fell below minus 40 degrees Celsius. In the spring of 1942, the mass evacuation of civilians was organized, and many children left Leningrad at this time.

A 1994 decree by President Boris Yeltsin, "On social guarantees and benefits for the citizens awarded with the medal 'For the Defence of Leningrad' and the designation 'To the Citizen of the Besieged City,'" equated both categories of the siege survivors – that is, "medalists" and "citizens" – with veterans of the Great Patriotic War and elevated the "citizen" category to national importance.[40] This decree marked the culmination of the struggle of Leningrad siege survivors to receive benefits that were equal to those of war veterans and to see laws honouring citizens of the besieged city enshrined at the federal level.

The "To the Citizen of Besieged Leningrad" designation inspired the proliferation of even further siege-survivor organizations not only in Leningrad but across Russia. This expansion helped to extend recognition and benefits to people who had lived in Leningrad during the war but who later moved elsewhere, and these new groups began to demand compensation from local and federal authorities. These societies spread quickly across other post-Soviet states, and, in 1991, activists formed an international association, the International Association of Siege Survivors' Organizations of the Hero City of Leningrad, to represent the movement at large. Of all survivor organizations, this group has been the most successful in bringing the history of the Siege of Leningrad to national prominence.

It is important to recognize that medals had served for many years as a socially convenient proof of heroism, so it is understandable that the creation of a new medal and a new category of recipients (Citizens of Besieged Leningrad) created new opportunities for survivors to revisit their memories of the event. Because most siege survivors had for so long not been officially recognized as heroes, they instead typically positioned themselves as victims, which added a new perspective for interpreting the war. This perspective of victimhood in some ways paralleled another discursive shift in the 1980s, whereby the memory of the Holocaust became a basis for understanding the Second World War and led to the founding of organizations for victims of National Socialism, and later, of communism. It seemed possible that this vision provided a model or "a frame of memory," as Maurice Halbwachs has called it, for Leningrad siege-survivor societies. This alternative frame made it possible for people who had endured the siege and who had contributed to the war effort in a military or industrial role to be admitted to survivors' organizations and, as a result, to be viewed in a heroic light. A 1994 appeal by activists from the society Blokadniki Leningrada (Siege Survivors of Leningrad) to the Ministry of the Social Protection of the Population of the Russian Federation drew a link between the narratives of the Holocaust and siege-related activism.[41] In that appeal, siege survivors hoped to gain the support of the Russian authorities in bringing a suit against the German government seeking compensation for their suffering. The survivors wrote in their appeal that the siege experience was comparable to life in Nazi concentration camps. Ultimately, the Russian authorities did not support this initiative, the ministry's response noting that German compensation was limited to specific groups targeted by the Nazi regime and did not extend to the victims of Leningrad. It was clear that Russian authorities were not going to broker the siege survivors' dialogue with the German government.

The language of victimhood can also be found in statements made by siege-survivor societies regarding the poor health of their members and their entitlement to better medical care. In numerous letters to state agencies, survivors explained that the irreversible damage inflicted by wartime starvation necessitated more generous health care benefits for themselves and their children. Several supporters sought to build a body of medical evidence to prove this assertion by organizing a centre in a St. Petersburg hospital where siege survivors could be examined and treated. Activists of the *blokadniki* movement insisted on the same benefits for all survivors, based on the fact that all inhabitants, including children and infants, had suffered from hunger during the siege. It is no coincidence that, in these years, that there was a proliferation of research on the medical effects of hunger. In the 1990s, activists from *blokadniki* organizations were involved with research undertaken by Dr. Boris M. Rachkov from the Vreden Russian Scientific Research Institute of Traumatology and Orthopedics, which was named after R.R. Vreden, who discovered so-called blockade syndrome. Rachkov monitored the health of siege survivors and members of their families and proved that "prolonged starvation has a negative effect on siege survivors' descendants up to the third generation."[42] In 2000, the city of St. Petersburg responded to activists' demands for improved health care by opening a special research centre for treatment and diagnosis at hospital No. 46 (Hospital St. Yevgenii), which offered medical assistance to siege survivors.[43]

The special attention that blockade activists paid to medical issues reflected not only their concern for the health of survivors and their families but also a broader struggle with Russian authorities. By proving a connection between the poor health of siege survivors in the 1990s and the hunger they had endured in 1941–2, the activists were able to claim financial compensation for the harm they endured during wartime, which was similar to the support given to individuals who had been injured at the front. At the same time, the Russian authorities were keen to stress the achievements and the heroism of the Leningrad siege survivors rather than the long-term ill effects the blockade had on them. Acknowledging responsibility for the health of people who had suffered hunger in the USSR would have facilitated further claims by representatives of other veteran groups and organizations, which would have been able to prove that they, too, had suffered from hunger under Soviet rule, be it the famine in the Volga region, the hunger and starvation caused by collectivization, or the famine of 1946. To avoid such confrontations, the authorities acknowledged the hunger resulting from the Leningrad Blockade as a special case in Soviet history and authorized two types of pensions for siege survivors: a general pension and a second based on their suffering during the war.[44]

Not all survivors' societies had the same goals or took the same approaches. Several constituent groups of the International Association of Siege Survivors' Organizations of the Hero City of Leningrad voted against bringing a lawsuit against Germany. The dissenting members, all of whom were recipients of the For the Defence of Leningrad medal, considered it unacceptable for victorious heroes – as they saw themselves – to appeal to former enemies, let alone defeated enemies, for compensation. Other groups avoided invoking the discourse of victimhood because they saw it as being in tension with their membership's established status as heroes: the label of victim would have implied that they had been passive in the face of their circumstances. Emphasizing a victim narrative would, they argued, lead to comparisons with victims of the Holodomor in Ukraine or of political repression, rather than with heroic veterans of the Great Patriotic War. Many siege survivors clearly rejected this possibility. New legal categories created during perestroika recognized victims of dictatorship, but they connoted a passive role in history. Moreover, few in Russia were eager to grant special social benefits on the basis of starvation and harsh living conditions, since those conditions affected the majority of elderly people in the last Soviet generation.

The siege survivors distinguished themselves by asserting that they had actively sacrificed themselves, as Assmann described, in order to defeat the enemy and determine the ultimate, victorious outcome of the war. It was on this basis that they were entitled to more generous assistance from the state and society. These themes of heroism and sacrifice could thus be combined into a coherent narrative without contradicting each other.

By the mid-1990s, there were several dozen siege-survivor societies representing thousands of members across Russia. The most important of these were the International Association of Siege Survivors' Organizations of the Hero City of Leningrad and the Society of Citizens of Besieged Leningrad, both of which advocated actively at the state level for siege survivors' interests. Russian authorities took the interests of the siege survivors into consideration during those years, and lawmakers were quite attentive to their requests, as is described below. This response is especially remarkable when compared to lack of attention devoted to similar initiatives from other groups such as the Association of the Juvenile Prisoners of Concentration Camps or the Children of Wartime Stalingrad. The relative prestige of the Leningrad survivors underscores the importance of the siege, and memories of it, for the political elite of the 1990s.

Heroes or Victims, 1994–2014

In 1994, the State Duma of the Russian Federation issued new legislation relating to various types of veterans, replacing numerous earlier laws that had regulated the social and economic status of siege survivors. In Russia, the term "veteran" includes not only military veterans but also those who worked in state service (such as police officers), in the Secret Service, and even in industry. The law therefore applied to practically all of Russia's elderly population. Although the new law clarified the hierarchy of various veterans' groups within Russian society, it annulled certain accepted standards regarding benefits for siege survivors. This federal law reaffirmed the legitimacy of the survivors' status but, at the same time, abolished their entitlement privileges, which had served as a material sign of equality on par with military veterans of the Second World War.

This law, "On Veterans," divided Russian pensioners into several categories: veterans of armed conflicts, veterans of public service, and veterans of labour, among others. Each group received benefits in amounts that reflected legislators' assessments of their service to the country. Indeed, the law enshrined a hierarchy that distinguished between "medal holders" and "citizens," which previously had been only a nominal distinction. Recipients of the For the Defence of Leningrad medal were declared to have been particularly heroic, and thus were given benefits on a par with those of military veterans. Meanwhile, Citizens of Besieged Leningrad were accorded a lower status and were given benefits roughly equal to those of young victims of Nazi concentration camps.

After this law was passed, the primary goal of siege-survivor societies was to make both medal holders and citizens – and the benefits that flowed to them – equal under the law. Organizations representing both groups joined forces in order to obtain the more favourable status and benefits afforded to military veterans. To this end, various societies published collections of memoirs and arranged conferences that purported to prove the heroism of all citizens of Leningrad. Thus, they tried to use both personal testimonies and historical scholarship to legitimate their membership's status as heroes of equal calibre.[45]

Throughout this period, the groups used the Soviet model of heroism to frame both their public and private memories of the siege. Examples of this include the 2002 address by the Eleventh Congress of the International Association of Siege Survivors' Organizations of the Hero City of Leningrad, which was directed to President Vladimir Putin, Head of the State Duma Gennadiy Seleznev, and Head of the Federation Council Sergey Mironov. It argued for a proposed companion bill, "On Victims," to rectify the problems of the "On Veterans" legislation. The address pleaded for the Duma "not to consider living siege survivors of Leningrad to be [mere] victims of war regardless of their current residence and awards." Rather, they should be considered heroes.[46] This statement is clear evidence that activists in the siege-survivor societies were reluctant to lose "hero" privileges by being placed by the state into a category of victims.

It was not only survivors who fought to keep alive the heroic narrative of the siege. Writers who had been present in Leningrad or at the front lines near it during the war as well as historians – many of them active supporters of perestroika – were also engaged in this struggle. Adherence to the heroic narrative meant, however, that survivors lacked a vocabulary other than that of socialist realism with which to describe their experiences. This explains why memoirs, produced under the aegis of survivor societies, are so similar to Soviet literary works dedicated to the war: they use the same paradigms of heroism.

Bourdieu's work on the history of cultural production and the habitus of the agents helps explain this reliance on a heroism narrative. Activists' use of this heroic narrative in formulating their demands on the state was embedded in existing traditions of representing the siege. It had been presented this way by survivor societies, heads of various movements and museums, and some historians. Successive survivor societies did not make any real attempts to formulate an alternative to the official version. It was easier – and in their interest – for them to describe new details of their own experience rather than to reconceptualize the edifice of the past that had been built throughout their lives. Joining this heroic pantheon – as opposed to joining a "victims" movement – remained the most efficient means of soliciting and obtaining material benefits. A variety of court decisions in the 1990s contributed to this approach, which authorities used to deflect lawsuits brought by those who had been persecuted in the Soviet period either in the form of dispossession, forced deportation, starvation (e.g., during the Holodomor), or besiegement.[47]

Despite this apparent consensus, survivor societies continued to engage in debates on topics such as the question of child siege survivors being considered equal to soldiers who had fought on the front lines. The groups were also forced to face the fact that membership in survivors' organizations exceeded the number of people who were trapped in Leningrad during the siege. One article reported on an initiative by a citizens' group demanding that the authorities of St. Petersburg "cleanse the numbers of siege survivors of persons who are not in any way connected to the siege." The author offered to publish her "own archival research that proves that roughly one-third of supposed siege survivors receiving benefits have no right of entitlement for them."[48] According to the author of that article, recent efforts to create a dialogue between siege survivors and the city administration were far from constructive: "Actually, there was no place for discussion. Holders of the medal 'For the Defence of Leningrad' dissociated themselves from holders of the designation 'Citizen of the Besieged City.' 'Adults' confronted 'children': the majority of the siege survivors' meetings end up in a loud slinging match over who is a genuine '*blokadnik*.'"[49]

As soon as the "On Veterans" bill was passed, it deepened the divide between the International Association of Siege Survivors' Organizations of the Hero City of Leningrad and the Citizens of the Besieged City. This split was in part due to differing world views between generations: the former organization was headed by an individual of the "adult generation" and focused on the interests of medal holders, whereas the latter organization fought for benefits of those who had been children during the siege, few of whom had been decorated. At the same time, all activists agreed on the heroic interpretation of the siege, even though they emphasized different aspects of it. This sort of divergence is typical of "social memory," as described by Assmann.[50] Personal conflicts between the groups' leaders also played an important role and came to eclipse the actual differences in the two societies' interpretations of the siege.

Despite the apparent endurance of the heroic narrative of the siege, there are concerns that it is not sufficient to maintain the work and membership of survivors' organizations as a vital concern. The organizations were concerned not only about preserving the heroic interpretation of the siege but also about increasing the number of their members by including new participants. Some groups lobbied for recognition to include people who were born during the siege but did not reach the four-month residency threshold the law required – the so-called toddlers of besieged Leningrad. Another group of survivors who had been children during the siege argued that they should be recognized as survivors because they were indirect victims of the starvation suffered by their mothers. Russian authorities in the past two decades have been more inclined to emphasize the heroic narrative over the assertions of suffering made by these groups. Thus, "toddlers of besieged Leningrad" has not been recognized as a category of siege survivors because their narrative did not comport with the heroic portrayal supported by the state.

During the past decade and a half, siege survivors have struggled without much success to change the legislative distinction between medal holders and citizens. Their numerous letters to the heads of the State Duma, the Federation Council, and the president have failed to yield positive results. Legislators have been reluctant to reconsider how pensions are calculated, and court appeals have not changed this. Thus, siege survivors with medals have remained privileged over Citizens of Besieged Leningrad.

Discontent with the state's policy was evident in the active protests against the government's effort to provide direct payments in lieu of certain benefits. A law that passed in 2004 meant that Russian pensioners would receive additional money rather than discounted goods and services (e.g., at pharmacies and hospitals, on public transport, etc.).[51] Such changes caused some pensioners to think that the government was going to abandon several of its social obligations to them. The siege survivors demanded that the government forego this move toward substituting payments for certain social services.

It is remarkable that, despite often heated protests, the relationship between siege-survivor organizations and the state has remained paternalistic. The main way these groups voice their appeals is through official letters to the governor of St. Petersburg and to the president of the Russian Federation, thus placing their hopes in the hands of those officials rather than in a more representative branch of power. This focus on the executive is a rather apt illustration of a larger recent political trend in Russian politics. There is a kind of understanding between survivor organizations and the current Russian authorities, and the organizations' wishes have sometimes been fulfilled. In effect, the survivors permit politicians to make use of the symbolic resource of their siege experiences, which recall the Great Patriotic War and its role in the national narrative, and, in return, the survivors are compensated with material aid and social status. The latter benefit is seen as an act of symbolic acknowledgment. For example, the sixtieth, sixty-fifth, and seventieth anniversaries of the siege's end have seen the production of new medals, special financial awards, and much solemn patriotic rhetoric. Russia's leaders use these opportunities to claim that the well-being of siege survivors is a constant priority. On the other hand, the siege survivors are able to lobby for their interests through direct appeals to the president of the Russian Federation, whereas most other groups have to follow formal procedures to make the authorities aware of their demands.

The status of siege survivors has not been seriously reconsidered since the law pertaining to categories of veterans was passed in 1994, which still provides for two groups entitled to different levels of benefits. Still, various gestures by the state, usually on anniversaries, have gradually improved the overall status of this group of survivors. For example, the Citizens of Besieged Leningrad received additional one-time payments of 500 rubles in 2005 in commemoration of the sixtieth anniversary of the end of the Second World War.[52] In January 2007, disabled siege survivors received two pensions, a labour pension and a disability pension, in commemoration of the siege's end.[53] Finally, all war veterans and siege survivors were awarded housing benefits on Victory Day 2008.[54] Presidential Decree RF No. 714, "On providing housing for veterans of the Great Patriotic War 1941–1945," issued on 7 May 2008, stated that a variety of veteran groups were entitled to better living conditions, and both groups of siege survivors were among them. In St. Petersburg, housing was granted to siege survivors who had lived in the city for a minimum of ten years and whose living conditions required improvement. This could mean exchanging a room in a communal flat for a private, one-bedroom flat. The program is still in operation, and, by 2015, the number of veterans whose living conditions were improved as a result totalled some 281,000.[55]

When new siege-survivor societies were being created in the 1980s, they aspired to recast remembrance of the siege and the experiences of their members during it. The deliberate desire of the central government to cease interfering too directly in the politics of memory created space in which new versions of the past – or at least criticism of Soviet versions of the past – could emerge. It seemed like circumstances were ripe for a reconsideration of the history of the Great Patriotic War and of the siege. But survivors' struggles for benefits prevented new versions of the siege story from becoming fully enshrined in law. At the same time, the perestroika era allowed many alternative versions of the siege to be articulated, and numerous previously taboo topics entered the public sphere. Nevertheless, in the end, only those narratives that upheld the notion that every siege survivor is a hero gained legal recognition.

The authorities did not divide siege survivors into heroes and victims. In their view, they were all heroes who, to a larger or lesser extent, had contributed to victory and were therefore entitled to benefits. It is rather telling that the Citizens of the Besieged City, who are less privileged than war veterans, receive considerably higher pensions than persons who, for instance, had suffered political repression and who are clearly classified as victims under law.

No one in Russia questions the authenticity of the memory of the Leningrad Blockade survivors. Appeals to authenticity aid their fight for benefits but also act as an obstacle to understanding the blockade as a disaster. In the public space of modern St. Petersburg, survivors' groups are considered experts with respect to historical memory and are among the most pro-government organizations. In Victory Day celebrations, they walk with portraits of Stalin, emphasize the victory of the USSR in the Second World War, and condemn attempts to consider the memory of the blockade in a different way. They do not take into account the fact that authentic blockade diaries present a different view of these events. The city has practically no independent platforms for free discussion of the blockade. Therefore, authenticity related to the blockade legacy is understood through the prism of the politics of memory administered by these associations and not through the prism of primary sources, such as diary entries of Leningraders who died of hunger.

NOTES

1 Alistair Thomson, "Anzac Memories: Putting Popular Memory Theory into Practice in Australia," in *The Oral History Reader*, ed. Robert Perks and Alistair Thomson (New York: Routledge, 2003), 301.

2 Ibid., 300.
3 Aleida Assmann, *Dlinnaya ten' proshlogo: Memorialnaya kultura i istoricheskaya politika* (Moscow: NLO, 2014), 21. Originally published as *Der lange Schatten der Vergangenheit: Erinnerungskultur und Geschichtspolitik* (Munich: C.H. Beck, 2006).
4 Ibid., 24.
5 Ibid., 76.
6 Nataliya Danilova, *The Politics of War Commemoration in the UK and Russia* (Basingstoke, UK: Palgrave Macmillan, 2015).
7 Charles Lindholm, *Culture and Authenticity* (Oxford: Blackwell Publishing, 2008); Lindholm, "The Rise of Expressive Authenticity," *Anthropological Quarterly* 86, no. 2 (2013): 361–95.
8 Irina Kaspe, "Certificate of What? Document and Documentation in Russian Contemporary Literature," *Russian Review* 69, no. 4 (2010): 563–84.
9 Alexandr Fadeev, *Leningrad v dni blokady: iz dnevnika* (Moscow: Sovetskiy pisatel, 1944).
10 M.A. Shishkin, *Universitet v blokadnom i osazgdennom Leningrade, 1941–1944.* (St. Petersburg: Gippokrat, 1996), 3.
11 Tatiana Voronina, *Pomnit to-nashemy: Sozsrealisticheskiy istorism i blokada Leningrada* (Moscow: Novoe literaturnoe obozrenie, 2018).
12 Paul Ricœur, *Pamyat, istoriya, zabvenie* (Moscow: Izdatelstvo gumanitarnoy literaturyi, 2004); originally published as *La mémoire, l'histoire, l'oubli* (Paris: Le Seuil, 2000).
13 Joachim Hösler, *Die sowjetische Geschichtswissenschaft 1953 bis 1991* (Munich: Verlag Otto Sagner, 1995); Nikolay Kopasov, *Pamyat strogogo rezhima: Istoriya i politika v Rossii* (Moscow: Novoe Literaturnoe Obozrenie, 2011), 90–102.
14 For more information, see *Vsesoyuznoe obschestvo politkatarzhan i ssyilnoposelentsev. Obrazovanie, razvitie, likvidatsiya, 1921–1935: byvshiye chleny obshestva vo vremya Bolshogo terrora: Materialy mezhdunarjdnoy nauchnoy konferenzii (26–28 Oct. 2001 g.) (sbornik)* ed. A.B. Roginskiy (Moscow: Zvenya, 2004).
15 The "Road of Life" (*Doroga Zhizny*) is a conventional name in Soviet historiography for a winter transport route across the frozen Lake Ladoga, which provided a supply and evacuation route for the besieged city.
16 The Monument to Heroic Defenders of Leningrad was founded at Pobeda Square in 1975. Its creators are laureates of Lenin's State Award, national artists of the USSR, including Sergey Speransky, Valentin Kamensky, and Michail Anikushin.
17 It is remarkable that groups with the same name were appearing almost simultaneously across the whole country. Some of them focused on searching for relatives and fellow soldiers; others searched for bodies of Soviet soldiers killed in battle, with the aim of reinterring them.

18 Interview with Marina Tkacheva, 12 April 2002, Archive of Oral History Center of the European University of St. Petersburg, interview number BL-1–014 (2003).

19 For example, Valeriy Selivanov, *Stoyali kak soldaty* (St. Petersburg: EGO, 2002); Irina Tetyueva, "Voyna, blokada, leningradskie deti," in *Deti i blokada: Vospominaniya, fragmenty dnevnikov, svidetelstva ochevidtsev, dokumentalnyie materialy*, ed. T.M. Golubeva (St. Petersburg: IPK Vesti, 2000), 9–22.

20 For more on the official interpretation of the siege, see Viktoria Kalendarova, "Formiruya pamyat: blokada v leningradskih gazetah i dokumentalnom kino v poslevoennyie desyatiletiya," in *Pamyat o blokade: Svidetelstva ochevidzev i istoricheskoe soznanie obshestva*, ed. M. Loskutova (Moscow: Novoe izdatelstvo, 2005), 275–96. See also Lisa A. Kirschenbaum, *The Legacy of the Siege of Leningrad, 1941–1995: Myth, Memories, and Monuments* (New York: Cambridge University Press, 2006).

21 Memorial alleys were a popular form of public commemoration in the USSR, consisting of a road lined on both sides with trees. They typically bore a name connected to the memory of a famous person or a historical event and are still used as a sites for commemorative rituals.

22 "V Peterburge begut marafon po 'doroge zhizni,'" *Baltinfo*, 30 January 2011, http://www.baltinfo.ru/2011/01/30/V-Peterburge-begut-marafon-po-Doroge-zhizni-185410.

23 "V pohod, molodezh!" *Smena*, no. 19 (12821), 24 January 1968, 1.

24 "Vstrecha v 16.00," *Smena*, no. 50 (12852), 29 February 1968, 4.

25 Ob'yavleniya (advertisements), *Smena*, no. 245 (13047), 18 October 1968, 2.

26 Interview with Oleg Akimushkin, leader of the group of siege survivors in one of the St. Petersburg organizations, 15 March 2003, Archive of the Oral History Center of the European University at St. Petersburg, BL-2A-019.

27 Assman, *Dlinnaya ten' proshlogo*, 24.

28 This was also the case, for example, in the siege-survivor section of the House of Scientists. Also, the interview with siege survivor Larissa Frolova, 19 June 2003, Archive of the Oral History Center of the European University at St. Petersburg, BL-2A-019, 3.

29 See also Tatiana Voronina and Ilya Utehin, "Rekonstruktsiya smysla v analize intervyu: tematicheskie dominanty i skrytaya polemika," in *Pamyat o blockade: Svidetelstva ochevidtsev i istoricheskoe soznanie obshestva*, ed. M. Loskutova (Moscow: Novoe izdatelstvo, 2005), 230–61.

30 Aleksandr Volodin and Nikolay Marley, *Medali SSSR* (St. Petersburg: Pechatnyiy Dvor, 1997).

31 The monument was designed by architects Alexandr Alimov and Filipp Gepner and created by sculptors Viktor Novikov and Ivan Kostyukhin.

32 Tatiana Voronina and Polina Barskova, "Unspeakable Truths: Children of the Siege in Soviet Literature," *A Companion to Soviet Children's Literature and Film*, ed. Olga Voronina (Leiden: Brill, 2019), 307–44.

33 Anatoliy Sobchak, *Iz Leningrada v Peterburg: puteshestvie vo vremeni i prostranstve* (St. Petersburg: Kontrfors, 1999).

34 Catriona Kelly, "'The Leningrad Affair': Remembering the 'Communist Alternative' in the Second Capital," *Slavonika* 17, no. 2 (2011): 103–22.

35 Voronina and Utehin, "Rekonstruktsiya smysla," 252.

36 "Postanovlenie TsKKPSS i Soveta Ministrov SSSR O rasprostranenii lgot, dlya uchastnikov Velikoy Otechestvennoy voyni, na grazhdan, rabotavshih v period blokady Leningrada na predpriyatiyah, v uchrezhdeniyah i organizatsiyah goroda, i nagrazhdennyih medalyu 'Za oboronu Leningrada'," in *Etapy zabveniya: Zaklyuchitelnaya glava k sborniku "Bol' pamyati blokadnoy,"* ed. Larisa Petrova (Moscow: MGUL, 2005), 11.

37 "Uchityvaya geroizm, projavlenniy leningradcami," 1994; *Leningradskaya Pravda*, no. 104 (228465), 5 May 1990, C. 1.

38 Decision no. 5 of the Executive Committee of the Leningrad City Council of People's Deputies "On the establishment of the sign 'Inhabitant of besieged Leningrad,' 23 January 1989," in *Etapy zabvenia*, 12.

39 Nataliya Barsova, "Blokadniki vtorogo sorta," *Moskovskiy komsomoletz v Peterburge*, no. 11/22 (777), 13 March 2008, , 3.

40 Decree of the president of Russian Federation, "About social guarantees and benefits for the citizens who have the medal "For the Defense of Leningrad" and the designation "To the Citizen of Besieged Leningrad," 18 January 1994, no. 163 in *Etapy zabvenia*, ed. Larisa Petrova, 22.

41 This organization is based in the town of Mytishchi (Moscow region). See letter from the head of Mytishchi region voluntary organization "Blokadniki of Leningrad" to the Ministry of the Social Protection of the Population of the Russian Federation in Petrova, *Etapy zabvenia*, 24.

42 Boris Rachkov and Yuriy Kolosov, "Vliyanie dlitel'nogo golodaniya na zdorov'e zhiteley blokadnogo Leningrada i ih potomkov," in *Uroki Vtoroy mirovoy voyny i problemy obespecheniya mira v 21 veke*, ed. Gennadiy Datchikov (St. Petersburg: RDK-Print, 2000), 135.

43 Petrova, *Etapy zabvenia*, 77.

44 Anastasia Kukuruzova, "Pensii i pesni dlya blokadnikov," *Fontanka*, 25 January 2007, http://www.fontanka.ru/2007/01/25/065/.

45 For more on this, see Viktor Demidov, ed., *Blokada rassekrechennaya* (St. Petersburg: Bojanych, 1995); Tatiana Golubeva, ed., *Deti i blokada: Vospominaniya, fragmenty dnevnikov, svidetel'stva ochevidcev, dokumental'nye materialy* (St. Petersburg: IPK Vesti, 2000); Victor Shapkin, ed., *Podvig Leningrada bessmerten: Trudy nauchno-prakticheskoy konferencii prepodavateley i studentov kolledzhey, posvyashhennoj 60-letiyu razgroma vraga pod Leningradom*

i Velikoy Pobedy nad fashizmom, 19–20 April 2004 (St. Petersburg: Gazieva L., 2004).

46 Petrova, *Etapy zabvenia*, 282.

47 This issue has been also studied by human rights observers in the context of rehabilitation of victims of political repression. See, for example, Veniamin Joffe, "Reabilitaciya kak istoricheskaya problema"; Aleksandr Danijel', "Koncepciya reabilitacii v kontekste politicheskogo razvitiya konca 1980-nachala 1990-h"; and Irina Flige, "Posle zakona o reabilitacii: transformaciya obshhestvennogo soznaniya," all in *Mir posle Gulaga: reabilitaciya i kul'tura pamyati. Mir posle Gulaga: reabilitacyja i kul'tura pamyatï. Vtoroy mezhdunarodniy simpozium pamyati V.V. Joffe. Syktyvkar, 10–11 sentyabrya 2003*, ed. Irina Flige (St. Petersburg: NIC Memorial, Nord-Vest, 2004), 6–9, 10–19, 55–61.

48 Olga Nikonova, "Novoe leningradskoe delo ili vseh ne pereschitaesh'?" *Nevskoe vremya*, no. 194 (1597), 23 October 1997, 3.

49 Ibid.

50 Assman, *Dlinnaya ten' proshlogo*, 22.

51 Petrova, *Etapy zabvenia*, 291.

52 "Doplata i pensiya dlya blokadnika," *Trud*, 15 March 2007.

53 Kukuruzova, "Pensii i pesni dlya blokadnikov."

54 N. Grivenkova, "Chinovniki formuliruyut zakony, blokadniki ostajutsya v kommunalkah," *ok-inform.ru obshhestvenniy kontrol'* 19 February 2013, http://ok-inform.ru/stroitelstvo-i-nedvizhimost/1128-chinovniki-formuliruyut-zakony-blokadniki-ostayutsya-v-kommunalkakh.html.

55 "Pobednye metry: obespechenie veteranov VOV zhil'em v RF idet bez sboev," *RIA Novosti*, 30 April 2015, http://ria.ru/victory70/20150430/1061895744.html#ixzz4AoBQedRq.

9 Victims, Perpetrators, or Both? How History Textbooks and History Teachers in Post-Soviet Lithuania Remember Postwar Partisans

BARBARA CHRISTOPHE

In 1991, at the climax of Lithuania's struggle for independence, a huge crowd in Vilnius joyfully cheered the removal of the monument to Lenin from the city's Lukiškės Square. The plaza, which had once served as a landmark in the public life of the Lithuanian capital, has been left with a gaping void since then. Several attempts to replace the statue of the heroic founder of the Soviet Union with one of an "unknown partisan" have failed. Lithuanian society apparently has still not reached a consensus regarding the legacy of the partisan war in the 1940s and 1950s.

In 2004, the Museum for the Victims of the Genocide in Vilnius, which is intended to cover the history of the entire Soviet period, opened an exhibition dealing with the anti-Soviet partisans. In this exhibition, partisans figure principally as victims who endured cruel torture. The cells on the ground floor, with all their carefully preserved narrowness and mustiness, help visitors immerse themselves in the dark world of Soviet repression. The cells feature belongings of former prisoners, among them many partisans. Eyeglasses, shoes, and photographs among bones from some burial sites are displayed on the floors. The curators of the exhibition have obviously learned something from the visual images used in representations of the Holocaust.[1] Cultural elites at the local level thus seem to have shaped the institutionalized memory of the partisans following global norms of remembrance.

In the same year, the film *Left Alone* (*Vienui vieni*) appeared in Lithuanian cinemas. It is centred on the tragic destiny of Juozas Lukša, a actual Lithuanian partisan who sets out on a difficult and dangerous journey to cross the Iron Curtain. In 1948, he reaches the United States, where he tries to mobilize support among Lithuanian emigrant communities for a fight that, by that time, had already been lost. In the end, he returns to his homeland, only to be shot in the back by a traitor who had infiltrated the ranks of the partisans. Almost immediately upon its release, the film triggered passionate debates. Critics blamed Jonas Vaitkus, the director, for having fallen back on outdated Soviet habits of telling stories about lonesome heroes ready to sacrifice their lives in the name of an honourable cause.[2] Proponents of the film claimed the opposite. For them, Vaitkus had finally overcome the distortions that Soviet narratives had inflicted on the historical consciousness of Lithuanians by portraying the partisans as bandits.[3] Glorification prompted vilification in return, and the dispute carried on for years. Some commentators recalled stories of innocent young Komsomol members who had been ruthlessly killed by members of the anti-Soviet resistance movement.[4] Others lamented that Lithuanian society was still very much in the grip of myths created by the Soviets.[5] These debates show that there is still no consensus on how to remember the partisans, but it is also through these disputes that one gets a sense of the issues at stake. Although all participants in the discourse equate victimhood with moral superiority, they differ with regard to the question of who really was the victim. Some say the partisans, and others favour ordinary people victimized by them.

This chapter takes these observations as points of departure in order to understand how the history of the armed resistance Lithuanian partisans mounted against the Soviets in the so-called war after the war is remembered in Lithuanian history textbooks and in biographical accounts of Lithuanian history teachers. Both teachers and textbooks are in many ways entangled with society in general.[6] Textbooks are located at the intersection of politics, scholarship, and pedagogy, and teachers specialize in conveying state-approved patterns of meaning to future citizens. Teachers use textbooks in their daily work, and they translate these texts into classroom practice. Hence, to investigate how both relate to one another allows a better understanding of how people engage with official memory culture.[7]

Taking into account the peculiarities of the Lithuanian culture of memory, I will address three interrelated issues. As the issue of how to remember the Lithuanian partisan movement seems to be rather contested in Lithuania, with various voices portraying them as heroes, perpetrators, or victims, I map similarities and differences by examining (i) individual textbooks, (ii) the relationship between textbook and teacher accounts, and (iii) the strategies applied in order to present a certain account as an authentic reflection of how things were. This third focus reflects the desire for the authentic that appears to grow particularly strong in situations of crisis, contestation, and uncertainty.

To this end, I will sketch the broader theoretical frameworks in which my research is situated by looking at recent developments in memory studies and paying attention to issues of contestation and victimhood. I continue by providing background information on the history of the partisan movement,[8] still relatively unknown to international observers, as well as on the politics of history adopted since the former Soviet republic of Lithuania regained independence in 1990. Subsequently, I analyse twelve Lithuanian history textbooks published by major publishing houses between 1994 and 2013 and pay particular attention to differences between books of different political affiliations as well as to slight changes occurring over time.[9] I will also explore the question of how history teachers position themselves vis-à-vis these accounts.[10] In the conclusion, I will reflect on the question of what can be learned from the Lithuanian case about the social dynamics in remembering a contested past and about the role narratives of victimhood as well as claims to authenticity play in these processes.

Memory Research

The field of memory studies has seen a significant shift in focus during recent decades. Roughly speaking, we can discern three major trends, all of which are relevant to the topical focus of this chapter.

First, researchers have urged us to attend not only to "institutionalized collective memory objects,"[11] such as museums, memorials, films, or textbooks, but also to take into consideration the many ways in which people engage with these objects. They have rediscovered the plurality of collective memory, which has become even more pronounced in the age of individualization and globalization. Hence, more emphasis is given to aspects of power and politics that are at stake when rival versions of the past vie for hegemony.[12] Some studies have also investigated how individuals position themselves with respect to hegemonic narratives, by reproducing, destabilizing, or otherwise interrupting them.[13] Scholars have also developed a special interest in the countermemories of marginalized or repressed groups, raising questions such as how experiences of the past that do not fit into the hegemonic frames of remembering the past can be voiced.

Second, some authors have come to realize how ambivalent manifestations of cultural memory tend to occur in response to contestation and conflict.[14] Ambivalence is seen as a resource that cultural elites drawn on in order to deal with the plurality of attitudes toward past events. To give just two prominent examples: Sturken has argued that the V-shaped Vietnam Veterans Memorial in Washington, DC, which consists of two black walls gradually disappearing into the ground, allows visitors to arrive at opposing interpretations of its symbolic character.[15]

Some take the construction as a reminder of the unjust and shameful war, whereas others view it as an expression of the symbolic castration of a nation that has failed to honour its soldiers in an adequate way. Beattie has offered a similar interpretation of the formula political elites in Germany came up with in order to head off a conflict over how to relate the history of Nazi Germany to the history of the former German Democratic Republic.[16] The formula found after intense debates calls for neither relativizing nor downplaying the crimes both regimes had committed. It is clearly meant to serve as a compromise in the still unresolved dispute between those who insist on the uniqueness of the Nazi regime and those who stress parallels between the two German dictatorships. What we can learn from this is that cultures of memories have become increasingly vague.

Third, current research has drawn attention to the emergence of "cosmopolitan memory." Levy and Sznaider have introduced this term to describe a double process, in the course of which "global concerns become part of local experiences," and local events are remembered "with reference to narratives generated outside the nation."[17] They have shown that transnational initiatives to promote the memory of the Holocaust on a global scale have resulted in crucial shifts in the way societies remember their pasts. Numerous institutionalized rules and unwritten conventions nowadays oblige national memory cultures to recall the exceptional crimes committed against the Jews. The suffering of a distant group is thus turned into a relevant concern. At the same time, the Holocaust increasingly serves as a model of how to recall other cases of massive violations of human rights. As a result, the hitherto rather marginalized figure of the victim has taken centre stage in many commemorative activities, slowly pushing the more conventional characters of the hero and the martyr into the background.

My analysis of the way the Lithuanian partisans are remembered in educational media and in the personal memories of history teachers responds to all three of these trends. It asks how individuals relate to textbooks as shortcuts to official memory, pays attention to the role of ambivalence and vagueness in reconciling rival versions of a contested past, and looks into the space given to heroes, martyrs, and victims.

A Brief History of the Lithuanian Partisans, 1944–1953

I have stressed how divided Lithuanian society is on the issue of the partisans. It is apparently the complexity of this historical experience that contributes to the unsettledness of these disputes.

The people who are described today as having belonged to the category of *the* partisans hardly represent a homogeneous group. We can recognize three different types of motives that led people, mostly young men, to join the resistance movement. The first groups consisted of those who had tried to escape military service in the Red Army. In 1944, Soviet officials organized a manhunt in order to capture them. Those who did not want to be sent to the front could choose between two options: they could go underground or they could join the armed squads formed by the Soviets in order to fight the partisans. These units were called *stribai*, a word derived from the Russian term for "terminator" (*iztrebitel*). Both choices had serious drawbacks. Joining the partisans meant embarking upon a dangerous life full of hardships; serving the hated Soviets meant losing social respect among fellow citizens or risking being killed by the partisans.

A second group of partisans consisted of those who had collaborated with the Germans while Lithuania was occupied between 1941 and 1944. Some of them, like Jonas Žemaitis, later the head of the partisans, had restricted their cooperation with the Nazis to a minimum. In June 1941, he was involved in the Lithuanian uprising staged with the support of the Nazi government just days before the German attack on the USSR. However, as soon as the Germans dissolved the provisional Lithuanian government that had emerged from the rebellion, Žemaitis changed locations and joined the ranks of the anti-German resistance movement. Others had served the Nazis willingly, and some had even been involved in the mass killing of Jews. They thus had good reason to fear severe punishment at the hands of the Soviets.

The third category of partisans included all those who still had vivid memories of the terror that had accompanied the first Soviet occupation in 1940.

This variety of stories behind individual partisans makes it difficult to come up with a single narrative that represents them all. In addition, it is necessary to distinguish between three different phases in the anti-Soviet struggle. The first phase, which lasted from 1944 to 1946, was characterized mainly by spontaneous acts of resistance against the Soviet army. Most of the young men who took to the woods did not follow a well-conceived plan. Quite a few were actually convinced that it would not take long until the Americans would turn their backs on their former Soviet ally and help the Lithuanians restore their independence.

The second phase, between 1946 and 1948, was characterized by a significant consolidation of the partisan movement and constituted the golden years of the Lithuanian resistance. It had acquired a centralized structure and consisted of units with combat strength of about one hundred men. Open battles with the Soviets were a normal occurrence. The partisans not only enjoyed broad support among the population, but, in many regions, they even controlled territory. Peasants offered them food and shelter during the night. Heads of local administrations were appointed only with the partisans' informal consent. They could move freely on the streets, whereas the Soviets had to be constantly on the alert, fearing attack.

All this was completely out of reach in the third and last phase. As soon as the Soviets had refined their counter-insurgency measures, the partisans lost their capacity to act and move. In addition, the collectivization of Lithuanian agriculture strengthened state control over the countryside. As a consequence, the partisans lost their retreats on private farms. As peasants struggled to survive deportations, villages were gripped by fear. In the end, the partisans were completely isolated. Soviet provocateurs infiltrated their ranks and discredited them by staging bloody attacks on the civil population. Ultimately, the Soviets managed to kill or arrest all the leaders. In 1953, the resistance movement had been completely stripped of its leadership cadre.

Politics of History, 1991–2008

In addition to the heterogeneity and the changing shape of the partisan movement, political controversies in the present make it difficult to arrive at a consensual understanding of the past. Generally speaking, debates on twentieth-century Lithuanian history are characterized by two features. First, the question of how to deal with the complex past repeatedly turned into an issue of intense political conflict. On the other hand, a precarious stalemate between the two rival camps of post-communists and conservatives, both of whom were able to mobilize an almost equal share of voters and thus replace each other several times in the government, generated a certain readiness for compromise.[18]

Differences in the approaches to history pertain mainly to the Soviet past. Although all political actors condemned the Soviet Union for having oppressed the Lithuanian nation and democracy, they blamed different people and institutions for the imposition of Soviet rule.[19] Post-communist governments attributed responsibility almost exclusively to the KGB. As a consequence, the whole Lithuanian population and even high-ranking party members appeared to have been victims of an oppressive regime. Moreover, the party leadership was credited with having defended the interests of the Lithuanian nation by preventing the arrival of too many Russian settlers or by supporting Lithuanian art and culture. According to this interpretation, the communist officials achieved much more than the partisans or later dissidents in terms of preserving national identity. The latter are said to have wasted time and energy in a hopeless fight. The celebrations on the occasion of the one-hundredth anniversary of the birth of Antanas Sniečkus, head of the Lithuanian Communist Party between 1940 and 1974, turned this point of view into a landmark event.[20]

The conservatives told a completely different story. They were convinced that the only morally legitimate thing one could have done during the whole Soviet period was to resist or retreat from Soviet organizations like the Komsomol or the Writers' Union. At the same time, conservatives were much more active in endeavouring to institutionalize their perspective on historical events.[21] In 1997, they introduced a memorial day for the partisans. In 1999, they officially commemorated the fiftieth anniversary of the founding of the Lithuanian Union of Freedom Fighters, the umbrella organization of all partisans set up during a secret meeting in 1949. A law adopted in 2008 banned the use of symbols of the Soviet Union, thus putting the treatment of that past on equal footing with that of the Nazi regime. In addition, the entire year 2009 was dedicated to the memory of the Lithuanian struggle for freedom.

However, beyond the determination to create a factual basis on which to base commemoration, we also can observe a certain constraint in the politics of history pursued by both sides. On some occasions, Lithuanian politicians abstained from pushing through their preferences on how to make sense of the past in order to avoid open conflict. In all their attempts to rehabilitate former comrades as nation-minded Lithuanians, the post-communists referred to arguments that even conservatives could acknowledge as legitimate. They thus articulated their position through dialogue with their political opponents.

Something similar can be observed with regard to the conservatives. For quite a long time, they hardly touched upon the contested issues related to the partisans. In the years following the declaration of independence in 1990, memory practices across the political spectrum were centred on the Molotov-Ribbentrop Pact of 1939 and the mass deportations from Lithuania in the 1940s and 1950s. Emphasis was thus given to events that upheld the idea of the Lithuanian nation as a unified community of victims.[22] The conservatives abandoned this restraint in commemoration only at the start of the new millennium, and this occurred partly in response to initiatives launched by the post-communists. But even then, conservatives were careful not to overstep the mark by unduly glorifying the partisans. When they did, they hurried to correct mistakes.

In 2000, the conservative majority of the Lithuanian parliament adopted a decree according to which all acts of the provisional government that had been formed in the course of the anti-Soviet uprising in June 1941 were recognized as legally binding. As was to be expected, this decision provoked a scandal. In the eyes of many Lithuanian and international observers, the insurgents of 1941 had long since lost all their credibility, some of them due to their anti-Semitic statements in the past.[23] This contentious move by the conservatives provoked vigorous public debate. At the height of the emerging political conflict, and before the president could use his right to veto, parliament rescinded the resolution. When the conservatives embarked upon another initiative in 2011 to commemorate the 1941 uprising, they did so in a much more cautious manner. On the one hand, they mentioned this hotly contested event as just one among a series of other attempts to defend the freedom of the Lithuanians. On the other, with an eye to global audiences, they declared the same year to be the year of remembering the Holocaust.

Based on these examples, we can tentatively conclude that being able to compromise and showing restraint in shaping the official memory culture according to one's own preferences appear to be important preconditions for those seeking to gain recognition from Lithuanian audiences as authentic voices of the past.

Textbooks

As is to be expected in a truly democratic society, Lithuanian textbooks exhibit both substantial common ground and numerous dissimilarities. All of the books uniformly reject the Soviet Union, characterizing it as the embodiment of foreign rule and totalitarian dictatorship, and all of them approve of the restoration of Lithuanian independence in 1990. At the same time, the stories they present about the partisan war reflect public controversies in at least two ways. First, textbooks show agreement to varying degrees with either the conservative or the post-communist version of the story. Second, all accounts contain a certain element of ambivalence.

Differences between textbooks can be understood by analysing the narrative perspectives from which they present their accounts and by identifying what is mentioned and what is omitted. They paint rather different pictures of the main categories of actors – in this case, the partisans, the representatives of Soviet power, and the general population. As a result, the dividing line that separates victims from perpetrators is drawn in different places, thus providing different answers to the question of whom to blame and whom to identify with.

These sorts of variations in narrative perspective can be illustrated best by a comparison of two fifth-grade textbooks, each of which represents distinctly contrasting approaches.[24] The more left-wing book narrates the story of the partisans through the eyes of Jonukas, an ordinary peasant boy, whereas the book representing more conservative views presents the same history from the angle of Juozas Lukša, one of the leading figures in the resistance movement.[25] As is to be expected, the views expressed by the boy and the hero on the same events could hardly be more different.

At first glance, the account given by Jonukas appears to be neutral. As a child, it is implied, he would hardly take sides. He is portrayed as listening to different positions. In one scene, he is eavesdropping on an argument between his parents and his elder brother, Pranas. His father blames Pranas for endangering the whole family. The Soviets, he fears, will take revenge for his son's decision to join the ranks of the resistance movement by deporting the entire family to Siberia. Pranas responds with great confidence that there are thousands of young men like him in the woods and that the Soviets could never hope to punish all of them, especially since the resistance will soon be supported by the Americans, who had promised to restore freedom. By this point in the story, at the latest, readers can be expected to have identified with one party in the family dispute. Unlike Jonukas, today's students understand how ill-conceived Pranas's hopes were, and how well-founded his father's fearse.

The textbook that focuses on the tragic fate of Juozas Lukša provides an ideologically unambiguous rendering of history meant to evoke sympathy for the story's hero. Lukša is described as outstanding in all respects. According to the author, he had personally liberated many brothers-in-arms who had been captured by the Soviets. The reader also learns that he accomplished the impossible by escaping to the other side of the Iron Curtain in 1948, and trying to raise funds among Lithuanian emigrants in the United States to support the partisans, by then a hopeless cause. His decision to return to his mother country and to a fight he could no longer hope to win is presented as one of the most noble and remarkable things a person could aspire to. This short episode climaxes with the detailed description of Lukša's dramatic death. As if the narrator was an eyewitness to the events, he describes how Lukša, having been lured into a trap by a traitor, is fatally struck by a bullet and then slowly collapses onto the cold and brittle ground. The beauty of the martyr's death is pushed front and centre. Another book, which describes how partisans preferred to blow themselves up instead of surrendering to the Soviets, describes their fate in a similar tone of almost breathless adoration.[26]

The politics of selection is also a vital consideration in understanding the stance taken by different authors. One can discover a great deal of variation between the more conservative and the more post-communist textbooks by exploring the decisions regarding what is worth mentioning and what is meant to be forgotten. To give just a few examples, all "right-wing" textbooks acknowledge the importance of the declaration adopted by the Supreme Council of the newly created umbrella organization of the partisans in 1949 that claimed that the partisans were the only legitimate representation of the Lithuanian people; the declaration was subsequently recognized as an official document of the Lithuanian state by a conservative majority of parliament in 2009. All books on the left ignore this political act. As the declaration mainly puts forward the claim of the partisans to be the only legitimate representation of the Lithuanian people, this discrepancy is quite significant.

Explanations of why so many young men took to the forests in the 1940s also serve as an example of the politics of selection. Some conservative authors, for instance, point explicitly to rather abstract values like patriotism,[27] whereas textbooks more closely aligned with post-communist positions focus exclusively on more mundane concerns, like the fear of being drafted into the Soviet army or of being persecuted by state security for past wrongdoings of one's own or for the decisions of other family members.[28] Again, these deviations have major consequences for the shape of the narrative. In the first case, the partisans are portrayed as outstanding personalities whose actions were the outcome of a firm belief in higher values. In the second, they are introduced as ordinary young men whose backs were up against a wall and who reacted rather spontaneously to the conscription order issued by the Soviets.

The refusal in conservative books to talk about the atrocities committed by the partisans is another case in point. Recalling stories of the partisans' victims seems to be almost exclusively the domain of authors on the left.

As the last examples show, the most important differences between the books involve the portrayal of the main actors and the politics of blaming. With respect to the actors, we can examine the management of responsibility – that is, the question of who is ascribed how much agency and control over events. We can also focus on how boundaries are drawn between different categories of actors. On both levels, the two types of books reveal clear dissimilarities.

Whereas left-wing textbooks tend to downplay the responsibility of Lithuanian communists for the terror and injustices of the Soviet regime, right-wing textbooks prefer to amplify it. Both sides use a variety of strategies to support their arguments. On the left, some stress the role of the Lithuanian office of the Communist Party of the Soviet Union (CPSU), which was staffed exclusively by non-Lithuanians, describing its chairman Michail Suslov as the "effective ruler" of the country, since he had sidelined the Lithuanian Communist Party. They draw attention to the fact that even those who were stalwart communists became victims of repression, and typically conclude that "party organs were effectively in the hands of foreigners" or that "Moscow did not even trust Lithuanian communists."[29] A complementary strategy of defending members of the former Lithuanian elite not only draws a line between Russian Communist perpetrators and the Lithuanian Communist victims but, in doing so, also distinguishes between the almighty Soviet security apparatus and the rather powerless and therefore – one is meant to infer – almost innocent Lithuanian party.[30]

Textbooks by authors on the right usually seek to undermine these versions. They remind their readers that the deportation lists were personally signed by Antanas Sniečkus, head of the Lithuanian Communist Party between 1940 and 1974. They even argue that it was Sniečkus who pushed the Soviets toward policies of genocide.[31] One author emphasizes that the power of the Moscow-based Lithuanian office of the CPSU came to an end as soon as the Lithuanian CP had gained sufficient strength.[32] Another argues that the Soviets were very much dependent on their Lithuanian counterparts for the execution of terror.[33]

Clear-cut differences are also reflected in the ways textbooks depict the relations among categories of actors. Textbooks that skew toward conservative preferences offer simplistic pictures with almost no shades of grey. Everybody belongs to a distinct category. Each individual is either a hero or a villain, and everybody acts according to their assigned roles. Partisans fight for freedom, defend their homeland against the evil empire, and make every sacrifice necessary in their rather desperate fight against the superior military power of the enemy. By waging a war they simply could not win, they prove to be the archetypical romantic hero so well known in Lithuanian culture, the person who will always be morally superior because he is inferior in the mundane categories of power and force.

Quite interestingly, the Soviets seem to be so alien and unacceptable as actors in this conservative telling of history that they are not even accepted as suitable objects for blame. Instead, conservatives direct their ire at the Western powers, which are portrayed as having made illusory promises of support for independence, only to abandon the Lithuanians when things became really tough.[34] The most important opponents of the partisans within Lithuania were the country's political and intellectual interwar elites, who are blamed for having sold out Lithuania to the Soviet enemy by 1940. Therefore, in these conservative accounts, the partisans are the only ones portrayed as having done something to save the heavily damaged reputation of the nation. The partisans are said to have "washed away the moral stain with their blood," a stain inflicted on Lithuania by all those who did not find the courage to resist the Soviets in 1940, the year of the nation's first occupation.[35] At times, and mainly between the lines, the accusations raised are also aimed at the majority of ordinary people who sooner or later began to adapt to the Soviet system. Textbook authors as a rule stop short of expressing open contempt for average people, but some of them portray those who had joined the ranks of the Soviet *stribai* (the collaborating "terminators") as opportunists who were happy to escape service in the Soviet army by helping the state security apparatus pursue the partisans – their fellow Lithuanians – in the woods.[36] They also claim that those who adapted to the Soviet regime were mainly in search of potential material benefits.[37]

In almost all aspects, textbooks closer to the post-communist version of the past tell the opposite story. Most importantly, they place great emphasis on identifying shades of grey. Partisans and representatives of Soviet power are both presented as perpetrators and victims simultaneously. The main dividing line does not separate political camps but, rather, runs right through them. We hear about partisans who did much to delay Sovietization and thus to protect Lithuanian tradition and culture. But we are also told how those same partisans killed not only suspected collaborators but also innocent children.[38] We learn that the partisans responded with excessive violence as their situation and their despair worsened.[39] Above all, we learn that the "freedom fighters" were hardly heroic masters of their destiny but, rather, desperate young men who tried to escape the atmosphere of terror and fear inflicted on ordinary Lithuanian villages by the Soviets. The reader can see how their situation went from bad to worse as they become confined to poorly ventilated underground shelters, hiding like animals, their bodies afflicted by thousands of parasites.[40]

There is no place for heroism in these narratives. Instead of feeling admiration for the brave, the reader is called upon to empathize with the weak. And this refers explicitly to persons on both sides of the war. Textbooks by authors on the left consistently remind us that Soviet officials are not always and only perpetrators. They are also described as human beings gripped by fear and despair, especially in the first year after the war, when partisans controlled much of the countryside and not a single supporter of the Soviet regime was safe.[41] Ambivalence sets the tone in these stories and prevents us from taking sides on behalf of one or the other of the warring parties. If the reader is meant to identify with somebody, it is the figure of the traitor, the one who is neither fish nor fowl, the one who has switched sides and is thus despised by one and all. It is through his eyes that we are made to look at the nightmare that troubled the country after the Second World War. We get to know him as the former partisan who was caught by the enemy and made to endure incredible torture until his will was broken and he agreed to spy on his former comrades.[42] We are made to understand how easy it was to recruit NKVD agents in times when people were driven crazy by fear, because, day after day, they would see the dead bodies of partisans put on display by local authorities in the marketplaces of rural towns. We are made to comprehend that those whose will has been broken, who proved to be all too human and were thus lacking the strength to withstand brutal force, are probably closest to us. It is they, most likely, who best embody post-heroic victimhood.

To sum up, a textbook closer to right-leaning political beliefs offer the story of a hero-turned-martyr, whereas a more left-wing textbook provides us with an account that is centred on ordinary people who were mainly powerless victims of a policy decided by others. While right-wing textbooks try to generate authenticity by offering coherent stories based on a clear-cut distinction between good and evil, left-wing books attempt to serve the same purpose by pursuing the opposite strategy, by pointing to ambivalences and shades of grey.

Thus far, I have mapped the contrasts between simultaneously polarized and politicized textbook accounts. I have described them as belonging to two types, each of which appears at first glance to be rather coherent. But upon closer examination, all of these accounts reveal disturbing cracks and fissures, and all of them can be described as being rather ambivalent. And it is this ambivalence, I argue, that shows where these types overlap.

Internal contradictions in conservative textbooks pertain mainly to the role ascribed to ordinary people. As I have shown, Lithuanians who did not choose the path of resistance but simply tried to adapt to circumstances beyond their own control are implicitly treated in conservative textbooks as cowards. There are, however, places in the same books where we observe the opposite, where the authors invoke the image of a unified Lithuanian nation, stating that "the majority of Lithuanian men" joined the fight, or stressing that the partisans, although defeated on the battlefield, achieved a moral victory for all Lithuanians who had never bowed to Soviet rule.[43] Conservative textbooks also put emphasis on the heroic features of the partisans by describing in detail how they paralyzed Soviet institutions,[44] showed courage in open battles, or righteously committed acts of violence against collaborators.[45]

Conservative texts also focus on political and cultural actions in a way that at times makes the armed resistance groups resemble more a civil society organization than combat units. In addition to highlighting the harshness of oppression and the horrifying conditions partisans had to live under, the authors also write about the establishment of a centralized leadership and the adoption of declarations.[46] They report on the considerable efforts made to raise the national and civic awareness of the population.[47]

Like their left-wing counterparts, some conservative authors give more attention to the last phase of the war and describe in detail how miserable the partisans were, living in wet, poorly ventilated underground shelters in which they almost died of starvation.[48] General, these books give much less attention to military actions and the fight with local enemies, the *stribai*.

Textbook authors leaning toward the political left provide slightly incoherent narratives by inconsistently assigning responsibility for the murder of innocent people. Depending on the account, they alternately place blame on the partisans themselves or on Soviet agents, who are described as having infiltrated the resistance movement only in order to commit crimes and to contribute to the propaganda image of the partisans as criminals.[49] A similar lack of clarity marks the depiction of Soviet actors. As in books by authors on the right, such individuals are portrayed largely as miserable victims of brute force, but, at times, they are also portrayed simply as greedy individuals keen to collect payment from the Soviets for each partisan handed over to them.[50]

Drawing a preliminary conclusion, I would like to point out three commonalities shared by the two groups of books. First, both left-wing and conservative textbooks become a bit more similar as time passes while, at the same time, preserving the opposing stances of each side. Both have embraced globally dominant narratives of victimhood, and both tend to authenticate the claims of their accounts by pointing from time to time to the complexity of historical reality. Second, both find it important to assign the role of victim, but they assign it to different types of actors. Whereas post-communist authors support an inclusive concept of victimhood, with ample space for literally everybody from collaborators to ordinary peasants to partisans, their conservative colleagues reserve the term exclusively for the partisans. Third, in both cases, the creation of victims serves political interests. Conservatives apparently sought to turn partisans into victims because it allowed them to transform Lithuanian communists into perpetrators. At the same time, they refused even to mention or to recognize those who had been victimized by the anti-Soviet underground. The post-communists, by contrast, blur the boundaries between victims and perpetrators because it enabled them to forget the crimes their political ancestors, the Lithuanian communists, had committed.

Teachers

We interviewed twenty teachers about the textbook historical accounts that they work with in the classroom. Their responses revealed one rather surprising observation regarding one aspect of the texts that is otherwise conspicuous and ubiquitous: despite the contradictions between and within the textbooks, almost all teachers seem to be deeply convinced that there is some kind of hegemonic narrative in which the partisans play a crucial role. All of the teachers try to invoke this narrative, and even those who were born long after the violent clashes would sooner or later mention the partisans as part of their family history. Some rushed to demonstrate their intimate knowledge of the history of the partisan movement. Some apologized for not having known about the partisans until after the Soviet era had ended. Others openly blamed old-fashioned teachers who, even nowadays, did not know how to distinguish between the good guys and bad, the partisans and the Soviets.

However, if we listen carefully to what they tell us, we arrive at a slightly different picture. For example, some teachers frequently favour the perspective of the Soviets when talking about the violent postwar years. It is through the eyes of officials serving the regime that we as listeners come to look at these events. As a rule, moreover, the Soviets appear to be the weak ones, those who must die in the end. They are referred to as victims.

The account given by Paulius, a rural teacher in his late 50s, is a good illustrative example. Paulius comes across as a typical right-wing conservative, who constantly complains about national minorities, Western consumerism, and the faked patriotism of power-hungry, post-communist elites, whom he describes as opportunists able to amass a fortune in any system. He displays great eagerness to demonstrate his knowledge of Lithuanian history, ranging from medieval kings and queens to the Lithuanian interwar army, a favourite topic in the conservative press. Most importantly, he portrays himself as a courageous man who was under constant surveillance by the KGB in Soviet times because he and his students had once visited one of the few statues of Vytautas the Great, a medieval ruler and epitome of Lithuanian national pride. This episode serves a double function. It was meant to turn him, the history teacher supposed to propagate the Soviet socialist ideology, into something of a dissident. But, at the same time, it also buys him cover for his more compliant moments, such as when he attended party meetings or confronted students who dared to joke about Brezhnev.

Paulius takes on an almost poetic tone in his other recollections, such as his childhood memories of a young Russian lieutenant who was decapitated by the low-hanging branches of a tree while on the back of a truck in hot pursuit of partisans. It is probably not by accident that Paulius offers us a narrative clearly reminiscent of typical Soviet stories about the Second World War, replete with young men bursting with energy, full of hopes and dreams, but whose lives were taken much too early at the hands of a merciless enemy. Implicitly we are invited to identify with this tragic hero, even though he happened to be a representative of the Soviet system.

Yet it is not only in regard to form and tone that Paulius slips back into Soviet patterns of remembering. Even with respect to content, he undermines the carefully constructed image of himself as a Lithuanian patriot who, from the bottom of his heart, hates all things Soviet. In all his narratives, the partisans are in full control of the situation. They are supported by the clergy. They always know in advance when and where the Soviet troops will leave their garrisons to attack them. They are always well prepared, and their opponents actually never really have a chance for victory. In the end, Paulius presents the partisans as perpetrators and the Soviets as victims who are helpless, if not innocent. In another recollection, he explains that his father did not fear the revenge of the partisans for playing cards with the local head of the Communist Party because an NKVD unit was located nearby. Here, Soviets are protectors against evil.

Adele, a female teacher about the same age as Paulius, tells slightly different stories, which nonetheless produce similar effects. She appropriates and radicalizes post-communist narratives. Almost everything she talks about during the interview is aimed at downplaying differences between the enemies and the followers of the Soviet regime in Lithuania. Adele wants us to understand that these categories are misleading and inappropriate because, in the end, everything boils down to whether someone is a good person or not. In order to make that point, she shows us that communists and anti-communists could be both saints and culprits. Priests could be understanding and empathetic, like the one who did not register the baptism of her children in the official parish book in order to save her trouble with the KGB, which was always checking up on teachers suspected of lacking a strong sense of atheism. On the other hand, clerics could also be bigoted and cruel, like the one who shouted at Adele's colleague during a funeral, blaming him for the evil Soviet system. In Adele's eyes, officials of the regime were the same. They could be helpful yet also an annoyance for ordinary people. One local official, she notes, shared his house with a deported woman upon her return from Siberia. In contrast, though, she recalls the chief of her parents' collective farm, who constantly cheated people.

This blurring of boundaries between political categories reaches a climax in the story Adele tells of her uncle, who had been head of the district administration during the partisan war. Adele describes in detail how he sometimes spent a week drinking heavily with the partisans, only to do exactly the same thing the next week with the NKVD officers, all in order to survive the years of chaos and unpredictability. In Adele's version of postwar events, we see him as the archetypical victim trying to walk the thin line between rival political camps. He is depicted as a largely helpless and powerless man.

These examples leave us with a rather ambivalent view. When they express explicit judgment, teachers try to argue in line with what they perceive to be the hegemonic discourse. In between the lines, however, when they are engaged in narrating and when they lose perspective of the way they talk, they are simultaneously subverting this hegemony. Paulius does so by denying the status of victims to the partisans. He describes them as the more powerful and even more violent party in the conflict. Adele lumps both partisans and communist officials together. To her, they were all of one kind, both fighting for power at the expense of ordinary people. Interestingly, she included even relatively high-ranking functionaries, like her uncle, in the category of the latter.

These stories are all based on the ideal of post-heroic victimhood. In Adele's case, we can even venture a guess about the sources these ideals and their respective images were taken from. The protagonist she introduces in her uncle as well as the plot structure she develops while telling this episode bear an intriguing resemblance to a famous Lithuanian film. In contrast to the official Soviet historiography, which would always paint a mostly stereotypical black-and-white picture of the partisans and the Soviets, the film *Nobody Wanted to Die* (*Niekas ne norėjo mirti*) aims at highlighting irritating nuances. Released at the end of the Khrushchev era, in 1966, it enjoyed great success all over the USSR. Many people appreciated it as the first Soviet film shot in the style of a Hollywood western. The plot unfolds in a Lithuanian village in 1947. The four sons of Lokys, the head of the local Soviet who had been killed by partisans, go on a bloody spree of revenge. In the end, they set in motion a ferocious dynamic that generates even more sorrow, even more senseless death. The main character of the film is

Vaitkus, a rather tragic person. He agrees to become the new village chief only under great pressure. He, a former partisan who had quit the ranks when he realized that they had long since mutated into assassins, is the one the audience is made to identify with. He alone tries to avoid any more bloodshed. To achieve this, he moves back and forth between partisans and Soviets, eating and drinking with them, in efforts to calm them down. When talking about her uncle, Adele appears to borrow scenes from this film in order to add colour and detail to a story she seems to know only in fragments. With the help of a famous work of Lithuanian-Soviet cinematic art, she thus presents a narrative vague enough to include even mid-ranking Soviet officials in the community of victims. This narrative meets not only global norms but also fulfils important functions in a post-communist present, helping to ward off potential accusations of collaboration.

Conclusion

What can we learn from the Lithuanian case about the dynamics of memory, the function that narratives of victimhood may assume, and the strategies actors may choose in order to present their accounts as authentic reflections of historical truth?

The analysis here offers mixed empirical evidence. Lithuanian society is deeply divided over questions of how to remember a violent past and how to lay claim to authenticity. Textbook authors offer competing narratives that reflect opposing political preferences. Under the spell of cosmopolitan discourses on victimhood, they vie for the attention of the public, telling stories of hitherto ignored victims. All these stories emphasize some facts and omit others. Conservative textbooks portray the partisans as victims and the communists as perpetrators. In order to preserve the dichotomy, they mention neither cruel acts of violence committed by the partisans nor the suffering endured by the communists. Textbooks closer to the post-communist version of the past dissolve dichotomies. In their accounts, partisans morph into collaborators, Lithuanian communists fall victim to the Soviets, and ordinary people suffer from the violence inflicted by all sides. As a result, boundaries are blurred. The reality of who did what to whom is almost lost. Both accounts serve political aims.

Teachers are as ambivalent as textbooks. They try to comply with what they perceive as the hegemonic discourse and, at the same time, strive to undermine it. They pay tribute to the memory of the partisans and simultaneously seek to diminish and tarnish their reputation as innocent victims by recalling disturbing facts. They probably do so because they fear being blamed for having served as pillars of the Soviet system of education. In a kind of pre-emptive strike, they try to defame those whom they envy as being beyond any doubt.

Does all this mean that narratives of victimhood once characteristic of politically correct counter-memories are transformed, and begin to support narrow interests as soon as they are appropriated by powerful actors? Looking at the Lithuanian case, this would appear to be only half the truth. The sheer existence of differing narratives allowed for a dialogue between competing memories. Through this dialogue, blind spots became visible and could be addressed. This also contributed to the emergence of more nuanced and differentiated accounts that, for this very reason, apparently hope to receive a stamp of authenticity from many Lithuanians.

NOTES

1 Katarina Frankovic, Johannes Kontny, Viola Pokriefke, and Ekaterina Makhotina, "Okkupation und Widerstand, Gewalt und Glauben: Visualisierung der sowjetischen Epoche im Museum für die Opfer des Genozids," in *Vilnius: Geschichte und Gedächtnis einer Stadt zwischen den Kulturen*, ed. Martin Schulze Wessel, Irene Götz, and E. Makhotina (Frankfurt: Campus, 2010), 50–63.

2 Saulius Macaitis, "Niekas nenorejo mirti," *Siaures Atenai*, 28 February 2004.

3 Petras Katinas, "Žuvusiems, nukankintiems, išniekintiems, bet nepalužusiems partizanams atminti," *XXI. Am žius*, 12 March 2004.

4 Jurgis Jurgelis, "Kas geriau – butu nusautam stribo ar partizano?" *Delfi*, 29 December 2011, https://www.delfi.lt/news/ringas/lit/jjurgelis-kas-geriau-buti-nusautam-stribo-ar-partizano.d?id=53367887.

5 Arvydas Anusauskas, "Partizanai ir stribai: atsakimas istorioje pasiklidusiam generolui," *Delfi*, 1 February 2012.

6 Alexandra Binnenkade, "Doing Memory: Teaching as a Discursive Node," *Journal of Educational Media, Memory, and Society* 7, no. 2 (2015): 29–43.

7 Felicitas Macgilchrist, Barbara Christophe, and Alexandra Binnenkade, "Memory Practices and Schooling: Introduction to the Special Issue," *Journal of Educational Media, Memory, and Society* 7, no. 2 (2015): 1–9.

8 Knowing that there is no such thing as neutral facts, I have tried to base my historical overview on a reading of a broad range of books representing divergent viewpoints in order to identify what is perceived to be undisputed in today's Lithuania. These books include Kestutis Girnius, *Partizanu kovos Lietuvoje* (Vilnius: Mokslo Leidykla, 1990); Kestutis Kasparas, *Lietuvos karas* (Kaunas: Lietuvos kalniniu ir tremtiniu sajunga,

1999); and Nijole Gaskaite-Zemaitiene, *Pasipriesinimas istorija, 1944–1953* (Vilnius: Mintis, 2006).

9 From the sample of twelve textbooks, the following six books were found to be reflective of positions articulated by post-communists: Viktoras Jakimevicius, *Gimtoji šalis Lietuva, 5. Klasei* (Vilnius: Alma Littera, 1994); Viktoras Jakimevičius, *Rodnoj kraj Litva. Vadovelis 5. Klasei* (Vilnius: Alma Littera, 1997); Algis Kasperevicius and Rimantas Jokimaitis, *Naujausiuju laiku istorija, 11–12 klasems* (Vilnius: Kronta, 1998); Rustis Kamuntavičius, Vaida Kamuntavičiene, and Remigijus Civinskas, *Lietuvos istorija, 11.–12. Klaesems* (Vilnius: Vaga, 2004); Algis Kasperevičius, Rimantas Jokímaítis, and Algirdas Jakubčíonis, *Naujausisuju laiku istorija. Vadovelis 10. Klasei* (Vilnius: Kronta, 2004); and Remigius Civinskas and Kastutis Antanaitis, *Lietuvos istorija 12 klasei* (Kaunas: Vaga, 2004). A more conservative approach to postwar history was identified in the following six editions: Juozas Brazauskas, *Lietuvos istorija. Vadovelis 5. Klasei* (Kaunas: Šviesa, 2000); Stanislovas Stašaitis and Jurate Šačkute, *Tevynes istorijos puslapiai. Vadovelis 5. Klasei* (Vilnius: Margi Raštai, 2001); Algirdas Gečas, Juozas Jurkynas, Genia Jurkyniene, and Albinas Visockis, *Lietuva ir pasaulis, Istorijos vadovelis 12. Klasei* (Kaunas: Šviesa, 2001); Evaldas Bakonis, *Lietucva pasaulye. Vadovelis 10. Klasei* (Kaunas: Šviesa, 2004/2005); Ignas Kapleris, Antanas Meištas, Karolis Mickevičius, and Zivile Tamkutonyte-Mikailiene, *Laikas. Istorijos vadovelis 12. Klasei* (Vilnius: Briedis, 2011); and Ignas Kapleris and Antanas Meištas, *Istorijos egzamino gidas. Nauja programa nua A iki ž* (Vilnius: Briedis, 2013). The categorization of textbooks according to the political preferences they express is based on the application of criteria that is discussed in detail later in this chapter.

10 This section on teachers is based on twenty narrative-biographical interviews. These interviews were conducted in 2008 and 2009 in the framework on the research project "Cultural Patterns of Remembering Socialism: History Teachers as an Interface between Cultural and Communicative Memory in Georgia, Kyrgyzstan and Lithuania," funded by the Volkswagen Foundation and headed by the author at the Georg Eckert Institute for International Textbook Research in Braunschweig, Germany. When selecting interview partners, we tried to achieve maximum variation by choosing teachers from both larger cities and rural areas as well as teachers who had come of age both prior to and after the death of Stalin.

11 Aaron Beim, "The Cognitive Aspects of Collective Memory," *Symbolic Interaction* 30, no. 1 (2007): 7–26.

12 Marita Sturken, "Memory, Consumerism and Media: Reflections on the Emergence of the Field," *Memory Studies* 1, no. 1 (2008): 74.

13 Johanna Ahlrichs, Katharina Baier, Barbara Christophe, Felicitas Macgilchrist, Patrick Mielke, and Roman Richtera, "Memory Practices in the Classroom: On Reproducing, Destabilizing and Interrupting Majority Memories," *Journal of Educational Media, Memory, and Society* 7, no. 2 (2015): 89–109.

14 Lorraine Ryan, "Memory, Power and Resistance: The Anatomy of a Tripartite Relationship," *Memory Studies* 4, no. 2 (2011): 154–89.

15 Marita Sturken, "The Wall, the Screen and the Image," in *Making Sense: Essays on Art, Science, and Culture*, ed. Bob Coleman, Rebecca Brittenham, Scott Campbell, and Stephanie Girard (Boston: Houghton Mifflin, 1999).

16 Andrew H. Beattie, *Playing Politics with History: The Bundestag Inquiries into East Germany* (New York: Berghahn Books, 2008).

17 Daniel Levy and Nathan Sznaider, "Memory Unbound: The Holocaust and the Formation of Cosmopolitan Cemory," *European Journal of Social Theory* 5, no. 1 (2002): 87; Daniel Levy and Natan Sznaider, "Memories of Universal Victimhood: The Case of Ethnic German Expellees," *German Politics and Society* 23, no. 2 (2005): 3.

18 Vasilijus Safronovas, "Lietuvos atminimo politicos tendencijos po 1990 metu," in *Nuo Basanavičiaus iki Vytauto didžiojo iki Molentovo ir Ribbentropo: Atminties ir atminimo kulturu transformacijos XX.–XXI. Amžiuje*, ed. Alvydas Nikžentaitis (Vilnius: LII leidykla, 2011), 65–113.

19 Rasa Čepaitiene, "Lietuviu istorines samones tyrimu perspektyvos: ideologinis problemos lygmuo," *Politologija* 3, no. 35 (2004): 84–100.

20 Kazys Blaževičius, "Antanas Sniečius. Kas jis?" *XXI. Amžius*, 24 January 2003.

21 Safronovas, "Lietuvos atminimo politicos tendencijos."

22 Barbara Christophe, *Staat versus Identität: Nation und nationales Interesse in den litauischen Transformationsdiskursen* (Cologne: Verlag Wissenschaft und Politik, 1997).

23 For example, the Lithuanian Activist Front, the organization founded in 1940 in Berlin that had organized the uprising, declared in its program that not a single Jew should be allowed to stay in a future Lithuania.

24 In general, these books are expected to offer a necessarily broad overview of Lithuanian history from the Middle Ages to the present. As a rule, they provide their young readers with snapshots presented in the form of personalized stories. Authors are typically under immense pressure to condense material and to distinguish between the trivial and the important. As a consequence, the textbook researcher can easily identify underlying plot structures by investigating the criteria on which the authors have based their selections. For an introduction to plot analysis in textbook research, see Elefterios Klerides, "Imagining Textbooks: The Textbook as Discourse and Genre," *Journal of Educational Media, Memory and Society* 2, no. 1 (2010): 31–54.

25 Jakimevičius, *Rodnoj kraj*, 211–13; Stašaitis and Šačkute, *Tevynes istorijos puslapiai*, 162–4.
26 Bakonis, *Lietuva pasaulye*, 115.
27 Kapleris and Meištas, *Istorijos egzamino gidas*, 395; Kapleris et al., *Laikas*, 113, 220.
28 See, for example, Kasperevičius, Jokímaítis, and Jakubčíonis, *Naujausisuju laiku istorija*, 197.
29 Jakimevičius, *Rodnoj kraj*, 426; Kasperevičius, Jokímaítis, and Jakubčíonis, *Naujausisuju laiku istorija*.
30 Kamuntavičius, Kamuntavičiene, and Civinskas, *Lietuvos istorija*, 428.
31 Kapleris and Meištas, *Istorijos egzamino gidas*, 401.
32 Bakonis, *Lietuva pasaulye*, 112.
33 Gečas at al., *Lietuva ir pasaulis*, 335.
34 Kapleris and Meištas, *Istorijos egzamino gidas*, 396; Stašaitis and Šačkute, *Tevynes istorijos puslapiai*, 163; Gečas et al., *Lietuva ir pasaulis*, 341.
35 Bakonis, *Lietuva pasaulye*, 113. See also Kapleris et al., *Laikas*, 221.
36 Brazauskas, *Lietuvos istorija*, 145.
37 Gečas et al., *Lietuva ir pasaulis*, 335.
38 Jakimevičius, *Rodnoj kraj*, 214; Kasperevičius, Jokímaítis, and Jakubčíonis, *Naujausisuju laiku istorija*, 198.
39 Kamuntavičius, Kamuntavičiene, and Civinskas, *Lietuvos istorija*, 434.
40 Kasperevičius, Jokímaítis, and Jakubčíonis, *Naujausisuju laiku istorija*, 197.
41 Ibid., 198.
42 Ibid., 202.
43 Brazauskas, *Lietuvos istorija*, 144; Kapleris et al., *Laikas*, 221.
44 Brazauskas, *Lietuvos istorjia*, 143.
45 Ibid., 145; Bakonis, *Lietuva pasaulye*, 114ff.
46 Kapleris and Meištas, *Istorijos egzamino gidas*, 396.
47 Kapleris et al., *Laikas*, 220.
48 Stašaitis and Šačkute, *Tevynes istorijos puslapiai*, 164.
49 Kasperevičius, Jokímaítis, and Jakubčíonis, *Naujausisuju laiku istorija*, 198, 202.
50 Ibid., 218, 219.

PART 4

Victims of Forced Migration and Deportations

10 In Search of a Usable Memory: The Politics of History and the Day of Commemoration for German Forced Migrants after the Second World War

MATHIAS BEER

"Flight and Expulsion" in Federal German Debates

The German Bundestag, the parliament of the Federal Republic of Germany, was constituted on 7 September 1949 and commenced work that day on a new state emerging from the aftermath of the Second World War. Two weeks later, on 20 September, Federal Chancellor Konrad Adenauer gave his first government declaration (*Regierungserklärung*) before the body. One of the focal points of his speech was the fate of German expellees (*Vertriebene*), which, as he put it, was a vital question for the German people that could be solved only internationally. Chancellor Adenauer addressed the issue of postwar borders and the expulsion of German populations in detail:

> I would like to point out that the deracination of the expellees has occurred in contravention of the terms of the Potsdam Agreement. This Potsdam Agreement concerned merely a resettlement of the remaining German population in Poland, Czechoslovakia, and Hungary, and ... it had been agreed that any resettlement should take place in an organized and humane manner. I find it quite difficult ... to speak with the necessary dispassionate restraint when I think of the fate of the expellees who have perished by the millions.

In his closing words, the chancellor emphasized that the government would accord this matter the utmost importance so that Germany's rights might be respected: "We will recapitulate all legal and factual data in a memorandum which shall be published and submitted to the Allied governments."[1]

On 27 August 2014, a German government spokesman announced the resolutions the federal cabinet had agreed on that day. Among other things, the government had decided "that as of the year 2015, the victims of flight and expulsion [were] to be commemorated on June 20. By choosing this date … the federal government joins in [recognizing] the World Refugee Day of the United Nations," which the UN General Assembly had established in 2001. The spokesman then made reference to the current figures on refugees worldwide and on displaced persons in Germany, to flight and expulsion as part of the history of the twentieth century, to forced migration as part of the Second World War initiated by Germany, as well as the expulsion of the Jews, which came to "its gruesome end in extermination camps." "Ultimately," he continued, "millions of Germans also had to leave their ancestral homes due to flight, expulsion, forced resettlement, and deportation. The federal government strongly supports the historical research of these events and the commemoration of the victims." In closing, he summarized the cabinet resolution: "On this new day of commemoration for the victims of flight and expulsion, the worldwide victims of flight and expulsion and especially the German expellees will be remembered."[2]

Both documents address the same key issue of recent European history in general and German history in particular: the forced migration of approximately 12.5 million German citizens and German minorities from east-central European states, who fled, were expelled, and were resettled during and after the Second World War.[3] In the German language, the cipher "flight and expulsion" is commonly used to refer to this process and encompasses multiple meanings. Only in their totality do they reveal the scale and the complexity of the topic, which includes the multifaceted remembrance of the process.

The term "flight and expulsion" refers to the violent relocation of millions of Germans, which claimed hundreds of thousands of lives and represents the numerically largest portion of European forced migrations at the end of the Second World War.[4] It evokes a process inextricably linked to that war and the National Socialist politics of conquest, occupation, and extermination. Its temporal and contextual dimension, however, reaches far beyond that: the historical context of flight and expulsion spans the entire first half of twentieth-century European history and its politics of ethnic cleansing, the roots of which reach far back into the nineteenth century and the era of nationalism.[5] As a catchall phrase, "flight and expulsion" encompasses a regionally diversified process with a wide range of manifestations. They range from resettlements on the basis of international treaties to evacuation, from flight to deportation, from "wild expulsions" to contractually regulated resettlements to the detriment of third parties. The phrase also encapsulates millions of life stories substantially impacted by this forced migration.

For those concerned, the age- and gender-specific experiences in the course of evacuation, flight, and expulsion represent some of the most drastic and traumatic ones of their lives. These memories are an enduring, heavy burden that is even passed on to refugee children and grandchildren.

Also embedded in this complex appellation are the inevitable short- and long-term effects of German forced migration. The latter represented an entire uprooting of demographic, social, economic, and cultural frameworks both in the east-central European states of origin and in the destinations of the refugees and expellees. The forcibly displaced represented between 20 and 25 per cent of the total population in their ultimate destinations and, as a consequence, significantly and permanently shaped the postwar societies of the two German states as well as of reunified Germany.[6]

Lastly, "flight and expulsion" implicates the intense political and social disputes in the Federal Republic of Germany concerning the forced migration of Germans at the end of the Second World War.[7] Contrary to the popular conception that the topic is taboo, flight and expulsion has been a constant topic of broad and controversial debates at all levels of society – in politics, interest groups, the media, academia, art, culture, and also among contemporary witnesses – ever since the foundation of the Bonn Republic in 1949. The arduous integration of the refugees and expellees laid a foundation to keep the fires of these debates kindled well into the present day of the Berlin Republic.[8] They are interdependent with the discourses on "flight and expulsion" of the Germans in the states of east-central Europe, especially Poland and Czechoslovakia or the Czech Republic respectively,[9] and they are prominent features running through the history of the Federal Republic that raise an eminent political question and constitute part of the German efforts to come to terms with its past before and after 1945.[10]

Both government documents mentioned above – Konrad Adenauer's government declaration of 1949 and the cabinet resolution of 27 August 2014 – address the same issue of flight and expulsion, but they differ fundamentally both in their arguments and in their priorities. Whereas the first is focused on purely legal questions concerning German forced migration – "Germany's rights," to which the Federal government intended to accord the utmost importance – the second is concerned with the status of German refugees and expellees in national memory culture. The latter has been highlighted by the new commemoration day for victims on which "the worldwide victims of flight and expulsion and especially the German forced migrants will be remembered."

Both documents can be considered milestones in the German debate on flight and expulsion in two respects. Chronologically speaking, they encompass the entire history of the Federal Republic. Thus, they include both the beginning of the highly politicized controversies over the issue, which have now been developing for more than seven decades, as well as the present status quo. In terms of content, they reveal a clear, fundamental shift in the assessment of forced migration by the Federal government and the Bundestag: the greatly prioritized legal questions at the core of the 1949 document are completely absent from the press conference of August 2014, at which the government emphasized an entirely new approach focused on the politics of memory. These fundamentally different perspectives and appraisals of the history of German forced migration are not the result of a linear development. They are, rather, points of departure and, for the time being, the point arrived at in German debates on flight and expulsion in international and national contexts from the late 1940s up to the present day. These debates reveal different strategies for gaining recognition in the culture of commemoration and display several characteristics. If we are to understand accurately the shift of perspective in its chronological development, and if we are to analyse its content appropriately, we must take a closer look at these characteristics; this closer inspection will follow in the second part of this chapter. These characteristics help to elucidate, first, how the identified shift came about by reframing "legal question" as a question of remembrance (the latter point will also be illustrated below). Second, the historical-political debates help us understand why the search for a usable, socially acceptable form of memory of flight and expulsion in the Federal Republic of Germany has been such a meandering process, which still has not been completed. Third, these characteristics explain the relatively recent establishment of a national commemoration day in Germany for the victims of the forced migration of Germans at the end of the Second World War. A fourth and final point is that this background accounts for the specific form ultimately taken by this commemoration day, which is, of course, tied to the existing World Refugee Day of the United Nations on 20 June.

The central thesis I would like to propose, and that I will pick up on again in the last part of the chapter, is that the introduction of this national day of commemoration cannot be regarded solely as an expression of the "boom of remembrance" that researchers have identified since the 1990s.[11] Rather, it is the result of the particularities of federal German politics of history,[12] in which "flight and expulsion" has been marked by controversy,[13] and a bitter struggle for memories that endures to this today. These debates on the politics of history and collective commemoration come into sharper focus when viewed through actions taken by the German Bundestag, which serve as the starting point of this inquiry.[14]

Aspects of the Debates, or How to Speak of a Catastrophe in the Shadow of an Even Greater One

The debates within Germany on flight and expulsion were long shaped by the frameworks of foreign affairs and were subordinated to those considerations. In 1949, this meant the political climate of the Cold War that tore asunder the anti-Hitler coalition of the Allies, split Europe, and divided Germany. Discourse on the forced migration of Germans subsequently reflected this dichotomy: in the Federal Republic, one spoke reproachfully – as the first government declaration of Chancellor Adenauer and the subsequent debate demonstrate – of expulsion, for which a large-scale, and seminal, not to mention controversial, research project was initiated.[15] The project used mainly oral interviews and was the first step in the authentication of flight and expulsion. In the states of the Eastern Bloc, however, the defensive words used were "relocation," "transfer," and "resettlement."[16] These programmatic terms corresponded to a supposedly clear assignment of responsibility for the flight, expulsion, and resettlement of German peoples, depending on which of the two systems of alliances one belonged to: in the West, it was considered to be the so-called expeller states; in the East, it was Nazi Germany.

The ensuing phase of détente between East and West caused by the atomic stalemate led to new circumstances in the 1960s and 1970s that provided the context for a reorientation of German foreign policy under a coalition of the Social Democrats (SPD) and Liberals (FDP). The Christian Democrats (CDU/CSU), the expellee interest groups, and notably those groups' mouthpiece, the Federation of Expellees (Bund der Vertriebenen, or BdV)[17] – which were operating according to German raison d'état – criticized the *neue Ostpolitik* and the new classification of flight and expulsion by the SPD-FDP coalition with equal vehemence.[18] No longer did the Federal government and the Bundestag accuse east-central European states alone of crimes *against* Germans in the context of forced migration. Rather, all crimes were now condemned indiscriminately, no matter by whom or by which side they had been committed during and after the war.[19] Flight and expulsion as discursive topics were subordinated to reconciliation with Eastern European neighbour states.

The fundamental changes in global political conditions in the last decade of the twentieth century – the collapse of the Soviet Union and thus the end of the bipolar world order, in addition to German reunification – also affected debates on flight and expulsion in the German Bundestag. Reunified Germany was no longer a frontline state and became a partner of the east-central European countries. In 2002, a red-green government coalition of the SPD and Bündnis 90/Die Grünen (Alliance 90/the Greens) planned to establish a centre against expulsions with a European perspective in order to create a greater sense of solidarity with Germany's neighbours but also – and not least of all – in order to proffer an alternative concept to the BdV's project for a similar centre that would have placed a greater emphasis on the German experience.[20] Engagement with the east-central European states, however, did not lead to a "European Centre against Expulsions" but, rather, to a German "Foundation Flight, Expulsion, Reconciliation" that was aimed at promoting dialogue with the neighbour states and was administered by the German Historical Museum in Berlin.[21] It was founded in 2008 and promoted by the grand coalition of CDU/CSU and SPD in power at that time. The official statement concerning the law that established the foundation clearly states that the Federal Republic's task of historically appraising the process of expulsion is shaped significantly by political conditions.

In addition, the debates on flight and expulsion were closely linked with the German political parties' assessment of territorial changes as a result of the Second World War. When referring to the western border of Poland in the government declaration of 1949, Chancellor Adenauer deliberately and exclusively employed the term "Oder-Neiße Line," thus substantiating the legal claim to the territories ceded by Germany and the right of return of expellees.[22]

The cross-party consensus regarding the German question dwindled during the 1960s. When the SPD-FDP coalition committed itself in the early 1970s to respecting the status quo in accordance with the *neue Ostpolitik*, it adopted the stance that German territory could not be restored to the borders of 1937. This politically highly controversial step added a new dimension to the discourse on flight and expulsion. The Federal government wanted to avoid by all means "discussions of compensation" and "balances of accounts of crime" with its neighbour states to the east,[23] but the political explosiveness of the topic did not wane. Quite to the contrary, the posture assumed by Germany vis-à-vis its neighbour states concerning the matter of flight and expulsion was complemented by a domestic one between the two major federal parties, the tracks of which, as we will see, can be traced up to the present day.

Twenty years later, the Iron Curtain fell. Due to the resolution of the long-standing "open German question" as a result of the

Two-Plus-Four Agreement on 14 November 1990 – that is, the final recognition of the postwar borders as envisioned in the Potsdam Agreement – all references to border concerns disappeared from discussions of flight and expulsion. The 2008 law establishing the Foundation Flight, Expulsion, Reconciliation emphasizes the notion of reconciliation and the joint transnational effort to deal with European forced migration in the twentieth century. In this respect, the name speaks for itself.

A third aspect of the debates in the Federal Republic concerns the preconditions for the act of expulsion, its causes, and the question of the victims who have perished. The government declaration of 1949 provides no indication of the causes for the forced migration of Germans, let alone the National Socialist politics of conquest, occupation, and destruction.[24] No background is offered – flight and expulsion appear simply to be a succession of repeated unlawful actions, without presuppositions, committed by multiple east-central European states and resulting in a death toll of millions, which was a great exaggeration on Adenauer's part.

A quarter of a century later, this assessment had changed. In the eyes of the SPD-FDP governments of the 1970s, the Nazi policies had laid the foundation for the forced migration of Germans. In view of this reappraisal of causes and consequences, in which the Holocaust was considered to be the absolute "point zero" – also largely as a result of the juridical processing of National Socialism in the Federal Republic[25] – the government strove to avoid a public discussion both in Germany and abroad of the crimes committed *against* Germans during the process of expulsion. They made every effort to keep under lock and key the "Documentation of Crimes of Expulsion," which the previous government had commissioned the Federal Archives to create and was completed in 1974.[26] To the extent that the Holocaust became the norm of the national remembrance and collective commemoration framework, flight and expulsion was also subordinated to it in the politics of remembrance.

At the beginning of the new millennium, causes and consequences were evaluated more judiciously. The reassessment opposed a narrative focused on German victims, as had been prevalent in the Federal Republic up to the early 1960s, as well as the general evasion of the issue during the SPD-FDP coalitions. Instead, a European perspective on flight and expulsion was called for, which would underline the reciprocity of the roles of victim and perpetrator. The causes were now stated clearly: the practice of resettlement and expulsion developed at the beginning of the twentieth century as a means of solving minority and border conflicts, the onslaught of the Second World War by the German Reich and the corresponding National Socialist politics of expansion, population transfer and extermination, and the new constellation of powers at the end of the Second World War.

A fourth aspect of the debates in the Federal Republic of Germany on flight and expulsion is their close connections to German society's self-examination concerning National Socialism, embodied by the term *Vergangenheitsbewältigung* (coming to terms with the past). In the government declaration of 1949, the German victims – wounded veterans, war widows and orphans, prisoners of war, abducted persons, and expellees – were the focus of attention. The Adenauer government hardly touched upon the mass slaughters directed by National Socialists. When the issue was addressed, it was often only by allusion and, even then, not by the ruling coalition but, rather, by the opposition SPD. Responding to Adenauer's government declaration, SPD vice-president of the Bundestag Carlo Schmid stated that the right to claim a moral basis for objecting to cruelties visited upon Germans at the end of the war belonged solely to those who "had been at least ashamed" about "the expulsion and eradication of the Jews and Poles, about Lidice, about Auschwitz and about Oradour."[27]

The interconnectedness of debates on flight and expulsion and the question of National Socialism intensified to the degree that, by 1960, Germany's coming to terms with the Nazi past was becoming the point of reference for dealing with the past altogether. If, at the founding of the Federal Republic, the focus had been on the crimes *against* Germans and the ensuing casualties, the balance, in the 1960s, of the "competition of crimes and victims" shifted that focus to the crimes committed *by* Germans.

This development continued to intensify in the ensuing years. Although the history of forced migration of Germans was acknowledged as an injustice, and the causalities of the expulsion process were commemorated, National Socialism and Nazi crimes became the primary point of reference for interpreting other historical events. To erect a site of remembrance commemorating expellees that was comparable to Berlin's Holocaust Memorial (approved in 1999 and dedicated in 2005) was therefore out of the question.[28] The permanent exhibition of the Foundation Flight, Expulsion, Reconciliation was thus charged to present the memory of German victims within a comprehensive historical context so as to counteract any suspicion of wanting to relativize the events.

A fifth important aspect is that the debates on flight and expulsion were not only exceedingly politicized, but they were also largely polarized ideologically. At the same time, the evolution of individual positions should not be overlooked, even if that was an admittedly slow process. The consensus that had existed among the major political parties during the 1950s regarding the political assessment of flight and expulsion – that is, that Germans were victims of the war – subsequently fell apart. The opposition to this view was essentially a partisan one composed of two camps. It had always been part of the basic philosophy of the conservative parties to consider Germans' victimization through flight and expulsion. The SPD, however, endorsed an opposing view: the injustices suffered by Germans were not only counterbalanced by Nazi crimes, but those crimes were also unquestionably at the top of the hierarchy of atrocities. This partisan discord intensified in the 1960s and 1970s. Bitter political altercations resulted that had yet to be fundamentally resolved even at the beginning of the twenty-first century. The establishment of the Foundation Flight, Expulsion, Reconciliation in 2008, however, indicates that they have been largely overcome. A stable, formal framework was found that reflected deep agreement in terms of the foundation's mission: remembrance, commemoration, and education in the spirit of reconciliation through "musealization," academic research, and documentation in the context of European and worldwide forced migrations. But the framework also accommodated the differing emphases of a primary focus on German flight and expulsion in an international context versus one on worldwide forced migration with a secondary focus on the German example. Thus, the complex matter, which had been mired for decades in partisan polarization, has to a certain degree been received and reintegrated into mainstream German historical narratives.

The foundation represented the first museum-based approach that acknowledges and deals with flight and expulsion as a part of German history. It is no longer a matter of legal questions, of balances of accounts and assignment of guilt, but of an academically based memorialization of German flight and expulsion in a European context and beyond. This result, however, does not answer the fundamental question of how global examples of flight and expulsion in the twentieth century in general and the specifically German variants relate to each other in the foundation's proposed permanent exhibition. Indeed, this question continues to be a bone of contention in ongoing academic and political disputes between the foundation's board of trustees and its advisory council.

The Path to a National Commemoration Day and the Politics of Memory in International Perspective

Progress toward establishing a commemoration day for the victims of flight and expulsion must be considered in the context of the nuanced debates described above. The question of how to commemorate this historical event adequately on a national level emerged after 1989/90. It provided the impetus for creating a permanent exhibition by the Foundation Flight, Expulsion, Reconciliation in 2008. A major push for establishing such a commemoration day also came from the BdV as part of its quest for victim status for German refugees and expellees. This advocacy group has played a considerable role in the national and international debates on flight and expulsion, by drawing on the strength created by the integration of refugees and expellees in the party landscape. It has served simultaneously as a driving and a braking force, both with regard to the legal positions adopted and to the commemorative goals.

The German Bundestag formed a commission in 1995 to examine the legacy of the East German past, and it published a final report in 1998 entitled *Overcoming the Consequences of the SED Dictatorship in the Process of German Unification*.[29] The commission recommended that the existing memorial site for victims of flight and expulsion on the Theodor-Heuss-Platz in Berlin, which had been constructed in 1955 on the initiative of the victim organizations, be used as the basis for the federal government's larger commemorative plans.[30] In view of the national significance of the expellee memorial, it was decided that the Federal government would be responsible for its maintenance costs. This suggestion was picked up on and amplified by the CDU/CSU parliamentary group in the Bundestag, which advocated for the Berlin memorial as a "central reminder against flight and expulsion." Erika Steinbach, president of the BdV and also a CDU member of the Bundestag at that time, responded to this as being merely a "small solution" and further proposed a more multifaceted plan for a "Centre against Expulsions." This plan was also the result of a ground-breaking insight of the expellee lobby. By embedding flight and expulsion in the national memory of the country, they saw a way to consolidate and mobilize their own dwindling group and to compensate for their diminished political influence, which had been on the wane since the 1970s, given the progressive integration of the expellees and the *neue Ostpolitik* of the SPD-FDP coalition. This meant changing direction from a course focused on legal questions to one geared toward the politics of memory.

The BdV's planned project, and especially the broad and controversial discussions that it triggered in Germany and abroad, significantly accelerated development of plans for a museum dealing with this topic.[31] It was, however, not the initiative of the expellee group, anchored on the idea of German uniqueness in victimhood, but, rather, the much differently conceived Foundation Flight, Expulsion, Reconciliation that was to become the definitive memorial and museum site in Germany for the forced migration of Germans. The group-specific commemorative interests of the BdV were not incorporated in their existing form into the ultimate representation of German cultural memory of flight and expulsion but nonetheless served as a catalyst for the creation of the Foundation Flight, Expulsion, Reconciliation. The BdV apparently does not fully identify with this development and continues to pursue its own project of a "centre against expulsions," despite the existence of the federal foundation.

In their efforts to shape the politics of memory, the BdV simultaneously strove toward establishing such a centre and advocating for a national day of commemoration;[32] it enjoyed the support of the CDU/CSU on both projects. The BdV built its efforts toward both objectives on the understanding that the resolution of the "German question" – that is, through reunification – meant that legal interests regarding expellees would no longer be in play. It therefore seemed advantageous to embed narratives regarding flight and expulsion in a broader narrative of German national memory.

Like the permanent exhibition, whose genesis drew in part on the memorial to expellees constructed in Berlin in 1955, the plans for a commemoration day also referred to historical precedent from the early years of the Federal Republic. The BdV sought to establish 5 August as the national day of commemoration for flight and expulsion. The BdV's predecessor organization, the Central Union of the Expelled Germans (Zentralverband der vertriebenen Deutschen, or ZvD), had observed a Homeland Day (*Tag der Heimat*) in Stuttgart in 1950 on this date, which had been chosen in connection with the anniversary of the resettlement of the German population formalized in the 1945 Potsdam Agreement.[33] On the first Homeland Day, the organization adopted the Charter of the German Expellees (*Charta der deutschen Heimatvertriebenen*).[34] The self-appointed expellee representatives crafted this declaration to renounce revenge and retaliation and referred to themselves as those "who have suffered most from the hardships of our times" – an obvious denial of the historical context. The group employed a narrative of salvation to buttress its demand for global recognition of a "right to homeland" as a human right, together with a demand, directed to the German people, for massive government aid for the integration of the expellees. The charter thus displayed a tension between the desired to return to a former homeland – now under the control of non-German states – and integrating into a new home (the Federal Republic). The charter as an expression of the expellees' political will at that point in time reveals the dilemma invariably faced by any potential resolution of the German refugee problem: claiming a right that could not be fulfilled and, at the same time, gradually putting down roots in Germany, which was initially a foreign and often hostile society in the eyes of many refugees and expellees.

The proposals at the beginning of this century that endorsed 5 August as the date for a national day of commemoration drew on Homeland Day, which all expellee organizations have continually observed since 1950, as well as on the Charter of Expellees, which they consider their "basic law" (using the same term as that designating the German constitution, the *Grundgesetz*). The Free State of Bavaria, with its traditional special relationship to the German expellees,[35] introduced a corresponding resolution in the German Federal Council (Bundesrat) on 11 July 2003.[36] The accompanying explanatory memorandum states that the "tragedy of deportation, flight and expulsion of approximately 15 million Germans from their homeland subsequent to World War II was one of the most drastic experiences in the history of our people." Using an explicit and deliberately selective reference to the Charter of the German Expellees and invoking present-day expulsions around the world, the resolution entreated the Federal government to "designate the fifth of August, the day the Charter of the German Expellees was signed, as the 'National Day of Commemoration for the Victims of Expulsion.'" The Bundesrat supported the resolution, but, in the ensuing years – during which the construction of the Holocaust Memorial was approved and the Foundation Flight, Expulsion, Reconciliation was created – it did not come to fruition.

Parliamentarians of the coalition formed between the CDU/CSU and FDP seized the opportunity presented by the sixtieth anniversary of the signing of the Charter of Expellees to make a new push for commemoration. On 15 December 2010, their proposal, "60 Years of the Charter of the German Expellees – Completing Reconciliation," called on the Federal government to, among other things, "support the reconciliation process of Germans concerning the issue of expulsion," to promote research on the culture and history of Germans in Eastern Europe more vigorously, and to promote the Foundation Flight, Expulsion, Reconciliation and especially its planned permanent exhibition.[37] These calls, however, were meant merely to buttress the underlying concern of the petition: drawing widely on the 2003 Bundesrat initiative, the content of the Charter of the German Expellees, the successful integration of refugees and expellees, and the arguments of both academia and political opponents, the petition exhorted the federal government to examine how "August 5th might be established as a nationwide commemoration day for the victims of expulsion."

The Bundestag's Culture and Media Committee (Ausschuss für Kultur und Medien des Deutschen Bundestags) supported the motion, and so it became the subject of a heated, hour-long debate on 10 February 2011.[38] The battle lines were clearly drawn from the outset: on one side, the reigning coalition of CDU/CSU and FDP and, on the other, the opposition parties of SPD, Greens, and the Left Party (DIE LINKE). The speakers from the government coalition emphasized the primary concern of their petition – namely, to commemorate the Charter of Expellees adopted on 5 August 1950 and to emphasize the accomplishments of the expellees. "We are seeking to ensure that the loss of homeland of 14 million Germans is made a symbol of warning [*Mahnmal*] for all expulsions of the present day."[39] The opposition parties made clear that, for them, the fundamental question was not the proper commemoration of flight and expulsion but, rather, when and in what way this should take place:

> The conflict in this debate does not concern the question whether we acknowledge the fate of the expellees or not. Nor does it concern whether we are interested in dealing with the history of expulsion in its historical context. The conflict fundamentally concerns the question whether we as the German Bundestag wish to make positive reference to the document of the Charter of Expellees and, moreover, underline that fact by making the day of its signing a commemoration day for the Federal Republic of Germany.[40]

The speaker of the SPD further pointed out the raison d'être of the Federal Republic of Germany, in which political practice and political culture must be understood as a consequence of the Nazi past. He derived from this a clear hierarchy of victims: "German sensitivity for the suffering and victims of expulsion and flight does not solely nor primarily result from Germans having been victims themselves, but from Germans having victimized others. It is from this twofold bitter experience that our permanent moral obligation stems."[41] Associating 5 August with a national day of commemoration for flight and expulsion was completely out of the question for the opposition – due both to the content of the charter and to the fundamental consensus in German society of assuming responsibility for the National Socialist past. The motion was nonetheless approved by the Bundestag on 10 February 2011, with the majority of votes of the coalition parties.

It was less the outcome of the vote and more the nuanced discussion of the motion in the plenary session of the Bundestag that illustrated that the debates over a commemoration day for flight and expulsion no longer focused on the question of whether such a day was expedient but, rather, the questions of when and how it should be observed. Thus, the adoption of the motion was not first and foremost a success for its exponents; it instead led to the insight that the BdV's endeavour to make 5 August a national day of commemoration, as supported by the government coalition, was not politically viable. This conclusion was reinforced by the fact that the project was fiercely criticized and rejected by parts of German society – including, for example, a petition of reputable historians[42] – as well as by the media and abroad. The parliamentarians of the government coalition would have to make a greater effort if they wanted to achieve their vision of a national commemoration day for the victims of flight and expulsion.

It took another two years before CDU/CSU and FDP made a new attempt. Apparently, those parties saw no suitable date in that period that could be used as a convincing basis for establishing a national day of commemoration. But by 2013, such a date arrived in the form of the sixtieth anniversary of the adoption of the Law on the Affairs of the Expellees and Refugees (Federal Expellee Law, for short; in German, *Gesetz über die Angelegenheiten der Vertriebenen und Flüchtlinge*, or BVFG), which had been approved by the Bundestag on 25 March 1953.[43] The law had come into effect on 5 June 1953 and, together with the Equalization of Burdens Act (*Lastenausgleichsgesetz*),[44] provided the decisive legal basis for the slow and arduous process of integrating the millions of refugees and expellees in the Federal Republic of Germany.

Capitalizing on the anniversary, the CDU/CSU and FDP parliamentary groups put forward a new motion in the Bundestag, called "60 Years Federal Expellee Law – Remembering the Victims of Expulsion,"[45] with the goal of establishing a national commemorative day for flight and expulsion. The preparation, content, structure, and wording of this motion indicate that its petitioners had drawn far-reaching conclusions from the simultaneous success and failure of 2011. Although this new motion pursued the same goal as its predecessor, it had undergone a complete makeover. First of all, in focusing on the Federal Expellee Law, the motion's supporters chose to anchor their efforts in an event of legislative history that was regarded positively across all party lines. From this starting point, the motion's proponents could attach the implication that Germany had a duty to support this group of persons as well as German minorities in Eastern Europe both materially and culturally. Second, the motion set out the hierarchy of victims in the Federal Republic of Germany's process of overcoming the consequences of war, albeit in a linguistically hair-splitting manner: "Reconciliation and making amends to the victims of National Socialism and the wars of aggression initiated by Germany is *of overriding importance*. It is *complemented* by solidarity with the Germans who have suffered a particularly heavy burden of fate in the wake of the war due to their ethnicity."[46] Third, the long-favoured date for a national day of commemoration was abandoned, and the Charter of the German Expellees was mentioned only in passing. The motion proposed to remember the victims of flight and expulsion in the context of an international commemoration day, namely "to expand the present World Refugee Day on June 20th to include the commemoration of the expellees."[47]

The motion was submitted only two days before the debate, and its name was changed three times by the petitioning coalition partners. When it was discussed in the Bundestag on 13 June 2013, it sparked a spirited and enthusiastic debate similar to the motion two years earlier, full of biographical references by the speakers present. Though nothing had changed concerning the fundamental partisan battle lines, parliamentarians of all parties – with the exception of the Left Party – seemed eager to overcome division, reinforce common ground, and build bridges. The opposition parties welcomed that by proposing World Refugee Day; the motion had picked up on a suggestion previously put forward by Alliance 90/the Greens. At the same time, the opposition parties criticized the motion for still containing a reference to the Charter of the German Expellees, even if it was a minor one. In addition, the concern was expressed that, in future, World Refugee Day might be used in Germany only to commemorate the German expellees: 20 June must "not be a day to remember German expellees only, but rather it must be a day that sends a message counter to the injustice of expulsions and encourages solidarity with all refugees and expellees"[48] – a sign of a potential new dimension of competition among victims.

In the course of the debate, BdV president Erika Steinbach took the floor for the CDU/CSU. She restated the central points of the motion, reminding parliamentarians that, prior to the adoption of the Federal Expellee Law in 1953, there had also been a struggle and heated arguments over practically every paragraph. Eventually, however, all members of the Bundestag – with the exception of those in the German Communist Party – had consented. She concluded her speech with the remarkable sentence: "It's not about August 5th. June 20th is just as good a day; all that matters is that this commemoration day happens."[49]

The BdV had apparently come to understand that insisting on 5 August could endanger the project of a national commemoration day for flight and expulsion altogether. Therefore they took advantage of the opportunity to push through its approval.

The vote on the motion reflected the consensus that had developed within the parties to choose World Refugee Day. It united the essential commemoration interests of all parties, with the exception of one, and also observed the shared understanding of the Federal Republic of Germany as a state born from the ashes of National Socialism. The CDU/CSU and FDP parliamentary groups voted in favour of the motion, SPD and Alliance 90/the Greens abstained, and only the Left Party opposed. This outcome was duly understood by the Federal government as a clear mandate to fulfil its executive role in establishing a national commemoration day for the victims of flight and expulsion.

That this was indeed a sustainable compromise across the old party lines was proven by the coalition agreement negotiated later the same year. The grand coalition of CDU/CSU and SPD that came into power at the end of 2013 titled its coalition agreement *Shaping Germany's Future*. One chapter, "Emigrants, Expellees, and National Minorities," succinctly states: "We will keep the chastening memory of flight and expulsion alive through a commemoration day."[50] (It is perhaps notable that this statement appeared in this chapter and not in another entitled "Social Cohesion," in which the support of Eastern European cultural heritage is laid out on the basis of the Federal Expellee Law.) Another chapter, "Responsibility in the World," adds: "At the United Nations, we advocate global condemnation of displacement and the expansion of World Refugee Day to include commemorations of the victims of displacements."[51]

These passages of the coalition agreement finally influenced the decision of the federal cabinet on 27 August 2014 to observe a "day of commemoration for the victims of flight and expulsion" on 20 June, beginning in 2015.[52] And so, seventy years after the end of the Second World War and after intensive parliamentary manoeuvring, a day of commemoration for these victims was made official in Germany for the first time.[53] In a very particular way, it unites national commemoration of German refugees and expellees with the international commemoration the United Nations' World Refugee Day.

Dual Integration of "Flight and Expulsion" in the German Politics of Memory

The historical path of German discourses on flight and expulsion began with the government declaration of Konrad Adenauer on 20 September

1949 and culminated with the Federal government's resolution of 27 August 2014. This path has at times been difficult, as it wound its way through competing narratives of victimhood related to the Second World War as well as to the legal rights of millions of German refugees and expellees, and, ultimately, to a nationally and internationally supported commemoration day for the victims of expulsion. It has not been a linear process, but it has generally pointed in the direction of justice and commemoration, even if many obstacles remain. Importantly, the commemoration of German expellees is kept distinctly subordinate to the commemoration of the victims of National Socialism and of refugees worldwide.

As a result of the territorial changes after the Second World War as well as the domestic and foreign political parameters of the Cold War, a legal perspective dominated the political debates of flight and expulsion in the Federal Republic up until the fall of the Iron Curtain and German reunification in 1990. The legal argument for restoring Germany to its 1937 borders corresponded to the demand for a right of German refugees and expellees to return to their home regions. Insistence on the right to their homeland was then part of Germany's raison d'état. At first, German political parties and the lobby of refugees and expellees were united in this demand. Correspondingly, the refugees were considered one of the groups of victims particularly afflicted by the war. This is illustrated by the adoption of the Federal Expellee Law and the Equalization of Burdens Act in the early 1950s, which paved the way for the integration of the new citizens. The recognition of the special victim status of the refugees and expellees was exemplified by a particular, government-endorsed culture of commemoration.

Although the non-recognition of the postwar borders, the condemnation of forced migration as a crime, and the demand for a right to homeland were goals that united the political parties of the young Federal Republic with expellee interest groups for quite some time, Homeland Day – introduced by expellees and founded on the basis of the Charter of the German Expellees that was adopted on 5 August 1950 – remained an exclusively expellee affair. On this day, they solidified their legal and political demands and displayed their cultural heritage. And yet the day always remained limited to the group of expellees and refugees, sustained by legal demands and group-specific commemoration, even though leading politicians have always been, and remain, welcome keynote speakers. The culture of commemoration for the refugees and expellees did not advance beyond the stage of a communicative group commemoration.

This status quo was not to change in the following years. The erstwhile consensus of the parties concerning the fundamental appraisal of flight and expulsion fell apart, leading to bitter and polarized disputes. Furthermore, the years around 1960 brought about a re-evaluation of the hierarchy of victims. The prominent status of the German victims of the Second World War, and notably of the German expellees and refugees, was ceded to the victims of National Socialism – above all, Jews – for whose suffering Germany was directly responsible. Not only did the Holocaust become the primary point of reference for German memory culture, but the "negative memory" of the crimes of National Socialism became the new German raison d'état.[54] Given the new international and national frameworks following 1990, all attempts to establish 5 August as a national commemoration day were destined to fail. The compromise finally agreed upon by the political parties of Germany, which were all forced to undergo a process of learning, is a hybrid commemoration day that connects national and international commemoration. On the one hand, it is linked to the anticipation that an acknowledgment of German refugees and expellees might be achieved by depoliticizing those issues; on the other, it is linked to the idea that national commemoration of flight and expulsion might best be carried out as a forward-looking admonition against human rights violations.

The national day of commemoration for flight and expulsion established in 2014 indicates a new stage in the acknowledgment of German refugees and expellees as victims that is genuinely motivated by the politics of memory. It has advanced the commemoration of these events in Germany to a new level characterized by two features. A remembrance formerly limited mostly to the communicative memory of the group of expellees has been elevated to national cultural memory by extricating the issue of flight and expulsion from being solely legal questions. These historical events have thus been accorded a place in official national memory for the first time and have been recognized by German society as part of its history. Furthermore, by choosing World Refugee Day as the date for the commemoration day, the federal government is making an effort to contextualize German flight and expulsion by embedding it in international commemorative practices.

By drawing a connection to an international day of commemoration, the Federal government is, in effect, building on considerations found in the context of the World Refugee Year proclaimed by the United Nations in 1959/60.[55] At that time, the Federal Republic of Germany participated in the World Refugee Year with the explicit expectation that the global community would acknowledge the German refugee and expellee question as an international one. This expectation was bound to unfulfilled, given the conditions of the Cold War and the specifically national interpretation of flight and expulsion. Within the framework of the particular characteristics of German commemoration culture and the international politics of memory in the early twenty-first century, however, this question is experiencing a renaissance.

It remains to be seen whether the simultaneously national and international contextualization and integration of flight and expulsion will be successful, considering that World Refugee Day, by definition, includes neither expellees in general nor German refugees and expellees in particular. It is in this context that we must understand the exhortation in the 2013 coalition agreement that the Federal government "advocate global condemnation of displacement and the expansion of World Refugee Day to include commemorations of the victims of displacements."

As long as this is not the case, the official German Commemoration Day for the Victims of Flight and Expulsion, observed for the first time on 20 June 2015, remains a day commemorating two distinctly defined groups of victims that also perceive themselves as such. Against this background, it is not surprising that two federal states, Bavaria and Hesse, introduced in 2013 their own commemoration days dedicated explicitly and exclusively to German refugees and expellees, while federal deliberations were still ongoing.[56] The Bund der Vertriebenen also continues to observe its Homeland Day (*Tag der Heimat*), which remains "the most important focal point in the annual calendar of the expellees and of our organization."[57] The ceremonies on the first national commemoration day in 2015 demonstrate that linking the national commemoration day for German refugees and expellees with the World Refugee Day of the United Nations can indeed be called a success, as was the government's ceremony in Berlin featuring the federal president as keynote speaker.[58] On the other hand, numerous memorial services for either of the two groups were simultaneously conducted throughout Germany. Therefore, the possibility cannot be ruled out that the new, both nationally and internationally embedded Commemoration Day for the Victims of Flight and Expulsion perpetuates the competition of victims through a competing commemoration day. For as yet, it is not a *single* day of commemoration but, rather, a day composed of two commemorations, as the combined commemoration ceremony on 20 June 2019 in Berlin showed. The search for a usable memory of flight and expulsion in Germany continues.

NOTES

1 Transcript of plenary proceedings of the German Bundestag (hereafter Bundestag plenary transcript), 1st electoral term, 5th plenary sitting, 20 September 1949, 28ff. Bundestag plenary transcripts can be retrieved by date at https://www.bundestag.de/protokolle.
2 "Regierungspressekonferenz vom 27. August 2014," http://www.bundesregierung.de/Content/DE/Mitschrift/Pressekonferenzen/2014/08/2014-08-27-regpk.html.
3 See Mathias Beer, *Flucht und Vertreibung der Deutschen: Voraussetzung, Verlauf, Folgen* (Munich: C.H. Beck, 2011); Ray M. Douglas, *Orderly and Humane: The Expulsion of the Germans after the Second World War* (New Haven, CT: Yale University Press, 2012).
4 On the controversial topic of the number of people who died during the process of flight and expulsion, see Beer, *Flucht und Vertreibung*, 127–34.
5 Norman M. Naimark, *Fires of Hatred: Ethnic Cleansing in Twentieth-Century Europe* (Cambridge, MA: Harvard University Press, 2001); Michael Mann, *The Dark Side of Democracy: Explaining Ethnic Cleansing* (New York: Cambridge University Press, 2004); Pertti Ahonen, Gustavo Corni, Jerzy Kochanowski, Rainer Schulze, Tamás Stark, and Barbara Stelzl-Marx, eds., *People on the Move: Forced Population Movements in Europe in the Second World War and Its Aftermath* (Oxford: Berg Publishers, 2008); Philipp Ther, *Die dunkle Seite der Nationalstaaten: "Ethnische Säuberungen" im modernen Europa* (Göttingen: Vandenhoeck & Ruprecht, 2011); Michael Schwartz, *Ethnische "Säuberungen" in der Moderne: Globale Wechselwirkungen nationalistischer und rassistischer Gewaltpolitik im 19. und 20. Jahrhundert* (Munich: Oldenbourg Verlag, 2013).
6 See Beer, *Flucht und Vertreibung*, 99–127.
7 The counterpart to "flight and expulsion" in the German Democratic Republic was the "resettler question" (*Umsiedlerfrage*), which is not discussed in this chapter. See Michael Schwartz, *Vertriebene und "Umsiedlerpolitik": Integrationskonflikte in den deutschen Nachkriegs-Gesellschaften und die Assimilationsstrategien in der SBZ/DDR 1945–1961* (Munich: Oldenbourg Verlag, 2004).
8 Andreas Kossert, *Kalte Heimat: Die Geschichte der deutschen Vertriebenen nach 1945* (Munich: Siedler, 2008).
9 Claudia Kraft, "Der Platz der Vertreibung der Deutschen im historischen Gedächtnis Polens und der Tschechoslowakei/Tschechiens," in *Diktatur – Krieg – Vertreibung: Erinnerungskulturen in Tschechien, der Slowakei und Deutschland seit 1945*, ed. Christoph Cornelißen, Roman Holec, and Jiří Pešek (Essen: Klartext Verlag, 2005), 329–53; Maren Röger, *Vertreibung und Umsiedlung: Mediale Erinnerungen und Debatten in Deutschland und Polen*

seit 1989 (Marburg: Herder-Institut Verlag, 2011); K. Erik Franzen, Martin Schulze Wessel, eds., *Opfernarrative: Konkurrenzen und Deutungskämpfe in Deutschland und im östlichen Europa nach dem Zweiten Weltkrieg* (Munich: Oldenbourg, 2012).

10 Beer, *Flucht und Vertreibung*, 139–61; Robert G. Moeller, *War Stories: The Search for a Usable Past in the Federal Republic of Germany* (Berkeley: University of California Press, 2001); Jörg-Dieter Gauger and Manfred Kittel, eds., *Die Vertreibung der Deutschen aus dem Osten in der Erinnerungskultur* (Sankt Augustin: Konrad-Adenauer-Stiftung, 2004); Christian Lotz, *Die Deutung des Verlusts: Erinnerungspolitische Kontroversen im geteilten Deutschland um Flucht, Vertreibung und die Ostgebiete (1948–1972)* (Cologne: Böhlau Verlag, 2007); Manfred Kittel, *Vertreibung der Vertriebenen? Der historische deutsche Osten in der Erinnerungskultur der Bundesrepublik (1961–1982)* (Munich: Oldenbourg, 2007); Peter Haslinger, K. Erik Franzen, and Martin Schulze Wessel, eds., *Diskurse über Zwangsmigrationen in Zentraleuropa: Geschichtspolitische Fachdebatte, literarisches und lokales Erinnern seit 1989* (Munich: Oldenbourg, 2009); Eva Hahn and Hans Henning Hahn, *Die Vertreibung im deutschen Erinnern: Legenden, Mythos, Geschichte* (Paderborn: Schöningh, 2010); Stephan Scholz, Maren Röger, Bill Niven, eds., *Die Erinnerung an Flucht und Vertreibung: Ein Handbuch der Medien und Praktiken* (Paderborn: Schöningh, 2015). On German efforts to come to terms with the past, see Aleida Assmann and Ute Frevert, *Geschichtsversessenheit: Vom Umgang mit deutschen Vergangenheiten nach 1945* (Stuttgart: Deutsche Verlags-Anstalt, 1999); Bill Niven and Chloe Paver, eds., *Memorialization in Germany since 1945* (Basingstoke, UK: Palgrave, 2010).

11 Ute Frevert, "Geschichtsvergessenheit und Geschichtsversessenheit revisited: Der jüngste Erinnerungsboom in der Kritik," in *Aus Politik und Zeitgeschichte* 53, nos. 40/41 (2003): 6–13. See also Bundeszentrale für politische Bildung, "Der jüngste Erinnerungsboom in der Kritik," http://www.bpb.de/apuz/27381/der-juengste-erinnerungsboom-in-der-kritik; Aleida Assmann, *Das neue Unbehagen an der Erinnerungskultur: Eine Intervention* (Munich: C.H. Beck, 2013); Klaus Naumann, *Der Krieg als Text: Das Jahr 1945 im kulturellen Gedächtnis der Presse* (Hamburg: Hamburger Edition, 1998); Lothar Kettenacker, ed., *Ein Volk von Opfern? Die neue Debatte um den Bombenkrieg 1940–1945* (Berlin: Rowohlt, 2003).

12 Peter Reichel, *Politik mit der Erinnerung: Gedächtnisorte im Streit um die Nationalsozialistische Vergangenheit* (Munich: Carl Hansen, 1995); Edgar Wolfrum, *Geschichte als Waffe: Vom Kaiserreich bis zur Wiedervereinigung* (Göttingen: Vandenhoeck & Ruprecht, 2001); Aleida Assmann, *Der lange Schatten der Vergangenheit: Erinnerungskultur und Geschichtspolitik* (Munich: C.H. Beck, 2006); Manuel Becker, *Geschichtspolitik in der Berliner Republik:*

Konzeptionen und Kontroversen (Wiesbaden: Springer, 2013); Stefan Troebst, "Geschichtspolitik," Docupedia-Zeitgeschichte, last modified 4 August 2014, http://docupedia.de/zg/Geschichtspolitik?oldid=106422.

13 Mathias Beer, "'Flucht und Vertreibung': Eine Streitgeschichte," in Haslinger, Franzen, and Wessel, *Diskurse über Zwangsmigrationen*, 261–77.

14 Mathias Beer, "'Flucht und Vertreibung': Debatten im deutschen Bundestag," in *"Doppelte Vergangenheitsbewältigung" und die Singularität des Holocaust*, ed. Lucia Scherzberg (Saarbrücken: Universitätsverlag des Saarlandes, 2012), 135–69.

15 Mathias Beer, "Im Spannungsfeld von Politik und Zeitgeschichte: Das Großforschungsprojekt 'Dokumentation der Vertreibung der Deutschen aus Ost-Mitteleuropa,'" *Vierteljahrshefte für Zeitgeschichte* 46 (1998): 345–89; Mathias Beer, "Dokumentation der Vertreibung der Deutschen aus Ostmitteleuropa," in *Lexikon der Vertreibungen: Deportation, Zwangsaussiedlung und ethnische Säuberung im Europa des 20. Jahrhunderts*, ed. Detlef Brandes, Holm Sundhaussen, and Stefan Troebst (Vienna: Böhlau, 2010), 215–18.

16 Bundestag plenary transcript, 20 September 1949, 28ff.; Robert G. Moeller, "The Politics of the Past in the 1950s: Rhetorics of Victimization in East and West Germany," in *Germans as Victims: Remembering the Past in Contemporary Germany*, ed. Bill Niven (Basingstoke, UK: Palgrave Macmillan, 2006), 26–42.

17 Pertti Ahonen, "The Expellee Organizations and West German Ostpolitik, 1949–1969" (PhD diss., Yale University, 1999), published in an extended version with the title *After the Expulsion: West Germany and Eastern Europe 1945–1990* (Oxford: Oxford University Press, 2003); Matthias Stickler, *"Ostdeutsch heißt Gesamtdeutsch": Organisation, Selbstverständnis und heimatpolitische Zielsetzungen der deutschen Vertriebenenverbände 1949–1972* (Düsseldorf: Droste, 2004); Anna Jakubowska, *Der Bund der Vertriebenen in der Bundesrepublik Deutschland und Polen (1957–2004): Selbst- und Fremddarstellung eines Vertriebenenverbandes* (Marburg: Verlag Herder-Institut, 2012); Michael Schwartz: *Funktionäre mit Vergangenheit: Das Gründungspräsidium des Bundes der Vertriebenen und das "Dritte Reich"* (Munich: Oldenbourg, 2013). See also the website of the BdV at http://www.bund-der-vertriebenen.de/.

18 Carol Fink and Bernd Schaefer, eds., *Ostpolitik 1969–1974: European and Global Responses* (Cambridge: Cambridge University Press, 2009); Stickler, *"Ostdeutsch heißt Gesamtdeutsch."*

19 Bundestag plenary transcript, 7th electoral term, 118th plenary sitting, 25 September 1974, 7906.

20 German Bundestag, Drucksache 14/9033, 16 June 2002. All *Drucksachen* (printed documents) can be retrieved by date or by document number at

https://www.bundestag.de/drucksachen. See also Bundestag plenary transcript, 14th electoral term, 248th plenary sitting, 4 July 2002, 25235–41.

21 German Bundestag, Drucksache 16/10429, 26 September 2008; "Stiftung Flucht, Vertreibung, Versöhnung," http://www.sfvv.de/.

22 Bundestag plenary transcript, 20 September 20, 1949, 28ff; Karin Böke, "Flüchtlinge und Vertriebene zwischen dem Recht auf die alte Heimat und der Eingliederung in die neue Heimat: Leitvokabeln der Flüchtlingspolitik," in *Politische Leitvokabeln in der Adenauer-Ära*, ed. Karin Böke, Frank Liedtke, and Martin Wengeler (Berlin: De Gruyter, 1996), 131–210.

23 Bundestag plenary transcript, 7th electoral term, 118th plenary sitting, 25 September 1974, 7906.

24 Bundestag plenary transcript, 20 September 1949, 28ff.

25 Edgar Wolfrum, *Geschichtspolitik in der Bundesrepublik Deutschland: Der Weg zur bundesdeutschen Erinnerung 1948–1990* (Darmstadt: Wissenschaftliche Buchgesellschaft, 1999); Daniel Levy and Natan Sznaider, *Erinnerung im globalen Zeitalter: Der Holocaust* (Frankfurt: Suhrkamp, 2007).

26 Mathias Beer, "Verschlusssache, Raubdruck, autorisierte Fassung: Aspekte der politischen Auseinandersetzung mit Flucht und Vertreibung in der Bundesrepublik Deutschland (1949–1989)," in Cornelißen, Holec, and Pešek, *Diktatur – Krieg – Vertreibung*, 369–401.

27 Bundestag plenary transcript, 1st electoral term, 10th plenary sitting, 29 September 1949, 181. See also Bundestag plenary transcript, 1st electoral term, 7th plenary sitting, 22 September 1949, 82.

28 Jan-Holger Kirsch, *Nationaler Mythos oder historische Trauer? Der Streit um ein zentrales "Holocaust-Mahnmal" für die Berliner Republik* (Cologne: Böhlau Verlag, 2003).

29 Final Report of the Enquete Commission, *Überwindung der Folgen der SED-Diktatur im Prozeß der deutschen Einheit*, German Bundestag, Drucksache 13/11000, 10 June 1998.

30 Stephan Scholz, *Vertriebenendenkmäler: Topographie einer deutschen Erinnerungslandschaft* (Paderborn: Ferdinand Schöningh, 2015).

31 K. Erik Franzen, "Der Diskurs als Ziel? Anmerkungen zur deutschen Erinnerungspolitik am Beispiel der Debatte um ein 'Zentrum gegen Vertreibungen' 1999–2005," in Haslinger, Franzen, and Wessel, *Diskurse über Zwangsmigrationen*, 1–29; Constantin Goschler, "Versöhnung und Viktimisierung: Der deutsche Opferdiskurs und die Vertriebenen," *Zeitschrift für Geschichtswissenschaft* 53 (2005): 873–84; Bill Niven, ed., *Germans as Victims: Remembering the Past in Contemporary Germany* (Basingstoke, UK: Palgrave Macmillan, 2006); Gregor Feindt, "Flucht und Vertreibung zwischen Kaltem Krieg und Universalisierung," in *Europäische Erinnerung als verflochtene Erinnerung: Vielstimmige und*

vielschichtige Vergangenheitsdeutungen jenseits der Nation, ed. Gregor Feindt, Félix Krawatzek, Daniela Mehler, Friedemann Pestel, and Rieke Trimçev (Göttingen: Vandenhoeck & Ruprecht, 2014), 153–77.

32 Stephan Scholz, "Gedenktage," *Online-Lexikon zur Kultur und Geschichte der Deutschen im östlichen Europa*, last modified 18 August 2015, http://ome-lexikon.uni-oldenburg.de/p32880.

33 Jeffrey Luppes, "The Commemorative Ceremonies of the Expellees: Tag der Heimat and Volkstrauertag," *German Politics and Society* 30, no. 2 (2012): 1–20.

34 Jörg Hackmann, "Die 'Charta der deutschen Heimatvertriebenen' vom 5. August 1950," *Themenportal Europäische Geschichte*, 2010, http://www.europa.clio-online.de/site/lang__de/ItemID__463/mid__11428/40208214/default.aspx; Matthias Stickler, "Charta der deutschen Heimatvertriebenen," *Online-Lexikon zur Kultur und Geschichte der Deutschen im östlichen Europa*, last modified 2 June 2015, http://ome-lexikon.uni-oldenburg.de/54028.html; Mathias Beer, "Die Charta der deutschen Heimatvertriebenen: Erinnerung und Ereignis," in *Baden-württembergische Erinnerungsorte*, ed. Reinhold Weber, Peter Steinbach, Hans-Georg Wehling (Stuttgart: Kohlhammer, 2012), 510–23.

35 K. Erik Franzen: *Der vierte Stamm Bayerns: Die Schirmherrschaft über die Sudetendeutschen 1954–1974* (Munich: Oldenbourg, 2010).

36 German Bundesrat, "Entschließung des Bundesrats zur Erhebung des 5. August zum 'Nationalen Gedenktag für die Opfer von Flucht und Vertreibung,'" Drucksache 460/03, 2 July 2003, http://dipbt.bundestag.de/doc/brd/2003/0460-03B.pdf.

37 German Bundestag, Drucksache 17/4193, 15 December 2010.

38 Bundestag plenary transcript, 17th electoral term, 90th plenary sitting, 10 February 2011, 10115–30.

39 Ibid., 10116.

40 Ibid., 10121.

41 Ibid., 10119.

42 "Erklärung zum Beschluss des Bundestages '60 Jahre Charta der deutschen Heimatvertriebenen – Aussöhnung vollenden,'" 13 February 2011, http://www.hsozkult.de/debate/id/diskussionen-1468. See also Stefan Berger, "On Taboos, Traumas and Other Myths: Why the Debate about German Victims of the Second World War Is Not a Historians' Controversy," in Niven, *Germans as Victims*, 210–24.

43 Mathias Beer, "Bundesvertriebenengesetz (BVFG)," in Brandes, Sundhaussen, and Troebst, *Lexikon der Vertreibungen*, 97–100.

44 Constantin Goschler, "Lastenausgleich in der Bundesrepublik Deutschland," in Brandes, Sundhaussen, and Troebst, *Lexikon der Vertreibungen*, 382–4.

45 German Bundestag, Drucksache 17/13883, 11 June 2013.
46 Ibid., emphasis added.
47 Ibid, 6.
48 Bundestag plenary transcript, 17th electoral term, 246th plenary sitting, 13 June 2013, 31275.
49 Ibid., 31280.
50 "Deutschlands Zukunft gestalten: Koalitionsvertrag zwischen CDU, CSU und SPD," 18th electoral term, 113, https://www.bundestag.de/resource/blob/194886/696f36f795961df200fb27fb6803d83e/koalitionsvertrag-data.pdf.
51 Ibid., 131.
52 Bundesgesetzblatt 2014, Teil I, Nr. 46, 14 October 2014.
53 Marco Dräger, "Ein Hoch auf Flucht und Vertreibung? Zur Einführung des neuen Gedenktages am 20. Juni," Bundeszentrale für politische Bildung, http://www.bpb.de/apuz/208013/zur-einfuehrung-des-neuen-gedenktages-am-20-juni?p=all.
54 Assmann, *Der lange Schatten*.
55 Peter Paul Nahm, "'Wir und das Weltflüchtlingsjahr': Die Reaktion der betroffenen Völker," in *Vertreibung, Annexion und Teilung als politische Weltprobleme: Referate des siebten Barsinghausener Gesprächs vom 29.–31. Januar 1960*, Arbeitskreis für Ostfragen Hannover (Leer: G. Rautenberg, 1960), 9–19; Arbeits- und Sozialministerium des Landes Nordrhein-Westfalen, *Weltflüchtlingsnot und Wir: Vorträge gehalten auf der Herbsttagung des Steinbacher Kreises ins Arnsberg im Weltflüchtlingsjahr 1959/60* (Düsseldorf, 1960); Arbeits- und Sozialministerium des Landes Nordrhein-Westfalen, *Tag der Heimat im Weltflüchtlingsjahr 1959: Heimat in Freiheit. 13. September 1959* (Düsseldorf, 1959); Peter Gatrell, *Free World? The Campaign to Save the World's Refugees, 1956–1963* (Cambridge: Cambridge University Press, 2011).
56 "Proklamation des Bayerischen Ministerpräsidenten zum Bayerischen Gedenktag für die Opfer von Flucht, Vertreibung und Deportation vom 27. August 2013," https://www.verkuendung-bayern.de/gvbl/jahrgang:2013/heftnummer:17/seite:574; "Proklamation des Hessischen Ministerpräsidenten zum Hessischen Gedenktag für die Opfer von Flucht, Vertreibung und Deportation vom 27. August 2013," https://soziales.hessen.de/ueber-uns/landesbeauftragte-fuer-heimatvertriebene-und-spaetaussiedler/gedenktag/proklamation.
57 *DO Deutscher Ostdienst. Nachrichtenmagazin des Bundes der Vertriebenen* 57, no. 4 (2015): 3.
58 "Federal President Joachim Gauck to Mark the First Day of Remembrance for Refugees and Expellees," 20 June 2015. German and English versions available at http://www.bundespraesident.de/SharedDocs/Reden/DE/Joachim-Gauck/Reden/2015/06/150620-Gedenktag-Flucht-Vertreibung.html.

11 Of Italian Perpetrators and Victims: Forced Migration in the Italian-Yugoslavian Border Region, 1922–1954

TOBIAS HOF

In the summer of 1941, Fascist Italy completed its largest territorial expansion. Yugoslavia and Greece were defeated, and the Axis powers in North Africa pushed back the British troops. On 10 June 1941, one year after Italy had entered the Second World War, Benito Mussolini bragged about these successes and predicted that the Axis would continue its victorious march. However, he also admitted that he had made a significant mistake in reorganizing the Balkans: "Recent events," he stated, "have shown that all states need to achieve the maximum ethnic and spiritual unity, to harmonize race, nation, and state." In conquering the Slavic populations of these territories, Italy had absorbed an alien, hostile element. The *Duce* already had a solution at hand to solve this problem: "When ethnicities do not correspond with geography, then the ethnicities have to be moved. Population transfers are part of God's will, because they allow us to bring the political boundaries into harmony with the ethnic ones."[1]

This chapter focuses on the questions of whether – and, if so, to what extent – this policy was carried out in the Italian-Yugoslavian border region and how it affected both ethnic minorities and Italians during and after the war. The history of this period in this region – characterized by shifting borders, changing occupation powers, and constant role reversals between perpetrators and victims – provides insight into the Italian conception, understanding, and practice of flight and expulsion. It also allows us to examine how the Italians eventually succeeded in creating the image of the "good Italian" and constructed a credible notion of Italian victimhood despite the multiple war crimes they had committed.

Even though numerous studies of forced migration in Europe during and after the Second World War have been published, the Italian case has been partly overlooked.[2] Moreover, the few studies that have dealt with Italy's experience are often limited in chronological and geographical scope.[3] Yet, recent scholarship on ethnic cleansing has convincingly illustrated that expanding chronological and geographical parameters to include colonial experience in analyses of European population transfers can produce new and important insights.[4] Therefore, this chapter will not only examine the forced migration that occurred in the border region during and after the war, but it will also link these events to key features of nineteenth-century Italy, including irredentism, racism, and Rome's colonial endeavours. This study also situates population transfers within the foreign and occupation policy of the Fascist regime and examines the role played by Italy's victimhood narrative in postwar memory.[5]

This chapter focuses primarily on the political macro-level for two reasons. First, the state is usually the driving, or at least legitimizing, factor of flight, expulsion, and deportation.[6] Second, the state also tries to shape education policy and public commemoration. The power of its own authority establishes the authenticity and credibility of acceptable victimhood claims.[7] Based on these hypotheses, the article will examine four questions: First, what were the reasons for flight and expulsion? Second, what were the political and social consequences of these migration movements? Third, how does the experience of flight and expulsion in Italy, including its political consequences, compare to the corresponding experience in Yugoslavia? And finally, how have the events of forced migration in the region been remembered by the Italian public after the war?

Irredentism and Italianization before the Second World War

Immediately after the creation of the Kingdom of Italy in 1861, Massimo d'Azeglio proclaimed – so it is said – that an Italian state had finally been achieved.[8] However, not all of his fellow citizens agreed. Many regarded the kingdom as an incomplete entity because thousands of Italians still lived outside its borders, so they sought to incorporate all areas with an Italian-speaking population – mostly territories that belonged to Austria-Hungary – into the newly created nation state. The Slavic people living in these areas were regarded as the main enemy because it was believed that they were conspiring against Italy with either the Habsburg Empire or the Bolshevists and thus had to be either assimilated or removed. Due to widespread nationalism in Europe, this irredentist mindset also appealed to the 350,000 Italians living in the Habsburg Empire, who took up the call for the unification of Italy. Given their self-perception as the rightful heirs of the Roman Empire, they felt like second-class citizens within the multi-ethnic state of Austria-Hungary.[9]

When the First World War broke out, the Italian government saw an opportunity to realize these irredentists' aspirations.[10] After secret negotiations with Great Britain and France, Rome was promised large parts of Istria and Dalmatia, among other territorial gains, in the Treaty of London, signed 26 April 1915. Less than a month later, Italy declared war on Austria-Hungary. After the armistice on 3 November 1918, the public spirit in Italy was effusive. The government, however, was unable to meet the great expectations for its territorial gains due to inconsistent diplomacy. Italy got South Tyrol, the Trentino, parts of Dalmatia, and areas around Trieste and Istria.[11]

An internationally binding border demarcation between Yugoslavia and Italy was formalized in the Treaty of Rapallo on 12 November 1920. As one of the victorious powers of the First World War, Italy forced the Yugoslavian government to accept all its demands in order to satisfy Italy's strategic and economic interests.[12] After the Treaty of Rapallo, ethnic minorities became a prominent element of Italy's political and social landscape. More than 470,000 Slavs lived in the new province of Venezia Giulia alone.[13] Most of the 15,000 Italians who remained in Yugoslavia lived along the coast. Whereas Yugoslavia was bound by the Treaty of Rapallo to protect all ethnic minorities, the Italian government made only informal promises to respect the rights of these Slavs.[14]

The Italian public, which had been exposed to pan-Italian propaganda for years, was disappointed by the scope of the territorial gains and blamed the West for denying Italy's rightful claims. The buzzword "mutilated victory" was born, created by the poet Gabriele D'Annunzio. He did not limit himself, however, to verbal attacks on the West and the government in Rome: from 12 September 1919 to 29 December 1920, he led the seizure of Fiume (now Rijeka), which, according to him, rightfully belonged to Italy. Fiume became a powerful rallying point for those who attacked what they viewed as unjust peace treaties. Many, including Mussolini, openly expressed their solidarity with the poet by visiting the city. After D'Annunzio was expelled from Fiume by the Italian army, the Independent Free State of Fiume was established, as had been agreed upon in the Treaty of Rapallo.[15]

Beginning in 1925, the Fascists intensified the Italianization policy initiated by liberal governments in order to abolish the Slavic minority as a political and social entity in the eastern regions.[16] They closed Slavic schools, gave streets and villages Italian names, forbade use of the Slavic language, and suppressed the local clergy, which was accused of preserving Slavic identity. Although these measures were intended to compel the Slavs to assimilate, they were not intended to cause mass emigration. Rome knew that the loss of thousands of residents would destabilize the local socio-economic system beyond the point where it could be counterbalanced by a resettlement of Italians in the short term.[17]

Among Slavs, the Italianization policy confirmed long-standing fears. Already during the Great War, they viewed Italian irredentism as the greatest threat to national self-determination and therefore sided with the Habsburg Empire. As a consequence of Rome's "cultural genocide" in the interwar period, Slavs distinguished less and less between Italians and fascists, and they developed a sweeping antipathy toward the entire Italian people.[18] In addition to Italianization projects, the economic crisis during the interwar period made life miserable in Venezia Giulia. Although flight was often seen as the last resort, recent studies have estimated that up to 100,000 people emigrated in the interwar years.[19]

The tensions in the eastern regions eased when Foreign Minister Galeazzo Ciano reversed the Italian policy toward Yugoslavia, which previously sought to weaken the multi-ethnic state in favour of increased Italian influence.[20] He intended to sign a treaty of friendship and bring Yugoslavia into the Axis in order to undermine France's postwar alliance system.[21] That Ciano was able to broach these projects was due to his good personal relationship with Yugoslavian prime minister Milan Stojadinović, who sought a rapprochement with Italy out of economic and strategic considerations.[22] To keep Stojadinović in power, Ciano even promised to respect the rights of the Slavs in Italy and to repatriate the Italians still living in Yugoslavia.[23]

Ciano's plans were part of a grand strategy to "bring home" all Italians who lived abroad. The reasons for this policy were manifold, including Rome's inability to utilize Italians abroad as advocates of its foreign policy, as well as its need for settlers in Abyssinia and North Africa.[24] Soon, however, Ciano had to abandon his plans. The Italian government lacked the necessary resources, and many Italians who lived abroad were unwilling to move back.[25] In the case of Yugoslavia, the situation was further complicated by Stojadinović's ouster in February 1939, which immediately damaged the bilateral relationship. Italy thus turned once again to Croatian separatists to weaken Yugoslavia and to strengthen its own presence in the region.[26]

The Axis Occupation, 1941–1945

Italy's entry into the Second World War finally offered the opportunity for it to occupy parts of Yugoslavia. However, Rome hesitated due to

German pressure and turned toward Greece instead. That campaign proved to be a disaster, and, after Peter II, the designated successor to Yugoslavia's throne, staged a coup d'état against the pro-Axis government in Belgrade in March 1941, Hitler saw his opportunity and gave the order to attack Yugoslavia on 6 April 1941.[27] Supported by Italian troops, the Wehrmacht defeated the Yugoslavian army eleven days later. Rome claimed for itself parts of the Yugoslavian coast as belonging to the province of Dalmatia and also deployed troops in Montenegro and in the southern areas of the newly created Independent State of Croatia under Ante Pavelić. In addition, Slovenia was split between Germany, Hungary, and Italy.[28] In violation of international law, Rome annexed the southwestern territories of Slovenia, encompassing a population of some 305,000, and created the province of Ljubljana.[29]

The newly appointed high commissioner of Ljubljana, Emilio Grazioli, promised to respect the inhabitants' right to practise their cultural and national traditions.[30] This policy derived from strategic and pragmatic considerations, not humanitarian ones. Grazioli feared that a harsh occupation policy would provoke resistance and endanger Italy's control and that Germany would then be able to consolidate its dominance with the help of Pavelić, who regarded Berlin as a partner against the Italians. Thus, Grazioli not only wanted to distinguish the Italians from the Germans by implementing a more tolerant policy, but he also wanted to win over the Slovenes as allies.[31] Yet, this strategy had an unintended side effect: seventeen thousand Slovenes and more than three thousand Jews tried to escape German and Croatian persecution by fleeing to the provinces of Ljubljana and Dalmatia.[32] Even though the Italian authorities were well aware of what the refugees' fates would be, they closed the borders and punished illegal immigration. The destabilization of public order and the heavy burden on sanitary facilities and the food supply were more risk than the Italians wished to assume.[33]

Despite the more lenient approach, Rome had no doubt that the Italians would eventually subjugate the Slavs, either with their cooperation or by force. This notion was based on the Italians' aforementioned feeling of superiority and aversion toward the Slavs and on a cultural racism that originated in the nineteenth century as a counter-narrative to Germany's biological racism.[34] Italians believed that it was their "white man's burden" to civilize people they deemed to be inferior. This civilizing mission was to be carried out by any means necessary. Groups who resisted would be deported or killed in the name of modernization and progress.[35] Decades of colonial endeavours, including the Abyssinian War, had further radicalized Italian racism.[36] Indro Montanelli, who later became a prominent conservative political commentator in postwar Italy, wrote in 1936, "We shall never be dominators, if we don't have an exact consciousness of our destined superiority."[37]

Italy's assimilation program in the carved-up Yugoslavia entailed three steps. First, a census was carried out to identify the politically trustworthy in order to distinguish them from the undesirables; the latter were to be deported. The second step was the Italianization of the annexed territories, followed by the colonization of the area by Italian settlers. These ideas, however, did not progress beyond a congeries of vague plans.[38] Although the regime had always flirted with the idea of occupying and annexing portions of the Balkans, it had no detailed plans for such a scenario. This discrepancy between words and deeds illustrates that it was often more important for the Italians to voice publicly a supposedly radical policy that negated the status quo rather than actually to implement it. Doing so, they feared, would endanger the compromises made among the church, the monarchy, and the army that stabilized the entire system.[39]

A lack of personnel, time, and resources, as well as the rise of resistance movements formed after the Axis invasion and the long-standing and deeply rooted suspicion of Slavs toward the Italians, all meant that these plans would go unfulfilled.[40] Yugoslav liberation movements, and in particular Tito's partisans, eventually turned against all occupying powers regardless of their policies.[41] This resistance was driven by the Italians' increasingly excessive counter-insurgency measures as well as the general fear that the existence of, respectively, the Slovene, Croatian, and Serbian nations were at stake. The Slovenian resistance grew to alarming dimensions by the end of 1941; in response, the general secretary of the Fascist Party, Aldo Vidussoni, wanted to "kill them all."[42] Although his radical ideas were never realized, the army took over the Province of Ljubljana.

The Italian military applied a twofold strategy to reclaim full control over the regions. One approach sought to exploit ethnic, religious, and ideological tensions among the various Slavic peoples. Many Catholic Slovenes sided with Italy because they feared Tito's communists. Rome was able to recruit many supporters from their ranks and, with their help, formed paramilitary units like the *Milizia Volontaria Anticomunista* (MVAC).[43] In addition, the military targeted the entire population with internment, shootings, and forced population transfers in order to isolate the resistance movements.[44] General Mario Roatta told his subordinates not to "shy away from using cruelty (if necessary). It must be a complete cleansing. We need to intern all inhabitants and put Italian families in their place."[45] He wanted to show the world that the Italians were fierce soldiers capable of suppressing rebellions and thereby debunk the stereotype of the good but incompetent Italian.[46]

These actions undoubtedly constituted war crimes. Nonetheless, there were still crucial differences between atrocities committed by the Italian occupiers in Yugoslavia and Germany's comprehensive war of extermination.[47] First, with qualifications such as "if necessary," Roatta's order appeared to allow for a more flexible occupation policy. Second, Rome did not have concrete plans prior to the invasion for how to manage the occupied territories; Italian analogues of the German General Plan East (*Generalplan Ost*) or of the Commissar Order (*Kommissarbefehl*) have yet to be discovered. The Italian army reacted when Italy's grip on power was in peril. In its attempt to regain control, the army did not refrain from escalating violence. As Isabel Hull has noted with respect to Germany, Italy's colonial history – such as the deliberate starvation of women and children on the Isole Tremiti during the Italo-Turkish War (1911–12) and the use of poison gas, camps, deportations, and executions in Libya and Abyssinia, which killed between 460,000 and 530,000 people by 1941 – reveals that this kind of behaviour against populations deemed to be inferior was nothing new.[48] These examples illustrate that the army under Generals Pietro Badoglio and Rodolfo Graziani, who were responsible for the atrocities committed in Africa during the 1920s and 1930s, could and did fall back on their colonial experience. Thus, as it had for many other countries, colonial policy "came home" to Europe.[49]

In the summer of 1942, the repression in Slovenia reached its peak with a nine-month military campaign against suspected partisans. Italian soldiers and paramilitaries shot civilians and hostages, taking pictures next to their victims before pillaging and burning down their villages.[50] Ljubljana was encircled by a thirty-kilometre barbed wire fence to cut off the capital from the rebels. A network of camps was created in which at least twenty-five thousand people, including women and children, were detained.[51] The most infamous concentration camp was on the island of Rab, which became a symbol for Italy's ruthless occupation policy. Even though Rab was not an extermination camp, its annual death rate was higher than that of Buchenwald because of the appalling conditions.[52]

After the Italian armistice with the Allies was announced on 8 September 1943, a short power vacuum emerged in Italy's eastern border region. Particularly in Istria, partisans took revenge against the former occupiers and their collaborators. Italians were shot and thrown into *foibe*, natural sinkholes commonly found in the karst topography of the region. The name *foibe* became a cypher for the atrocities that were committed against Italians in the Balkans at the end of the war. Between five hundred and seven hundred people were murdered within two days before the Wehrmacht invaded the territories and created the operation zone *Adriatisches Küstenland* (Adriatic Coastal Area, consisting of the former provinces of Ljubljana and Venezia Giulia). After Mussolini's liberation in mid-September, the region officially became part of the newly proclaimed Repubblica Sociale Italiana (RSI); it remained, however, under Berlin's de facto control.[53]

Italian Fascists, Yugoslavian Communists, and German National Socialists used simplistic labels of class and ethnicity in order to categorize the various groups living in the contested area. These artificial divisions turned "the region into a German, Slavic and Italian condominium of oppression, of racist, ethnic and ideological persecution – and the victims were Jews, Slavs and Italians."[54] The Germans, for example, simultaneously cracked down on partisans and Italians they did not trust. To consolidate their rule, they also deployed the Slovene Home Guard, an anti-communist paramilitary unit created in September 1943. Many of its members had been part of the MVAC and were now used against their former Italian handlers. Under the auspices of SS commander Odilo Globočnik, a merciless fight against partisans was waged, and the systematic deportation of Jews began. The Risiera di San Sabba concentration camp in Trieste was used to intern partisans, Italians, and political prisoners. Twenty-five thousand people were deported via the camp to Germany, and up to five thousand people were killed there. The remaining Italian Fascists tried to hold their ground against partisans, Italian anti-fascists, the Germans, and their collaborators.[55]

From Perpetrator to Victim

At the end of April 1945, Tito's National Liberation Army occupied most parts of the Adriatic Coastal Area. On 1 May, it reached Trieste and was met there one day later by the British army, which had liberated the western areas of Venezia Giulia. The region once again entered into a period of ill-defined power relations. Tito's troops immediately began to arrest, deport, and execute people. During the "forty days of Tito," a mixture of spontaneous and planned violence seemed to be settling accounts with everything that was regarded Italian, but the situation was in fact more complex. Although Tito launched a pre-emptive nationwide purge against every social, professional, and cultural group he considered to be dangerous,[56] he also tried to obtain the support of Italian Communists by propagating an Italian-Slavic brotherhood. As part of his efforts, he invoked a proclamation by the Italian Communist

Party (PCI) from 1926 that had promised the Slovenes their national sovereignty. Only in May 1945, when Italian Communist leader Palmiro Togliatti nullified this declaration and declared his support for Rome's claim to Istria and Venezia Giulia, did Tito abandon his notion of collaborating with the PCI.[57] From the beginning, conservative Italian anti-fascists, whose only sin was "not sharing Communists' ideals," were persecuted. This conversion of a former ally into an enemy left the Italian conservatives shocked and wary.[58]

Tito's army also persecuted members of the Home Guards as well as Slovenian Catholics. Often one's religious belief was enough to prove suspected collaboration with the Germans and Italians. In May 1945, 17,000 Slovenian paramilitaries and civilians fled to Austria and surrendered to the British army. Even though the British knew about atrocities committed by the National Liberation Army, they sent 11,000 of them back; these men were immediately interned by the Yugoslav army, and many died in camps. Those who were permitted to stay in Austria became part of the collection of displaced Europeans who never returned to their homeland out of fear for their lives.[59] Though the British army's behaviour was heavily criticized both at the time and in subsequent scholarship, its motive is still disputed.[60] The British justified their actions by claiming that they would have lost in a confrontation with Tito's troops.[61] It should also be mentioned, however, that many politicians in London deemed the "separation of ethnicities" the only way to reduce ethnic tensions, which had been a huge burden for international relations in the interwar period.[62]

After the signing of the Paris Peace Treaty in 1947, Italy lost most of its territories in Istria and all islands in the eastern Adriatic to Yugoslavia. Parts of the province around Pola (Croatian: Pula) and Trieste formed the Free State of Trieste, which was divided into Zone A, administered by the Americans and the British, and Zone B, occupied by the Yugoslavians. The people living in the border region were allowed to choose their citizenship freely, but those who opted for the citizenship of the neighbouring country had to move within a year. Belgrade and Rome were obliged to respect the rights of the ethnic minorities.[63] It was under these preconditions that the flight and expulsion of Italians from Italy's former territories took place.

Although the Yugoslavian regime expelled the entire German minority, a similar decision was not taken in regard to the Italians.[64] However, the government in Belgrade still drew a clear distinction between the "honest anti-fascist" and the "reactionary Italian." While the former could stay, the latter had to leave, despite the provisions in the peace treaty. The emigration wave began in late 1945 in the Fiume region. In other regions, such as Zone B of the Free State of Trieste, the flight did not begin until 1956. This delay was not due to a more tolerant approach by Yugoslav authorities – they acted with the same oppressive measures they used elsewhere – but, rather, to the Italians' hope that the territory would be returned to them because of its proximity to Trieste.[65]

Most recent estimates point to as many as 250,000 Italian refugees in total by 1956. Only 8 per cent of the former Italian-speaking population remained in Yugoslavia, and they were mostly elderly workers or peasants. From the Istria regions alone, which were handed over to Yugoslavia, the entire Italian population of some 27,000 people fled.[66] Tens of thousands boarded ships for Trieste, which became a transit point, with more than 50,000 refugees.[67] Once again, an entire minority, and its entire social structure, was forced to abandon its homeland.[68] Pola is a good example of this: more than 82 per cent of its 32,000 Italian residents chose to leave. Journalist Anne O'Hare McCormick was shocked by "the chill of death [that] hangs over Pola."[69]

Despite these migration movements, ethnic minorities remained an element of postwar Italy. Slovenes and Croats living in Italy faced hostility and pressure to assimilate, although Rome had promised to protect them. Flight to Yugoslavia or elsewhere was often seen as the only possible way out. A small number of Italian workers and left-wing intellectuals moved to Yugoslavia to help build its burgeoning socialist state, but, after a few years, many became disillusioned and returned to Italy. Additionally, Italian refugees from the lost territories faced mistreatment and hostility in their homeland. They were defamed, especially by the left-wing milieu, as fascists who had got what they deserved.[70] The government only reluctantly reintegrated these displaced persons into postwar society. It should be noted, however, that, after Germany, Italy had to accommodate the most refugees. Recent estimates suggest that 850,000 people legally or illegally immigrated to Italy after the war.[71]

Politics of Remembrance: The Italian Victim Narrative

A victim narrative had already spread among the Italian population during the short-lived power vacuum in September 1943, but it gained momentum in the aftermath of the war. Italians reported that their fellow citizens interned by Tito's Communists were treated the same way the Germans had treated their prisoners.[72] Italians who lived in Istria and Venezia Giulia sent telegrams to the British troops and the Italian Foreign Ministry in Rome, pleading for intervention. They accused Yugoslavia of ethnic cleansing and stated that they had no choice but to emigrate. British sources mention 20,000 Italian refugees and nearly

3,000 deportees who were all forced to serve in Tito's army – 2,100 never returned.[73] But while Italians stressed their own victimhood, they ignored the atrocities they had inflicted upon the Slavic population for decades.

Tony Judt remarks that, after the war, every nation in Europe in one way or another highlighted the sacrifices they made and the suffering they had experienced because of the Germans.[74] Although Italy seems to follow this trend, the case was more complex: Rome had been Berlin's closest ally, had committed many war crimes, and was ruled by a Fascist dictator for over twenty years.[75] Additionally, Italy experienced a bloody civil war and referred to crimes committed not only by Germans but also by Yugoslavians in order to authenticate its victimhood. Consequently, a struggle over who was entitled to assign the roles of victim and perpetrator erupted between the Italian and Yugoslav governments in the last months of the war.[76] The history of forced migration, assimilation policies, and war crimes in the eastern border region is a perfect case study illustrating how and why Italians self-identified as victims and, most importantly, why they were recognized as such by others.

Italy's notion of victimhood was born in the summer of 1943, when Mussolini was overthrown by the monarchy and the military. Yet, many protagonists who were responsible for the coup d'état had been involved in war crimes in the Balkans and elsewhere: King Vittorio Emanuele III (as one of the supreme commanders of the army), former Chief of General Staff Pietro Badoglio, and Chief of Staff Vittorio Ambrosio to name only a few. Consequently, to become an essential part of the founding myth of the Italian Republic, the army, personified by Badoglio, had to be portrayed as a positive institution that had always opposed the *Duce* and the Germans.

In order to achieve this goal, the army and the monarchy created and spread the myth of the "good Italian" versus the "despicable German criminal," etched in the collective memory by Louis de Bernières's novel *Captain Corelli's Mandolin* (1994) and a subsequent movie starring Nicolas Cage (2001).[77] This myth not only blamed the Germans for all atrocities committed during the war but also accused them of betraying Rome and dragging Italians into a war they never wanted. Everything before the summer of 1943 was framed as having been forced upon an unwilling Italian populace, thus absolving all Italians of any guilt for crimes committed before Mussolini's downfall. What mattered for Italians was the war they fought against Nazi Germany after the armistice because that was the only war they ever wanted. Of course, it was in those last two years of the war that Germans and Yugoslavians committed most crimes against the Italians. The story of the "two wars" allowed Italian politicians and academics to acknowledge only the cruelties their own nation suffered – not those they inflicted – thus lending authenticity to their victimhood claim. Any historical research or acknowledgment of atrocities committed by Italians would have compromised this artificial notion. Instead, scholars and politicians engaged only with the history of the resistance, which was "performed by few, [but] served as a cleansing of the conscience for all."[78]

Italy's state-mandated amnesia concerning everything that happened before 1943 also helped a great many civil servants and officers continue their work after 1945. These men and women, who had served during the Fascist era but made a timely change in allegiance, would in turn help lend authenticity to the victim narrative and the image of the good Italian by promptly publishing their memoirs. These accounts, which are often taken at face value even today, recalled manifold stories of how Italians helped people in need while being subjected to German and Slavic cruelty.[79]

These memoirs were important to authenticating notions of victimhood within Italy, but help consolidating such ideas internationally came from an unlikely ally: directors of the neorealist cinema were crucial in spreading this founding myth of the Italian Republic. In movies like Roberto Rossellini's *Roma città aperta* (*Rome, Open City*, 1945), most Italians were portrayed as resistance fighters and innocent victims of German brutality. References to their own fascist past or the persistence of fascist ideology were omitted. Whereas eleven-year-old Edmund in Rossellini's *Germania anno zero* (*Germany, Year Zero*, 1948) was seduced by Nazi ideology and later committed suicide, Italian children in neorealist movies such as *Ladri di biciclette* (*Bicycle Thieves*, 1948) by Vittorio De Sica focused on themes of dignity and maturity in the face of unbearable hardship. Those movies were critically acclaimed international box-office hits, particularly in the United States, and their success in turn contributed to Western public recognition of the "innocent" Italian and lent credibility to the Italian notion of victimhood.[80]

The cultural politics of remembrance and victimhood is very much a politics of narratives created during times of suffering. Using effective terminology was crucial for the victims in successfully establishing their narrative authority in order to seek justice. The expulsion of the Italians is known by the name "exodus," which intentionally conjures a biblical scale. The usage of this term and that of *foibe*, which evoked a feeling of terror and angst, became metaphors for the cruelties committed by the Tito's partisans.[81] But it was not only the comparison to German atrocities that helped to sear horrific images into the minds of Western audiences; Western anti-communism had for decades successfully promoted the image of the blood-thirsty and uncivilized communist. Furthermore, renowned journalists such as O'Hare McCormick reported on the suffering of Italians, thus authenticating Italy's claims. Accusations levelled by the Italian communist press at their "ideological comrades" in Belgrade for having committed horrible crimes helped dispel any lingering doubt regarding Italian victimhood.[82] The government in Belgrade countered with terms such as "traitor" or "fascist" in order to justify its actions against Italians and deflect blame for the atrocities. The problem with these counterattacks, however, was that they also implicated Slovene citizens and well-known anti-fascists among their targets. By the beginning of the Cold War, these labels became so frequently used in communist propaganda they became vague and lost credibility in the West.[83]

Another key component of the Italian Republic's founding myth is Germany's betrayal of Italy. This was not the first instance of betrayal in Italian collective memory: irredentists had accused the Habsburg regime of having betrayed the Italian-speaking citizens of Austria-Hungary; they promulgated the "mutilated victory" myth blaming the Western allies for the denial of Italy's territorial claims after the First World War; and the Italians accused the British army of betrayal for not protecting their compatriots living in the Italian-Yugoslavian border regions after 1945. By emphasizing a historical narrative of betrayal that contained at least some emotional truth, Italians were again able to enhance their victimhood claim.

An irony of history is that the Italians were convincingly able to revert back to the stereotype of the good but innocent Italian, a stereotype they had wished to jettison since the late nineteenth century – and, moreover, one of the reasons they committed war crimes in the first place. This stereotype of being innocuous and perhaps pitiable was popular in Europe after Italy's defeats at Larissa (1866) and Adwa (1896) – Otto von Bismarck's comment on Italy's colonial endeavours was that "the Italians have a big appetite but they have poor teeth"[84] – and Italy's performance in the two world wars did nothing to alter it. During the Second World War, the Allies would actually use this stereotype in a propaganda campaign "aimed at breaking support on the home front": they sought to drive a wedge between Mussolini and the Germans, who were blamed for the war, by providing Italians a cover of innocence by which to escape their predicament.[85] The propaganda corroborated and reaffirmed the authenticity of the victimhood narrative by emphasizing the image of the good Italian.

Political decisions made in the postwar period regarding Italy's rehabilitation gave further credibility to the victimhood narrative. In

Germany, the Allied re-education and denazification processes, with all their flaws, together with war-crimes trials called for by the international community, all served to portray the Nazi period as the endpoint in a narrative of German national development. This framing attracted intense scrutiny of Germany by scholars, and facts surrounding German atrocities committed under the Third Reich were established as early as the late 1940s. In the Italian case, there was no re-education program, no "Italian Nuremberg," and no pressure to disclose Italian crimes. Instead, Badoglio's takeover was used to perpetuate a narrative that was founded on Italian resistance, civilization, and victimhood. This allowed the new Italian state to become a founding member of NATO in 1949 and an ally against the Eastern Bloc.[86] To complete the picture of the Italian-Yugoslavian relationship, it should be noted that, while Rome's amnesia about its war crimes and the victimhood narrative was protected, or at least tolerated, by the West, Yugoslavia's counter-narrative never received the same support from the Soviet Union. With Yugoslavia's expulsion from the Cominform in 1948, Tito lost his most influential ally in his country's attempt to shape commemoration of the war on the global stage.[87]

Italian diplomats, officers, and politicians attempted to exploit the victimhood narrative in various ways "to further political, social, and economic objectives."[88] Above all, they were instrumental in helping those responsible to avoid prosecution. They threatened to withhold reparations from foreign governments if they did not free captured Italians accused of war crimes, and they formed their own commission of inquiry into war crimes in Yugoslavia.[89] This commission concluded that the perpetrators were to be found on the side of the Yugoslavian partisans, and that Italians had acted honourably. Instances of violence at the hands of Italians were ignored, though a few were justified as acts of self-defence. These findings were incorporated into a government report covering Italy's occupation in the Balkans, illustrating the authority the state held over the authenticity of victimhood. The government in Rome wanted to buy time, hoping that the pressure to extradite war criminals to Belgrade would subside as the world's attention was focused on the rising tensions of the early Cold War.[90] Indicting their fellow countrymen for committing war crimes was never the commission's purpose. Approximately 1,200 Italians accused of atrocities in Africa and the Balkans, including Mario Roatta, never faced justice.[91]

The Italian government also used the victimhood narrative to stress Rome's claim to the lost Balkan territories, particularly Trieste. They argued that these areas were given to Italy as compensation after the First World War and thus rightfully belonged to Italy. Italians, so their argument went, were brutally murdered and deported in defending what rightfully belonged to them. The British were evidently irritated by these presumptuous demands. However, the postwar Italian diplomats' behaviour and worldview should not be surprising, as most of them began their careers during the Mussolini era and simply continued them after war.[92]

Conclusion

Flight and expulsion were daily phenomena in the Italian-Yugoslavian border region beginning in the late nineteenth century. They reached their peaks during the Italianization policy in the interwar period, during the Axis occupation of Slovenia, and immediately after the Second World War. They drew on a modern apparatus of administration and bureaucratic controls, such as identity documents or census rolls, and would have not been possible without technological innovation and governmental organization.[93] Several factors have changed over time that must be taken into consideration in order to achieve a nuanced understanding of these population movements.

The myth of ethnic homogeneity and the notion that the exchange or resettlement of entire ethnic groups can make political and ethnic frontiers coincide are key in explaining forced migration. In the beginning, Italian cultural racism was based on the presumed superiority of the Italians. They believed that other races would eventually assimilate, giving up their cultural, political, and societal identities. When the Fascists realized the limits of this policy, agreements with Yugoslavia were intended to initiate a massive population transfer.[94] In contrast to the many cases of population transfers triggered by mutual distrust – like, for example, the "Option" for the German-speaking people of South Tyrol – the Rome-Belgrade understanding resulted from newly gained, albeit short-lived, trust.

Moreover, wartime frustration, military defeats, and insurgencies led to Italy's "policy of elimination," which was realized through deportations, internments, and executions.[95] Italian conduct is thus another example of Michael Geyer's thesis that ethnic cleansing can be a weapon of a group that is, or believes itself to be, in a subaltern position and seeks to (re)claim space.[96] Yugoslavia's policy at the end of the war shows similarities: deportation and persecution of ideological opponents were meant to present a fait accompli in order to reclaim lost territories.

Furthermore, war provided cover for an escalation of violence, which often resulted in flight and expulsion.[97] Although the ideology of fascism lowered the threshold at which violence was considered permissible and legitimized many of those atrocities in the aftermath of the war, the Italian military's colonial experience should not be neglected in explanations of why atrocities were committed in the first place.[98] To date, however, we still lack in-depth biographies of Italian military leaders and studies exploring the experience of the individual soldier. These are crucial to understanding the extent to which fascist ideology, racial theories, a lack of national self-confidence, or counter-insurgency strategies were decisive in overcoming officers' inhibitions against ordering or carrying out war crimes.

The cessation of wars also triggered forced population movements. After the First World War, Italy forced Yugoslavia to accept its territorial demands and to guarantee the rights of the Italian minority, whereas Rome made only informal promises about protecting Slavs, allowing Italy to assimilate ethnic minorities ruthlessly within its own borders. After the Second World War, the victorious powers intended to define a new status quo by confirming or altering existing borders, including a possible population transfer.[99] However, the peace treaties did not call for an orderly population transfer between Italy and Yugoslavia. It was instead left up to individuals to declare their citizenship. Nevertheless, the Western Allies did not want to relinquish all control over local migration, so they forbade Italians from settling in the regions around Gorizia out of fear of future ethnic conflicts.[100]

Economic coercion and the subversion of traditional social, religious, and cultural hierarchies also forced people to flee. The importance of religion in maintaining cohesion of local communities is illustrated by the persecution of the clergy in the wake of Italianization programs since the 1920s. Furthermore, in the eastern regions, Catholics of all ethnicities were subjected to reprisals after 1945 because communists regarded them as collaborators and a reactionary force. Therefore, a sense of being out of place in what should have been one's own country often became the main reason for the decision to leave, regardless of which ethnic group was affected.[101]

Last but not least, the question of inclusion and exclusion of ethnic minorities was also of crucial importance. Which criteria were applied in deciding who belonged to the nation and who did not? In this regard, the cultural politics of forced removal, and the power of images played a decisive role in forging the Italian us-versus-them narrative and making removals acceptable.[102] Language played a vital role in decisions as to whether a person belonged to the "Italian race" or not. In the east, racial antagonism was aggravated by other considerations such as ideology, class, and religion.[103] The power of language and the equation of race and ideology are best reflected in the fascist neologism of *slavobolscevismo*.[104] The mere existence of these different criteria sometimes led to a very arbitrary interpretation of inclusion and exclusion.

Deportations and expulsions destroyed local communities and social structures. This was not only a heavy burden for the future development of the region but also for the persons affected, who had to leave their homelands and ways of life behind. The act of expulsion itself led to feelings of trauma, grief, anger, and powerlessness. Many of the forcibly displaced began to realize that they would never be able to return to their homeland, a realization that had devastating psychological consequences on the individual level.

Similar consequences can be found on the level of collective memory. The loss of Istria was as painful for the Italians as relinquishing Gorizia to Italy was for the Slovenes.[105] This collective sense of loss in both countries is similar to other stories of forced migration. However, the reappropriation of the stereotype of the "good Italian" after 1943, though previously despised by Italian nationalists and fascists, can be seen as a uniquely Italian response to the question of how to remember the events in the Italian-Yugoslavian border region. This myth, combined with the victimhood narrative, not only offered a common identity for a divided nation after the civil war; it also allowed Italy to become an integral part of NATO during the Cold War.

In 1943, a struggle between Italians and Yugoslavians erupted over who was the victim and who was the perpetrator. The Italian victimhood narrative eventually triumphed not only among Italians but also among Western audiences. Above all, it was the manifold testimonies from various actors that ascribed a sense of validity to Italy's claim. They included not only Italian conservative politicians and diplomats but also Italian Communists, academics, and artists; Western authorities and journalists; and even Slavs who had been persecuted by Yugoslavian partisans and who corroborated stories of Tito's crimes and Italy's helpfulness.

The downfall of the Italian First Republic in the 1990s opened the door for scholarly research on Italian war crimes. The establishment of a joint Italian-Slovenian commission of historians also contributed to a better understanding of these acts. However, even today, historians often concentrate on singular territorial or chronological case studies and thus tend to present their findings as a peculiarity. This approach neglects the *longue durée* of forced migration since the early days of the Kingdom of Italy as well as the long persistence of the victimhood narrative. The continuing efficacy of this narrative in regard to the events in the eastern border region was illustrated in 2004: Berlusconi's government, along with the support of the centre-left, established a day of remembrance for the victims of the *foibe* killings and the Italian "exodus."[106] Thus, much remains to be done to deconstruct the one-sided interpretation that still dominates Italian public memory and replace it with a better understanding of why and how Italians committed, and then suffered from, atrocities in the eastern border regions.

NOTES

I would like to thank the Gerda Henkel Foundation as well as the Volkswagen Foundation for supporting this work.

1 "Il Discorso alla Camera dei Fasci e delle Corporazioni nell'annuale della Guerra," in *Opera Omnia di Benito Mussolini*, vol. 30, ed. Duilio Susmel and Edoardo Susmel (Florence: La Fenice, 1960), 97.

2 See Gustavo Corni, "The Exodus of Italians from Istria and Dalmatia, 1945–56," in *The Disentanglement of Populations: Migration, Expulsion and Displacement in Postwar Europe, 1944–9*, ed. Jessica Reinisch and Elizabeth White (New York: Palgrave Macmillan, 2011), 71.

3 Gaia Baracetti, "*Foibe*: Nationalism, Revenge and Ideology in Venezia Giulia and Istria, 1943–5," *Journal of Contemporary History* 44, no. 4 (2009): 660; Marina Cattaruzza, "L'esodo istriano: questioni interpretative," *Ricerche di Storia Politica* 9 (1999): 27–8; Marina Cattaruzza, Orietta Moscarda, and Gabriele D'Ottavio, "L'esodo istriano nella storiografia e nel dibattito pubblico in Italia, Slovenia e Croazia: 1991–2006," *Ventunesimo Secolo* 7, no. 16 (June 2008): 9–29. Only Cattaruzza has examined the Italian-Yugoslavian border region within a broader time frame. Based on a "spatial turn" approach, she focuses on "space" in her analysis. See Cattaruzza, *L'Italia e il confine orientale 1866–2006* (Bologna: Il Mulino, 2007).

4 Michael Schwartz, "Ethnic 'Cleansing' and Modernity: Global Interactions of Forced Migrations in 19th and 20th Centuries" (paper presented at Conference on Forced Migration in Global Perspective, 1943–1951, Munk School of Global Affairs, University of Toronto, 11 October 2013), 2–4.

5 For the occupation policy, see Eric Gobetti, *L'occupazione allegra: Gli italiani in Jugoslavia (1941–1943)* (Rome: Carocci, 2007); Amedeo Osti Guerrazzi, *L'esercito italiano in Slovenia 1941–1943: Strategie di repressione antipartigiana* (Rome: Viella, 2011); Davide Rodogno, *Fascism's European Empire: Italian Occupation during the Second World War* (Cambridge: Cambridge University Press, 2006). On postwar memory, see the following works by Filippo Focardi: "Italy's Amnesia over War Guilt: The 'Evil Germans' Alibi," *Mediterranean Quaterly* 25, no. 4 (2015): 5–26; "Italy as Occupier in the Balkans: Remembrance and War Crimes after 1945," in *Experience and*

Memory: The Second World War in Europe, ed. Jörg Echternkamp and Stefan Martens (New York: Berghahn 2010), 135–46; "Prefazione," in *Italiani senza onore: i crimini in Yugoslavia e i processi negati (1941–1951)*, ed. Costantino Di Sante (Verona: Ombre Corte, 2005), 7–11.

6 The state is understood neither as a monolithic structure nor as an entity that can operate in insolation from society. See Alf Lüdtke, "Explaining Forced Migration," in *Removing Peoples: Forced Removal in the Modern World*, ed. Richard Bessel and Claudia B. Haake (London: Oxford University Press, 2009), 19, 25; Joanna De Groot, "Removing Peoples in the 'Modern' World: A Comparative Perspective," in *Removing Peoples*, 424.

7 See the introduction to this volume.

8 Stephanie M. Hom, "On the Origins of Making Italy: Massimo D'Azeglio and 'Fatta l'Italia, bisogna fare gli Italiani,'" *Italian Culture* 31, no. 1 (2013): 1–16; Silvana Patriarca, *Italian Vices: Nation and Character from the Risorgimento to the Republic* (Cambridge: Cambridge University Press, 2010), 8.

9 Shalom Reichman and Arnon Golan, "Irredentism and Boundary Adjustments in Post–World War I Europe," in *Irredentism and International Politics*, ed. Naomi Chazan (Boulder, CO: Lynne Rienner, 1991), 57.

10 See R.J.B. Bosworth, *Mussolini* (London: Bloomsbury Academic, 2002), 107; Michael Mann, *Fascists* (Los Angeles: University of California Press, 2004), 93.

11 Hans Woller, *Geschichte Italiens im 20. Jahrhundert* (Munich: C.H. Beck, 2010), 65–9, 79–80.

12 Reichman and Golan, "Irredentism," 57–9.

13 Arrigo Petacco, *A Tragedy Revealed: The Story of the Italian Population of Istria, Dalmatia, and Venezia Giulia, 1943–1956* (Toronto: University of Toronto Press, 2005), 11.

14 Glenda Sluga, *The Problem of Trieste and the Italo-Yugoslav Border: Difference, Identity, and Sovereignty in Twentieth-Century Europe* (Albany: SUNY Press, 2001), 42.

15 Alexander De Grand, *The Hunchback's Tailor: Giovanni Giolitti and Liberal Italy from the Challenge of Mass Politics to the Rise of Fascism, 1882–1922* (London: Greenwood, 2001), 236–8.

16 Sluga, *Problem of Trieste*, 47–8; Woller, *Geschichte Italiens*, 80.

17 *Slovene-Italian Relations, 1880–1956: Report of the Slovene-Italian Historical and Cultural Commission* (Trieste, 2004), 15, http://www.kozina.com/premik/poreng.pdf.

18 Baracetti, "*Foibe*," 661. On "cultural genocide," see A. Dirk Moses, "Raphael Lemkin, Culture, and the Concept of Genocide," in *The Oxford Handbook of Genocide Studies*, ed. Donald Bloxham and A. Dirk Moses (Oxford: Oxford University Press, 2010), 19–41. See also *Slovene-Italian Relations*, 10–11.

19 Zdenko Čěpič, Damjan Guštin, and Nevenka Troha, *La Slovenia durante la seconda guerra mondiale* (Udine, IT: Istituto Friulano per la Storia del Movimento di Liberazione, 2012), 25; Corni, "Exodus," 74; *Slovene-Italian Relations*, 16.

20 H. James Burgwyn, *Italian Foreign Policy in the Interwar Period, 1918–1940* (Westport, CT: Praeger, 1997), 108; Zara Steiner, *The Triumph of the Dark: European International History 1933–1939* (Oxford: Oxford University Press, 2011), 75.

21 "Der Botschafter in Rom von Hassell an das Auswärtige Amt, 14.1.1937," in *Akten zur deutschen Auswärtigen Politik, 1918–1945*, series C, vol. 6, bk. 1 (Göttingen: Vandenhoeck & Ruprecht, 1981), 309–10.

22 Dejan Djokić, "Leader or Devil? Milan Stojadinović, Prime Minister of Yugoslavia (1935–39), and His Ideology," in *In the Shadow of Hitler: Personalities of the Right in Central and Eastern Europe*, ed. Rebecca Haynes and Martyn Rady (London: I.B. Tauris, 2011), 155, 163–4; Tobias Hof and *Galeazzo Ciano, The Fascist Pretender* (Toronto: University of Toronto Press, 2021), 162–3.

23 "Colloquio col Presidente del Consiglio di Jugoslavia Stoiadinovic, Belgrad, 26.3.1937," in Galeazzo Ciano, *L'Europa verso la Catastrofe: 184 Colloqui con Mussolini, Hitler, Franco, Chamberlain, Sumner Welles, Rustu Aras, Stoiadinovic, Göring, Zog, Francois-Poncet ecc. verbalizzati di Galeazzo Ciano con 40 documenti diplomatici inediti* (Milan: Mondadori, 1948), 160–1.

24 Galeazzo Ciano, *Hidden Diary 1937–1938*, trans. Andreas Mayor (New York: I.P. Dutton, 1953), 195; "Telegramm Mackensen (Rom) an AA (Berlin), 27.11.1938," Botschaft in Rom, Bd. 809c, Politisches Archiv des Auswärtigen Amtes.

25 Luca De Caprariis, "I fasci italiani all'estero," in *Il fascismo e gli emigranti*, ed. Emilia Franzina and Matteo Sanfilippo (Bari: Laterza, 2003), 20.

26 See Ciano Diaries, 9, 17, 19, and 30 March 1939, Working Papers Relating to the Publication of the Ciano Diaries, cont. 4, Library of Congress (hereafter, "Ciano Diaries").

27 Cited in H. James Burgwyn, *Mussolini Warlord: Failed Dreams of Empire, 1940–1943* (New York: Enigma Books, 2012), 76.

28 By the end of January 1942, the Third Reich resettled 11,500 Germans from the Gottschee region – a part of the Province of Ljubljana – to the area between the Sava and Sutla Rivers. Around 37,000 Slovenes then living in the region were deported to 500 different camps in Germany. See Telegramma Grazioli a Ministero degli Interni, 6.6.1941, RG 40.002, reel 6, United States Holocaust Memorial Museum (hereafter USHMM); Mitja Ferenc, "Die Gottscheer Deutschen – ihre Umsiedlung und die Folgen," in *Zweiter Weltkrieg und ethnische Homogenisierungsversuche im Alpen-Adria-Raum*, ed. Brigitte Entner and Valentin Sima (Klagenfurt: Drava Verlag, 2012), 86.

29 Janez A. Arnež, *Slovenia in European Affairs: Reflections on Slovenian Political History* (New York: League of CSA, 1958), 82.
30 *Slovene-Italian Relations*, 19.
31 Sluga, *Problem of Trieste*, 58.
32 Rodogno, *Fascism's European Empire*, 365.
33 Ministero della Guerra, Gabinetto, Oggetto: Attività Ustasci, Roma, 23.8.1941, RG 40.003*03, USHMM; Telegramma De Renzo a Comando Supremo, Oggetto: Ingresso clandestino di ebrei, 31.8.1941, RG 40.003*12, USHMM; Rodogno, *Fascism's European Empire*, 367.
34 Aristotle Kallis, *Genocide and Fascism: The Eliminationist Drive in Fascist Europe* (New York: Routledge, 2009), 68–70.
35 Alexander De Grand, "Mussolini's Follies: Fascism in Its Imperial and Racist Phase, 1935–1940," *Contemporary European History* 13, no. 2 (2004): 142.
36 Woller, *Geschichte Italiens*, 151.
37 Cited in Bosworth, *Mussolini*, 307.
38 Pertti Ahonen, Gustavo Corni, Jerzy Kochanowski, Rainer Schulze, Tamás Stark, and Barbara Stelzl-Marx, eds., *People on the Move: Forced Population Movements in Europe in the Second World War and Its Aftermath* (Oxford: Bloomsbury Academic, 2008), 47.
39 R.J.B. Bosworth, "War, Totalitarianism and 'Deep Belief' in Fascist Italy, 1935–43," *European History Quarterly* 34, no. 4 (2004): 475–505, 497.
40 Ahonen et al., *People on the Move*, 47.
41 Baracetti, "*Foibe*," 661; *Slovene-Italian Relations*, 20.
42 Ciano Diaries, entry 5 January 1942.
43 John Corsellis and Marcus Ferrar, *Slovenia 1945: Memories of Death and Survival after World War II* (London: I.B. Tauris, 2005), 3.
44 Ahonen et al., *People on the Move*, 47.
45 Cited in Corsellis and Ferrar, *Slovenia 1945*, 26.
46 H. James Burgwyn, "General Roatta's War against the Partisans in Yugoslavia: 1942," *Journal of Modern Italian Studies* 9, no. 3 (2004): 316–17; David M. Crow, *War Crimes, Genocide, and Justice: A Global History* (New York: Palgrave Macmillan, 2014), 148.
47 Focardi, "Italy's Amnesia," 7–8.
48 Isabel Hull, *Absolute Destruction: Military Culture and the Practices of War in Imperial Germany* (Ithaca: Cornell University Press, 2005). On the Italo-Turkish War, see R.J.B. Bosworth, *Mussolini's Italy: Life under the Dictatorship* (London: Penguin Books, 2005), 50–1. On North African, see Aram Mattioli, "Die vergessenen Kolonialverbrechen des faschistischen Italiens in Libyen 1923–1933," in *Völkermord und Kriegsverbrechen in der ersten Hälfte des 20. Jahrhunderts*, ed. Fritz-Bauer-Institut (Frankfurt: Campus, 2004), 203–26; James Walston, "History and Memory of the Italian Concentration

Camps," *Historical Journal* 40, no. 1 (1997): 173–4; Woller, *Geschichte Italiens*, 54–6, 133–5.

49 Schwartz, "Ethnic 'Cleansing,'" 5.

50 Corsellis and Ferrar, *Slovenia 1945*, 26.

51 Comando II Corpo d'Armata, Oggetto: Programma dei provvedimenti e delle operazioni da attuare in Slovenia, 27.5.1942, RG 49.002*03, USHMM; *Slovene-Italian Relations*, 20.

52 Focardi, "Italy as Occupier," 136; Walston, "History and Memory," 176–7.

53 Baracetti, "*Foibe*," 659.

54 Feliks Gross, *Ethnics in a Borderland: An Inquiry into the Nature of Ethnicity and Reduction of Ethnic Tensions in a One-Time Genocide Area* (Westport, CT: Greenwood Press, 1978), 98–9.

55 Ibid, 93; Berndt Rieger, *Creator of Nazi Death Camps: The Life of Odilo Globocnik* (London: Vallentine Mitchell, 2007), 149–55; Susan Zuccotti, *The Italians and the Holocaust: Persecution, Rescue, and Survival* (New York: Peter Halban, 1987), 185.

56 See Baracetti, "*Foibe*," 659, 664–8, 674.

57 Corni, "Exodus," 77–8; *Slovene-Italian Relations*, 17–18, 23, 30.

58 Letter Prunas (Rome) to Sir Noel Charles (Rome), 12 May 1945, RG 59.063, box 1, 18–20, USHMM; "Istrian Death Pits," appendix I to report no. 186/780, 25. August 1945, RG 59.063, box 6, 7, USHMM.

59 Corsellis and Ferrar, *Slovenia 1945*, 242.

60 See documents in RG 59.063, box 6, USHMM.

61 HQ AMG Eighth Army Report, 16.5.1945, RG 59.063, box 1, 14–17, USHMM.

62 Donald Bloxham, "The Great Unweaving: Forced Population Movement in Europe, 1875–1949," in Bessel and Haake, *Removing Peoples*, 185. The Foreign Office had already prepared a memorandum in 1942 in which it argued for a limited population transfer. See Cattaruzza, "L'esodo istriano," 38.

63 Cattaruzza, "L'esodo istriano," 32–3.

64 Baracetti, "*Foibe*," 664.

65 For details, see Corni, "Exodus," 80–4.

66 *Slovene-Italian Relations*, 30.

67 Pamela Ballinger, "'National Refugees,' Displaced Persons, and the Reconstruction of Italy: The Case of Trieste," in Reinisch and White, *The Disentanglement*, 115–40.

68 Corni, "Exodus," 84; Raoul Pupo, *Il lungo Esodo. Istria: le persecuzioni, le foibe, l'esilio* (Milan: BUR Biblioteca Univ. Rizzoli, 2005), 139.

69 Cited in Joseph Schechtman, *The Refugees in the World: Displacement and Integration* (New York: Barnes, 1964), 69; Pupo, *Lungo Esodo*, 188–9.

70 Pamela Ballinger, "Borders of the Nation, Borders of Citizenship: Italian Repatriation and the Redefinition of National Identity after World War II,"

Comparative Studies in Society and History 49, no. 3 (2007): 723–4, 737; Corni, "Exodus," 81; *Slovene-Italian Relations*, 26–7.

71 Malcolm Proudfoot, *European Refugees, 1939–52: A Study in Forced Population Movement* (Evanston, IL: Northwestern University Press, 1956), 206. For the migration between Italy and Albania, see Pamela Ballinger, "A Sea of Difference, a History of Gaps: Migrations between Italy and Albania, 1939–1992," *Studies in Society and History* 60, no. 1 (2018): 90–118.

72 Letter to the Committee of the Italian Red Cross and for the Information to the Allied Military Government, Triest, August 1945, RG 59.063, box 6, 30, USHMM.

73 Documents relevant here can be found in RG 59.063, USHMM: Comitato d'Azione Giuliano a Ministero degli Affari Esteri, box 1, 19; Information Note for H.E. the British Ambassador, Rome, 28 June 1945, box 4, 6; letter of the Julian Committee for National Liberation to Admiral Stone, Rome, 17 May 1945, box 1, 3–4. See also Gross, *Ethnics in a Borderland*, 101–2.

74 Tony Judt, "The Past Is Another Country: Myth and Memory in Postwar Europe," in *The Politics of Retribution in Europe: World War II and Its Aftermath*, ed. István Deák, Jan Gross, and Tony Judt (Princeton, NJ: Princeton University Press, 2000), 293–323.

75 Focardi, "Italy's Amnesia," 7.

76 Baracetti, "*Foibe*," 673; Pamela Ballinger, *History in Exile: Memory and Identity at the Borders of the Balkans* (Princeton, NJ: Princeton University Press, 2002), 144–5.

77 Focardi, "Italy's Amnesia," 9.

78 Claudio Pavone, "Introduction," *Journal of Modern Italian Studies* 9, no. 3 (2004): 272–3.

79 Focardi, "Italy as Occupier," 138–9.

80 See Ulrich Dröge, *Barbaren mit humanen Zügen: Bilder des Deutschen in Filmen Roberto Rossellinis* (Trier: Wiss. Verl. Trier, 2009), 198–253; Robert S.C. Gordon, *Bicycle Thieves* (Basingstoke, UK: Palgrave Macmillan, 2008), 9–12; Tobias Hof, "Ein Land auf der Suche nach sich selbst: Italiens Zukunft in *Ladri di Biciclette* (1948)," in *Verfilmte Trümmerlandschaften: Nachkriegserzählungen im internationalen Kino 1945–1949*, ed. Johannes Hürter and Tobias Hof (Berlin: DeGruyter Oldenbourg, 2019), 227–48.

81 Baracetti, "*Foibe*," 659.

82 Focardi, "Italy as Occupier," 141.

83 Cattaruzza, Moscarda, and D'Ottavio, "L'esodo istriano," 13; Corsellis and Ferrar, *Slovenia 1945*, 1.

84 Cited in Hendrik L. Wesseling, *Teile und herrsche: Die Aufteilung Afrikas, 1880–1914* (Stuttgart: Franz Steiner Verlag, 1999), 25.

85 Focardi, "Italy's Amnesia," 10–11.

86 Michele Battini, "Sins of Memory: Reflections on the Lack of an Italian Nuremberg and the Administration of International Justice after 1945," *Journal of Modern Italian Studies* 9, no. 3 (2004): 356. For postwar trials in Italy, see Andrea Martini, *Dopo Mussolini: I processi ai fascisti e ai collaborazionisti (1944–1953)* (Rome: Viella, 2019). Similar arguments can be made regarding Turkey and its remembrance of the Armenian genocide, or regarding Japan's silence about its war crimes. Similar to Italy, both countries were important allies in American strategy against the Soviet Union, and thus the West did not pressure the governments in Ankara or Tokyo to confront their pasts. Any discussions that might have caused friction within the NATO alliance were judiciously avoided from the beginning.
87 Focardi, "Italy as Occupier," 140.
88 See the introduction to this volume.
89 Rory Carroll, "Italy's Bloody Secret," *Guardian*, 25 June 2001.
90 Costantino Di Sante, "Introduzione: Crimini senza giustizia né memoria," in *Italiani senza onore: I crimini in Yugoslavia e i processi negati (1941–1951)*, ed. Costantino Di Sante (Verona: Ombre Corte, 2005): 21–3; Focardi, "Prefazione," 8–9.
91 Carroll, "Italy's Bloody Secret"; Di Sante, "Introduzione," 40.
92 Letter Prunas (Rome) to Sir Noel (Rome), 12 May 1945, RG 59.063, box 1, 26–7, USHMM; Di Sante, "Introduzione," 21–3.
93 De Groot, "Removing Peoples," 418.
94 Ahonen et al., *People on the Move*, 46.
95 Bloxham, "Great Unweaving," 196.
96 Lüdtke, "Explaining Forced Migration," 28.
97 Kallis, *Genocide and Fascism*, 29–30; Norman M. Naimark, *Fires of Hatred: Ethnic Cleansing in Twentieth-Century Europe* (Cambridge, MA: Harvard University Press, 2001), 187–90.
98 Tobias Hof, "Extreme Violence and Military Identity: The Italians in the Balkans (1941–1943)," *Zeitschrift für Genozidforschung* 16, no. 1 (2018): 57–84.
99 Bloxham, "Great Unweaving," 199. For the relationship between new borders and expulsion, see Marina Cattaruzza, "Endstation Vertreibung: Minderheitenfrage und Zwangsmigration in Ostmitteleuropa, 1919–1949," *Journal of Modern European History* 6, no. 1 (2008): 6.
100 Schechtman, *Refugees in the World*, 70.
101 Ahonen et al., *People on the Move*, 110; Corsellis and Ferrar, *Slovenia 1945*, 8.
102 De Groot, "Removing Peoples," 428.
103 Appreciation of Political Situation Venezia Giulia, 17 June 1945, RG 59.063, box 3, 6, USHMM.

104 Nevenka Troha, "Ethnopolitische Flurbereinigungen im italienisch-slowenisch-kroatischen Grenzgebiet," in Entner and Sima, *Zweiter Weltkrieg*, 59–77, 60.

105 *Slovene-Italian Relations*, 26.

106 Cattaruzza, Moscardo, and D'Ottavio. "L'esodo istriano," 11, 17–20.

12 Defiant Victims: The Deportation of the Chechen and the Memory of Stalinism in the Soviet Union and Russia

MORITZ FLORIN

In his seminal project documenting life in Soviet forced labour camps, Alexander Solzhenitsyn attempted to do justice to all the victims of Stalinism. *The Gulag Archipelago*, written between 1958 and 1968, became not only an "experiment in literary investigation" but also a "memorial" to the victims of Stalinist dictatorship. According to Solzhenitsyn, the victims of Stalinism were equal in the suffering and subjugation they endured, except for the Chechen:

> There was one nation which would not give in, would not acquire the mental habits of submission – and not just individual rebels among them, but the whole nation to a man. These were the Chechen … The Chechen never sought to please, to ingratiate themselves with the bosses; their attitude was always haughty and indeed openly hostile. They treated the laws on universal education and the state curriculum with contempt, and to save them from corruption would not send their little girls to school, nor indeed all of their boys … They were capable of rustling cattle, robbing a house, or sometimes taking what they wanted by force. As far as they were concerned, the local inhabitants, and those exiles who submitted so readily, belonged more or less to the same breed as the bosses. They respected only rebels.[1]

In other words, according to Solzhenitsyn, the Chechen resisted oppression during their years of exile more strongly than, for example, Germans, Koreans, Ukrainians, Poles, or Russians who had also experienced deportation. When the Soviet regime tried to destroy the Chechen nation, the deported heroically resisted. They were not only unwilling to accept their supposed guilt, but they also refused to speak Russian, to go to school, to work, or to vote in the Soviet elections. Many authors have followed in Solzhenitsyn's footsteps, arguing that, during their years of exile, the Chechen were the most "defiant" or "resistant" of all deported groups.[2] Some have even spoken of a Chechen "cultural and ethnic revitalization" that occurred in exile. Even if the Stalinist state succeeded in breaking most of its victims, the Chechen supposedly remained unbended, unchanged, and, in this primordial and existentialist sense, true and authentic to themselves.[3]

This chapter attempts to situate the history of Chechen commemoration of the 1944 deportations within Soviet, European, and global contexts. On the one hand, such commemoration belongs firmly in the history of Soviet and post-Soviet memory cultures. As citizens of the Soviet Union, the Chechen lacked connections to the history of Holocaust memorialization and global discourses of victimhood for most of the twentieth century. Instead, the Chechen case was entangled with a larger history of what has variously been labelled the "distorted," "deformed," "warped," or "false" memories of Stalinism in Russia.[4] Outbreaks of memory during the so-called thaw (*ottepel'*) after Stalin's death and during perestroika were quickly superseded by new phases of repression, culminating in the near-total erasure under the current pro-Russian regime of Ramzan Kadyrov of any memorial culture honouring the victims of Stalinism.[5] The decision in February 2014 to destroy the memorial for the victims of the Chechen deportations may be seen as an extreme case of the repression of memories, but it nevertheless fits into a larger picture of the troubled relationship of the Russian state with the Stalinist past.

On the other hand, the history of Chechen commemoration can also be situated in a global context in which victims have often failed to rid themselves of the rhetoric of heroic nationalism and to escape the racialization upon which atrocities and genocide were based. Even if, in recent years, scholars have started to challenge images of Chechen "defiance," with its attendant connotations of not only resistance but also childlike stubbornness,[6] the history of the deportations has hardly been reassessed. The idea of Chechen "defiance" can be read as a particularly striking case of a group of victims reclaiming their subject-oriented historical authenticity. Images of Chechen stubbornness and bravery date back to the Russian wars of subjugation and colonization in the nineteenth century.[7] The image of the Chechen not only as exceptional warriors but also as victims of Stalinism has been adopted by many Chechen themselves.[8] This image played an important role in mobilizing the Chechen people for two wars that have sometimes been described as the last wars of decolonization worldwide.[9] The notion of defiant resistance provided the basis on which to reclaim a special place within a community of victims.[10] In other words, it might be true that the ways in which anti-colonial images of violence have been projected onto later representations of authenticity and victimhood are unique to the Chechen deportees.[11] The underlying logic, however, is not: the claim of singularity and authenticity and the struggle for recognition of this (national) uniqueness are also what make the Chechen case quite ordinary in the context of twentieth-century commemoration and victimhood.

This chapter is about the Chechen people, but parallel developments among other deported groups should, of course, not be overlooked. When Solzhenitsyn speaks of the "Chechen," for example, it is likely that he was referring to all the deported "mountain people" (*gortsy*) from the North Caucasus (for example, the Balkars, Karachays, Chechen, and Ingush), the Chechen being the most numerous and best-known among them. All of these groups were deported in 1944 as supposed or potential traitors of the Soviet fatherland. Not only Chechen, Balkar, and Ingush individuals were deported but, rather, whole ethnonational groups, including those who had served as soldiers in the Red Army in the fight against Germany. In other words, these groups were targeted in their entirety, which is also why the deportations have sometimes been labelled "genocidal."[12] It is against this background that all later attempts to achieve recognition and to reclaim authenticity in the name of imagined collectives of victims must be understood. The experiences of the different deported groups are inseparable one from another, and the histories of the so-called Vaynakh group of mountain people – for example, the Chechen and Ingush – are especially closely related.[13] Nevertheless, this chapter also aims to highlight some of the specific qualities of Chechen commemoration. In fact, within the larger culture of Soviet and post-Soviet commemoration, the Chechen case most clearly demonstrates a specific claim of authenticity and singularity.

Rehabilitation and Return, 1955–1957

One of the prime characteristics of Chechen mourning was that, because it took place in a Soviet context, it could never escape the strictures of Soviet speech. It was "warped" not only because it was suppressed but also because it had to follow the rules of Soviet commemorative culture.[14] Just as in postwar Germany, the question of responsibility remained hard to address in a society in which both victims and perpetrators were everywhere. Unlike in Germany, however, the very state that had been responsible for the terror remained intact, and it was imperative for the victims of Stalinism to follow its discursive rules.[15] This also holds true for the Chechen and Ingush civil rights movement (the so-called movement for rehabilitation) that began after Stalin's death. The members of this movement were the first who tried to make sense of what had happened. However, their attempt to invent a narrative of collective and national suffering would soon come into conflict with the discursive restraints of Soviet commemoration.

After the deportations in February 1944, the Chechen and Ingush were dispersed across Central Asia and were not allowed to communicate with each other. Their experiences were far more varied than has often been acknowledged. The old elites among the deportees were sent to cities such as Frunze (present-day Bishkek) or Alma-Ata (Almaty), where a majority of the population was Russian.[16] Others were sent to kolkhozes (collective farms), where a majority of the population was Central Asian and Muslim (e.g., Kyrgyz, Kazakh, or Uzbek).[17] Most had to work in agriculture, though some worked in mining, construction, or evacuated industries.[18] A majority of the deported people ended up in "special settlements," most of whose inhabitants belonged to one or another group of the victims of Stalinism (e.g., kulaks or various ethnic groups).[19] Depending on location, the Chechen and Ingush "traitors of the fatherland" arrived to find established societies of victims – but also sometimes societies of self-declared "Soviet patriots."[20] In some places, the deported tried to organize resistance; in others, they simply had to struggle to survive.[21]

Nevertheless, some shared experiences would later form the basis for a narrative of collective suffering. With some exceptions, the Chechen were all deported on the same day and on the same trains. This is one of the reasons why epidemics spread quickly among them: according to some estimates, at least 25 per cent of all the deported Chechen died during the first two years of exile.[22] Even though deportees hardly had a chance to make sense of their experience collectively, they of course knew that they had been deported on the basis of their national identities. Prior to their arrival, the Central Asian *kolkhozes* were at least vaguely aware of the official reasons for the deportation. Supposedly, the Chechen people (like the Ingush, Balkars, Karachays, Crimean Tatars, Kalmyks, and so on) had collectively "betrayed" the Soviet fatherland during the war.[23] In many places, old stereotypes of the Chechen as supposed "bandits" and "thieves" played an important role in justifying cruelty against them.[24] From the beginning, it was clear that the Chechen (just like the Ingush and others) had been deported as a supposedly homogeneous ethnic group.

From this perspective, it is not surprising that the first letters that individuals wrote to the Soviet government after Stalin's death express a very clear idea about the deportations as a collective experience. The authors of most letters referred to both groups, the Chechen and the Ingush, as one "people" (*Checheno-Ingushskiy narod*), although they did sometimes note that most of the accusations of betrayal and banditry had been aimed specifically at the Chechen.[25] It is important to note that the authors of such letters usually belonged to a small, literate elite. But even though this elite was small, it purported to represent all Chechen and Ingush people, who had been deported together and who were accused of the same crime. Ingush writer Idris Bazorkin sent his first long letter (around forty typed pages) to the government in 1953. Although he was the only signatory, he added that, "if it is required, any one of us will add his signature."[26] According to Bazorkin, the goal of the unified Chechen and Ingush rehabilitation movement was national. They wanted to return to their homelands and to regain an autonomous status. They petitioned in the name of the Chechen and Ingush – together, the "Vaynakh" people – but rarely in the name of all deported ethnic groups.

In seeking "rehabilitation," however, the Chechen and Ingush peoples could not escape confronting the accusations that the Soviet state had brought against them. They not only sought to refute the narrative of betrayal but, moreover, wanted to be reaccepted into the Soviet family of nations. From this perspective, the deportations had been not only about exile but also about the deliberate suppression of Chechen culture and history. The nation could exist only if it were allowed to uncover the historical "truth" and to speak out against the "falsification" of its past during the years of exile. According to those leading the rehabilitation movement, the Chechen and Ingush not only had *not* betrayed the Soviet fatherland but, collectively, had supported the Bolshevik project from the very beginning. The aspirations of the suppressed people of the North Caucasus had coincided with the Bolshevik struggle against tsarist oppression.[27] During the Second World War, any traitors among them had been only a minority. Lengthy discussions revolved around questions such as who the traitors had been (were they Chechen, Ingush, or just simply deserters from the Soviet army?), how many traitors there had been (a hundred, a thousand, or the entire nation?), how much support they had received from the Germans, how many Chechen and Ingush soldiers had fought in the Soviet army, and how many had deserted.[28] In other words, the rehabilitation movement asked the Soviet state not only to admit a mistake but also to re-establish a positive and pro-Soviet historic image of the Chechen and Ingush as Soviet nationalities.

Even though the members of the rehabilitation movement clearly understood the deportations in national terms, they also knew that they should not single themselves out. They did not argue that their fate was singular but instead compared themselves to the Crimean Tatars, the Balkars, and the Kalmyk people – and sometimes even to the kulaks. They also frequently mentioned how many good Russians they had met during their years in exile. Even if Russian women had been allowed to divorce their deported Chechen husbands, "not a single one of them" decided to do so.[29] And although there had been many Russians among the perpetrators, the Chechen and Ingush had also met Russian victims of Stalinism in exile.[30] In this sense, the deportation was not part of an age-old colonial conflict between Russia and the mountain people of the North Caucasus, but instead, was about Stalinism, and specifically the Stalinist "cult of personality."

It is significant that the Chechen and Ingush elites refrained from using the word and legal concept of "genocide." The Chechen civil rights movement did not have any contact with the Chechen diaspora abroad (in Western Europe, the United States, or Canada), and it was unaware of attempts to bring the attention of a wider international public to the deportations. In 1948, Abdurakhman Abdrakhmanov, who had fled from the USSR during the war, wrote a short pamphlet for the United Nations entitled *Narodoubiystvo v SSSR*, the term *narodoubiystvo* paralleling the German term *Völkermord*, or "genocide."[31] In 1955, a group of Chechen in exile in the United States tried to bring the deportations to the attention of the United Nations.[32] Although this might have helped the Chechen cause at a time when they were lobbying for rehabilitation and return to the North Caucasus, it is unlikely that the Chechen still in the Soviet Union knew anything about these attempts to bring international attention to their fate; they likely learned of these efforts only later, during perestroika.

In fact, the Chechen and Ingush letter writers firmly rooted their arguments in Soviet discourse. They argued, for example, that "we would not write if we had anyone to turn to, if we did not live in the Soviet Union and instead in a capitalist state."[33] It could be that they framed arguments for gaining recognition this way based solely on strategy; deportees, as everyone else in the Soviet Union, had to follow the rules of the standard discourse in order to achieve anything. And what they sought to achieve was clear: their return to the North Caucasus.

It is important to remember, however, that, under Khrushchev, the Soviet state did in fact openly discuss and atone for some "mistakes" made under Stalin. Especially among the literate (and usually socialist) elites, there was gratitude for Khrushchev's "Secret Speech," and, throughout the USSR, there was hope that the state could admit the complete truth about Stalinism.[34] Rehabilitation also meant that the Chechen could wash themselves of the guilt forced on them for having supposedly betrayed the Soviet Union. Thus, the idea was often accepted that Stalin alone – and not the Soviet system or Russians in general – had been responsible for the deportations. In a Chechen song about the deportations, such an idea took centre stage:

Of sunrises you deprived us, Stalin,
Of sunsets you deprived us, Stalin,
Of our motherland you deprived us, Stalin,
May God conceal you in your coffin.

So that you are deprived of sunrises, Stalin,
So that you are deprived of sunsets, Stalin,
So that you are deprived of all that is most precious to you
Just as you deprived us of our native land.

Should we forget that morning?
Should we forget that evening?
We must never forget our native land
And that black day which befell it.

The bleating of sheep, the whine of dogs,
The weeping of children and old men,
As long as we live on this earth.
We will not forget them.[35]

The idea that only Stalin and the small clique around him had been responsible was an acceptable way of telling the story of the deportations without discussing some of the more delicate issues of perpetration, Russian chauvinism, Marxist-Leninist ideology, or the role that the local, Central Asian population had played in the everyday discrimination against the deported people.

Return and Incomplete Mourning since 1956

The civil rights movement had set two related goals for itself. First, it demanded "rehabilitation" or, in other words, for the Soviet state to admit that the deportations had been based on false assumptions and accusations. Second, they wanted to be allowed to return to their ancient homelands. In many respects, they succeeded. In the years after 1956, most Chechen and Ingush were allowed to return to the North Caucasus, and their national autonomy was reinstated. After years of exile and silence, they had become part of the Soviet "empire of nations" again.[36] However, the Chechen and Ingush were forced to accept the terms of Soviet commemorative culture, and they thus had to agree not to seek out a differentiated or privileged place among the other groups of victims. The only Soviet *lieu de mémoire* allowing for memories of grief, desperation, and loss was the Great Patriotic War. Although the Soviet history of the war was written as a story of collective heroism, some space was allowed for memories of loss and hardship that people went through in order to achieve victory.[37] However, the Chechen and Ingush had to accept – as did Jews, so-called gypsies, Soviet Germans, kulaks, and the Ukrainian and Kazakh victims of famine – that they would not be accorded a special place within the culture of Soviet commemoration. In one sense, the deported peoples were further disadvantaged because they could not be accepted as members of the collective war effort. As described further below, the image of the deported as notorious traitors persisted after their collective return.

From a Chechen and Ingush perspective, rehabilitation was not only an attempt to reinstate the status quo that had prevailed before the deportations; it was also intimately linked to a need to mourn. The living as well as the dead could now return to their homelands, to the ancient "lands of their fathers." From the very beginning of the "thaw" era of the 1950s, the deportees were clear in their desire not to stay in Central Asia. They argued that "neither in terms of language nor culture" did they have anything in common with the Kyrgyz or Kazakh peoples.[38] Later, during perestroika, some of the victims recalled how they exhumed the remains of their relatives in order to bury them at "home."[39] During the 1990s, historian Michaela Pohl interviewed Chechen and Ingush individuals who were still living in Kazakhstan, and she frequently heard people say, "It cannot be that our graves will be here."[40] To many Chechen and Ingush, return was about loss, burial, and overcoming grief.

After their return, it seemed for a very short period as if the Chechen and Ingush would be allowed to speak about their past suffering. Some authors called upon party officials to remove the monument for the "harriers" and "killers" of the mountain people.[41] At a writer's conference in 1957, Chechen author Saidbey Arsanov spoke about the horrendous suffering during the deportations and asked his listeners never to forget.[42] Arbi Mamakayev wrote a poem about an old Chechen man who had spent thirteen years in Siberian exile under the tsars. Only after the October Revolution was he allowed return to his native village near the Terek River. On the surface, this was a poem about the tsarist era, but most people immediately understood its metaphorical meaning. According to the KGB, when Mamakayev read his poem on the local Grozny radio, people wept: "We were eight people listening … This poem made such a strong impression that I could not withstand [it], and barely holding back my tears I went away from the radio, especially when in the poem they spoke about the Terek and about a man who has spent 13 years in a foreign land and now returns to his beloved Terek."[43]

The idea that the dead deportees had to be buried in their native soil emerges repeatedly in literature, memoirs, and films. Kazakh filmmaker Shaken Aymanov broached this topic in one of the few Soviet films containing any mention of deportations. *The Land of Our Fathers* is the story of an old Kazakh man whose only son has fallen during the war. He wants to return the remains of his son to his native Kazakh lands in order to bury him according to the laws of their ancestors. On his way to Leningrad, the old Kazakh meets many people, among them a stowaway travelling on the roof of a train. It turns out that this stowaway had been deported to Kazakhstan in 1944 and is now making a desperate attempt to return to the North Caucasus in order to die "in the land of his fathers." Neither the stowaway nor the old Kazakh succeed: the old Kazakh makes it to Ukraine, only to find out that his son's remains lie buried in a mass grave. The stowaway dies when the train enters a tunnel.[44] Aymanov's film was one of the very rare attempts to create an inclusive vision encompassing the memories of war and Stalinism that crossed boundaries between different groups of victims.

The significance of return as an aspect of mourning and grief also helps explain why so many conflicts of the late Soviet era revolved around the idea of incomplete return. Even though the Chechen and Ingush succeeded in regaining most of their "ancient lands," some parts of the pre-war Chechen-Ingush Autonomous Socialist Republic remained within the borders of neighbouring republics. In the Chechen case, the district of Aukh remained within the republic of Dagestan, and, in the Ingush case, the region of Prigorodny was absorbed into the Republic of North Ossetia. These decisions were a constant source of friction that provoked repeated protests and streams of letters to Moscow.[45] Aza Bazorkina, an Ingush author, later accused the Soviet government of a "second genocide" that was even worse than the first because it was an ongoing injustice.[46] Incomplete return meant incomplete mourning, and the loss of ancient lands thus also symbolized the incompleteness and insufficiency of mourning in the Soviet context.

The returnees also did not succeed in shedding the reputation of being traitors. During the 1960s, discussion of the crimes of Stalinism was again repressed, and the Second World War became increasingly inescapable as the "dominant myth" of the Soviet state.[47] Thus, after the "thaw," it also became almost impossible to address questions of guilt. This might also be one of the reasons why the stain of being "traitors" did not fade. In 1958, a major conflict erupted in Grozny between the returnees and the Russian population, and two Chechen men killed a Russian in a fight. Thousands of Russian (also labelled "European") inhabitants of Grozny attended the funeral, and it turned into a political gathering directed not only against "the Chechen who kill the Russians" but also against the regional committee of the Communist Party (*obkom*) and the KGB. The Russian rioters demanded that the Chechen-Ingush ASSR be renamed Grozny region and that the proportion of Chechen and Ingush in this region not exceed 10 per cent.[48] In other words, just like so many other victims of Stalin's terror, the Chechen were rejected by those who had taken their place.[49] However, unlike many other victims, they were not rejected because exile had transformed them so much that they had become unrecognizable. The trope of "misrecognition" that Alexander Etkind has so insightfully analysed played no role here.[50] Instead, they were rejected precisely because they were perceived to be Chechen, and because the stereotype of the Chechen traitor and bandit persisted.

Arguably, by keeping silent, the state missed a great opportunity to use rehabilitation for reintegration. Many Chechen wanted to be reaccepted into the Soviet family. However, the state feared the consequences of an open debate in a society in which not only victims but also perpetrators, collaborators, informants, bystanders, and profiteers were everywhere, and in which the boundaries between victim and perpetrator were not always clearly defined. Because the state forced the deportees to keep silent, public commemoration itself could become an act of defiance or dissidence. Memoirs and interviews collected during perestroika and after reveal that, behind the official veil of silence, people shared stories about the deportations. Such stories about forced exile, cultural survival, and return often contained an element of heroic resistance, of cultural self-preservation and defiance.[51] As Brandenberger and Park have argued, the deportations became the Chechen's first "commonly held" experience as a "modern nation."[52] However, only during the process of rehabilitation did the Chechen people get a chance to make sense of the deportations as a collective experience. Rehabilitation and return became a process in which the Chechen could reorient their self-image toward collective mourning.

Perestroika and Chechen Exceptionalism

Russian author Anatoly Pristavkin is sometimes credited for first speaking openly about the deportations in his 1987 novel *A Golden Cloud Spent the Night* (*Nochevala tuchka zolotaya*).[53] Following this partly fictional, partly autobiographical account, deportees started to tell their own versions of the events. Authors such as Nikolai Bugay began to publish archival sources. Others collected oral testimonies and memoirs and founded the Confederation of Repressed Peoples.[54] In the beginning, the Chechen were part of an all-Soviet movement to recover the past and to speak about the "blind spots" (*belye pyatna*) of memory. Organizations such as MEMORIAL were for all victims of Stalinism and did not single out the Chechen.[55] The authors of a "white book" on the deportations, published in 1991, called upon their readers not to "judge your tormentors." The Chechen and Ingush should do everything to "strengthen their friendship with all peoples." According to the authors, memories did not have to be divisive. Instead, the victims of the "Stalinist-Berievist" crimes – that is, those committed by Stalin and his chief of the secret police, Lavrentiy Beria – should be commemorated collectively in a spirit of "solidarity" and "human compassion."[56]

Nevertheless, memories of Stalinism always entailed the potential of an ethnic hierarchization of memories. Each national group of the Soviet Union had been subjected to the Stalinist politics of social cleansing, but the dividing lines between social and ethnic terror sometimes blurred. This was the case, for example, in the Ukrainian and Kazakh famines of 1932–3, or the "national operations" of 1937–8, which had targeted the elites of the Soviet national republics. In the case of the punished people (the deported nationalities), ethnic classifications most clearly superseded social ones.[57] It is telling that in her famous book *Tak eto bylo* (This is how it was), published in 1993, Karachay author Svetlana Alieva grouped the memoirs of individual victims according to ethnicity. The book contained separate chapters for deported Korean, German, Karachay, Balkar, Kalmyk, Crimean Tatar, Greek, Meskhetian Turk, Kurdish, Chechen, and Ingush peoples. Though Alieva tried to avoid a hierarchization of victim groups, she nevertheless provided each group with a platform to tell their specific national stories. Generally, she stayed true to her intention of letting victims among the various national groups speak for themselves. Nevertheless, she also reserved a special place for Solzhenitsyn and for his thoughts about the particularities of the Chechen, quoted at the beginning of this chapter.[58]

As in many places throughout the USSR, public protest movements in Chechnya started in earnest after the Chernobyl catastrophe, when the public debates surrounding glasnost took on a new dynamic. In April 1988, protesters gathered in Gudermes, a village thirty kilometres east of Grozny, and demanded that construction of a nearby biochemical plant be terminated.[59] Such protests can be called eco-nationalist in the sense that they were not about ecology as such but, instead, about the destruction of national landscapes.[60] As in most other republics throughout the USSR, protesters quickly identified a whole range of unresolved "national" issues, such as the social gap between Russified cities (e.g., Grozny) and the countryside.[61] At the same time, historians and journalists started to re-examine the recent and distant past. Protesters challenged, for example, the official narrative that most national minorities had "voluntarily" joined the Russian Empire during the nineteenth century. The local press did its best to dismiss the protests as "nationalist" and thus arguably helped deepen the gap between the protesters and the government.

Most significantly, glasnost also enabled a discussion about commemoration across the Soviet Union. In 1988, Ruslan Tulikov, a Chechen party member from Urus-Martan, initiated a movement with the aim of reconstructing destroyed Chechen cemeteries. He said in an August 1990 interview:

> As a child I heard from old people that we trample underfoot the memory of our ancestors. Everywhere in Chechnya-Ingushetia tombstones were used for building houses, bridge supports, or as curb-stones. These tombstones, painstakingly carved from solid blocks, skillfully painted in Arabic script, used to stand in our cemeteries as annals of past generations. But in 1944 Stalin's vandals suddenly expelled the Chechen and the Ingush from their homes. And in order to also erase the memory of them, they destroyed the cemeteries. It is our goal to restore all the gravestones – every single one of them.[62]

According to the diary of Sherip Asuev, a correspondent for the Russian news agency Itar-Tass, many people at first kept their distance from Tulikov. But by September 1990, a mass movement had formed for the reconstruction of tombstones, and approximately five hundred stones had already been recovered.[63]

Around the same time, Tulikov heard about mass graves in his native village of Urus-Martan. According to an elderly woman working in the local hospital, the sick and elderly considered to be unfit for the long trip to Kazakhstan had been executed nearby in 1944. Tulikov found the mass grave and, together with his group, started to exhume the dead. Only then did others inform him about the existence of yet another mass grave, at Khaibakh, where the population of a whole village had been locked in a stable and then burned alive.[64] The basic facts of the massacre had been known among the Soviet leadership since 1956, when an eyewitness to the events, Ziyauddin Malsagov, had written a letter to

Khrushchev. A state commission had opened the mass grave that same year but then decided to keep its existence a secret.[65] Only during perestroika did the wider public learn of the events, and, in August 1990, a Chechen state commission started to exhume the remains.[66] Even though atrocities of a similar scale had taken place elsewhere, and even though searches for mass graves took place across the Soviet Union,[67] Tulikov had laid the foundation for a national interpretation of past suffering. Graves and tombstones became the central symbol of Chechen commemoration and came to symbolize the genocidal dimension of the deportations.[68] The Stalinist regime had not only deported the Chechen but also tried to erase their culture. The tombstones pointed not only to Stalin's responsibility for these crimes but also to the complicity of those who had stolen Chechen lands and vandalized their cemeteries.

The first memorial to the Chechen victims of Stalinism, unveiled in Grozny in 1992, consisted of tombstones. A sculpture of a fist clutching a dagger stood at the centre, and the background featured a red wall inscribed with the words "We won't cry! We won't lose our courage! We won't forget!"[69] In contrast to the memorial in Magas, the capital of the Ingush republic, which consisted of nine towers that represented each deported ethnic group, the Chechen memorial conveyed a highly specific idea about Chechen identity. According to the inscription on the memorial, the Chechen never surrender to the outside world. They will neither cry nor mourn; they will never bow and will always resist. The Chechen people remained true to themselves and did not change – or, if they did, it was unrelated to the regime's attempts to break them. The memorial became an indicator of the ethnicization and politicization that the memory of the deportations had acquired.

Chechen Defiance and the Russian-Chechen War

Glasnost started as a general debate throughout the Soviet Union, but, around 1988, it was becoming increasingly nationalistic. Mark Beissinger has spoken of "tides of nationalism" sweeping through the USSR, and the Chechen and Ingush did not escape its waves.[70] The most important difference between these two groups of deportees was the fact that their nationalist energies went into different directions: Ingush nationalists' main concern was for their "historic lands" and the "graves of their fathers" within neighbouring North Ossetia, whereas Chechen nationalists were concerned mainly about their autonomy and, later, independence from Russia. Even though former Soviet Air Force general Dzhokhar Dudayev took over the Chechen government during a coup d'état in 1991, he gained wide support for his pursuit of independence during subsequent elections. However, the Russian government was not willing to grant Chechen independence, and two bloody wars followed. There is a wide range of estimates of casualties, but it is safe to say that between 65,000 and 75,000 civilians died, and almost a million were displaced during the two wars, which took place from 1994 to 1996 and from 1999 to 2009.[71] In 2001, the Committee on Conscience of the United States Holocaust Memorial Museum put Chechnya on its alert list of areas facing the potential for genocide.

The chaos and urgency created by these events pushed the memory of the deportations to the background. Any attempt nowadays at recording oral histories of the deportations faces the problem that memories of different horrors – during the Second World War and the more recent ones – blur and overlap. Most archival sources were destroyed in the air raids of the First Russian-Chechen War.[72] However, many observers agree that the Russian attacks in these conflicts themselves evoked memories of deportation. British journalist Anatol Lieven conducted a series of interviews during the wars, some of them in air raid shelters. Some people had already started to make sense of the new war as a continuation of the old. Some feared that, if resistance failed, the Chechen would again face mass deportation, as they had in 1944.[73] According to historian Yusha Aidaev, a Chechen "deportation syndrome" played an important role in the "stubbornness" during the war.[74] Many Chechen likened the Russian invasion of 1994 to the 1944 deportations, fifty years earlier.[75] On a political level, this idea of renewed suffering and heroism was translated into a historical narrative of repeated genocides. According to this narrative, there had been at least three attempts at genocide: one in the early nineteenth century during Russian general Aleksey Yermolov's wars of subjugation, one in 1944 under Stalin, and the third in the 1990s under Yeltsin.[76] The destruction of the Grozny memorial to the victims of the 1944 deportations, and of the national archives with newly declassified documents on the deportations, added to the perception that Yeltsin had attempted to commit "culturecide" of the Chechen nation.[77] These events were thus integrated into the narrative of a centuries-long struggle against Russia.[78]

The image of the defiant Chechen received additional fodder during the battle of Grozny. Anatol Lieven wrote: "The longer I knew them, the more the Chechen seemed to me a people who had rejected not just much of the Soviet version of modernisation and the modern state – with all its works and all its empty promises – but modernisation in general ... Since December 1994, I have come to look on the Chechen people almost as on the face of Courage herself – with no necessary relation to justice or morality, but beautiful to see."[79] Such a self-image of resistance certainly helped in mobilizing the Chechen for war.[80] During the years of exile, the perception of Chechen and Ingush "banditry," "backwardness," and "treason" had been a way of blaming the victims for their own fate, and of justifying cruelty against them.[81] Treason now became heroic resistance, banditry became love of freedom, and anti-Soviet behaviour became cultural self-preservation. In this interpretation, the Chechen were exceptional victims who did not belong to the Stalinist community of victims or the communities of Soviet and post-Soviet people. It was easy, however, for the Russian state to exploit such images in justifying the First Russian-Chechen War, and stereotypes of Chechen backwardness and incorrigibility have acquired a life of their own in the Russian media and public.[82]

The memories promoted respectively by Russia and Chechnya seemed increasingly irreconcilable. When Russia celebrated the fiftieth anniversary of the Soviet victory over Nazi Germany, in May 1995, the war in Chechnya had not yet ended. Of course, the Chechen republic – now called the Chechen Republic of Ichkeria – did not participate in the celebrations, and Shamil Basaev even ordered raids and guerrilla strikes in Russia in June 1995. After the First Russian-Chechen War ended in August 1996, the exclusion of the Chechen from Russian commemorative culture appeared to be total. The independent Chechen government of the interwar period not only rebuilt the memorial in Grozny to the victims of Stalinism but also encouraged a new commemorative culture with respect to the recent war. Soon, new monuments started to appear, dedicated to Dzhokhar Dudayev, the first president of independent Ichkeria (Chechnya), and to a whole range of "martyrs" of the war. According to Brian Glyn Williams, these memorials acted as "communal monuments" and "reminders to the Chechen of the suffering they have endured at the hands of their great neighbour to the North, Russia."[83] The memories of past horrors became so intimately linked to the self-image of the Chechen nation that it seemed almost impossible to differentiate between the 1944 deportation and the recent past, let alone to reconcile Chechen and Russian commemorative cultures.

The Second Russian-Chechen War and the (Re-)Creation of an Inclusionary Myth

Unlike the Soviet and Russian governments, the Chechen independence movement had found answers to the past that seemed acceptable to many people. The 1992 memorial to deportation victims was a place that many Chechen acknowledged as an authentic representation of national grief.[84] However, it also was a symbol of Chechen independence from Russia and, as such, seemed inappropriate if Chechnya were to stay within the Russian Federation. This may help explain why the current pro-Russian puppet regime of the Chechen republic, which was installed during the Second Russian-Chechen War, has again decided to transform, and repress, the commemoration of the past. Aude Merlin speaks of a form of "symbolic violence" and "foreclosure" silencing any vivid memory of past horrors.[85]

As paradoxical as it may sound, Ramzan Kadyrov's pro-Russian puppet regime attempts to use the "Great Patriotic War" as a foundation on which to construct an acceptable past. Like everywhere else in the Russian Federation, annual veterans' parades commemorating the Second World War were reinstated in Grozny after it had been reconquered in 2003, and 9 May again became a day of collective celebration in Chechnya. In 2014, Putin even conferred the title "city of military glory" (the post-Soviet variant of the Soviet "hero city") on Grozny.[86] In the interpretation of Chechnya's current government, the city deserved this title in recognition of its endurance during the Second World War as well as the valour of its inhabitants in fighting "terrorism" more recently. In other words, the current Russian state has extended its narrative of collective Soviet (or, more specifically, Russian) heroism to include the Chechen. Like the Ingush, Balkars, and Karachays, Chechen authorities have published official textbooks about the Second World War, emphasizing the Chechen "contribution" to the war effort.[87] There is a notable revival of the old idea of "people's friendship" among Soviet peoples through war and suffering.[88] Although most of this might seem like a gross misinterpretation of historical facts, the basic idea that the Chechen did not collectively betray the fatherland – but, instead, heroically fought on the front lines – has some appeal. It dates back to the Chechen civil rights movement of the 1950s and 1960s, and, in this interpretation, the collective myth of people's friendship is not only pro-Russian but also anti-Stalinist and anti-racist. Indeed, Chechen outrage over recent attempts of neo-Stalinist apologists to justify Stalin's decision to deport the Chechen "traitors" in 1944 seems genuine.[89]

But when the Second World War was reinstated as a source of inclusive pride, conflict surrounding the history of the 1944 deportations was almost inevitable. At the beginning of his term, Ramzan Kadyrov seemed to encourage discussions on the deportations. On 23 February 2010, he issued a decree that made that date the official "Day of Memory and Mourning." The next year, the government launched an official website, which, under the slogan "Forbidden to Forget," presented interviews, reports, and articles that were later published in as a book. The Chechen government also sponsored a new edition of a book on the 1944 Khaibakh massacre.[90] Nevertheless, contradictions soon emerged. In 2011, Kadyrov decided to move the official Day of Memory and Mourning from 23 February to 10 May. The official reason given was that 23 February was not only the date associated with the 1944 deportations but was also the Russian Defender of the Fatherland Day (the former Soviet Red Army Day). Yet, the tenth of May also happened to be the day commemorating the death of Ramzan Kadyrov's father, Akhmad, who had died in a terrorist attack on 9 May 2004, during the annual Victory Day parade in Grozny. It seems that Ramzan Kadyrov was attempting to conflate the commemoration of the deportations and the celebration of the Chechen contribution to the victory in the Great Patriotic War. Parades on 9 May featured Chechen war veterans, and, the next day, these same veterans would commemorate the deportations. On the second day, a train symbolizing the deportations was placed on the "Avenue of Glory," and an exhibition on the deportations was erected in one of its cars.[91]

Even if Kadyrov did not completely suppress all public memory of the deportations, he nevertheless tried to control certain types of memory that were associated with the image of Chechen defiance and the independence movement. The most important decision concerned the above-mentioned deportation memorial that had been erected under Dudayev, was destroyed twice, rebuilt twice, and, in 2014, was finally removed. A film on the deportations and the Khaibakh massacre, entitled *Ordered to Forget*, was shelved by the Russian Ministry of Culture in February 2014, on the seventieth anniversary of the deportations. The ministry argued that the film did not present any "proof" of the massacre and that its story was "inaccurate" from a historical perspective (*istoricheskiy fal'shiviy*).[92] Anybody who dared to publicly protest these decisions was jailed or driven out of Chechnya.[93] The Chechen government uses such tactics in its attempts to decontextualize the deportations, thus conflating the heroic memory of past wars against German "fascists" and "terrorists" with the commemoration of victims of "fascism" (e.g., deportees) and "terrorism." Kadyrov even tends to avoid mentioning Stalin's responsibility for the deportations and to hint at anti-Semitic conspiracy theories.[94]

Many observers agree that people in Chechnya strongly disapprove of Kadyrov's politics of memory. Olga Reznikova, who has conducted ethnographic research during the commemorative May days in Chechnya, has noted a general sense of misapprehension and disapproval. The problem seems to be not only the repression of memories but also the gap between official and individual memories. The memories of the deportations and the commemoration of Akhmad Kadyrov's death on 10 May remained largely disconnected. People complained about the "hollowness" (*pustota*), "facelessness" (*bezlikost'*), and "deadness" (*mertvennost'*) of the new rituals. Some perceived the new Avenue of Glory in Grozny as a "menace" (*ugroza*). In general, there was nothing *rodnoy* about the new ways of celebrating the past,[95] the word *rodnoy* referring not only to an idea of a nativity and home but also of affection and authenticity. In this sense, an insurmountable gap between what seems officially acceptable and individual ways of mourning has not been overcome.

Conclusion

Stalinist terror was not always or even primarily about race or ethnicity. Nevertheless, the Chechen victims of Stalinism did belong into a group of ethnic victims created by the regime (rather than ones defined by social class). Mainly because the Soviet and Russian states sought to repress attempts to accept the Chechen as a group of victims, a self-image of defiant victimhood spread among them. Attempts to connect the Chechen story of deportation to larger debates about genocide in the twentieth century inevitably met opposition, since the term "genocide" itself seemed to liken the crimes of Stalinism to those of the Germans during the Second World War. Authenticating oneself as a member of a Chechen group of victims, as opposed to the broader group of victims of Stalinism, has itself become an act of defiance that supports the basic imagery of the Chechen, characterized variously by stubbornness, self-preservation, and heroic resistance.

In fact, the Chechen pursuit of independence has been conflated with questions of loyalty and guilt during the Second World War, and the discussion of the past has thus been tied to the legitimacy of Russian rule in the North Caucasus. The Soviet and Russian states have never succeeded in creating a more inclusive vision of heroism and suffering that encompasses all the different groups of victims of Stalinism. The general failure to address questions of culpability has made it difficult to accept and to accommodate conflicting claims of authenticity and victimhood within Soviet and post-Soviet cultures of commemoration. This ongoing politicization of memory on both sides seems to leave little room for post-heroic representations of guiltless suffering to this day.

NOTES

1 Alexander Solzhenitsyn, *The Gulag Archipelago*, trans. Harry Willets, vol. 3 (New York: Harper Collins, 1992), 401–2.

2 See Michaela Pohl, "'It Cannot Be that Our Graves Will Be Here': The Survival of Chechen and Ingush Deportees in Kazakhstan, 1944–1957," *Journal of Genocide Research* 4, no. 3 (2002): 401–30; Birgit Brauer, "Chechens and the Survival of Their Cultural Identity in Exile," *Journal of Genocide Research* 4, no. 3 (2002): 387–400. Solzhenitsyn's words have often been taken at face value.

3 Marc Elie, "La vie en déportation (1943–1953)," in *Les déportations en héritage: Les peuples réprimés du Caucase et de Crimée hier et aujourd'hui*, ed. Aurélie Campana, Grégorie Dufaud, and Sophie Tournon (Rennes: Presses Universitaires de Rennes, 2009), 54. See also Vladimir A. Kozlov, ed., *Vaynakhi i imperskaya vlast': Problema Chechni i Ingushetii vo vnutrenney politike Rossii i SSSR* (Moscow: ROSSPEN, 2011), 692–9.

4 See Antony Kalashnikov, "Stalinist Crimes and the Ethics of Memory," *Kritika* 19 (2018): 600. See also Alexander Etkind, *Warped Mourning: Stories of the Undead in the Land of the Unburied* (Stanford, CA: Stanford University Press, 2013); Maria Tumarkin, "The Long Life of Stalinism: Reflections on the Aftermath of Totalitarianism and Social Memory," *Journal of Social History* 44 (2011): 1051.

5 On the Soviet period, see Aurélie Campana, "The Chechen Memory of Deportation: From Recalling a Silenced Past to the Political Use of Public Memory," in *Public Memory, Public Media, and the Politics of Justice*, ed. Philip Lee and Pradip N. Thomas (Basingstoke, UK: Palgrave Macmillan, 2012), 141–62. On the more recent events, see Aude Merlin, "Remembering and Forgetting in Chechnya Today: Using the Great Patriotic War to Create a New Historical Narrative," in *Chechnya at War and Beyond*, ed. Anne Le Huérou, Aude Merlin, Amadine Regamey, and Elisabeth Sieca-Kozlowski (London: Routledge, 2014), 37–57.

6 Jeronim Perovic, *From Conquest to Deportation: The North Caucasus under Russian Rule* (Oxford: Oxford University Press, 2018), 3–10; Ehren Park and David Brandenberger, "Imagined Community? Rethinking the Nationalist Origins of the Contemporary Chechen Crisis," *Kritika* 5 (2004): 543–60.

7 On images of the Caucasus in nineteenth-century Russian literature, see Susan Layton, *Russian Literature and Empire: Conquest of the Caucasus from Pushkin to Tolstoy* (Cambridge: Cambridge University Press, 2000).

8 Aurélie Campana, "Collective Memory and Violence: The Use of Myths in the Chechen Separatist Ideology, 1991–1994," *Journal of Muslim Minority Affairs* 29 (2009): 43–56.

9 See, for example, Moshe Gammer, *The Lone Wolf and the Bear: Three Centuries of Chechen Defiance of Russian Rule* (London: Hurst, 2006); John B. Dunlop, *Russia Confronts Chechnya: Roots of a Separatist Conflict* (Cambridge: Cambridge University Press, 1998); Emil Souleimanov, *An Endless War: The Russian-Chechen Conflict in Perspective* (Frankfurt: Lang, 2007); Robert Seely, *Russo-Chechen Conflict, 1800–2000: A Deadly Embrace* (Portland, OR: Frank Cass, 2001).

10 For a comparative perspective, see Rebecca Jinks, "Thinking Comparatively about Genocide Memorialization," *Journal of Genocide Research* 16, no. 4 (2014): 423–40.

11 Rebecca Gould has shown that such images were not only projected upon the Chechen and other peoples of the North Caucasus but, in the early Soviet Union, became ingrained in vernacular "literatures of insurgency." On a local level, the Soviet project was accompanied by a tendency to aestheticize and, in this sense, glorify anticolonial violence. See Rebecca Gould, *Writers and Rebels: The Literature of Insurgency in the Caucasus* (New Haven, CT: Yale University Press, 2016), 33–91.

12 Norman Naimark, *Stalin's Genocides* (Princeton, NJ: Princeton University Press, 2010), 80–98. See also Perovic, *From Conquest to Deportation*, 2–3.

13 See Aurélie Campana, "Les Tchétchènes et Ingouches, entre résilience et résistances passives, 1956–1991," in Campana, Dufaud, and Tournon, *Les déportations en héritage*, 97–116.

14 Etkind, *Warped Mourning*, 12–24.

15 Analyses of this process of de-Stalinization include Miriam Dobson, *Khrushchev's Cold Summer: Gulag Returnees, Crime, and the Fate of Reform after Stalin* (Ithaca, NY: Cornell University Press, 2009) and Polly Jones, *Myth, Memory, Trauma: Rethinking the Stalinist Past in the Soviet Union* (New Haven, CT: Yale University Press, 2013).

16 Moritz Florin, *Kirgistan und die sowjetische Moderne: 1941–1991* (Göttingen: V&R unipress, 2015), 54–9.

17 See Elie, "La vie en déportation," 54.

18 "Memorandum on the economic situation and political attitudes of the special settlers in the Kazakh SSR," in Kozlov, *Vaynakhi*, 748–74.

19 Pohl, "It Cannot Be," 401–4.

20 Florin, *Kirgistan*, 58–9.

21 Ibid.

22 Dalkhat Ediev, *Demograficheskie poteri deportirovannykh narodov SSSR* (Stavropol: ARGUS, 2003).

23 Pohl, "It Cannot Be," 410.

24 Examples include: Report on Propaganda and Education among Special Settler in Frunze Oblast, 12 August 1946, TsGAPDKR, f. 406, op. 2, d. 198, ll. 26–8; Protocol on the Economic Situation of Special Settlers in the

Kyrgyz Republic, 12–14 August 1946, TsGAPDKR, f. 56, op. 4, d. 564, ll. 35–42; 227–334; and Report on Propaganda and Education among the Special Settlers in Talas, 13 February 1947, TsGAPDKR, f. 921, op. 4, d. 1, l. 31. These documents are reprinted in V.M. Ploskikh and M.K. Imakeev, eds., *Deportirovannye narody Kavkaza v Kyrgyrzskuyu Respubliku: sbornik dokumentov i materialov* (Bishkek, KG: Kyrgyz-Russian Slavic University), 200–45.

25 See, for example, J.S. Patiyev, *Ingushi: Deportatsiya, vozvrashchenie, reabilitatsiya, 1944–2004: Dokumenty, materialy, kommentarii* (Magas, RU: Izdat. Serdalo, 2004), 366.

26 Ibid., 350.

27 See, for example, the letter from a group of Chechen and Ingush to Khrushchev, March 1956, first reproduced without a date in L. Yakh'yaev, ed., *Belaya kniga: Iz istorii vyseleniya chechentsev i ingushey 1944–1957 gg.* (Grozny / Alma-Ata: Örken / Gorizont, 1991), 182–95. See also Patiyev, *Ingushi*, 369–82.

28 Letter of Nalayev and Khamiev to Mikoyan, 30 March 1956, in Patiyev, *Ingushi*, 351.

29 Patiyev, *Ingushi*, 325.

30 Ibid.

31 Aleksandr Uralov [Abdurakhman Abdrakhmanov], *Narodoubiystvo v SSSR* (Munich: Svobodnyi Kavkaz, 1948).

32 Pis'mo-obrashchenie gruppy kavkaztsev, zhivushchikh v SShA v organizatsiyu ob'edinennykh natsiy, in *Deportatsiya Chechenskogo naroda: Fakty, svidetel'stva, dokumenty*, ed. Islam Khatuev and Isa Sardalov (Grozny: Grozny University Press, 2012), 574–6.

33 Letter of a group of Chechen and Ingush to the Central Committee, 1956 (exact date missing), in Yakh'yaev, *Belaya kniga*, 166–73.

34 Jones, *Myth, Memory, Trauma*, 259.

35 Quoted in Svetlana Alieva, *Tak eto bylo: Natsional'nye repressii v SSSR 1919–1952 gody. V 3-kh tomakh* (Moscow: Insan, 1993), 173.

36 Francine Hirsch, *Empire of Nations: Ethnographic Knowledge and the Making of the Soviet Union* (Ithaca, NY: Cornell University Press, 2005).

37 Catherine Merridale, *Night of Stone: Death and Memory in Twentieth-Century Russia* (New York: Penguin, 2000), 212.

38 Patiyev, *Ingushi*, 364.

39 Aza Bazorkina, "Terpenie," in Alieva, *Tak eto bylo*, 2, 107–44, 133.

40 Pohl, "It Cannot Be."

41 M. Mamakayev speech at a history conference, Moscow, 16 November 1956, in Yakh'yaev, *Belaya kniga*, 203–8.

42 Speech of A. Shmoylov, head of the KGB of the Chechen-Ingush ASSR, 4 December 1957, quoted in Kozlov, *Vaynakhi*, 912.

43 Ibid.

44 *Zemlya otsov*, directed by Shaken Aymanov (1966, kazakhfil'm).
45 See Bazorkina, "Memoirs," in Alieva, *Tak eto bylo*, 138.
46 Bazorkina, "Memoirs," 139–40.
47 Amir Weiner, "The Making of a Dominant Myth: The Second World War and the Construction of Political Identities within the Soviet Polity," *Russian Review* 55 (1996): 638–60.
48 Materialy o massovykh besporyadkakh v g. Groznom 26 avgusta 1958 g., 5 marta 1959 g. – 25 iyunya 1960 g., in Kozlov, *Vaynakhi*, 926–32. See also Nicolas Werth, "The 'Chechen' Problem: Handling an Awkward Legacy, 1918–1958," *Contemporary European History* 15 (2006): 347–66.
49 For an analysis of such attitudes, see Dobson, *Khrushchev's Cold Summer*, 109–32.
50 Etkind, *Warped Mourning*, 44–59.
51 Pohl, "It Cannot Be," 380. See also Campana, "Chechen Memory of Deportation," 147–53.
52 Park and Brandenberger, "Imagined Community," 558.
53 Anatoly Pristavkin, *Nochevala tuchka zolotaya* (Moscow: Knizhnaya palata, 1987); published in English as *The Inseparable Twins* (London: Picador, 1991).
54 Brian Glyn Williams, "Commemorating 'The Deportation' in Post-Soviet Chechnya: The Role of Memorialization and Collective Memory in the 1994–1996 and 1999–2000 Russo-Chechen Wars," *History and Memory* 12, no. 1 (2000): 107.
55 On the memorial-society, see Nanci Adler, *Victims of Soviet Terror: The Story of the Memorial Movement* (Westport, CT: Praeger, 1993). See also Kathleen E. Smith, *Remembering Stalin's Victims: Popular Memory and the End of the USSR* (New Haven CT: Yale University Press, 1996).
56 Yakh'yaev, *Belaya kniga*, 5, 13.
57 Nicolas Werth, "Mass Deportations, Ethnic Cleansing, and Genocidal Politics in the Russian Empire and the USSR from the mid-Nineteenth Century to the mid-Twentieth Century," in *The Oxford Handbook of Genocide Studies*, ed. Donald Bloxham and A. Dirk Moses (Oxford: Oxford University Press, 2010), 386–407; Terry Martin, "The Origins of Soviet Ethnic Cleansing," *Journal of Modern History* 70, no. 4 (1998): 813–61.
58 Alieva, *Tak eto bylo*, 245–50.
59 Sherip Asuev, *Tak eto bylo: Grozny 1988–1991*, https://www.litmir.co/br/?b=231146, last accessed 18 December 2019.
60 Jane I. Dawson, *Eco-Nationalism: Anti-Nuclear Activism and National Identity in Russia, Lithuania, and Ukraine* (Durham, NC: Duke University Press, 1996), 162–77.
61 Georgi M. Derluguian, *Bourdieu's Secret Admirer in the Caucasus: A World-System Biography* (Chicago: University of Chicago Press, 2005), 243–7.

62 Asuev, *Tak eto bylo*, 4.
63 Ibid.
64 Ruslan Tulikov, "Nedoskazannost', polupravda, lozh' – grabli, na kotorye nastupayut snova i snova," *Kavpolit*, 29 January 2014, http://kavpolit.com/articles/ruslan_tulikov_nedoskazannost_polupravda_lozh_grab-641/.
65 Salamat Gayev, *Khaibakh: Sledstvie prodolzhaetsya* (Grozny: Kniga, 1994). According to another NKVD document, Khaybakh was not the only place where people were burned alive. See Patiyev, *Ingushi*, 68.
66 Patiyev, Ingushi, 23–60.
67 Merridale, *Night of Stone*, 297–323.
68 Gayev, *Khaibakh*, 4. This also holds true for the Ingush. A special commission seeking facts of the genocide was established in 1990; it later investigated, among other things, the destruction of graveyards. See "Akt chrezvychaynoy komissii po fakty genotsida v otnoshenii ingushskogo naroda, 14 August 1990," in Patiyev, *Ingushi*, 143–4.
69 Photographs of the memorial can be found at "Zayavlenie Mezhdunarodnogo obshchestva 'Memorial.' Razrushenie pamyati," *voinenet.ru*, http://www.voinenet.ru/voinenetinform/nashi-reportazhi/21143.html.
70 Mark Beissinger, *Nationalist Mobilization and the Collapse of the Soviet State* (Cambridge: Cambridge University Press, 2002).
71 Emma Gilligan, *Terror in Chechnya: Russia and the Tragedy of Civilians in War* (Princeton, NJ: Princeton University Press, 2010), 3.
72 T.I. Bondareva, "Chto stalo s arkhivami Chechenskoi Respubliki," *Otechestvennye arkhivy* 3 (1995): 22–4.
73 Anatol Lieven, *Chechnya: Tombstone of Russian Power* (New Haven, CT: Yale University Press, 1998), 223–30. See also Anatoly Shabad, "A First-Hand Account of Russian Military Actions in Chechnya," in *Central Asia: Conflict, Resolution, and Change*, ed. Roald Sagdeev and Susan Eisenhower (Chevy Chase, MD: Eisenhower Institute, 1995), 19.
74 Yusha A. Aydaev, *Chechentsy: Istoriya i sovremennost'* (Moscow: Mir Tvoyemu Domu, 1996), 12.
75 Williams, "Commemorating," 124.
76 Dzhokhar Dudayev, "*Kontseptsiya* natsional'no gosudarstvennoy politiki Chechenskoy respubliki Ichkeriya," no date or publisher, https://chechen-government.com/концепция-национально-государстве, last accessed 18 December 2019. Dudayev does not explicitly name Yermolov, but this is presumably what he is referring to when he mentions two genocides, one in the nineteenth century and another under Stalin. See also Said-Khasan Abumuslimov, "Rossiya i Chechnya: Chetyre veka *protivostoyaniya*, prestupleniye bez nazakaniya," 24 March 2011, http://www.ichkeria.info/index.php/analytics/9165-2011-10-09-00-14-59.

77 Williams, "Commemorating," 126–7.
78 For analyses of different variants of this narrative (which has also been taken up by many Russian and Western scholars), see Park and Brandenberger, "Imagined Community," 543–5; Perovic, *From Conquest to Deportation*, 21–52.
79 Lieven, *Chechnya*, 22.
80 Aurélie Campana, "The Effects of War on the Chechen National Identity Construction," *National Identities* 8, no. 2 (2006): 129–48.
81 Florin, *Kirgistan*, 54–9.
82 John Russell, "Terrorists, Bandits, Spooks and Thieves: Russian Demonization of the Chechens before and since 9/11," *Third World Quarterly* 26, no. 1 (2005): 101–16.
83 Williams, "Commemorating," 125.
84 Merlin, "Remembering and Forgetting," 54; Olga Reznikova, "Skorb' i prazdnik v (post)kolonial'nom kontekste: Etnograficheskie zametki," *Neprikosnovennyy zapas* 3 (2015), https://www.nlobooks.ru/magazines/neprikosnovennyy_zapas/101_nz_3_2015/article/11516/.
85 Merlin, "Remembering and Forgetting," 50.
86 "Putin prisvoil Groznomu zvaniye 'Gorod voinskoy slavy'," *Novaya gazeta*, 6 April 2015, http://www.novayagazeta.ru/news/1692945.html.
87 It is noteworthy that these books are full of references to Soviet symbols and phraseology. A volume on the German, Karachay, Kalmyk, Chechen, Ingush, and Balkar peoples bears a five-pointed star as well as a hammer, and sickle on its front cover. See B.B. Boromangnaev, ed., *Vklad repressirovannykh narodov SSSR v pobedu v velikoy otechetsvennoy voyne, 1941–1945 gg.* (Elista, RU: ZAOr NPP "Dzhangar," 2010). The same symbols have been used for the cover of another publication on the Chechen: Movsur Ibragimov and Islam Khatuev, *Pravda ob uchastii narodov Chechenskoy Respubliki v Velikoy Otechestvennoy voyne* (Grozny, 2007).
88 The new official Chechen textbook is Musa M. Ibragimov, *Istoriya Chechni s drevneyshikh vremen do nashikh dney. Istoriya Chechni XX i nachala XXI vekov* (Grozny: Kn. Izdat, 2008). This idea also plays a central role in the Central Asian debates on the deportations. See Z.A. Ermekbaev, ed., *Chechentsy i Ingushi v Kazakhstane* (Almaty, KG: Daik-Press, 2009).
89 The most notorious book in this context is Igor Pykhalov, *Za chto Stalin vyselyal narody? Stalinskie deportatsii – prestupnyy proizvol ili spravedlivoe vozmezdie?* (Moscow: Yauza-Press, 2008). On the reaction, see Merlin, "Remembering and Forgetting."
90 Although the website is no longer available, a book with facsimiles of the Russian archival documents has been published. In the introduction, the publishers expressed their "special gratitude" to Ramzan Kadyrov, who had supported the edition. Khatuev and Sardalov, *Deportatsiya chechenskogo naroda.*

91 Reznikova, "Skorb' i prazdnik." See also "70 let traura v den' prazdnika," *Radio svoboda*, 10 October 2014, http://www.svoboda.org/content/article/25271249.html.

92 V Chechne net voprosa – byla ili net tragediya v Khaybakhe, *gazeta.ru*, 6 June 2014, http://www.gazeta.ru/culture/2014/06/25/a_6085921.shtml.

93 V Chechne ne provoditsya ofitsial'nye meropriyatiya po sluchayu 70-letiya deportatsii vaynakhov, *Kavkazskij uzel*, 2 February 2014, http://www.kavkaz-uzel.ru/articles/238585/.

94 Reznikova, "Skorb' i prazdnik."

95 Ibid.

13 East Asian Victimhood Goes to Paris: A Consideration of Second World War–Related Chinese, Japanese, and Korean Nominations to UNESCO's Memory of the World Project

LORI WATT

In 2014, China, Japan, and South Korea made two nominations each for documentary collections from their countries to be inscribed in UNESCO's Memory of the World Register. Existing entries in the register from these countries – nine from China, three from Japan, and eleven from Korea – almost all come from pre-industrial times and are related to the distinct cultural heritage of East Asia. One notable aspect of the 2014 nominations was that four of the six – the two from China, one from Japan, and one from Korea – are all related to problems stemming from the Second World War and its aftermath. Three of the nominations grappled, directly or indirectly, with issues of dislocation, forced migration, and repatriation. These proposals all date from the same year, 2014, and are of the same genre, a Memory of the World (MOW) nomination of about ten pages each.[1] For these reasons, they provide us with a snapshot of how each country, at least in this particular form, narrates its Second World War documentary heritage and seeks international authentication of victim experiences. The stakes are high in public expressions of the war's history in East Asia. History and memory wars, which emerged with particular fervour from about 1991, continue to shape diplomatic, political, and, at times, economic relations throughout the region and remain a highly emotional issue for many. People in China and the Koreas continue to draw attention to Japan's wartime past, but responses from the Japanese state are viewed as unsatisfactory.

Established in 1992, UNESCO's Memory of the World Programme seeks to protect the documentary heritage of the world. The Memory of the World Register, the list of collections in the project, is its best-known element. As of 2014, the register contained three hundred items, including, for example, the Declaration of the Rights of Man and of the

Citizen (1789–91), a canonical document in the history of human rights. As explained on the UNESCO website, the premise of the project is that the world's documentary heritage belongs to all. The project has three goals – preservation, access, and raising awareness – which are mutually reinforcing.[2] Preserving the materials and making them accessible may stimulate wider interest. Raising awareness about heritage-related materials stimulates demand for access that, in turn, may encourage preservation efforts. Inscription in the register recognizes the importance of the materials and brings prestige to the organizations and countries that preserve them. The use of the word "memory" in the register's name draws our attention to the fact that, although the materials were produced in the past and are useful in understanding the past, the process of inscribing them brings the past into the present. The "past made present" is perhaps the most succinct definition of memory.[3]

The MOW website emphasizes that the program's focus is on the historical materials themselves, but, as we know, sources are mediated from the moment they enter the world and may be used for present-day political purposes. The nominations under consideration here embed the materials for which they seek recognition in national narratives of the war, narratives that emphasize Chinese, Japanese, or Korean national suffering. The process of authenticating national victimhood in three of the nominations involved drawing a boundary around a group of victims and then seeking recognition of the suffering of those victims. In places, the narratives of the proposals conflict, as if one might cancel out another. Moreover, they seem to compete for what is understood as a limited supply of sympathy and recognition. The MOW process, which evaluates the relative worth of the proposals, inadvertently facilitates a confrontation of different national histories in the public sphere.

Applying for MOW inscription, however, requires that the nominators present their documentary heritage not simply in a competitive context. All nominations are required to explain the "world significance" of their materials.[4] In claiming the ability to judge that significance, the MOW program asserts itself as an arbiter in the global public sphere, and others treat it as such. One conceivable way to demonstrate world significance would be to argue that the materials show a degree of suffering so great that they are unquestionably worthy of attention. Another principle of the program is that the heritage of the world "belongs to all." This puts some pressure on the nominators to show how their materials, almost always presented as part of a national heritage, can be relevant to others.

These conflicting demands create an intriguing internal tension – a struggle between the more familiar process of authenticating national victimhood and the need to reach, and perhaps even include, a universal audience. These two impulses can be understood in terms of two approaches to memory theorized by Michael Rothberg.[5] Authenticating national victimhood conforms to what Rothberg calls "the competitive memory model," in which advocates operate with the sense that space in the public sphere is limited and that narratives of suffering tend to cancel each other out in what amounts to a "zero-sum game over scarce resources."[6] In this model, the boundaries of memory and the boundaries of group identity tend to be the same. Yet, the MOW process requires that a group show how its documentary heritage belongs to all, which challenges the boundaries of the group – in this case, the nation. Rothberg proposes an alternative to the competitive memory model: the dynamic of multidirectional memory. This dynamic is "multidirectional" in that it can incorporate cross-referencing and negotiation, and challenge the "straight line" that links identity to history. It is temporally multidirectional, facilitating links between events and memory across time. The dynamic of multidirectional memory, according to Rothberg, can allow for a wider range of difference in debates about memory and belonging, and it can serve as a potential source for solidarity. Because multidirectional memory can facilitate a broader range of interpretations of the past, drawing on this dynamic can strengthen an MOW nomination by arguing more persuasively that a particular set of materials belongs to all.

With the competitive memory model and the dynamic of multidirectional memory in mind, let us turn to an evaluation of the four Second World War nominations. In addition to familiar national narratives, the authors of the proposals used techniques to try to reach international, although not necessarily universal, audiences. The research and writing of this chapter took place in the months before the International Advisory Committee, the group that makes recommendations to the director-general of the program concerning the inscription of documentary heritage in the MOW Register, met in Abu Dhabi in early October 2015. The results of the 2014–15 round of nominations were therefore unknown to me. Not yet knowing the outcome of the process created a productive vacuum for evaluating the nominations and introduced of a heightened sense of curiosity. The model of competitive memory or the dynamic of multidirectional memory – which would prevail in determining the Memory of the World?

"Nanjing" and the "Comfort Women": Proposals from China

In 2014, China nominated two sets of archives for inscription in UNESCO's Memory of the World Register: "Documents of Nanjing Massacre" and "Archives about 'Comfort Women': The Sex Slaves for Imperial Japanese Troops." The materials that the nominations seek to inscribe are related to two of the most notorious and sustained examples of extraordinary violence committed by the Japanese military in its war on Asia – the Nanjing Massacre and the "comfort women" system of sexual slavery.[7] The first event consisted of approximately six weeks of depraved and indiscriminate violence inflicted on the people of Nanjing, China, in 1937–8. The second example involved the establishment and maintenance of a system that ensnared women from across the empire who were transported, held captive, and forced to provide sex to troops, often at stations near the battlefield. The Nanjing Massacre and the comfort women have since come to serve as the two most recognizable events in the conflicts over history and memory between Japan and its neighbours, conflicts that unfold in political and academic venues across Asia, Europe, and North America.[8]

Historian Daqing Yang has written extensively on the Chinese and Japanese historiographies of these events in ways that help us to understand the 2014 Chinese nominations.[9] As Yang points out, obstacles such the absence of documentation prevent a comprehensive historical understanding of the Nanjing Massacre. People killed could not speak of it, and the same was true of the women who did not survive sexual slavery. But absence is not the only problem with documentation. As Yang also shows, many historians in China and Japan who research these historical events tend to favour positivist forms of inquiry. In this method, scholars identify facts in the documentary record and then present those facts as historical truth. The problem with this approach is that it leaves room for sceptics and deniers to attack what is presented as historical truth by questioning the documentary evidence and the facts it produces. In the case of the Nanjing Massacre in particular, sceptics and deniers have done precisely this – questioned the veracity of the documents, facts, and, therefore, the truth. One response to them has been to try to find more documents to prove more facts to fortify, beyond a doubt, a given historical truth. This is the fraught historiographical context of the Nanjing Massacre and comfort women nominations, a context that helps to explain the Chinese nominators' emphasis on new documents and facts as a means of proving the truth.

The materials related to the Nanjing Massacre and comfort women that China sought to register in the MOW were generated by Japanese military officials, local witnesses, and war crimes tribunals during and after the war. A total of eleven municipal, provincial, memorial, and national archives worked to develop the two nominations from China; seven from this group produced the Nanjing nomination, and a combination of eight worked on the nomination regarding comfort women.

The Nanjing nomination sets forth what is now a standard presentation of the historical event. It begins by asserting China's preferred name for the event, the "Nanjing Massacre," instead of alternatives, including the "Rape of Nanking," the "Nanjing Atrocity," or the "Nanjing Incident." The nomination identifies 13 December 1937 as the key date, both in history and as the national memorial day that commemorates the event. The nomination states the number of victims killed as 300,000 plus 20,000 women raped; it references the numbers established by the International Military Tribunal for the Far East number ("over 200,000") and by the Nanjing War Criminals Tribunal ("at least 300,000 Chinese" killed).[10] It was the Chinese themselves who arrived at the number 300,000 killed, and it has since taken on symbolic significance. The refusal of some outside of China, especially in Japan, to agree on this number as historical fact remains a flash point in debates on the event.

The nomination describes the perpetrators of the Nanjing Massacre variously as "Japanese troops," "Japanese soldiers," or the "Japanese army." It describes a range of victims, including the pregnant Li Xiuying. It also profiles heroes: Tsen Shui-fang, who kept a diary of the events; Luo Jin, a photography studio apprentice who made extra copies of photographs of the violence from film submitted for processing by a Japanese officer; and John Magee, an American who filmed the events and went to great lengths to preserve his recordings. The heroes in this Chinese nomination are presented as ordinary people who created and preserved documentary evidence, unlike the Japanese, who "destroyed many archival materials." That documentary evidence, the nomination asserts, is invaluable because it proves facts. On the first page, the nomination states that the items "have indisputable authority and authenticity" in showing the Nanjing Massacre as "historical fact." Elsewhere, the nomination reiterates that these archives record historical facts.[11] As discussed below, the comfort women nomination, too, relies on the archives as invaluable sources of historical facts. And the facts are important, the nominations assert, because they prove the truth.

Readers familiar with the work of the film scholar Michael Berry may notice similarities among the key issues and narrative strategies that appear in both the Nanjing nomination and films on the Nanjing Massacre. In his presentations and publications, Berry has identified elements shared by almost all films on the Nanjing Massacre, arguing that an identifiable genre exists.[12] Those elements include an emphasis on the date of 13 December, the number of victims as 300,000 killed and 20,000 raped, the importance of photographic and filmic evidence recording the massacre, and attention to the importance of documentary evidence and testimony. The Nanjing nomination shares the concerns of Nanjing Massacre cinema, both of which may reflect and shape concerns of society at large. The same kind of effort that filmmakers have put into "documenting" the massacre is reproduced in the archivists' 2014 MOW proposal.

Although the Nanjing nomination reflects the current understanding of Nanjing's place in China's national narrative, the nomination of the archives related to comfort women does something new by making an explicitly Chinese claim on that issue. Historians believe that many of the women who were incorporated into the system of sexual slavery came from the Korean peninsula, and the issue is often associated with Korea. Symbolized by the statue of a defiant young woman gazing across the street at the Japanese embassy in Seoul, this issue captures much of the Korean-Japanese tension surrounding the problems with history and memory.[13] China's comfort women nomination, however, places the archives – and the historical problem – squarely within a Chinese narrative of "the Japanese Aggressive War upon China and other countries," periodized from 1931 to 1945. Because most of the "comfort stations" operated in China, it makes good historical sense to pay more attention to how the system functioned there, and not only to Korea, the place of origin of many of the women who were forced into the system. The 2014 nomination regarding comfort women appears to have been stimulated by political as well as historical concerns, including the ongoing effort to "prove" Japanese victimization of others.

The nomination for "Archives about 'Comfort Women' for Japanese Troops" asserts that the archives are of great historical value "because they unequivocally disclose the historical fact that the Japanese troops set up 'comfort women lodges' and forcibly recruited 'comfort women' in China and Southeast Asia during the war."[14] Elsewhere, the nomination asserts that the documents are of value "in restoring historical truth," are "true records," and "disclose" and "show the historical fact" that the Japanese military was responsible for the system.[15] Japan, the nomination continues, destroyed materials to cover up the historical truth, but the documents in the archives form the "complete chain of evidence" of Japanese troops' involvement with the system as "historical fact," and these historical facts are important in order "to objectively restore and record authentic history."[16] The Nanjing nomination, too, notes that Japanese troops deliberately covered up the truth and that Japan destroyed evidence.[17] As noted, some of that material was dug up from where it was buried, evoking a sense of uncovering the past. The sources are disparate, but, taken together, they, too, "form a complete chain of evidence." We see the imperative of positivist history here to uncover documents that provide facts, which, in turn, prove the truth.

Most historians welcome the availability of new sources. Those who work on the history of the comfort women may be interested in newly discovered documents, such as those produced by the Japanese Kwantung Army and the Bank of Manchuria, that may serve to clarify the relationship of the Japanese state to the system. New sources might also be useful in the ongoing struggle of activists in seeking recognition and compensation for victims from the Japanese state. That said, the nomination presents the documents in support of a singular "authentic history," an idea that many historians would reject. Moreover, the nomination claims partial credit for bringing the history of the comfort women into public consciousness. As we know from the work of Carol Gluck, it was not the state in late-twentieth-century mass societies that controlled public memory about these women. Rather, "vectors of memory change" from below and outside brought the comfort women into view, with state responses lagging behind.[18]

A perhaps more productive way to engage with the Chinese nominations is to ponder their emphasis on the destruction and recovery of historical materials. Berry has noted that people who make films about the Nanjing Massacre may feel forced to respond to Japanese deniers of the event.[19] Despite the existence of a few who would publicly deny or downplay the massacre and comfort women, most professional historians share a more-or-less common understanding of these events: that Japanese troops perpetuated a massacre in Nanjing and that the Japanese state was involved in the sexual slavery system.[20] Both the Nanjing and comfort women nominations point out that "Japan" destroyed historical materials to cover up the truth and destroyed evidence that could be used in war crimes trials. These nominations show an apparent continuation of the strategy of responding to deniers, with an emphasis on "Japan" as a destroyer of historical materials. The Japanese military's systematic destruction of documents is well known to historians and is described most succinctly in a widely cited article by Japan's leading historian of the war, Yoshida Yutaka.[21] The assertion that the military destroyed documents is not especially controversial. Japanese scholars including Yoshida, Yoshimi Yoshiaki, and others have made efforts to make extant materials available to all, especially through the Center for Research and Documentation on Japan's War Responsibility. They also work to train graduate students from other parts of Asia in using Japanese-language historical materials to research the war. The emphasis, in China's nominations, on the Chinese as rescuers in contrast to the Japanese as destroyers – similar to the idea of the Chinese as challengers to the Japanese as deniers – presents a circular and potentially unproductive trap, especially in the context of the MOW's imperative that the world's documentary heritage belongs to all.

The MOW nomination form asks for an explanation of the social, spiritual, or community significance of the materials. The Chinese nominations are notable for their insistence that the materials are important because they represent Chinese victimization. The Nanjing nomination, for example, states that the materials "mean so much emotionally to the descendants of the victims of the massacre, to the citizens of the victimized city of Nanjing, and to the people of the once injured country."[22] Here, we see the competitive memory model at work, with a straight line drawn from the memory of the event to the national identity of the Chinese people. The comfort women nomination notes the fact that women from many different places, including Japan, Europe, and the Americas, were enslaved in the system.[23] But in response to the question of social, spiritual, and community significance, the nomination indicates that the system was a "bitter memory" that brought harm and pain to the people of China, Korea, and Southeast Asia. One is left to observe that many have been excluded from this "bitter memory" – above all, the comfort women from places outside of China, Korea, and Southeast Asia, but also anyone who might have encountered the system and found it appalling. The nomination states that it wants people around the world to have "knowledge" about the misery of the women affected, but there is no call for empathy.[24]

The Nanjing nomination reaches beyond Chinese points of reference – it notes, for example, that Tsen Shui-fang's diary is known as China's "Diary of Anne Frank" – and seeks to universalize its concerns by stating that "these solid evidences had a profound appeal to the global community and helped people around the world to better understand the cruelty of war."[25] The nomination therefore attempts multidirectionality, but the main thrust is to state that the materials establish facts that then prove the truth of these events, which can best be understood as affirming Chinese and other Asian suffering at the hands of the Japanese. The nominations seek recognition of fact-based national suffering, with an impermeable line drawn around the designated sufferers.

Most scholars would welcome any new materials on the contested events of the Nanjing Massacre and comfort women that these Chinese archives are willing to preserve, make accessible, and promote. It may be possible to delink these new sources from the narratives in which they have been embedded. But, as my analysis has shown, these two nominations illustrate the limitations of the competitive memory model and the trap created by the perceived need to respond to deniers and destroyers of evidence.

Maizuru: The Proposal from Japan

In 2014, Japan submitted two MOW nominations for consideration, the first of which was "Archives of Tōji temple contained in one-hundred boxes (763 to 1711)," which consisted of materials from the archipelago's pre-industrial past. The second, "Return to Maizuru Port – Documents Related to the Internment and Repatriation Experiences of Japanese (1945–1956)," nominated a collection of documents related to the immediate post–Second World War internment of Japanese soldiers and civilians in the Soviet Gulag and problems associated with their subsequent repatriation. After the Japanese surrender on 15 August 1945, Japanese soldiers were to be disarmed and repatriated. The Soviets, who accepted the Japanese surrender in Northeast China and Korea north of the thirty-eighth parallel, disarmed the Japanese soldiers but then transported as many as six hundred thousand of them to Siberia and throughout the USSR as a captive labour force. Survivors coming home in the postwar period passed through Maizuru, a port city on the eastern side of Japan, facing the Chinese continent. Maizuru, in Kyoto Prefecture, was the site of the longest-operating postwar repatriation centre, in existence from 1945 to 1958. Because of the paucity of writing materials in general and the threat of punishment and extended captivity for producing written documents of any kind, detainees were unable to keep records while in the camps. One exception is a diary, composed as poetry, that Seno Osamu recorded on white birch bark, using soot as ink. He then succeeded in smuggling the diary home. The *Shirakaba Nisshi* (white birch diary) is one of the most important sources in the collection.

Two memorial museums in Japan seek to recognize the suffering of repatriates, with special attention to those who had been interned in Siberia. The newer of the two, the Memorial Museum for Soldiers, Detainees in Siberia, and Postwar Repatriates, opened in a Tokyo high-rise in Shinjuku in 2000.[26] It was originally sponsored by the prime minister's office in what some critics have suggested was mainly a political gesture to representatives of three groups: soldiers who did not serve long enough to qualify for pensions, those who had been detained by the Soviets, and civilian repatriates. The exhibits in the Tokyo museum are divided precisely into thirds, one for each of the three representative groups, a choice that substantiates the idea that the museum was established partly to meet the demands of these constituent groups. The older of the two museums, the Maizuru Repatriation Memorial Museum, houses the collection of materials related to Siberian detention and submitted the nomination. The Maizuru Museum emerged organically on the site of the repatriation port, one that was transformed into a memorial park in 1958 and where a museum was established in 1988.[27]

The Maizuru nomination, like the Chinese nominations, presents its materials in a national narrative, one that emphasizes the Japanese as the victims, and not the aggressors, in the Second World War.[28] The story begins in 1945, in a nation "absolutely devastated by the war,"[29] and continues with the people of the Japanese nation suffering postwar deprivation together, a common suffering that produced an abhorrence of war and, in turn, an aspiration for world peace.

The nomination then strives to integrate the Siberian internees, their families, and other repatriates into this war-to-peace story of postwar Japan and does so by making some modifications to the narrative. First, it asserts that all Japanese suffered after the war, especially those abroad. This emphasis is somewhat unusual, since most versions of the national narrative focus on victims on the home islands, especially those who suffered the consequences of atomic and incendiary bombings. Then, combining these two forms of suffering, abroad and at home, adds up to the abhorrence of all war: "The hardships that repatriates experienced on their way home, combined with the extreme difficulties experienced by people in a land that had turned to ashes, led the Japanese people to abhor all forms of warfare," noting also that the problems associated with repatriation shaped the "peace-oriented post-war mentality among the Japanese people."[30] The experiences of internment and repatriation also influenced the Japanese mindset, "providing a basis for post-war nation building as a peaceful, culture-oriented nation."[31] In this way, the story of Siberian internment is integrated retroactively into an already familiar telling of the postwar period.[32]

The conclusion of this revision to the national narrative is stated in the nomination's opening paragraph, which avers that the experiences of the internees "form an important part of the collective memory of the Japanese people."[33] In the version of history presented by the nomination, internees have been incorporated into the nation of sufferers, and, from them, we can draw a "straight line" to the collective memory of the Japanese people. The nomination hastens to qualify that collective memory, because it is a collective memory with a purpose: it aspires for permanent world peace.[34] The nomination does not directly seek world recognition of Japanese suffering, but it does seek recognition of the Japanese as a peace-loving people resulting from their abhorrence of war, which was born of suffering – that is, an indirect recognition of their suffering.[35] In this way, the nomination defines the boundaries of the Japanese nation, or at least of its national collective memory.

The nomination does attempt to reach beyond the national memory of collective Japanese suffering, on the basis that "similar experiences endured at the same time are part of the collective memory of people in nations in Europe."[36] The Japanese experience, it asserts, "holds historical meaning similar to that of their European counterparts" and, therefore, shares the common ground of suffering with the nations of Europe, especially Germany.[37] In a 2019 article, historians Jonathan Bull and Steven Ivings situate Japan's "Return to Maizuru" MOW application in the context of several changes at the Maizuru museum, including responding to the imperative of attracting more visitors. They then explain how the proposal was generated, noting that one of its main authors included references to German and Hungarian prisoners of the Soviets as a way to address the problem of "victim's consciousness" in Japan.[38] It is clear that the nomination tried to reach outside the Japanese national community by drawing parallels with the European experience, in what might be seen as an attempt to use the dynamic of multidirectional memory, but the effort is circumscribed.

The nomination nonetheless does make a case for universal human experiences: "the human determination to survive in the face of great hardship"; "the humanity maintained by people in extremely inhumane situations"; and "the universal nature of humanity, particularly love for families and homelands, friendships, aspiration for permanent peace, and zest for living, embraced by people living in desperate situations."[39] Histories of people in Soviet camps suggest that there was something universally human – or, rather, inhuman – about them.[40]

The nomination's strategy of creating parallels between the Japanese experience and European suffering, and, later, drawing universal connections, leaves one group conspicuously absent: other Asians. Although the nomination makes a fleeting reference to "Chinese foster parents,"[41] families in Northeast China who raised orphans of Japanese colonial settlers after the war, it does so to draw attention to the problems of war-displaced Japanese children. The authors of the nomination made a strategic decision to try to appeal to two audiences: the UNESCO assessment committee and a domestic Japanese audience.[42] This meant that the nomination did not acknowledge the fact that some Koreans who served in the Japanese military were also interned in Siberia until they were able to persuade the Soviets to release them, and that approximately two million Koreans and other non-Japanese Asians suffered in a devastated postwar Japan. A 2014 submission to the global public sphere of a nomination related to the Second World War that is periodized from 1945 and emphasizes Japanese suffering and redemption, all the while excluding the rest of Asia, shows that continued insensitivities persist when it comes to seeking recognition of Japanese suffering after the war.[43]

The Maizuru museum developed naturally, and from the bottom up, on the site of a former regional repatriation centre. It has been funded by donations from the general public. It serves as the key site that repatriates visit when reliving their return to Japan and reflecting on the circumstances of the war. The museum has served its constituency well by providing a place to which ordinary people can entrust their materials related to repatriation, including personal memorabilia, with the knowledge that the museum will care for them and treat them respectfully, and it has done this consistently over time with scarce resources. The idea that a relatively small local archive and museum could be recognized internationally for its persistence in collecting and preserving a wealth of relevant social history documents is appealing. Like the Chinese nominations, however, the materials have been pre-interpreted and are embedded in a national narrative that leads to a particular, predetermined conclusion: the people in our nation suffered. Critical readers of the nomination might sense that the appeal for world recognition of Japanese pacifism also includes an appeal for world recognition of carefully periodized Japanese suffering that is made distinct from the period of Japanese aggression during the Second World War. Such readers might hesitate to endorse any narrative that presents the Japanese nation as monolithic, even if that appeal is made in the name of world peace.

"Finding Dispersed Families": The Proposal from South Korea

In 2014, South Korea submitted two proposals to UNESCO's MOW Programme, one on Confucian printing woodblocks, and the other entitled the "Archives of the KBS Special Live Broadcast 'Finding Dispersed Families.'" The archival materials referenced in the latter proposal were generated over several months in 1983, when the Korean Broadcasting System (KBS) first decided to produce a one-time segment on families who had remained separated long after the end of the Korean War, to be shown on a regular morning program. While seeking candidates to appear on the show, the producers at the station discovered a widespread and intense longing among people to be reunited with long-lost family members. KBS then decided to produce a two-hour special broadcast on the topic that featured fifty people seeking relatives, strategically seated behind the announcers so that they were visible to viewers. The broadcast set off a deluge of responses. People telephoned the station, claiming to be relatives of the fifty on the broadcast or seeking help finding relatives of their own; when they could not get through on the telephone, they went in person to the studio by taxi. The show was extended for another two hours, resulting in thirty-six reunions. The following day, people "swarmed" the KBS headquarters and the plaza in front of the station. It continued its programming on dispersed families live for 138 straight days. Over 100,000 people applied, and more than 10,000 reunions were facilitated by the programming.

Most of the nomination is devoted to this moving description of the circumstances of these materials' origins and the outpouring of pent-up desire among ordinary people to find family members from whom they were separated in the 1940s and 1950s.[44] The nomination is based primarily on the KBS materials, which are wide ranging and include records of live broadcasts of reunions of war-dispersed families, producers' journals, applications to participate, broadcast ephemera, audiotapes, and photographs. The nomination also provides some historical background. It places the "history of dispersed families" in the context of Japanese colonial rule, Stalin's ethnic relocation practices, forced migration for labour during "the Pacific War," the postwar partition of the Korean peninsula, and the subsequent Korean War. While all of these factors contributed to the dispersals, the nomination ultimately pins the blame for the continued separations on one thing: the Cold War. The narrative it presents, therefore, is of grieving and powerless working- and middle-class families who suffered the misery of the Cold War. Many throughout the world can sympathize with this story.

One could find fault with the nomination in terms of its politics. The proposal criticizes North Korea for obstructing reunions between families divided by the Demilitarized Zone but does not acknowledge that anti-communism in South Korea also inhibited the ability of people to seek relatives freely. Moreover, it presents a story of national suffering, demanding recognition of Korean suffering: "the tragedy of families separated in this way must be remembered."[45] Unlike the Chinese and Japanese nominations, however, it wants others to join in Korea's collective memory, stating that Korean family separation should be "remembered, not only by Koreans but by the whole world."[46] The dispersed family nomination seeks to bring the whole world in.

The nomination makes several arguments for the global significance of the materials. The program won many awards and has served as course material in classes on television production in several different countries. It also makes the case that these materials "belong to all" by pointing out that many of the materials are already accessible on the KBS website, where one can easily view images of individuals seeking family members during the broadcasts. Moreover, the expansive language used in the application invites everyone to share in the grief of separations and the joy of reunion.

South Korea and North Korea both joined the United Nations in 1991, at the end of the Cold War. Since then, South Korea has been active in UN programs, seeking and securing UNESCO recognition for aspects of its cultural heritage. As described by anthropologist Hyung Il Pai, South Korea has an extensive bureaucracy that preserves and promotes the country's heritage.[47] It has succeeded in having eleven collections inscribed on the MOW Register. As of 2014, this was more than China (nine) and Japan (three). South Korea had collections inscribed before either China and Japan – China's and Japan's first collections were inscribed in 2011, joining South Korea's seventh and eighth collections that same year. South Korea's fourth inscription, in 2001, was the Jikji, formally known as the "Anthology of Great Buddhist Priests' Zen Teachings." The Jikji is the world's oldest book printed with moveable type, predating the Gutenberg Bible. It is the namesake of the Jikji Prize, a MOW award of US$30,000 given to institutions contributing to the preservation and accessibility of documentary heritage. Since 2009, South Korea has been active in training people in other parts of Asia in how to prepare nominations, sponsoring training workshops in Cambodia (2013) and the Kyrgyz Republic (2015). South Korea has been successful in the UNESCO World Heritage Site program as well, securing recognition for twelve historically significant places. This combination of an active heritage bureaucracy, enthusiasm for UNESCO recognition, and experience with the organization all may have contributed to its compelling nomination of a remarkable set of materials. But it was more than just these circumstances that led to a persuasive nomination, crafted by the Cultural Heritage Administration. The spirit of the proposal emphasized the pathos of ordinary people separated from their loved ones by ideological and political forces. The proposal was grounded in a particular time and place – South Korea from 30 June to 14 November 1983, and it makes a national case. But, more so than the three other proposals discussed above, it invited people outside of the peninsula to experience the universally human aspects of suffering endured by Korean families torn apart by war. In its effort to engage others in a Korean story, it makes use of the dynamic of multidirectional memory. Rothberg has argued that "when the productive, intercultural dynamic of multidirectional memory is explicitly claimed … it has the potential to create new forms of solidarity and new visions of justice."[48]

The use of this dynamic gives more substance to the claims for the organic humanitarianism of the event and the materials themselves.

Conclusion: Collective Memory and National Suffering Claims in the Global Public Sphere

The Chinese and Japanese nominations made bold claims on their nations' collective memory. The Nanjing nomination asserted a straight line between the Nanjing Massacre and the people of China. The comfort women nomination attested that its materials "truthfully reflect human beings' memory."[49] The Japanese nomination claimed that the experiences of the detainees were part of Japanese collective memory – the stories of internment "have become part of the enduring collective memory of the Japanese people"[50] – and that these memories have engendered a culture that aspires for world peace. The nominations did not concern themselves with debates on the meaning of national collective memory but, rather, simply stated that it existed.[51]

The Korean proposal, however, did something different. It did not claim a national collective memory tied to a history of dispersals, but it did describe an event in which much of the nation took part. As the nomination explained, one hundred thousand people gathered in the plaza in front of KBS to seek reunions with family members. Many more came as volunteers to care for them and support the process. The nomination presents a few statistics on the number of viewers that were somewhat difficult to decipher, but those figures suggest that many people throughout the nation watched the programming and wept.[52] Without making claims on national collective memory, the proposal nevertheless describes members of a nation simultaneously participating in an event that was emotionally meaningful to many of them, an event that comes close to a nationwide act of collective remembrance.

In East Asia, national committees select MOW nominations before forwarding them for international consideration. More research on the domestic process of generating the proposals in China, Japan, and Korea – following the lead of Bull and Ivings's research on the Maizuru nomination – would enrich our understanding of the extent to which these nominations reflect national views.[53] Investigation into how these particular nominations were chosen over others at the national level would enhance our understanding of how domestic evaluators understand the differences between a nomination that is targeted for a national audience and one that might resonate with an international panel. In the Japanese case, the two nominations submitted in 2014 beat out at least two others, one of which was nominated by the Chiran Peace Museum and sought recognition of its collection related to that city's role as a base for launching kamikaze pilots during the Second World War. It remains to be seen whether the world is ready to accept the kamikaze collection as something belonging to all. Another potentially productive avenue of research might be to analyse the nature of the protests that people in China and Korea, for example, have launched against Japanese proposals, and how civic groups in Japan, apparently with some kind of state backing, have protested the Chinese nominations.[54]

The four nominations analysed here were among a total of 88 nominations, submitted by 54 different countries, 1 organization, and 1 individual. The countries participating in 2014 nominated one or two collections, conforming to the limit of a maximum of two nominations per country per year. Eight countries, however, submitted more than two entries, which was made possible under two circumstances. First, countries can apparently make joint nominations above that quota. Germany, for example, nominated two collections on its own and participated in three further joint nominations. Second, there are cases of resubmitted applications seeking reconsideration. Italy, for example, nominated a total of four collections: three sets of materials by itself, including two new nominations for 2014 and one previous nomination from 2012, plus a joint nomination with Mexico. This combination of factors led to 77 nominations by individual countries and 9 joint nominations, plus 1 each from an organization and an individual, for a total of 88 nominations in 2014.[55]

One can gain a very rough sense of the percentage of proposals accepted by reviewing the rate of acceptance during the past two evaluations. In the 2010 round, 44 nominations were recommended for inscription, 8 were provisionally accepted, and 23 were not recommended.[56] In the 2012 round, 55 nominations were recommended for inscription, 1 was provisionally accepted, and 24 were not recommended.[57] Using these figures, it appears that, including provisional acceptance, roughly two out of three nominations in recent years have been accepted for inscription.

All four proposals are intriguing in how they describe the materials they are seeking to place on the MOW register and how they attempt to express domestic concerns while also laying claim to world significance. The proposals from China and Japan are hampered by well-worn national narratives of the Second World War, ones that attempt to place limits on the use of the materials they are promoting. The proposal from Korea, on the other hand, was effective in focusing in on a particular moment in a particular place – 1983 at the KBS offices – and then explaining that moment's historical and present significance to create a story to which a person of any nationality can relate. To reiterate, officials in China, Japan, and Korea usually draw upon the competitive memory model when claiming national victimization, but the MOW application process forced them to practise the dynamic of multidirectional memory. Korea's application, perhaps because of the relatable topic of the joy of family reunification, effectively integrated the latter dynamic. Based on these nominations, it appears that the competitive memory model is still alive and well in practice but that the dynamic of multidirectional memory has potential in terms of expanding a nation's documentary heritage to include all, perhaps even leading to new forms of solidarity.

As a historian, I believe that the more materials that are available to the public, the better. The archives and other units that are the custodians of these materials deserve recognition and support. When I first conducted the research for this chapter, my hope was for the acceptance of all four proposals. Another possibility was that members of the International Advisory Committee would be feeling productively mischievous on the day that they made their decisions, and, in the spirit of peace and reconciliation, would recommend provisional acceptance of all of the nominations, on the condition that all four be resubmitted as joint China-Japan-Korea nominations for 2017.

According to UNESCO's MOW website, three of the four nominations discussed above were accepted for inscription on the register for 2015: Documents of Nanjing Massacre; Return to Maizuru Port; and the Archives of the KBS Special Live Broadcast "Finding Dispersed Families." The MOW program rejected China's nomination for "Comfort Women." That rejection has gone on to generate substantial controversy. In 2017, Korea and Japan did collaborate on a successful joint nomination of materials, "Documents on Joseon Tongsinsa/Chosen Tsushinshi: The History of Peace Building and Cultural Exchanges between Korea and Japan from the 17th to 19th Century." People of the twenty-first century may have much to learn from the history of peace building in previous centuries.

NOTES

1 The four proposals, all accessed in August and September 2015, include: "Documents of Nanjing Massacre," http://www.unesco.org/new/en/communication-and-information/memory-of-the-world/register/full-list-of-registered-heritage/registered-heritage-page-2/ (hereafter Nanjing nomination); "Archives about 'Comfort Women': The Sex Slaves for Imperial

Japan," http://www.unesco.org/new/fileadmin/MULTIMEDIA/HQ/CI/CI/pdf/mow/nomination_forms/china_comfort_women_en.pdf (hereafter Comfort women nomination) (this item is no longer on the UNESCO MOW website, as the nomination was unsuccessful; the pdf is in the author's possession); "Return to Maizuru Port – Documents Related to the Internment and Repatriation Experiences of Japanese (1945–1956)," http://www.unesco.org/new/en/communication-and-information/memory-of-the-world/register/full-list-of-registered-heritage/registered-heritage-page-7/return-to-maizuru-port/ (hereafter Maizuru nomination); and "The Archives of the KBS Special Live Broadcast 'Finding Dispersed Families,'" http://www.unesco.org/new/en/communication-and-information/memory-of-the-world/register/full-list-of-registered-heritage/registered-heritage-page-8/the-archives-of-the-kbs-special-live-broadcast-finding-dispersed-families/ (hereafter Dispersed families nomination).

2 See "Programme Objectives" on the Memory of the World website, https://en.unesco.org/programme/mow.

3 Richard Terdiman, *Present Past: Modernity and the Memory Crisis* (Ithaca, NY: Cornell University Press, 1993).

4 See the section "World Significance" in each of the proposals cited in note 1.

5 Michael Rothberg, *Multidirectional Memory: Remembering the Holocaust in the Age of Decolonization* (Stanford, CA: Stanford University Press, 2009).

6 Ibid., 3.

7 "Comfort woman," the literal translation of the historical Japanese-language euphemism *ianfu*, refers to the victims of this system and has taken on historical and political layers of meaning over time and therefore is, in my view, a more meaningful term than the alternative "sex slave."

8 Scholarship on the history, historiography, and memory of these events is vast. For Nanjing, see Daqing Yang, "Revisionism and the Nanjing Atrocity," *Critical Asian Studies* 43, no. 4 (2011): 625–48. For the comfort women, see Sarah C. Soh, *The Comfort Women: Sexual Violence and Postcolonial Memory in Korea and Japan* (Chicago: University of Chicago Press, 2008), and Carol Gluck, "Operations of Memory: 'Comfort Women' and the World," in *Ruptured Memories: War, Memory, and the Post-Cold War in Asia*, ed. Sheila Miyoshi Jager and Rana Mitter (Cambridge, MA: Harvard University Press, 2007), 47–77.

9 Daqing Yang, "Review Essay: Convergence or Divergence? Recent Historical Writings on the Rape of Nanjing," *American Historical Review* 104, no. 3 (1999): 842–65.

10 Nanjing nomination, 9.

11 Ibid.

12 Michael Berry, "Shooting the Enemy: Photographic Attachment in Nanjing Massacre Cinema and the Curious Case of Scarlet Rose," paper presented

at the Conference on Authenticity and Victimhood in Twentieth-Century Commemorative Culture, Berlin, 10–12 December 2014; Michael Berry, "Cinematic Representations of the Rape of Nanking," *East Asia: An International Quarterly* 19, no. 4 (2001): 85–108.

13 Choe Sang-Hun, "Statue Deepens Dispute over Wartime Sexual Slavery," *New York Times*, 15 December 2011. Much to the dismay of the Japanese state, replicas of this statue have proliferated in many places including Glendale, California; Wiesent, Germany; and Sydney, Australia.

14 Comfort women nomination, 1.

15 Ibid., 3, 9.

16 Ibid., 3, 10.

17 Nanjing nomination, 4, 9–10.

18 Gluck, "Operations of Memory," 70.

19 "Perhaps the greatest tragedy of the Rape of Nanjing is that even today, some six decades after the fact, the Chinese cultural, and cinematic, memory of the massacre continues to be dictated by Japan's denial." Berry, "Cinematic Representations," 108.

20 Yoshimi Yoshiaki, *The Comfort Women*, trans. Suzanne O'Brien (New York: Columbia University Press, 2000).

21 Yoshida Yutaka, "Haisen zengo ni okeru Kōbunsho no yakkyoku to intoku," *Sensō sekinin kenkyū* no. 14 (1996): 2–7; reproduced in Yoshida Yutaka, *Gendaishi Rekishi-gaku to sensō sekinin* (Tokyo: Aoki Shoten, 1997), 127–34.

22 Nanjing nomination, 10.

23 Comfort women nomination, 4, 7, 9.

24 Ibid., 10.

25 Nanjing nomination, 1, 8.

26 Takashi Yoshida, *From Cultures of War to Cultures of Peace: War and Peace Museums in Japan, China, and South Korea* (Portland, ME: Merwin Asia, 2014). The original name of this museum was the Exhibition and Reference Library for Peace and Consolation, as described by Yoshida, *From Cultures of War*, 193–6. See also the website of the Memorial Museum for Soldiers, Detainees in Siberia, and Postwar Repatriates, http://www.heiwakinen.jp/english/index.html.

27 Website of the Maizuru Repatriation Memorial Museum, http://m-hikiage-museum.jp/.

28 Dower, Orr, and other scholars have identified the contexts that facilitated the emergence of the narrative that suffering in war was then transformed into the basis for pacifism. They then show how it was sustained in various forms throughout the postwar period. John Dower, *Embracing Defeat: Japan in the Wake of World War II* (New York: W.W. Norton, 1999);

James J. Orr, *The Victim as Hero: Ideologies of Peace and National Identity in Postwar Japan* (Honolulu: University of Hawai'i Press, 2001).

29 Maizuru nomination, 8.

30 Ibid.

31 Ibid., 3.

32 My research on the political, social, and cultural labelling of repatriates, including the Siberian detainees, as perceived threats to a post-imperial and anti-communist nation shows that they were not immediately welcomed in to the circle of sufferers. Lori Watt, *When Empire Comes Home: Repatriation and Reintegration in Postwar Japan* (Cambridge, MA: Harvard University Asia Center, 2009).

33 Ibid., 1.

34 Ibid.

35 The nomination states: "The hardships that repatriates experienced on their way home, combined with the extreme difficulties experienced by people in a land that had turned to ashes, led the Japanese people to abhor all forms of warfare. Based on this new world-view, the Japanese people came to foster strong aspirations to create a peaceful, culture-oriented nation. In other words, the experiences of the repatriates provided a spiritual background for post-war peace movements and nation rebuilding." And, "the experience of the repatriation continues to serve as a cornerstone for Japanese people's aspirations to sustain a peaceful nation that shall not engage in warfare, and which works to seek permanent world peace. At the same time, the experiences of the internees have formed extremely important, collective memories, which should be handed down to future generations." Maizuru nomination, 8, 10.

36 Ibid., 1.

37 Ibid., 2–4.

38 Jonathan Bull and Steven Ivings, "Return on Display: Memories of Postcolonial Migration at Maizuru," *Japan Forum* 31, no. 3 (March 2019): 336–57.

39 Maizuru nomination, 1, 3, 6.

40 Andrew Barshay, *The Gods Left First: The Captivity and Repatriation of Japanese POWs in Northeast Asia, 1945–56* (Berkeley: University of California Press, 2013).

41 Maizuru nomination, 8.

42 Bull and Ivings, "Return on Display," 349.

43 Mariko Asano Tamanoi has analysed the tendency to periodize Japanese narratives of the war beginning on 9 or 15 August 1945. Tamanoi, *Memory Maps: The State and Manchuria in Postwar Japan* (Honolulu: University of Hawai'i Press, 2009).

44 Author Helie Lee's portrait of her grandmother's life in Korea and China during the colonial period and the Korean War depicts the many ways that family members could become separated from one another. According to Lee, her grandmother participated in the KBS programming. For her, it was one part of a decades-long search for her first-born son. Helie Lee, *Still Life with Rice* (New York: Touchstone, 1997).
45 Dispersed families nomination, 10.
46 Ibid.
47 Hyung Il Pai, *Heritage Management in Korea and Japan: The Politics of Antiquity and Identity* (Seattle: University of Washington Press, 2013).
48 Rothberg, *Multidirectional Memory*, 5.
49 Comfort women nomination, 3.
50 Maizuru nomination, 7.
51 Jay Winter and Emmanuel Sivan, "Introduction: Setting the Framework," in *War and Remembrance in the Twentieth Century*, ed. Winter and Sivan (Cambridge: Cambridge University Press, 1999), 1–38; Franziska Seraphim, *War Memory and Social Politics in Japan, 1945–2005* (Cambridge, MA: Harvard University Asia Center, 2006).
52 "From October 10 to 20, 1983, Gallup Korea carried out a random survey of 1,450 households of which 53.9 per cent said they watched the live broadcast till 1 a.m.; 88.8 per cent reported they shed tears while watching the program." Dispersed families nomination, unnumbered page 7.
53 Bull and Ivings, "Return on Display."
54 "Sekai isan NEWS 15/08/01: Nankin jiken, ianfu tōroku ni taishi hanron shokan," analysis in a blog post by Hasegawa Dai, last modified 16 August 2015, http://www.hasegawadai.com/world-heritage.
55 These figures are based on the information for 2014–15 available on the MOW website. These numbers conflict slightly with information made available for the IAC meeting, held in Abu Dhabi, which indicated that they would consider eighty-nine nominations from sixty-one countries. "UNESCO International Advisory Committee to Meet in Abu Dhabi to Nominate Documentary Heritage of World Significance," https://en.unesco.org/news/unesco-international-advisory-committee-meet-abu-dhabi-nominate-documentary-heritage-world.
56 Appendix 3, Final Report of the 10th Meeting of the International Advisory Committee, 10th session, 22–5 May 2011, available under "Meeting documents" and "International Advisory Committee" at https://en.unesco.org/programme/mow/documents.
57 Appendix 3, Final Report of the 11th Meeting of the International Advisory Committee, 11th session, 18–20 June 2013, available under "Meeting documents" and "International Advisory Committee" at https://en.unesco.org/programme/mow/documents.

Contributors

Mathias Beer conducts research at the Institute of Danube Swabian History and Regional Studies, focusing on German and east-central and southeastern European history. More specifically, he is interested in issues of migration and refugees, the national state and minorities, memory culture, museum studies, the politics of history, and historiography.

Barbara Christophe is the coordinator of the memory cultures research forum at the Georg Eckert Institute for International Textobook Research. With a background in history and Slavonic studies, she has focused primarily on the post-Soviet area, particularly the Baltic states, the Caucasus, and central Asia. Some of her research also examines Germany and eastern Europe.

Moritz Florin is a researcher in recent and contemporary eastern European history at the Friedrich-Alexander-Universität Erlangen-Nürnberg. His current research focuses on right-wing terrorism and violence in the early age of the mass press, while past research has focused on central Asia and the propaganda related to the Hitler-Stalin Pact.

Randall Hansen is the director of the Centre for European, Russian, and Eurasian Studies at the Munk School and Canada Research Chair in Global Migration in the Department of Political Science, University of Toronto. His research focuses on immigration and citizenship, demography and population policy, and the effects of war on civilians.

Tobias Hof joined the Ludwig-Maximilians-Universität in February 2019 as a *Privatdozent* in modern and contemporary history after completing his Habilitation in 2018 at the same institution. His research focuses on the history of Germany and Italy, international relations, security, and fascism.

Ingo Loose conducts research at the Leibniz Institute for Contemporary History (IfZ). Focusing on history and Slavic studies, he has conducted research projects on central and eastern Europe, antisemitism, and the Łódź Ghetto.

James Orr is an associate professor of East Asian Studies at Bucknell University. His focus is on modern and premodern Japanese history, the remembrance of Hiroshima in Japan and the United States, constructions of national identity in East Asia, international relations in East Asia, and Japanese history through film.

Nakano Satoshi is a professor of history at Hitotsubashi University's Graduate School of Social Sciences. His past research has included studies of Philippine-US relations and the lived experiences of Japanese military officers and civilians in Southeast Asia during the Second World War. Currently, he is studying the Japanese occupation while continuing to focus on Philippine-US relations, specifically regarding war memory.

Achim Saupe is a historian and research fellow at the Centre for Contemporary History in Potsdam and also acts as the coordinator of historical authenticity for the Leibniz Research Alliance. His research interests include modern European history, twentieth-century German history, historiography, conceptual history, digital history, memory, identity, and commemoration culture.

Michael Schwartz conducts research at the Leibniz Institute for Contemporary History (IfZ). His research projects focus on German history, ethnic cleansing, and the history of sexuality.

Tatiana Voronina is a historian at the European University in St. Petersburg whose research interests include the social and cultural aspects of Soviet history, oral history, and memory studies. Some of her past projects have focused on socialist realism, the Siege of Leningrad, and Soviet repressions.

Lori Watt is an associate professor of history and international area studies at Washington University in St. Louis, Missouri. She specializes in Japanese history and is currently working on a book project regarding Allied-managed population transfers through East Asia at the end of the Second World War. In the past, she has written about repatriation and reintegration in postwar Japan and on other post-colonial and postwar issues in East Asia.

Andreas Wirsching is the director of the Leibniz Institute for Contemporary History (IfZ). His research focuses on democracy, twentieth-century German history, and the period of National Socialism.

Daqing Yang is an associate professor at George Washington University, Washington, DC, teaching in the Department of History and at the Elliott School of International Affairs. His research focuses on modern Japanese history, Sino-Japanese relations, colonialism, memory, and reconciliation.

Jürgen Zarusky was a research fellow at the Leibniz Institute for Contemporary History (IfZ), and editor-in-chief of the quarterly journal *Vierteljahrshefte für Zeitgeschichte,* published by the institute. His research focused on National Socialism, Stalinism, German-Soviet relations, dictatorship and totalitarianism, and the politics of European memory and history.

Index

GERMAN AND EUROPEAN STUDIES

General Editor: Jennifer L. Jenkins

1 Emanuel Adler, Beverly Crawford, Federica Bicchi, and Rafaella Del Sarto, *The Convergence of Civilizations: Constructing a Mediterranean Region*
2 James Retallack, *The German Right, 1860–1920: Political Limits of the Authoritarian Imagination*
3 Silvija Jestrovic, *Theatre of Estrangement: Theory, Practice, Ideology*
4 Susan Gross Solomon, ed., *Doing Medicine Together: Germany and Russia between the Wars*
5 Laurence McFalls, ed., *Max Weber's "Objectivity" Revisited*
6 Robin Ostow, ed., *(Re)Visualizing National History: Museums and National Identities in Europe in the New Millennium*
7 David Blackbourn and James Retallack, eds., *Localism, Landscape, and the Ambiguities of Place: German-Speaking Central Europe, 1860–1930*
8 John Zilcosky, ed., *Writing Travel: The Poetics and Politics of the Modern Journey*
9 Angelica Fenner, *Race under Reconstruction in German Cinema: Robert Stemmle's Toxi*
10 Martina Kessel and Patrick Merziger, eds., *The Politics of Humour: Laughter, Inclusion, and Exclusion in the Twentieth Century*
11 Jeffrey K. Wilson, *The German Forest: Nature, Identity, and the Contestation of a National Symbol, 1871–1914*
12 David G. John, *Bennewitz, Goethe,* Faust: *German and Intercultural Stagings*
13 Jennifer Ruth Hosek, *Sun, Sex, and Socialism: Cuba in the German Imaginary*
14 Steven M. Schroeder, *To Forget It All and Begin Again: Reconciliation in Occupied Germany, 1944–1954*
15 Kenneth S. Calhoon, *Affecting Grace: Theatre, Subject, and the Shakespearean Paradox in German Literature from Lessing to Kleist*
16 Martina Kolb, *Nietzsche, Freud, Benn, and the Azure Spell of Liguria*
17 Hoi-eun Kim, *Doctors of Empire: Medical and Cultural Encounters between Imperial Germany and Meiji Japan*
18 J. Laurence Hare, *Excavating Nations: Archeology, Museums, and the German-Danish Borderlands*
19 Jacques Kornberg, *The Pope's Dilemma: Pius XII Faces Atrocities and Genocide in the Second World War*

20 Patrick O'Neill, *Transforming Kafka: Translation Effects*
21 John K. Noyes, *Herder: Aesthetics against Imperialism*
22 James Retallack, *Germany's Second Reich: Portraits and Pathways*
23 Laurie Marhoefer, *Sex and the Weimar Republic: German Homosexual Emancipation and the Rise of the Nazis*
24 Bettina Brandt and Daniel L. Purdy, eds., *China in the German Enlightenment*
25 Michael Hau, *Performance Anxiety: Sport and Work in Germany from the Empire to Nazism*
26 Celia Applegate, *The Necessity of Music: Variations on a German Theme*
27 Richard J. Golsan and Sarah M. Misemer, eds., *The Trial That Never Ends: Hannah Arendt's* Eichmann in Jerusalem *in Retrospect*
28 Lynne Taylor, *In the Children's Best Interests: Unaccompanied Children in American-Occupied Germany, 1945–1952*
29 Jennifer A. Miller, *Turkish Guest Workers in Germany: Hidden Lives and Contested Borders, 1960s to 1980s*
30 Amy Carney, *Marriage and Fatherhood in the Nazi SS*
31 Michael E. O'Sullivan, *Disruptive Power: Catholic Women, Miracles, and Politics in Modern Germany, 1918–1965*
32 Gabriel N. Finder and Alexander V. Prusin, *Justice behind the Iron Curtain: Nazis on Trial in Communist Poland*
33 Parker Daly Everett, *Urban Transformations: From Liberalism to Corporatism in Greater Berlin, 1871–1933*
34 Melissa Kravetz, *Women Doctors in Weimar and Nazi Germany: Maternalism, Eugenics, and Professional Identity*
35 Javier Samper Vendrell, *The Seduction of Youth: Print Culture and Homosexual Rights in the Weimar Republic*
36 Sebastian Voigt, ed., *Since the Boom: Continuity and Change in the Western Industrialized World after 1970*
37 Olivia Landry, *Theatre of Anger: Radical Transnational Performance in Contemporary Berlin*
38 Jeremy Best, *Heavenly Fatherland: German Missionary Culture and Globalization in the Age of Empire*
39 Svenja Bethke, *Dance on the Razor's Edge: Crime and Punishment in the Nazi Ghettos*
40 Kenneth S. Calhoon, *The Long Century's Long Shadow: Weimar Cinema and the Romantic Modern*
41 Randall Hansen, Achim Saupe, Andreas Wirsching, and Daqing Yang, eds., *Authenticity and Victimhood after the Second World War: Narratives from Europe and East Asia*

www.ingramcontent.com/pod-product-compliance
Lightning Source LLC
LaVergne TN
LVHW090149080826
844660LV00013B/724/J

* 9 7 8 1 4 8 7 5 2 8 2 1 8 *